Reincarnated as a Sword

1

story by
YUU
TANAKA

art by
TOMOWO
MARUYAMA

original
character
design by
LLO

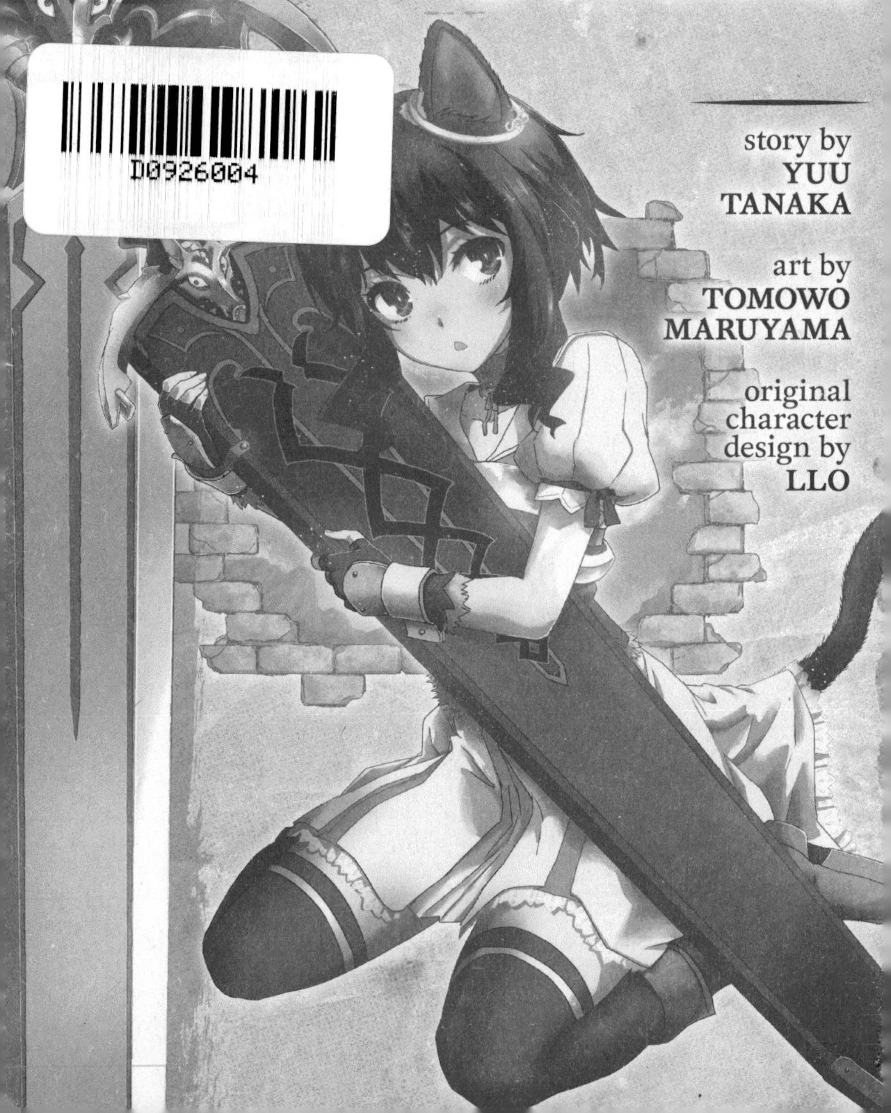

Reincarnated as a sword

1

Chapter 1: Black Cat Without a Name

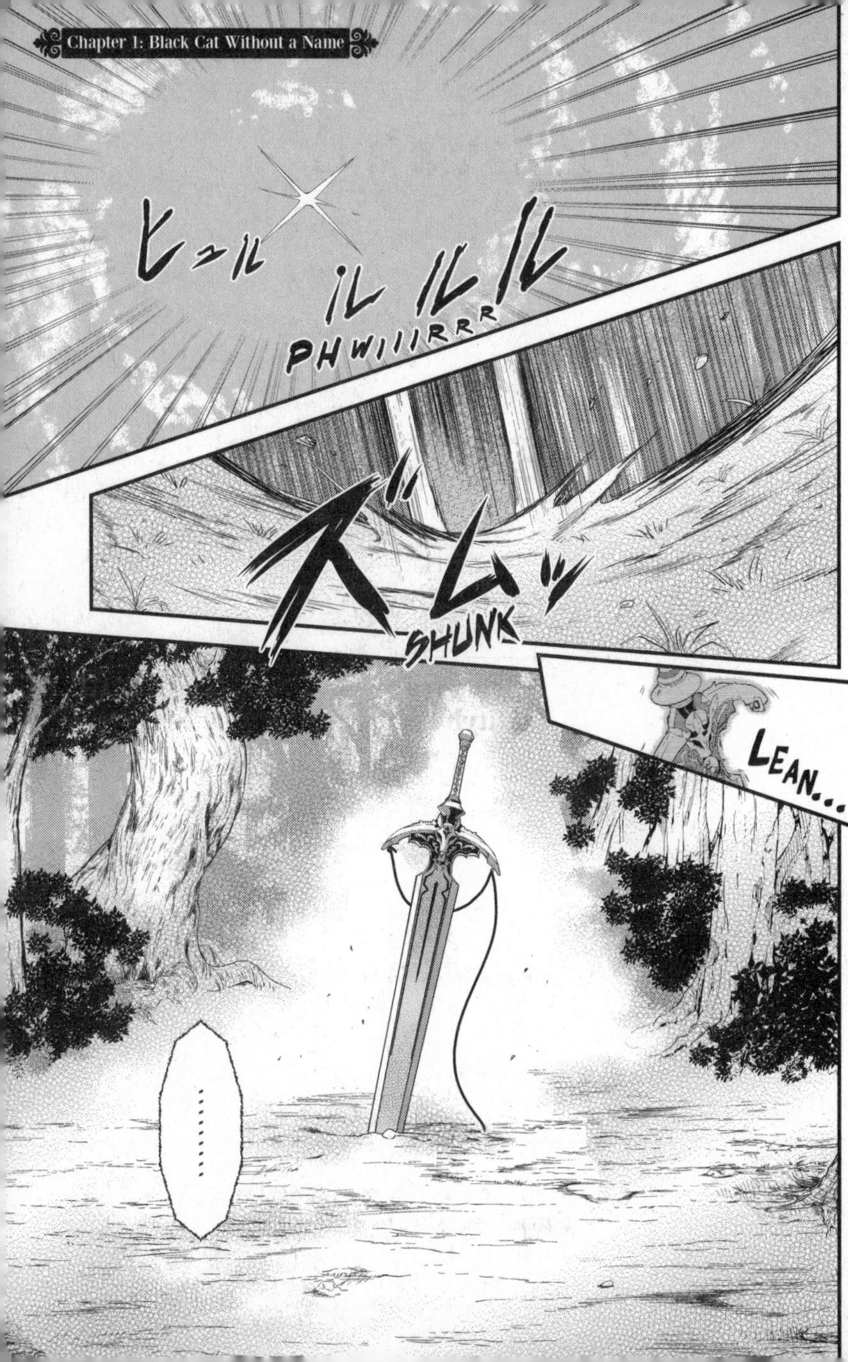
ヒュルルルル
PHWIIIRRR
ズムッ
SHUNK
LEAN...
......

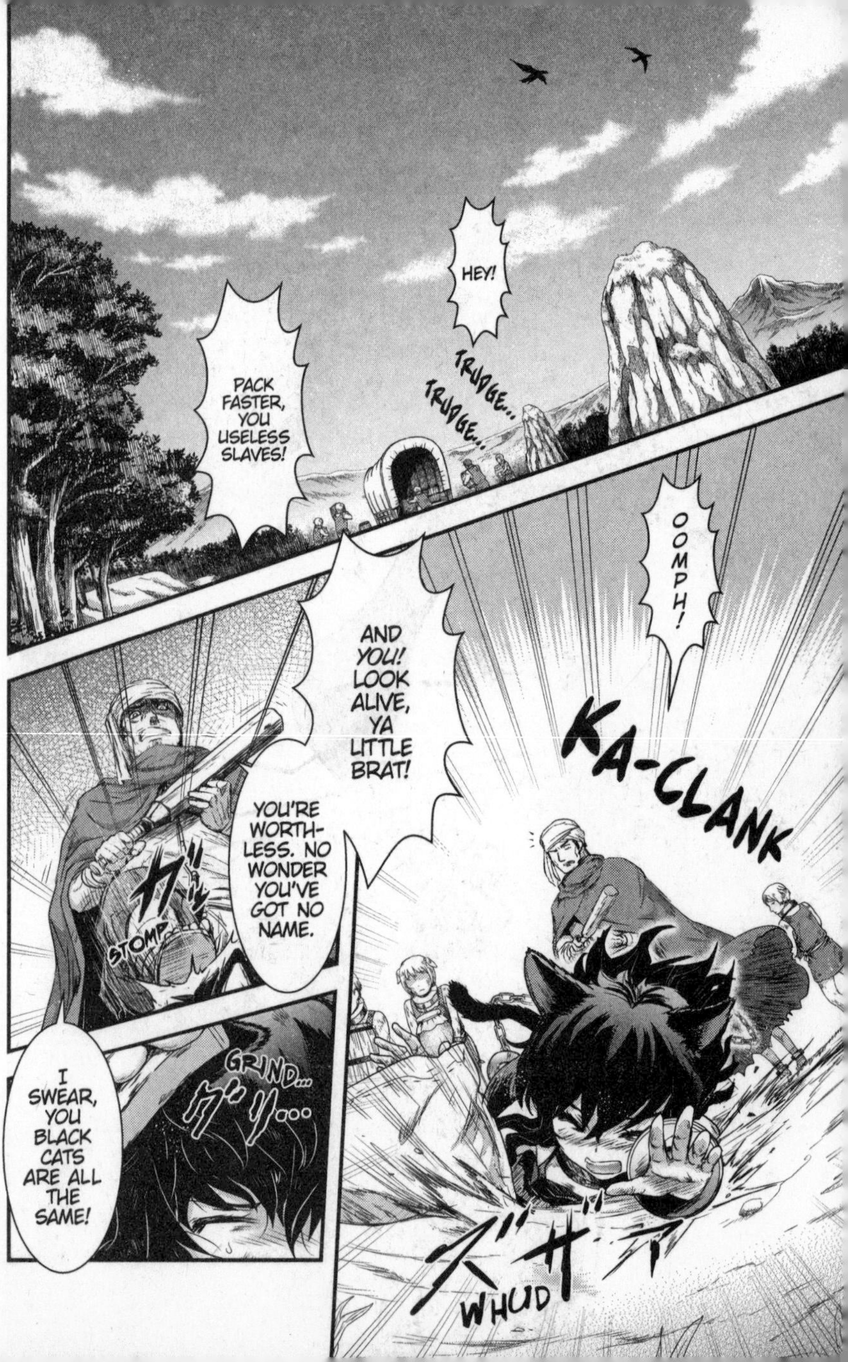
HEY!
TRUDGE...
TRUDGE...
PACK FASTER, YOU USELESS SLAVES!
OOMPH!
KA-CLANK
WHUD
AND YOU! LOOK ALIVE, YA LITTLE BRAT!
STOMP
YOU'RE WORTH-LESS. NO WONDER YOU'VE GOT NO NAME.
GRIND...
I SWEAR, YOU BLACK CATS ARE ALL THE SAME!

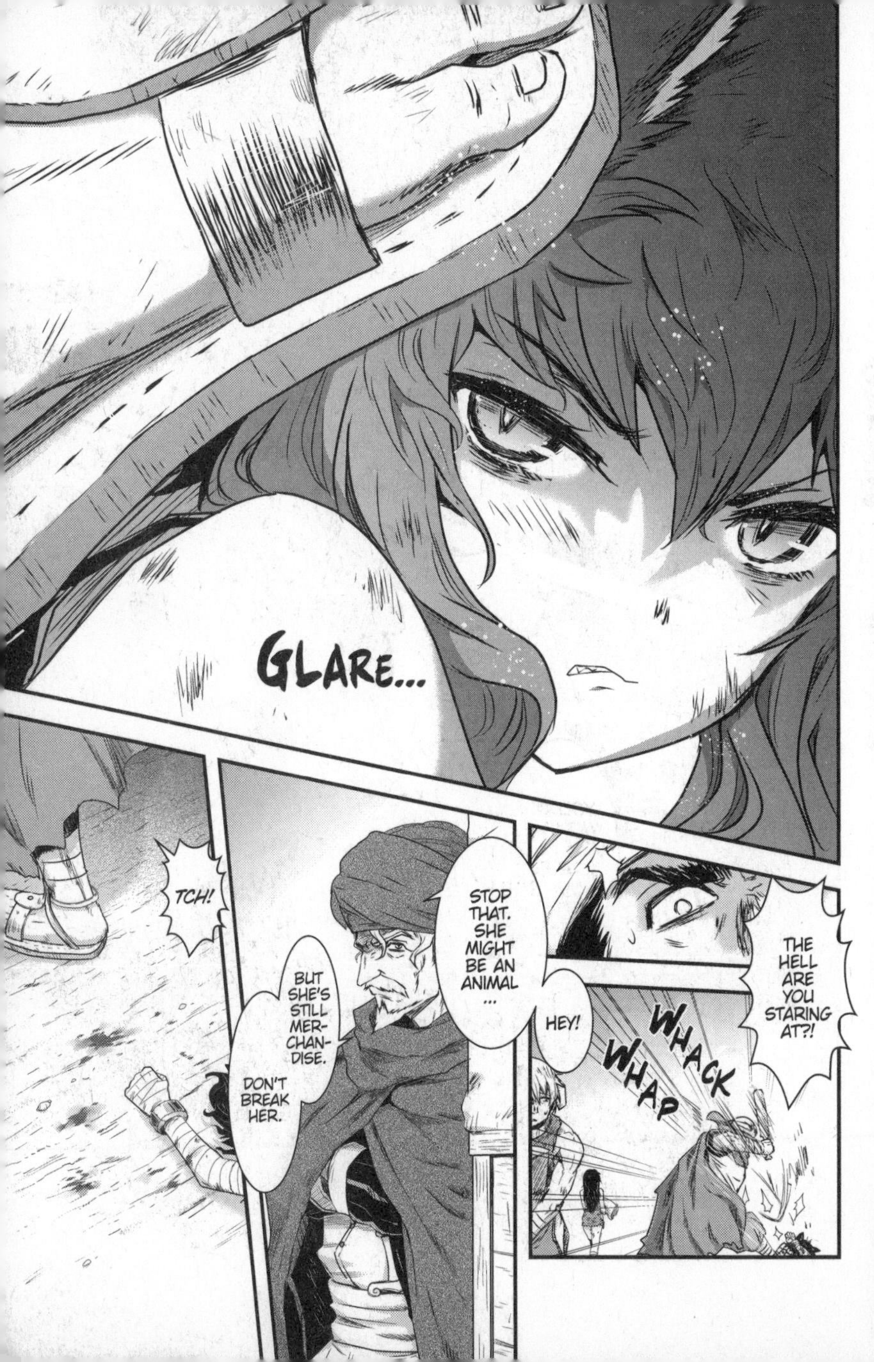
GLARE...
THE HELL ARE YOU STARING AT?!
WHACK
WHAP
HEY!
STOP THAT. SHE MIGHT BE AN ANIMAL...
BUT SHE'S STILL MER-CHANDISE.
DON'T BREAK HER.
TCH!

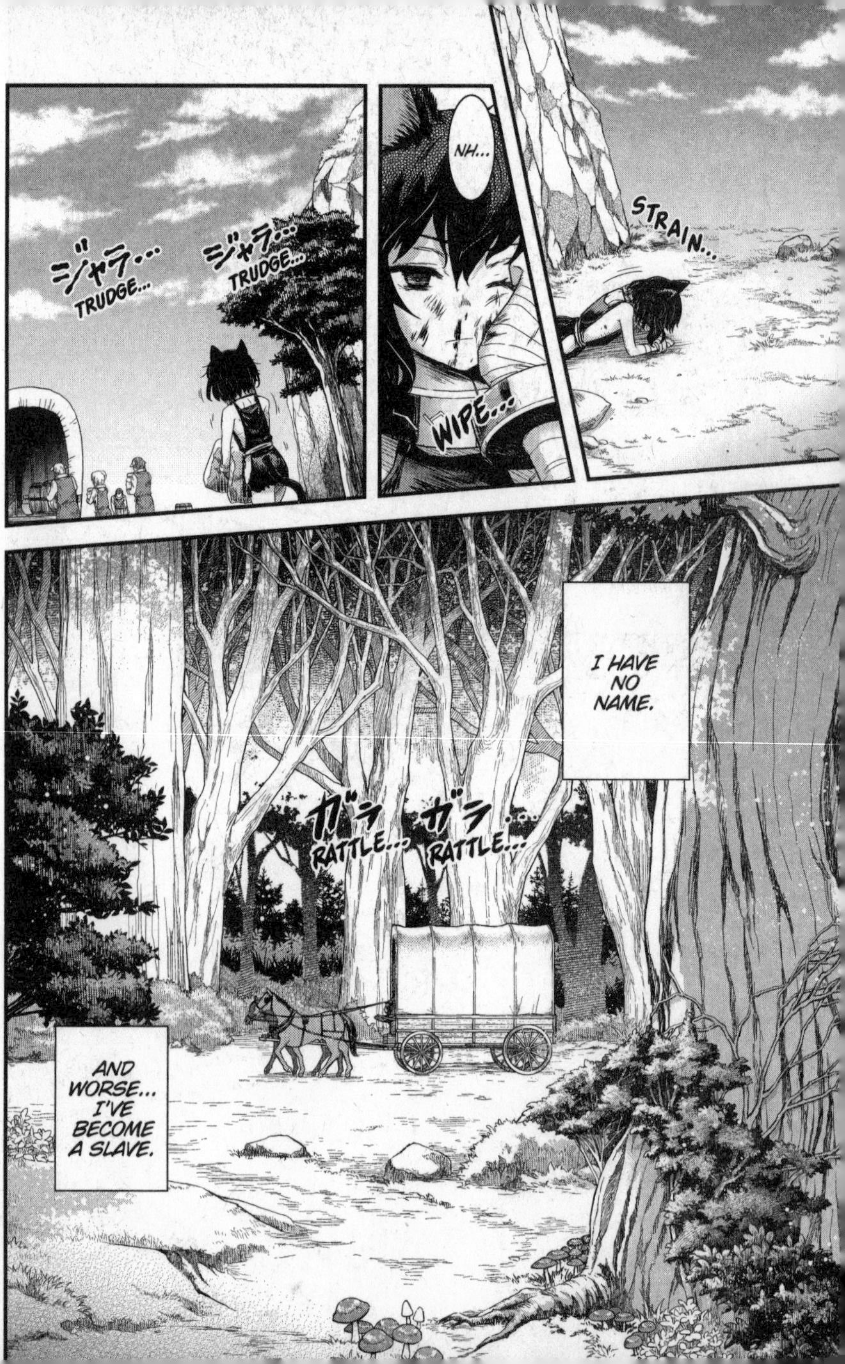
STRAIN...
NH...
WIPE...
ジャラ・・・
TRUDGE...
ジャラ・・・
TRUDGE...
I HAVE NO NAME.
ガラ ガラ・・・
RATTLE... RATTLE...
AND WORSE... I'VE BECOME A SLAVE.

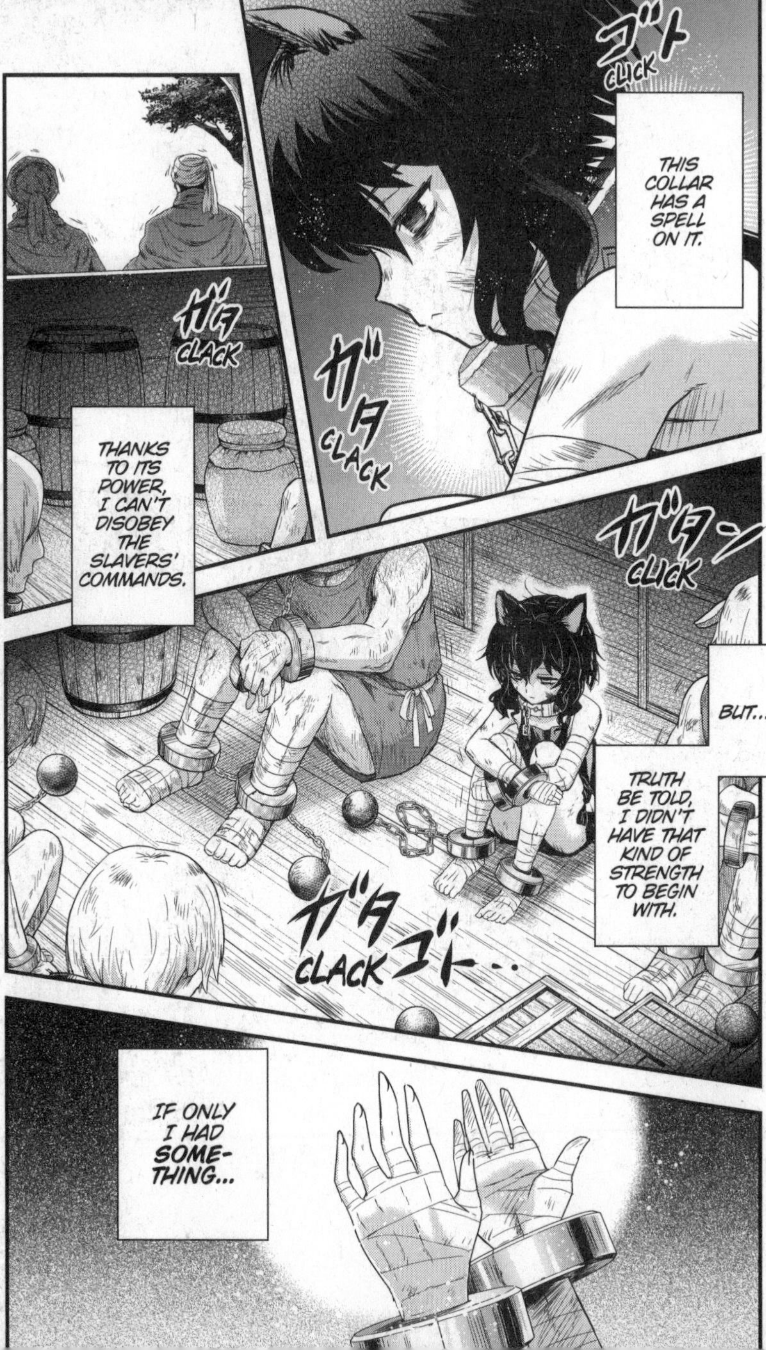
ゴト
CLICK
THIS COLLAR HAS A SPELL ON IT.
ガタ
CLACK
ガタ
CLACK
THANKS TO ITS POWER, I CAN'T DISOBEY THE SLAVERS' COMMANDS.
ガタン
CLICK
BUT...
TRUTH BE TOLD, I DIDN'T HAVE THAT KIND OF STRENGTH TO BEGIN WITH.
ガタ
CLACK
ゴト…
IF ONLY I HAD SOME-THING...

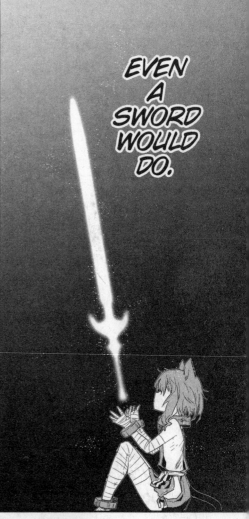

EVEN A SWORD WOULD DO.

SKSH...

SKSH...

SNIFE...

SNIFE...

SKSH...

GURR...

HELP...

PLEASE...

CAN ANY- ONE ...

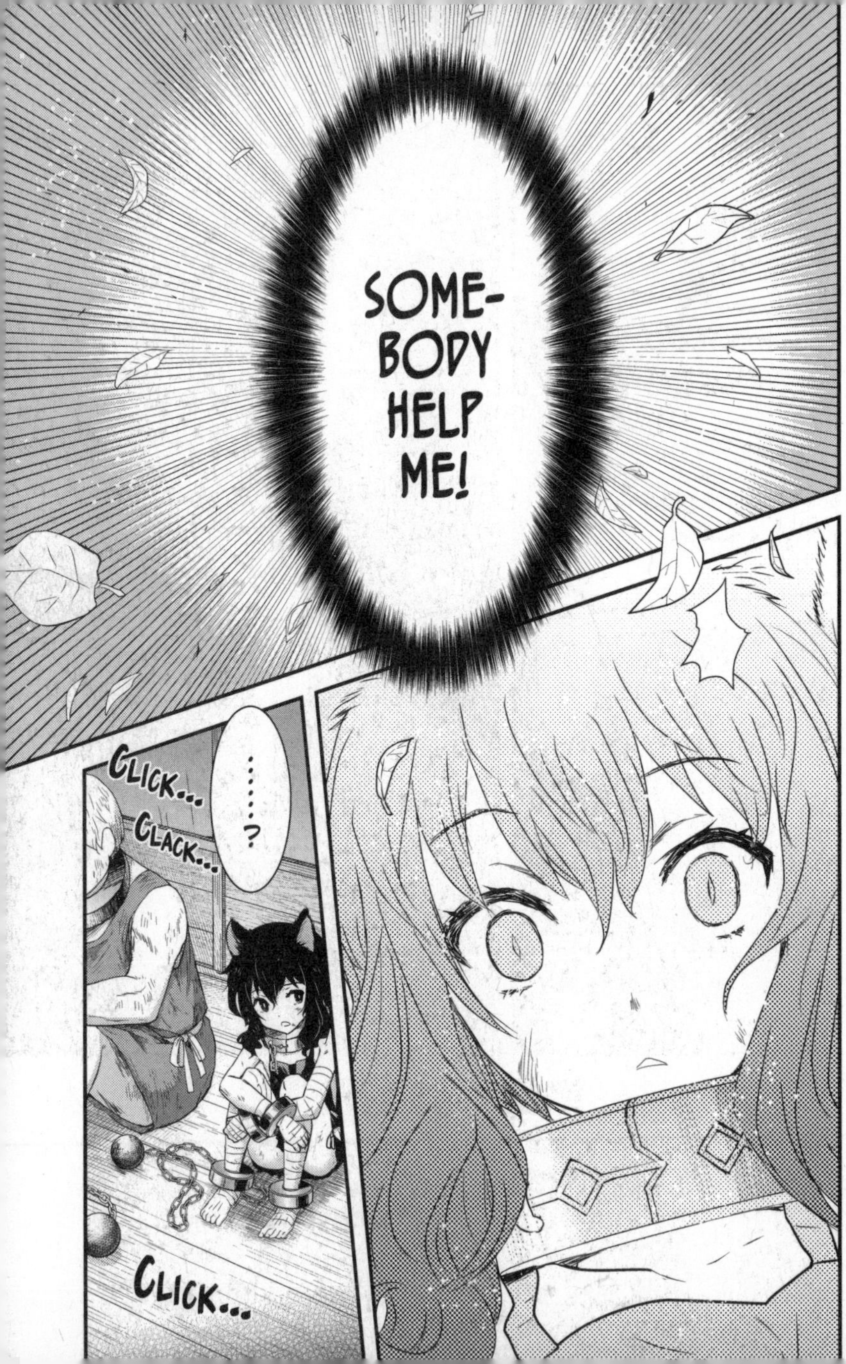
SOME-
BODY
HELP
ME!
......?
CLICK...
CLACK...
CLICK...

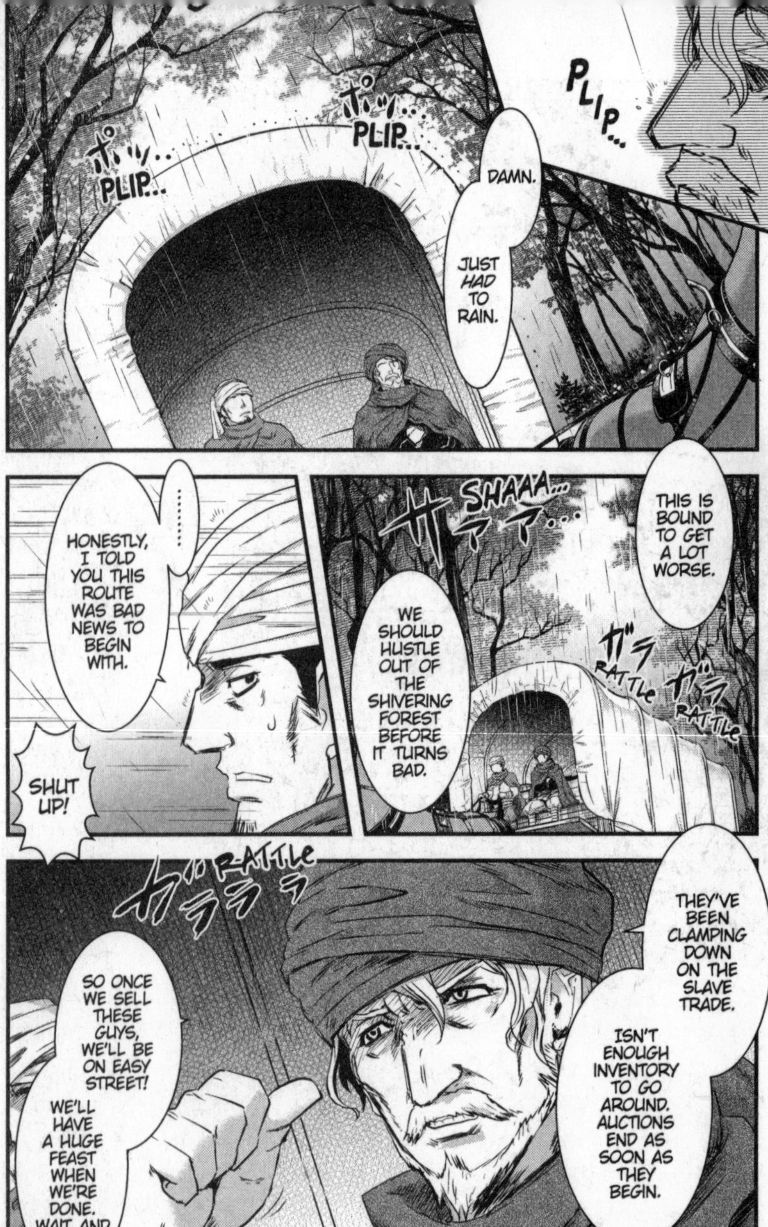
PLIP...
DAMN.
JUST HAD TO RAIN.
PLIP...
PLIP...
SHAAA...
THIS IS BOUND TO GET A LOT WORSE.
WE SHOULD HUSTLE OUT OF THE SHIVERING FOREST BEFORE IT TURNS BAD.
RATTLE
RATTLE
......
HONESTLY, I TOLD YOU THIS ROUTE WAS BAD NEWS TO BEGIN WITH.
SHUT UP!
THEY'VE BEEN CLAMPING DOWN ON THE SLAVE TRADE.
ISN'T ENOUGH INVENTORY TO GO AROUND. AUCTIONS END AS SOON AS THEY BEGIN.
RATTLE
SO ONCE WE SELL THESE GUYS, WE'LL BE ON EASY STREET!
WE'LL HAVE A HUGE FEAST WHEN WE'RE DONE. WAIT AND SEE!

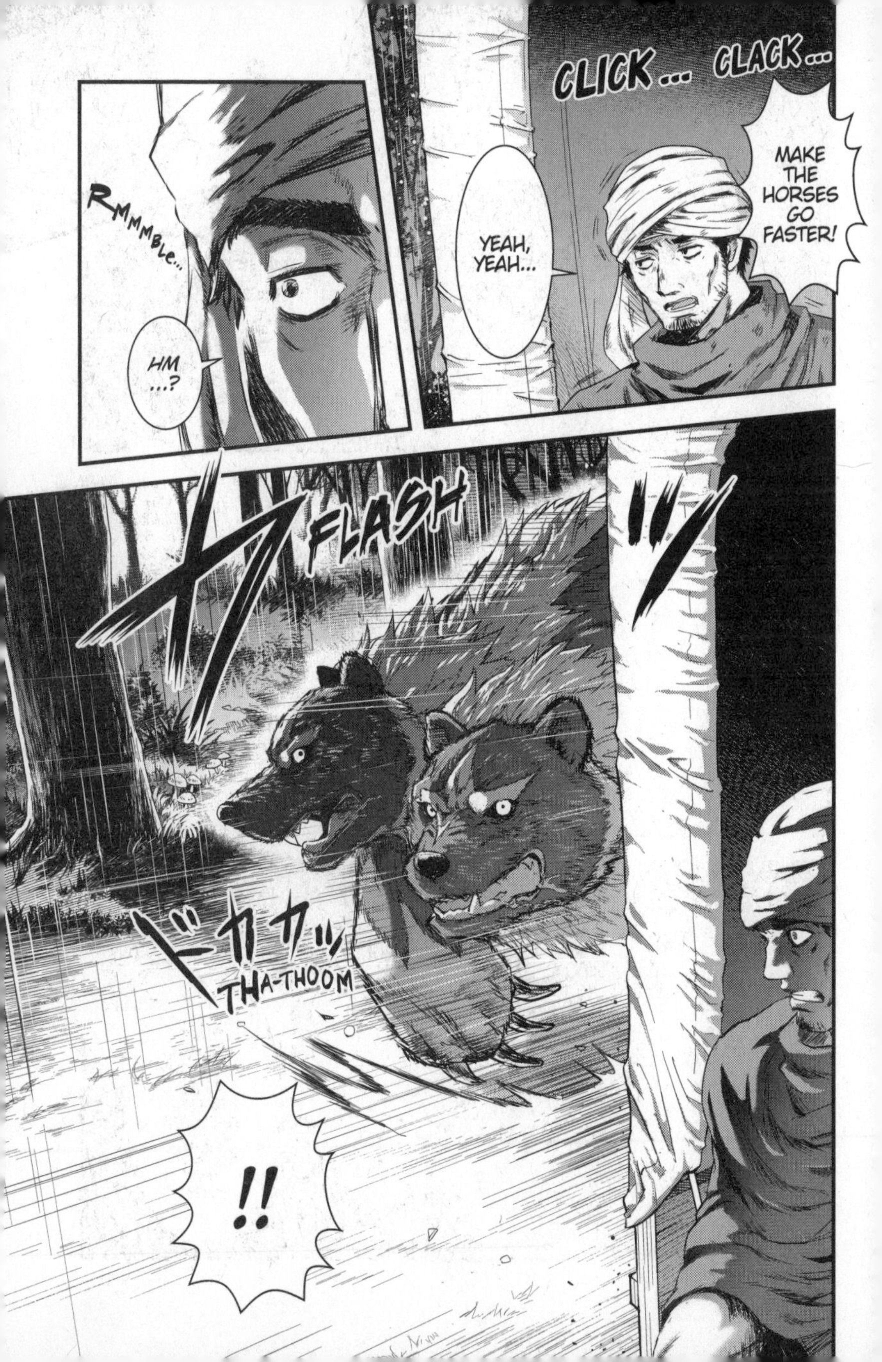
CLICK... CLACK...
MAKE THE HORSES GO FASTER!
YEAH, YEAH...
RMMMBLE...
HM ...?
FLASH
ドカカッ
THA-THOOM
!!

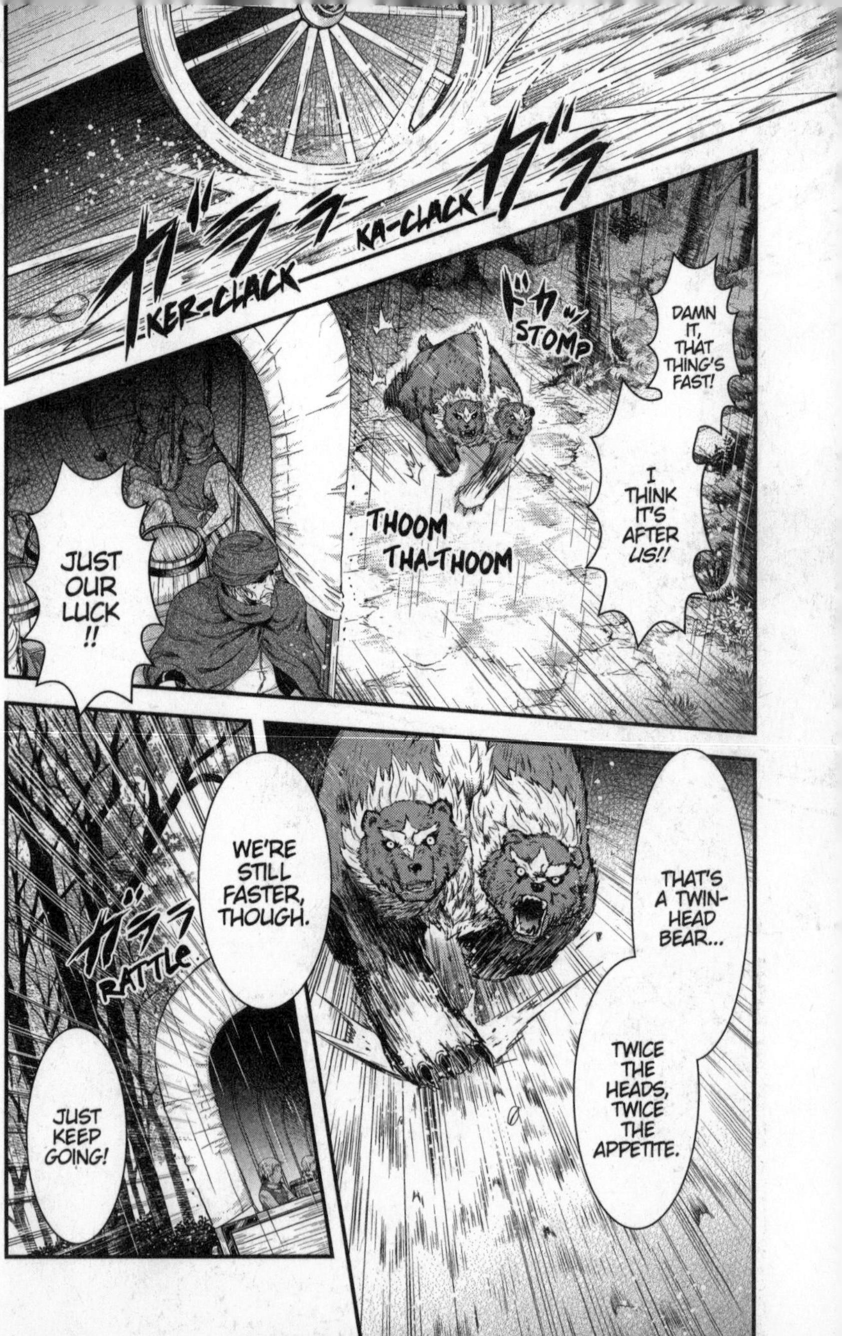

ガラ
KA-CLACK
ガラララ
KER-CLACK
ドカッ
STOMP
DAMN IT, THAT THING'S FAST!
I THINK IT'S AFTER US!!
THOOM THA-THOOM
JUST OUR LUCK!!
THAT'S A TWIN-HEAD BEAR...
TWICE THE HEADS, TWICE THE APPETITE.
WE'RE STILL FASTER, THOUGH.
ガラララ
RATTLE
JUST KEEP GOING!

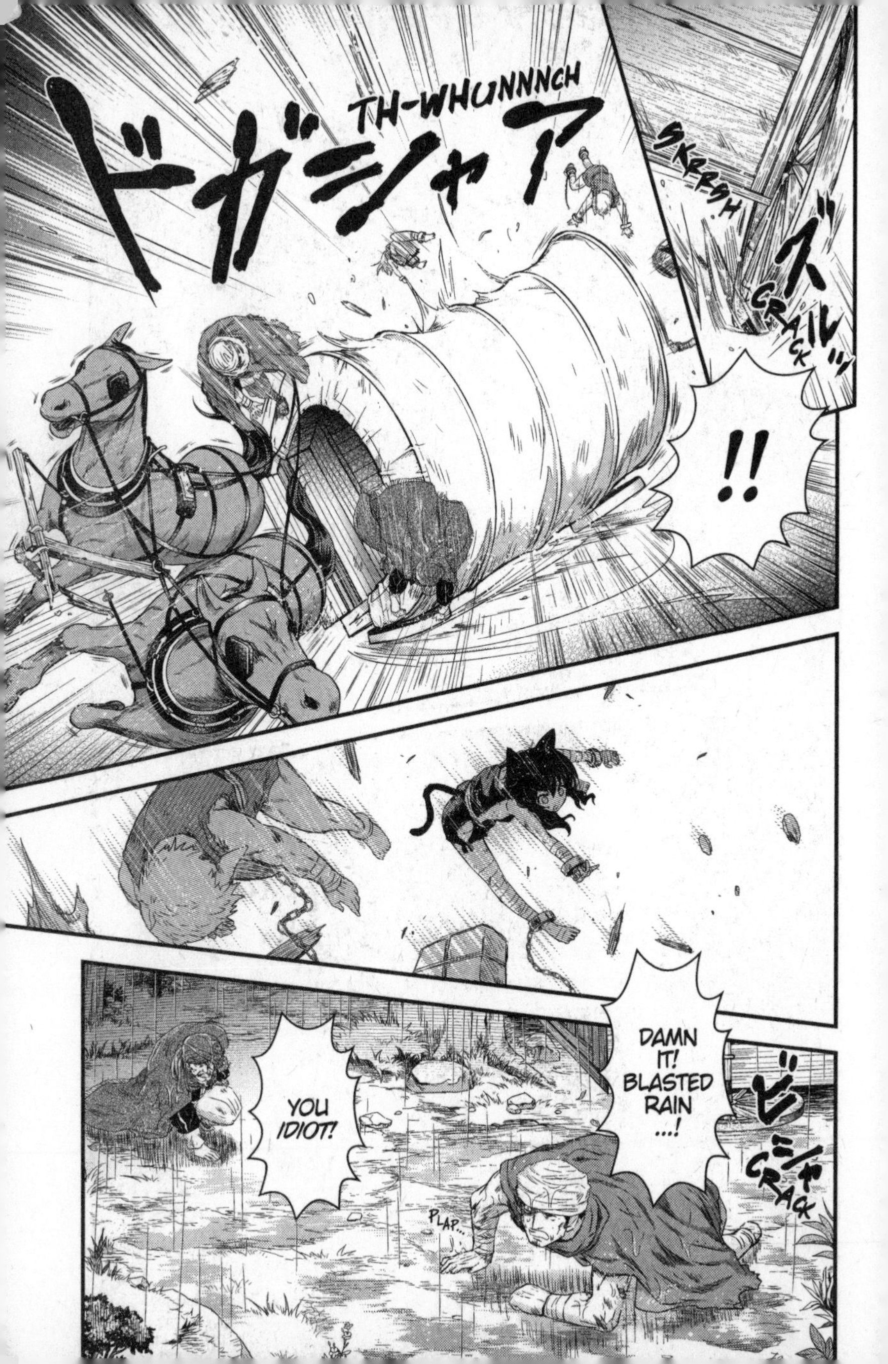

SKRRSH
ズ
CRACK
ル
!!
ドガシャア
TH-WHUNNNCH
DAMN IT! BLASTED RAIN ...!
ビ
CRACK
YOU IDIOT!
PLAP...

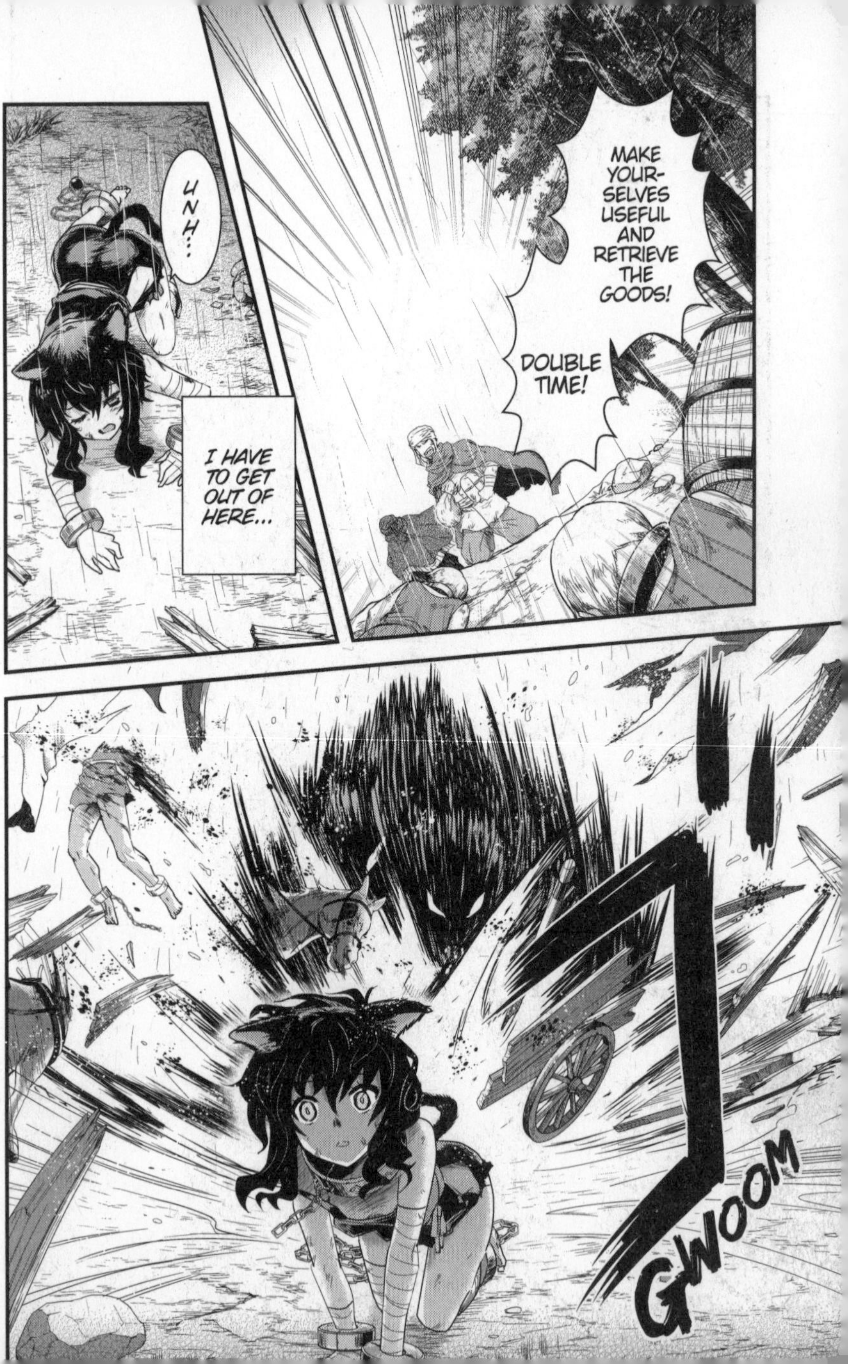
MAKE YOUR-SELVES USEFUL AND RETRIEVE THE GOODS!
DOUBLE TIME!
UNH...
I HAVE TO GET OUT OF HERE...
GWOOM

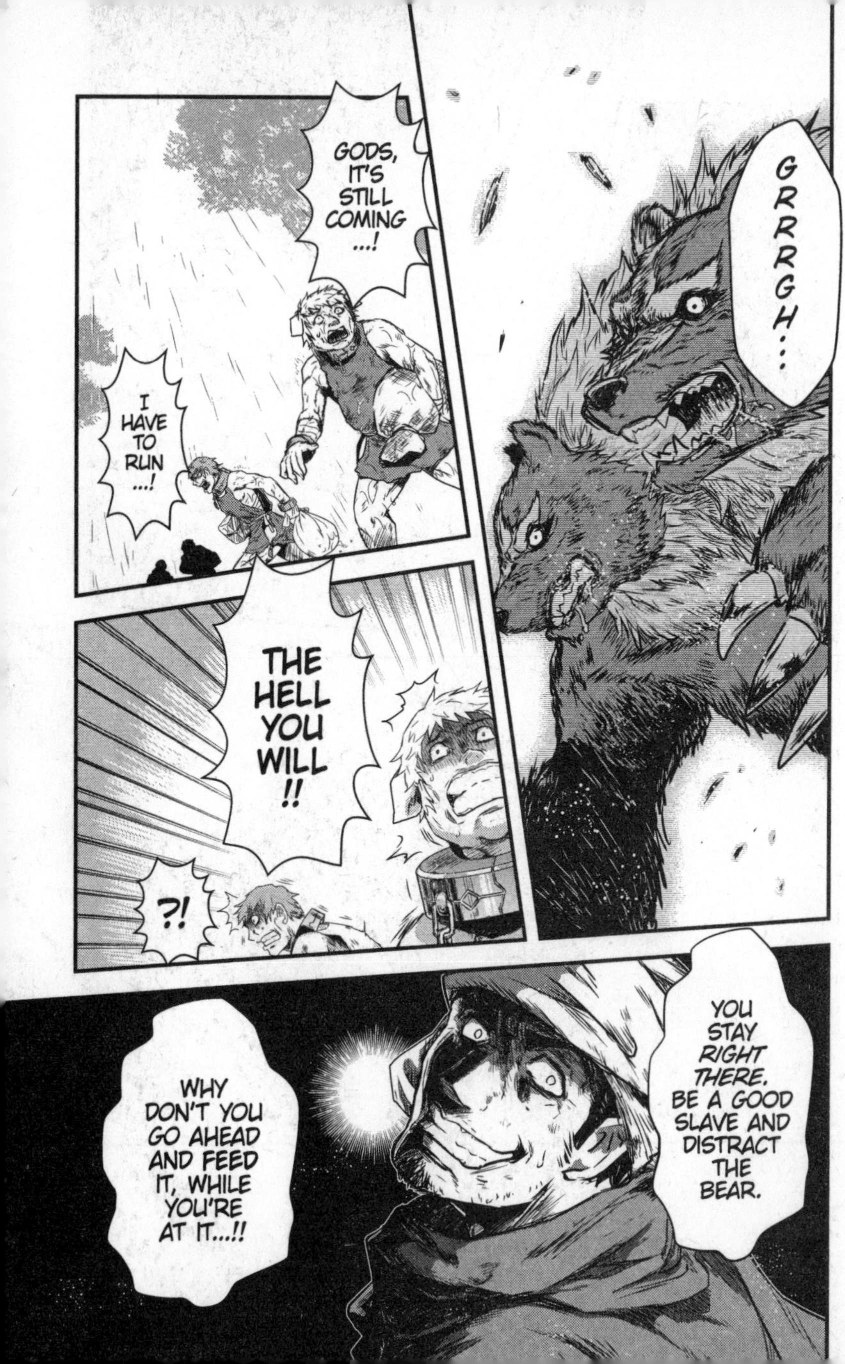
GRRRGH...
GODS, IT'S STILL COMING ...!
I HAVE TO RUN ...!
THE HELL YOU WILL !!
?!
YOU STAY RIGHT THERE. BE A GOOD SLAVE AND DISTRACT THE BEAR.
WHY DON'T YOU GO AHEAD AND FEED IT, WHILE YOU'RE AT IT...!!

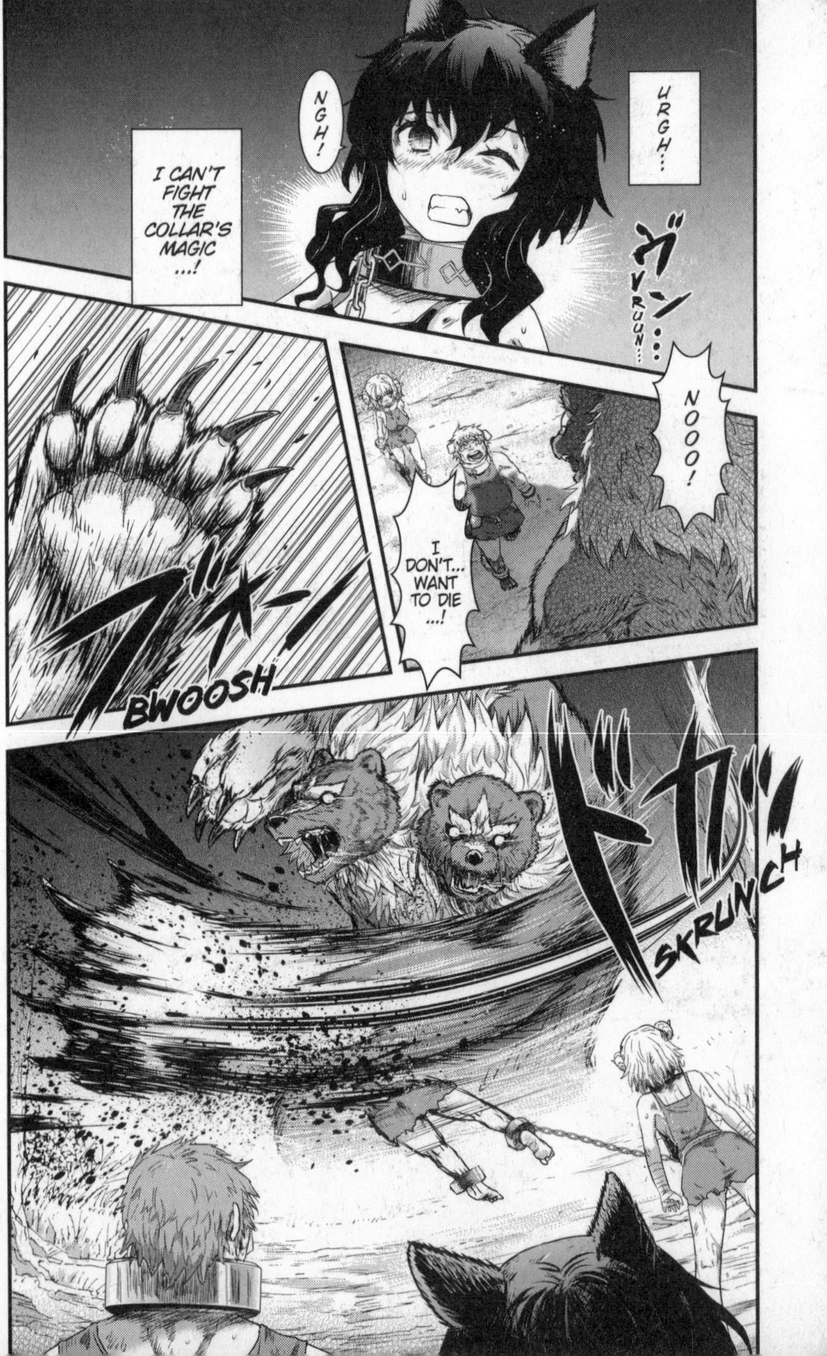
URGH...
NGH!
I CAN'T FIGHT THE COLLAR'S MAGIC ...!
VRUUN...
NOOOO!
I DON'T... WANT TO DIE ...!
BWOOSH
SKRUNCH

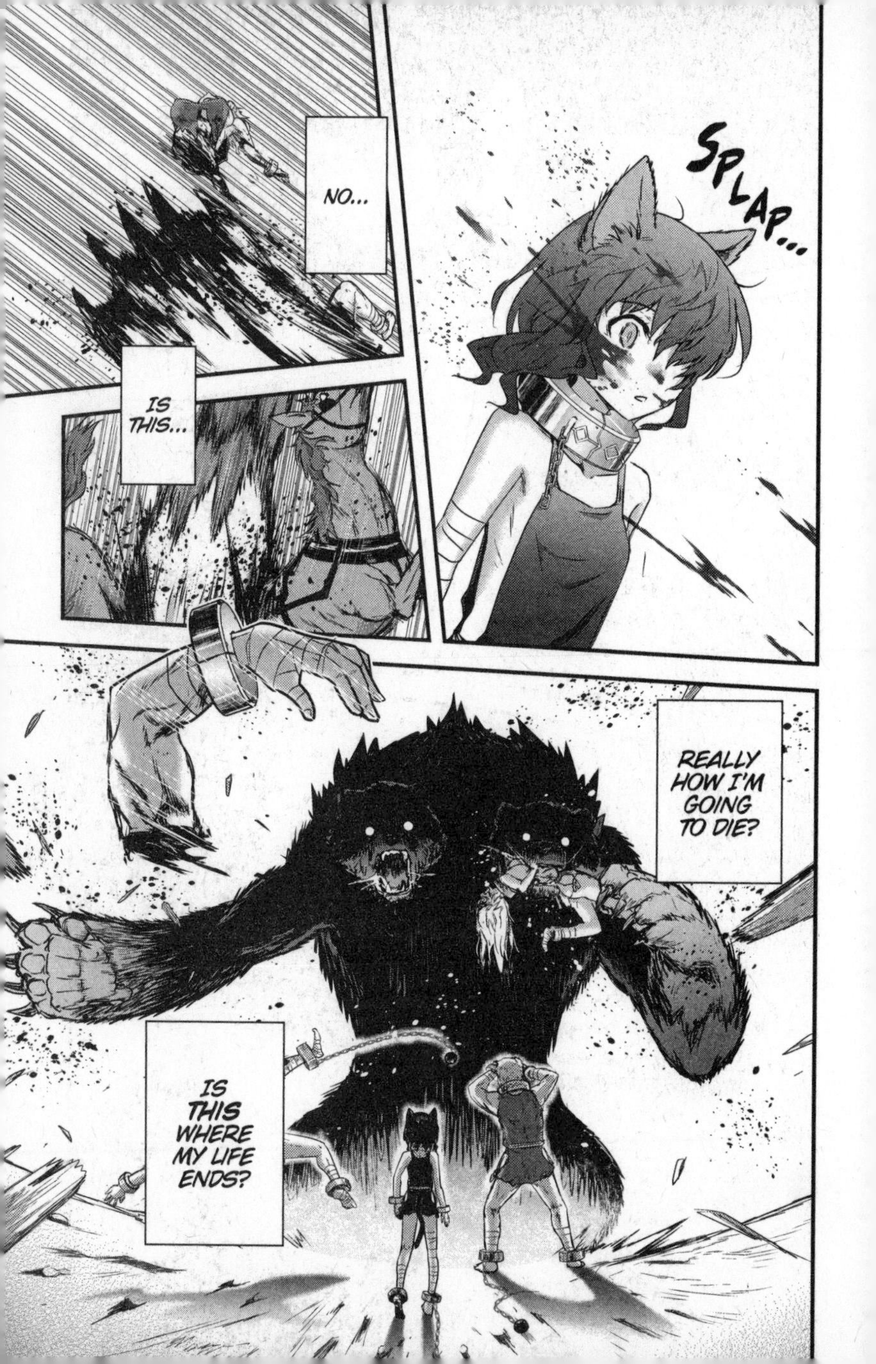
SPLAP...
NO...
IS THIS...
REALLY HOW I'M GOING TO DIE?
IS THIS WHERE MY LIFE ENDS?

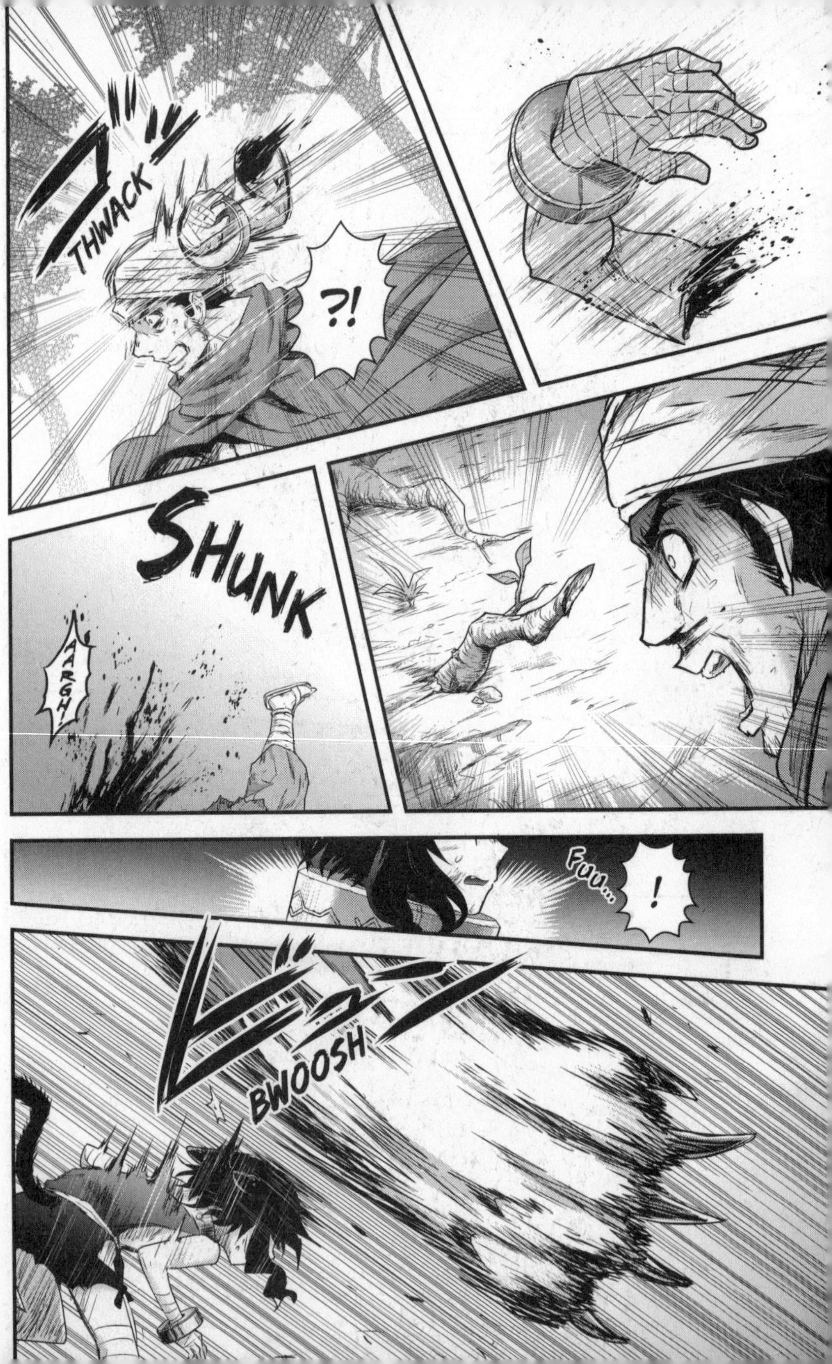
THWACK
?!
SHUNK
AARGH!
!
Fuu...
BWOOSH

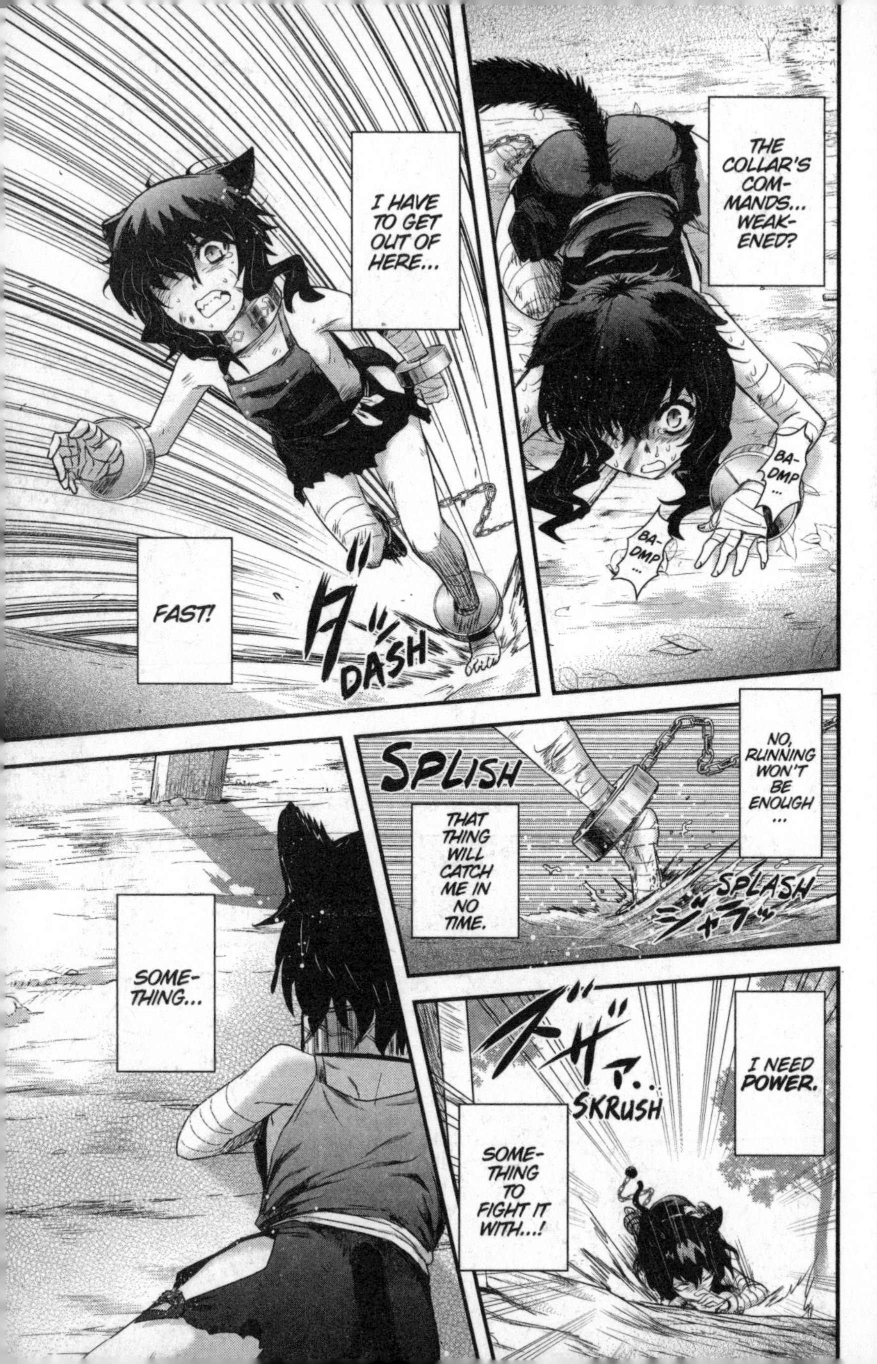
THE COLLAR'S COM-MANDS... WEAK-ENED?
BA-DMP...
BA-DMP...
I HAVE TO GET OUT OF HERE...
FAST!
DASH
NO, RUNNING WON'T BE ENOUGH...
SPLISH
THAT THING WILL CATCH ME IN NO TIME.
SPLASH
I NEED POWER.
SKRUSH
SOME-THING TO FIGHT IT WITH...!
SOME-THING...

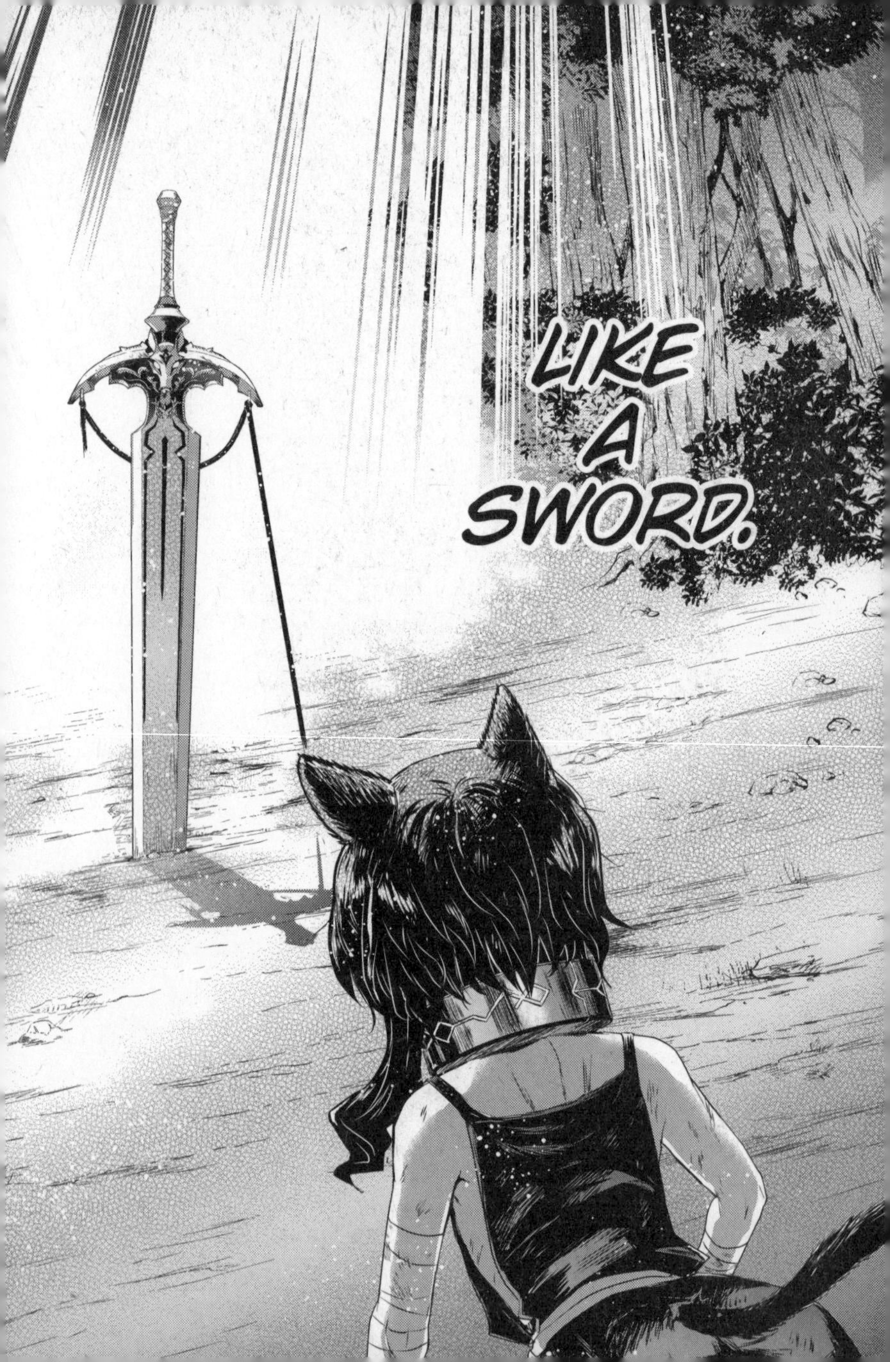
LIKE A SWORD.

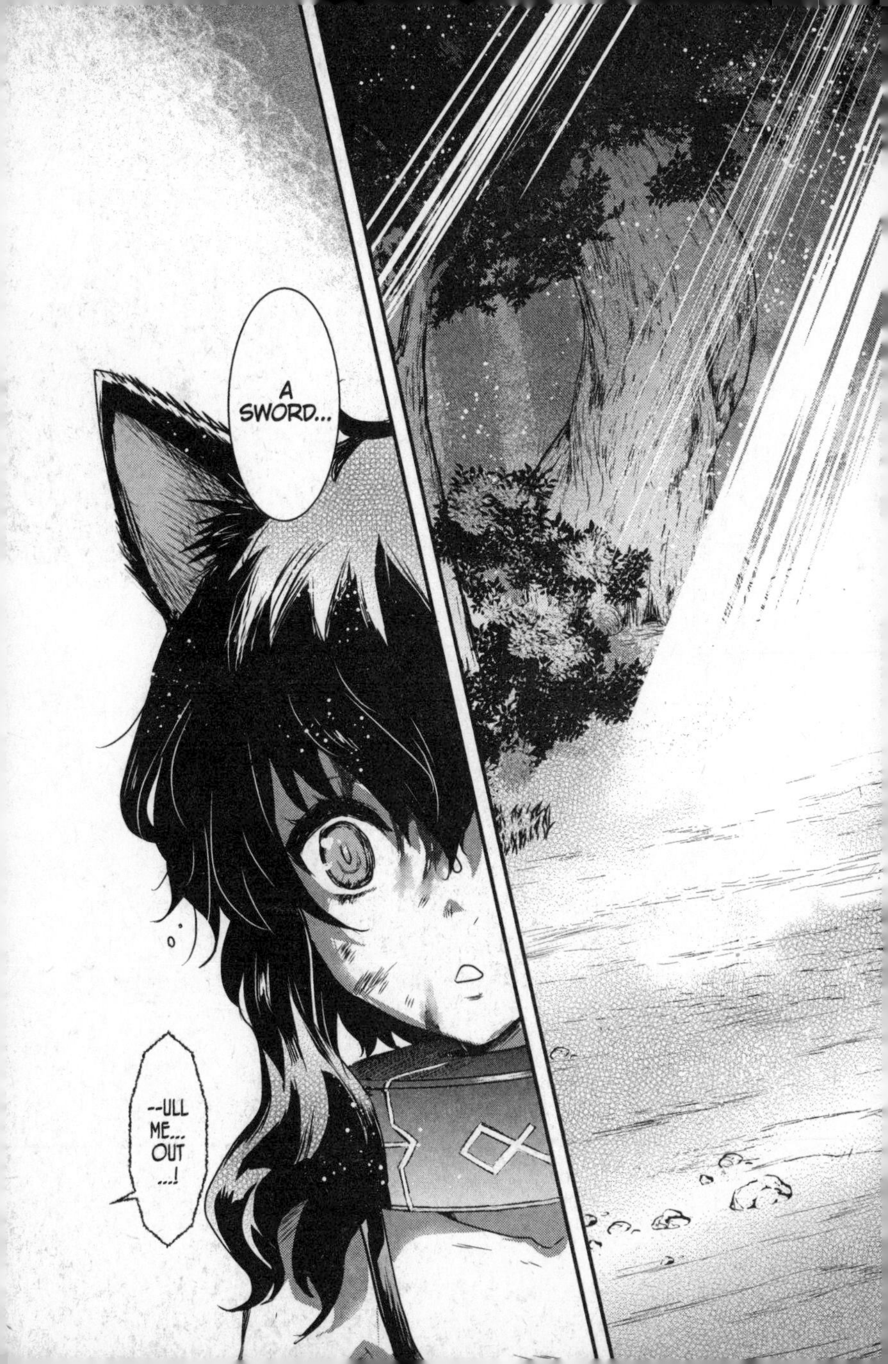
A SWORD...
--ULL ME... OUT ...!

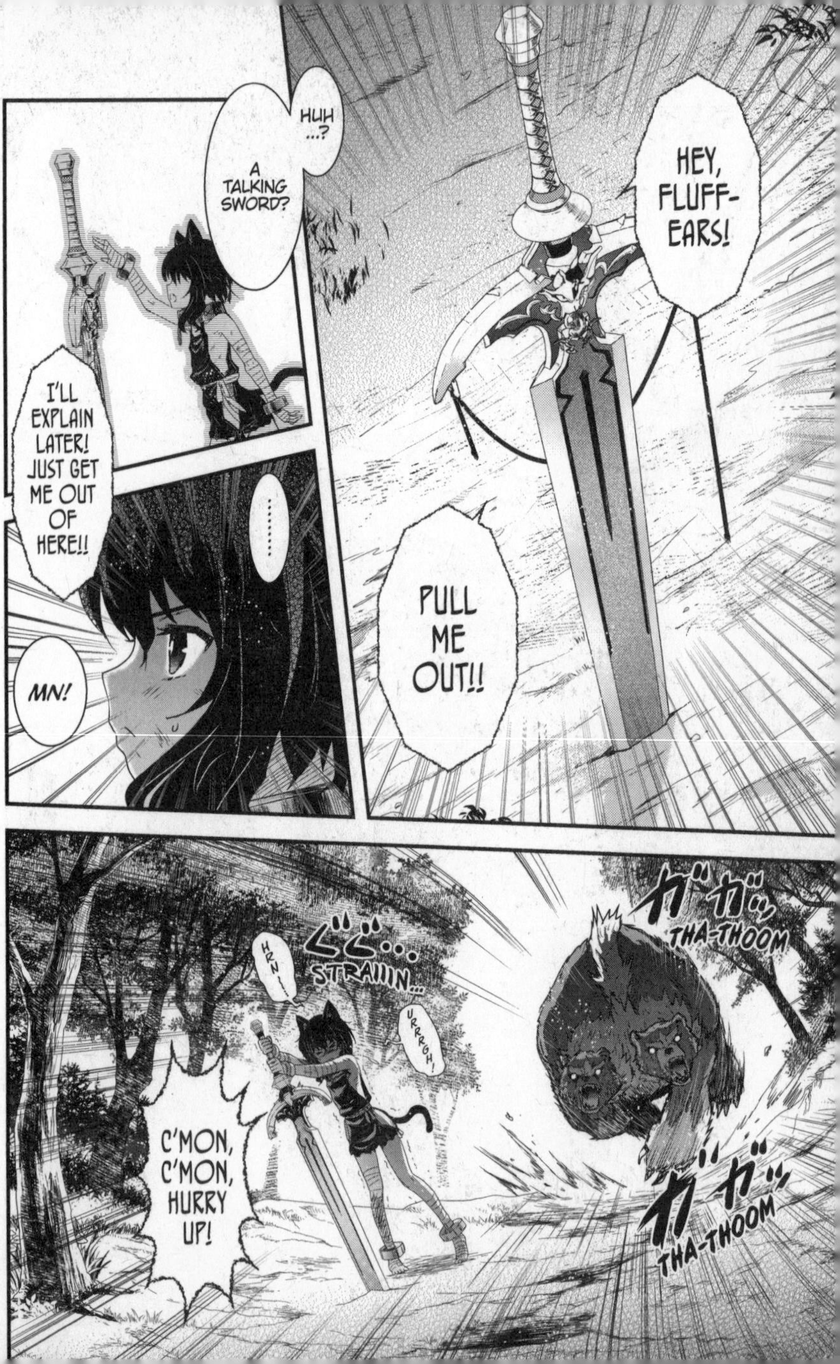
HEY, FLUFF-EARS!
PULL ME OUT!!
HUH ...?
A TALKING SWORD?
I'LL EXPLAIN LATER! JUST GET ME OUT OF HERE!!
......
MN!
ガガッ
THA-THOOM
ガガッ
THA-THOOM
ぐぐ...
STRAIIIN...
HRN...
URRRGH!
C'MON, C'MON, HURRY UP!

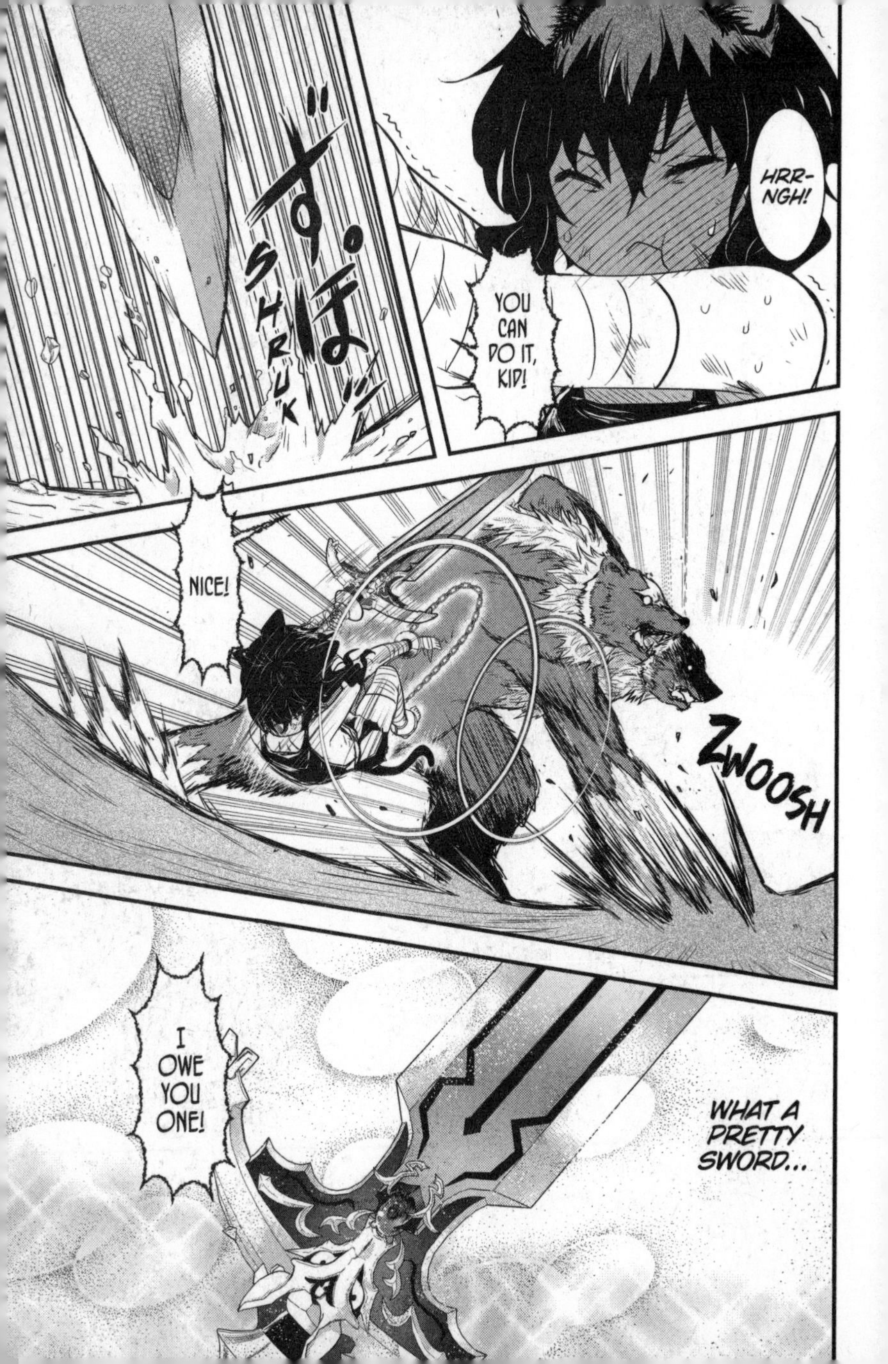

HRR-NGH!
YOU CAN DO IT, KID!
ずぽ
SHRUK
NICE!
ZWOOSH
WHAT A PRETTY SWORD...
I OWE YOU ONE!

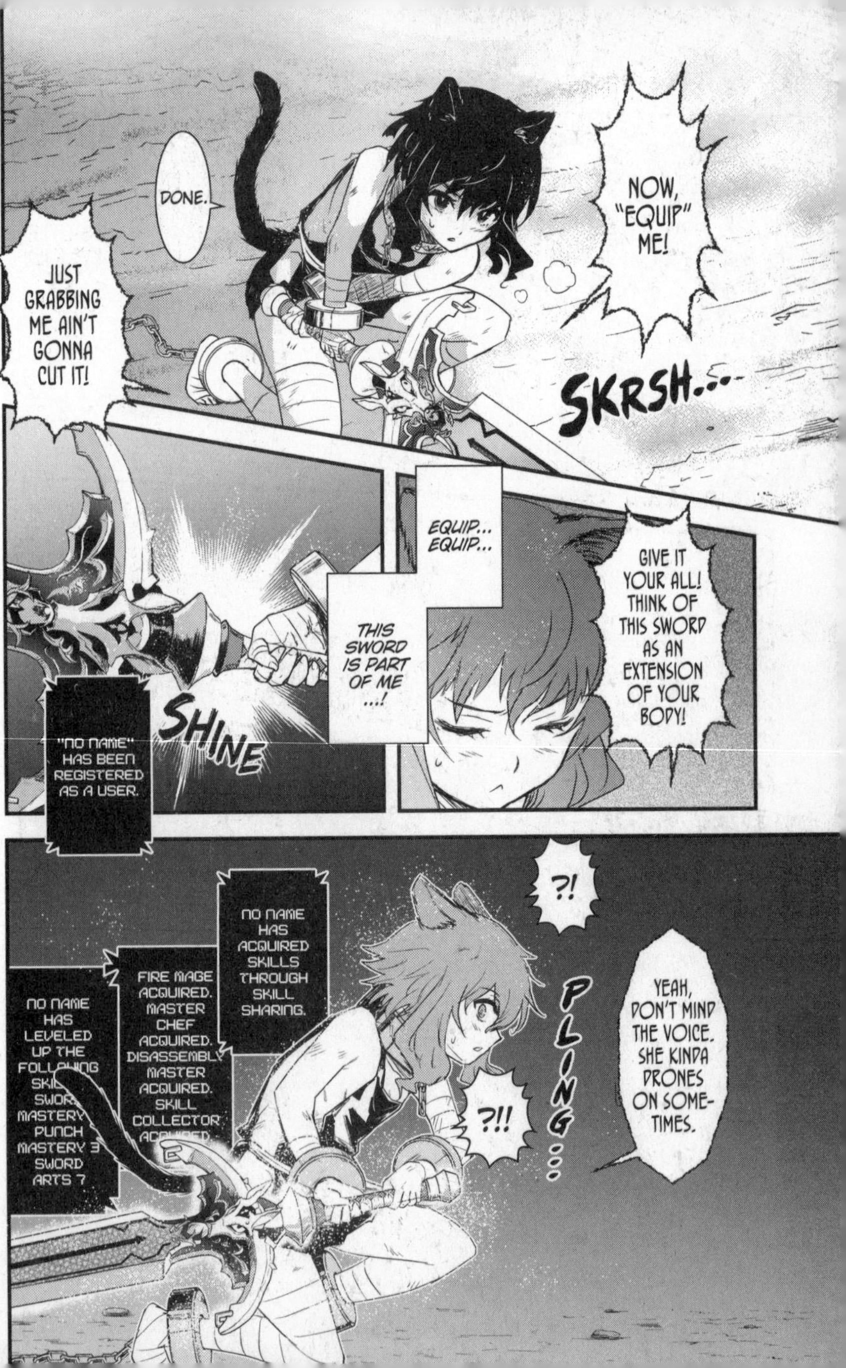
NOW, "EQUIP" ME!
DONE.
JUST GRABBING ME AIN'T GONNA CUT IT!
SKRSH...
GIVE IT YOUR ALL! THINK OF THIS SWORD AS AN EXTENSION OF YOUR BODY!
EQUIP... EQUIP...
THIS SWORD IS PART OF ME ...!
SHINE
"NO NAME" HAS BEEN REGISTERED AS A USER.
?!
YEAH, DON'T MIND THE VOICE. SHE KINDA DRONES ON SOME-TIMES.
PLING...
?!!
NO NAME HAS ACQUIRED SKILLS THROUGH SKILL SHARING.
FIRE MAGE ACQUIRED. MASTER CHEF ACQUIRED. DISASSEMBLY MASTER ACQUIRED. SKILL COLLECTOR ACQUIRED.
NO NAME HAS LEVELED UP THE FOLLOWING SKI SWOR MASTERY PUNCH MASTERY 3 SWORD ARTS 7

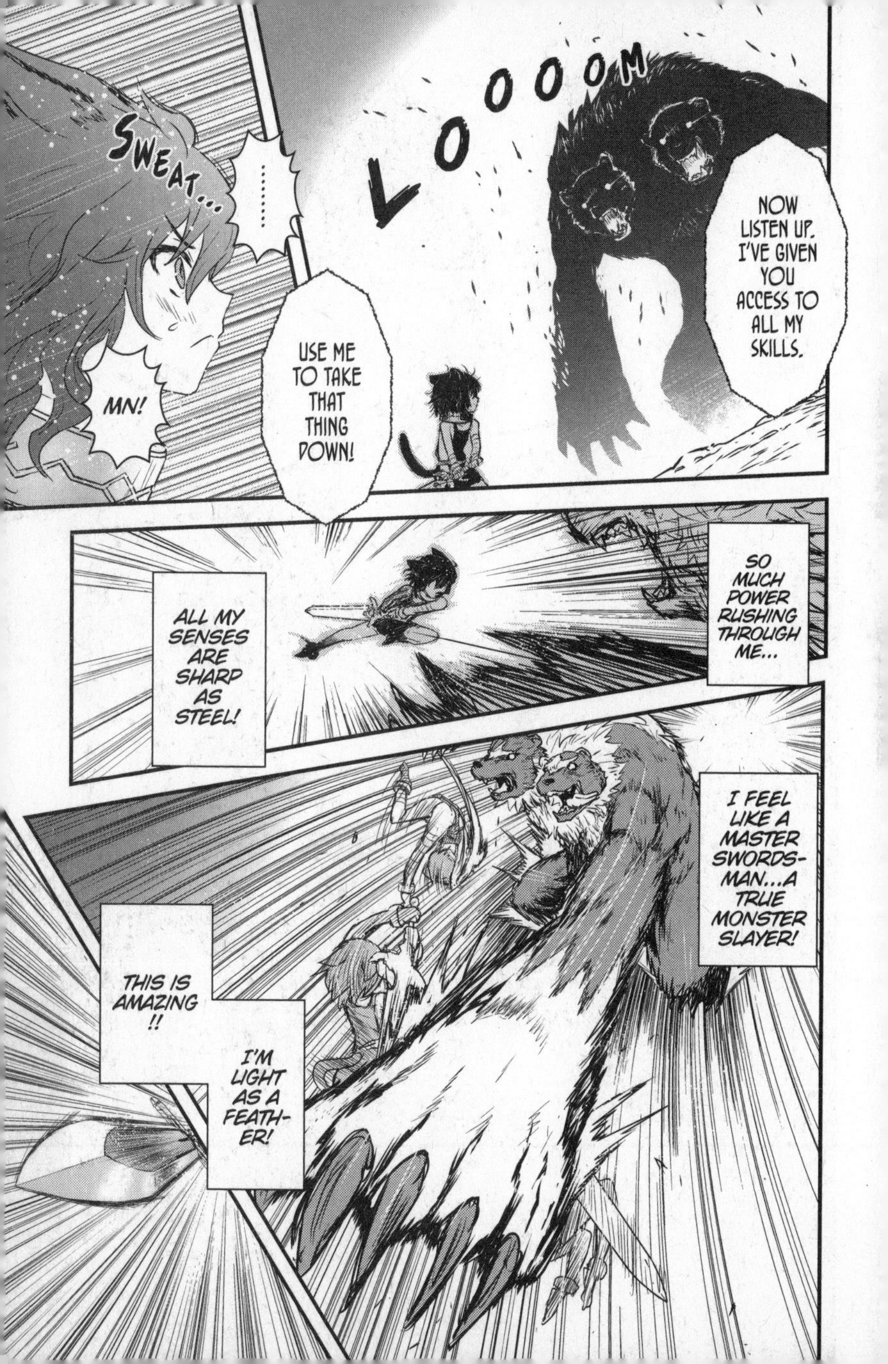
LOOOOM
NOW LISTEN UP. I'VE GIVEN YOU ACCESS TO ALL MY SKILLS.
USE ME TO TAKE THAT THING DOWN!
SWEAT...
......
MN!
SO MUCH POWER RUSHING THROUGH ME...
ALL MY SENSES ARE SHARP AS STEEL!
I FEEL LIKE A MASTER SWORDS-MAN...A TRUE MONSTER SLAYER!
THIS IS AMAZING!!
I'M LIGHT AS A FEATHER!

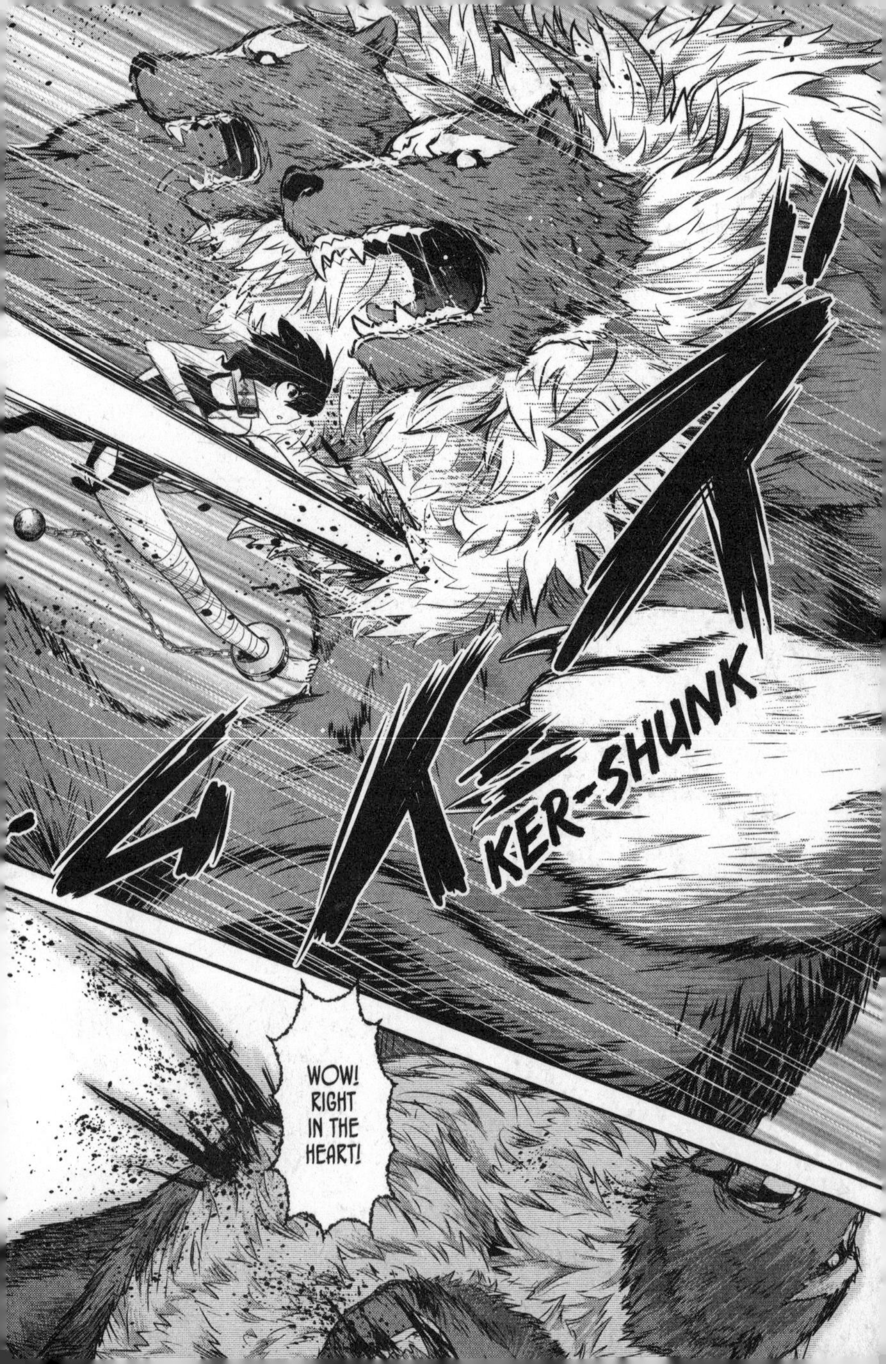
KER-SHUNK
WOW! RIGHT IN THE HEART!

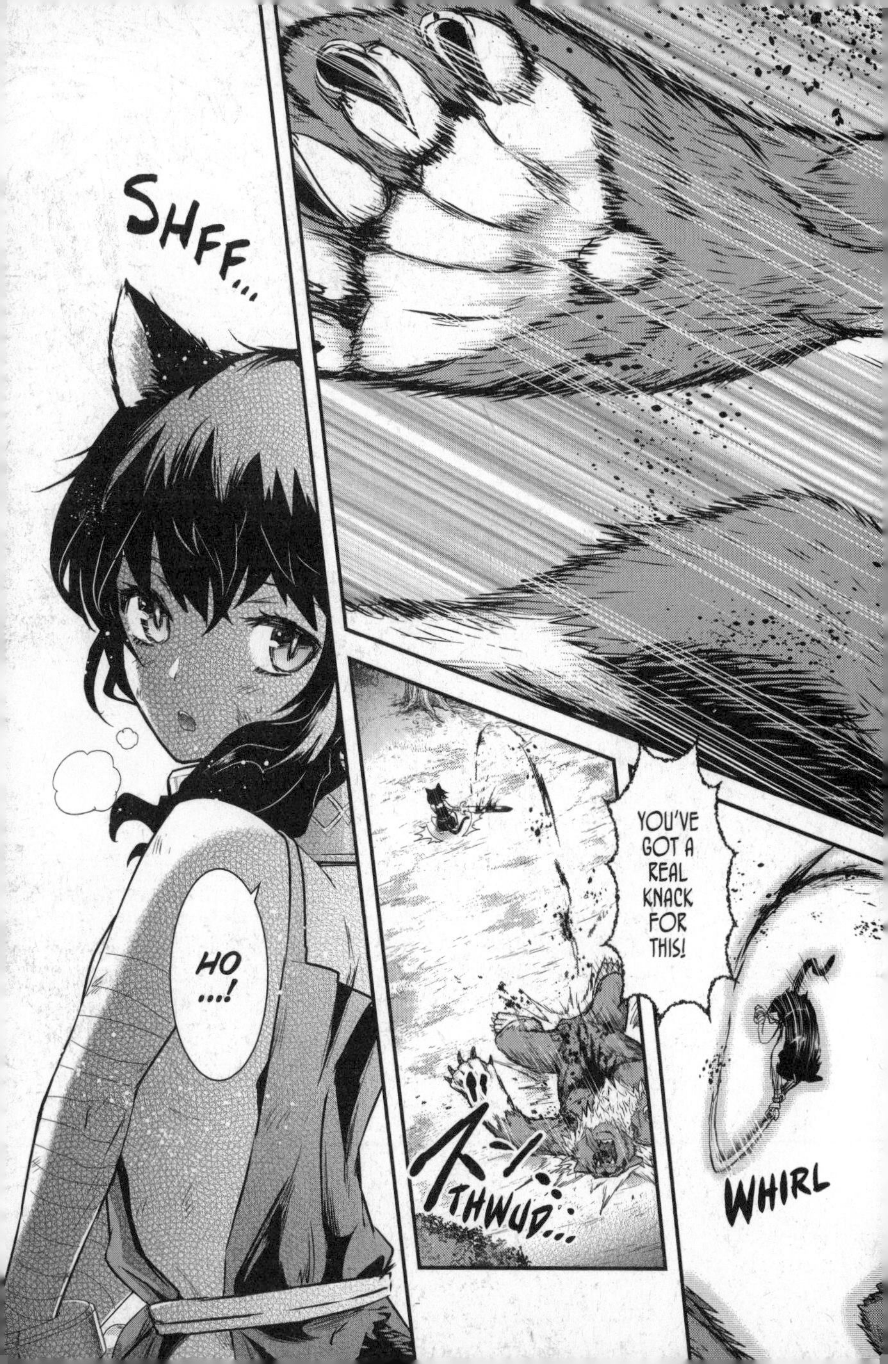
WHIRL
YOU'VE GOT A REAL KNACK FOR THIS!
THWUD...
SHFF...
HO ...!

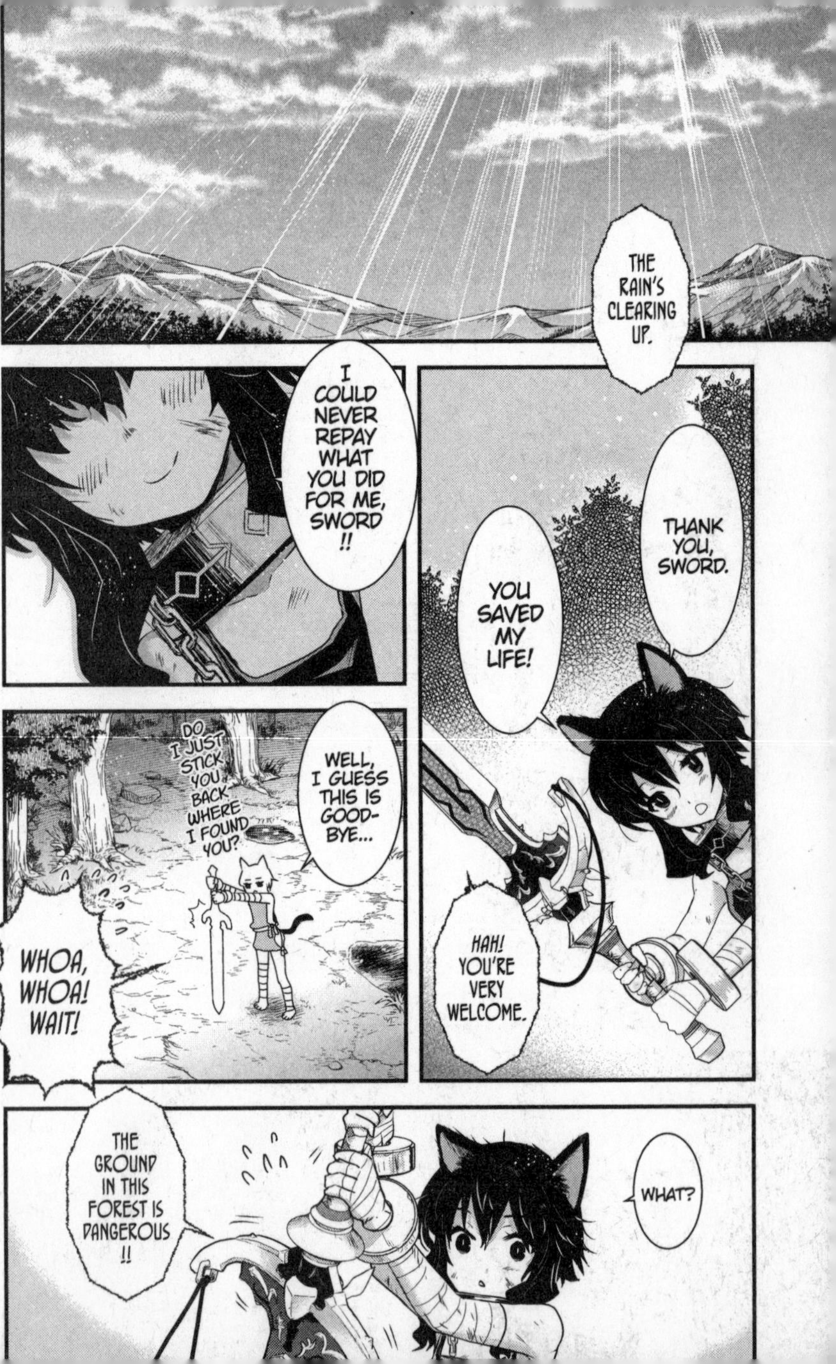
THE RAIN'S CLEARING UP.
THANK YOU, SWORD.
YOU SAVED MY LIFE!
HAH! YOU'RE VERY WELCOME.
I COULD NEVER REPAY WHAT YOU DID FOR ME, SWORD!!
WELL, I GUESS THIS IS GOOD-BYE...
DO I JUST STICK YOU BACK WHERE I FOUND YOU?
WHOA, WHOA! WAIT!
WHAT?
THE GROUND IN THIS FOREST IS DANGEROUS!!

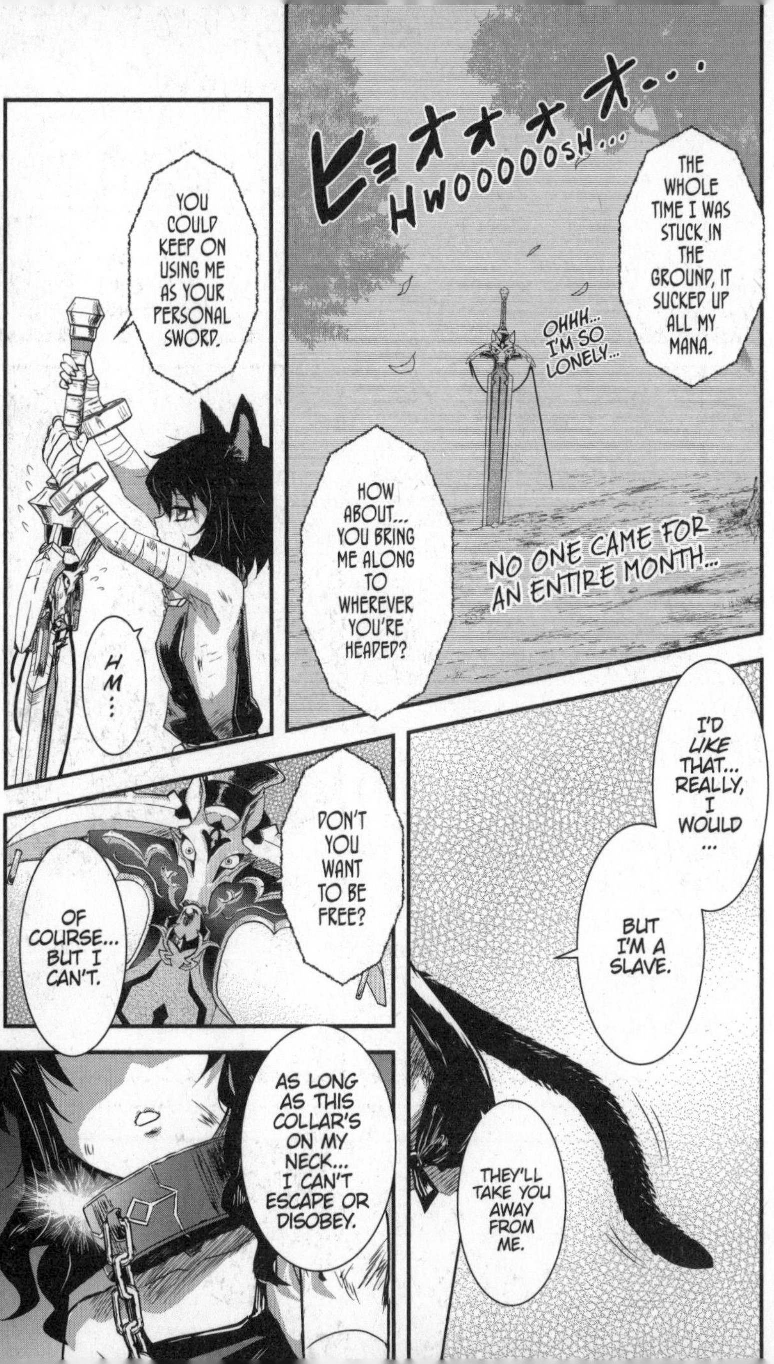
ヒョオオオオ…
HWOOOOOSH...
THE WHOLE TIME I WAS STUCK IN THE GROUND, IT SUCKED UP ALL MY MANA.
OHHH... I'M SO LONELY...
NO ONE CAME FOR AN ENTIRE MONTH...
HOW ABOUT... YOU BRING ME ALONG TO WHEREVER YOU'RE HEADED?
YOU COULD KEEP ON USING ME AS YOUR PERSONAL SWORD.
HM...
I'D LIKE THAT... REALLY, I WOULD...
BUT I'M A SLAVE.
THEY'LL TAKE YOU AWAY FROM ME.
DON'T YOU WANT TO BE FREE?
OF COURSE... BUT I CAN'T.
AS LONG AS THIS COLLAR'S ON MY NECK... I CAN'T ESCAPE OR DISOBEY.

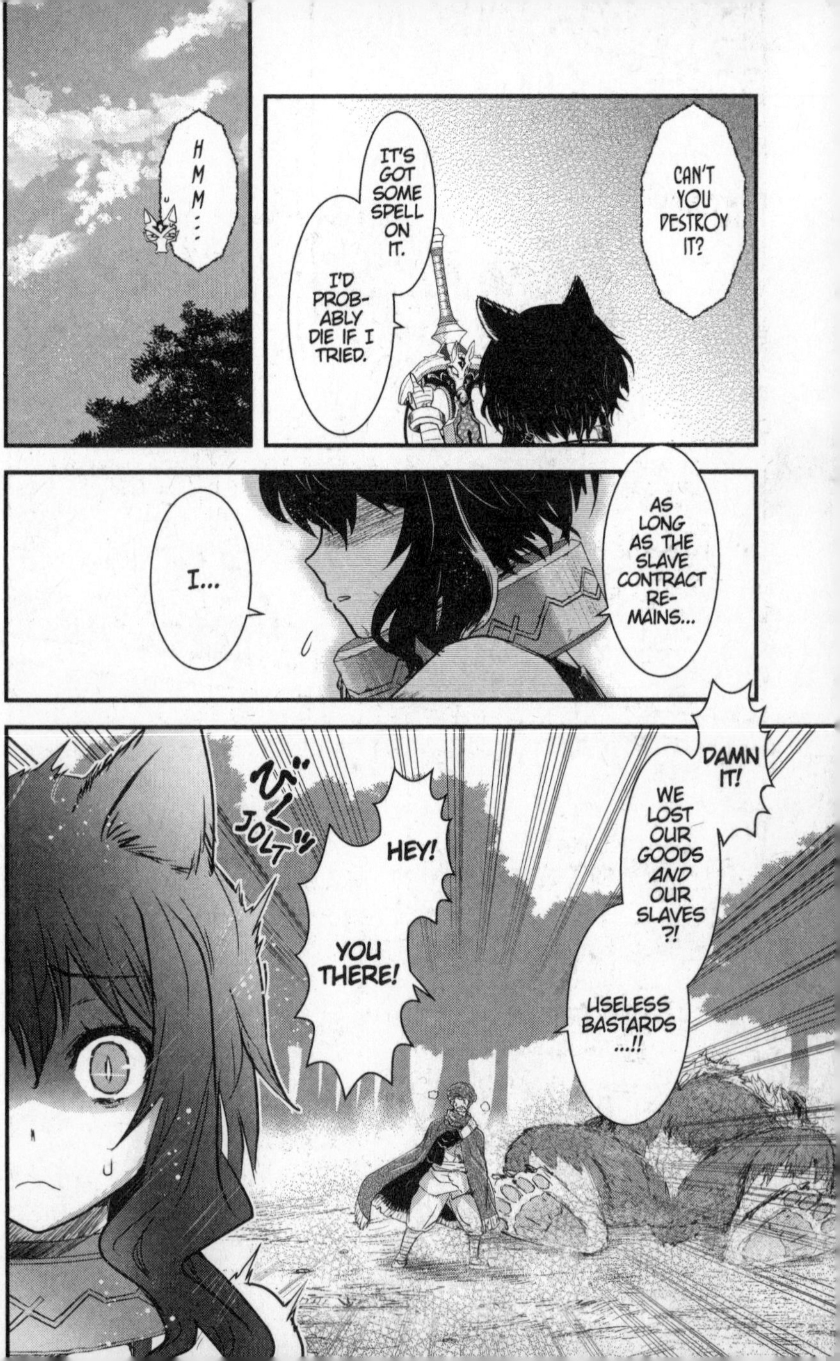
CAN'T YOU DESTROY IT?
IT'S GOT SOME SPELL ON IT.
I'D PROBABLY DIE IF I TRIED.
HMM...
AS LONG AS THE SLAVE CONTRACT RE-MAINS...
I...
DAMN IT!
WE LOST OUR GOODS AND OUR SLAVES?!
USELESS BASTARDS...!!
HEY!
YOU THERE!
JOLT

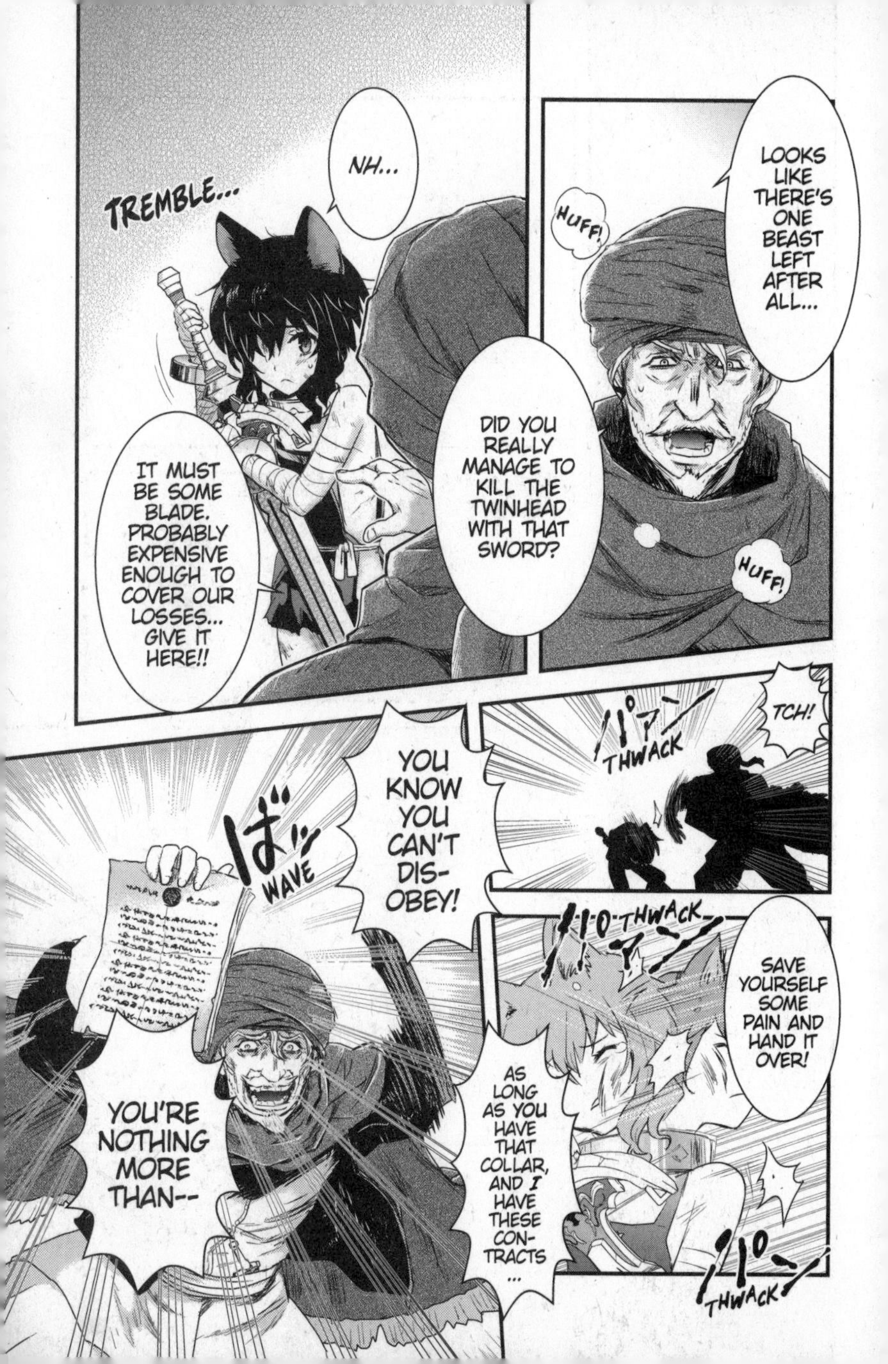
LOOKS LIKE THERE'S ONE BEAST LEFT AFTER ALL...
HUFF!
HUFF!
NH...
TREMBLE...
DID YOU REALLY MANAGE TO KILL THE TWINHEAD WITH THAT SWORD?
IT MUST BE SOME BLADE. PROBABLY EXPENSIVE ENOUGH TO COVER OUR LOSSES... GIVE IT HERE!!
TCH!
パァン
THWACK
THWACK
SAVE YOURSELF SOME PAIN AND HAND IT OVER!
AS LONG AS YOU HAVE THAT COLLAR, AND I HAVE THESE CONTRACTS...
THWACK
YOU KNOW YOU CAN'T DIS-OBEY!
ばっ
WAVE
YOU'RE NOTHING MORE THAN--

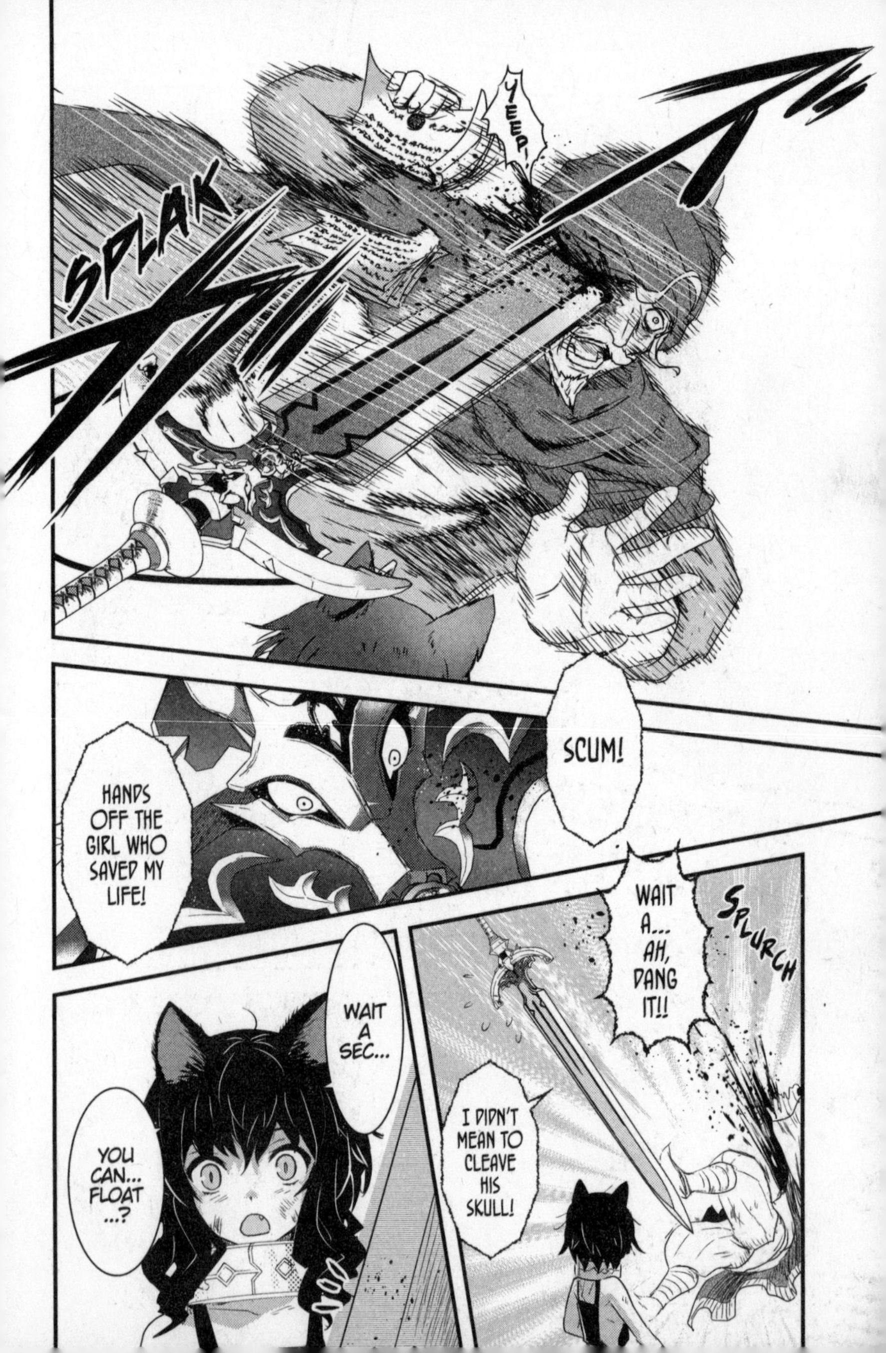
YEEP!
SPLAK
SCUM!
HANDS OFF THE GIRL WHO SAVED MY LIFE!
WAIT A... AH, DANG IT!!
SPLURCH
I DIDN'T MEAN TO CLEAVE HIS SKULL!
WAIT A SEC...
YOU CAN... FLOAT ...?

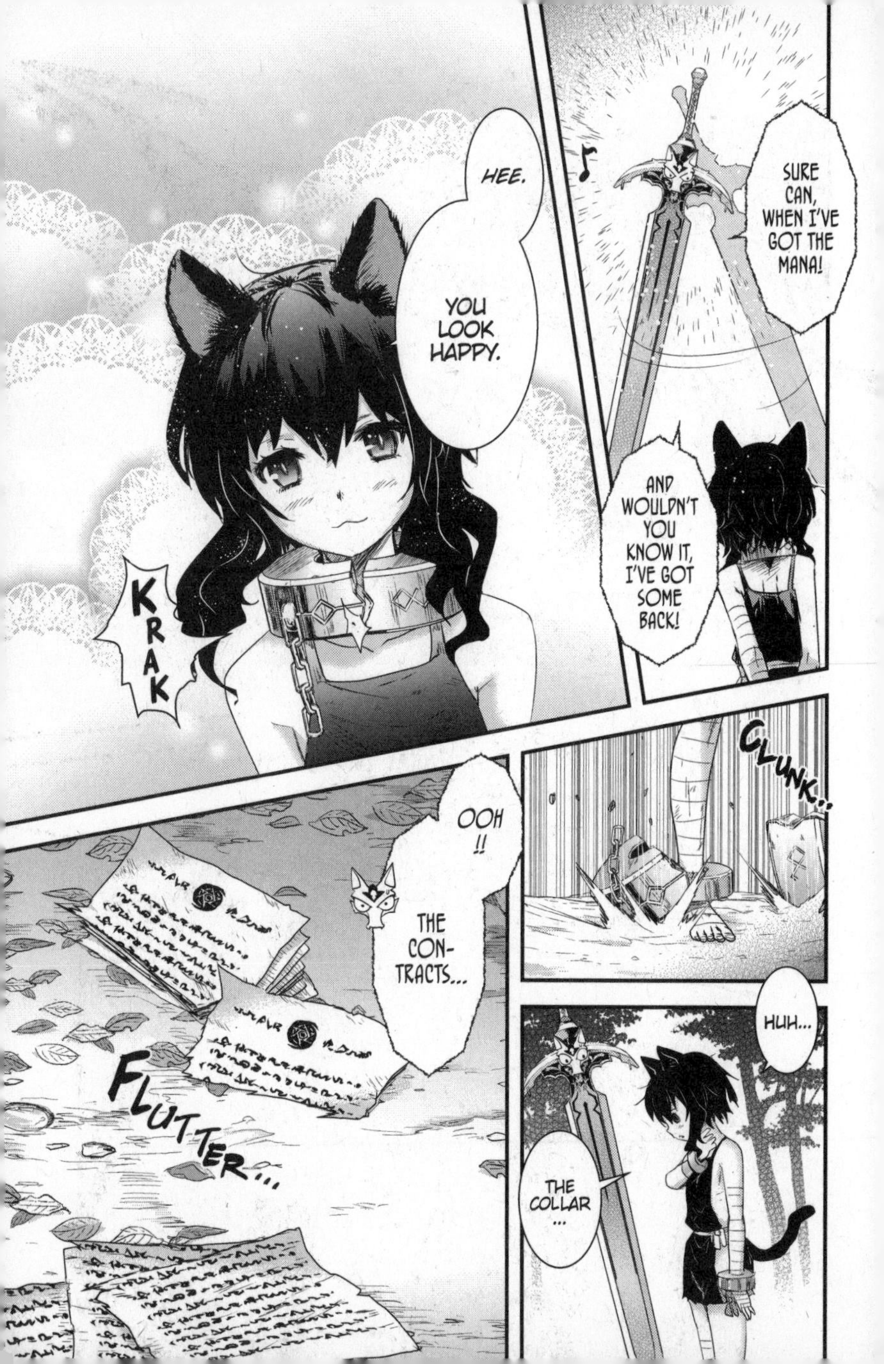
SURE CAN, WHEN I'VE GOT THE MANA!
AND WOULDN'T YOU KNOW IT, I'VE GOT SOME BACK!
HEE.
YOU LOOK HAPPY.
KRAK
CLUNK...
HUH...
THE COLLAR...
OOH!!
THE CONTRACTS...
FLUTTER...

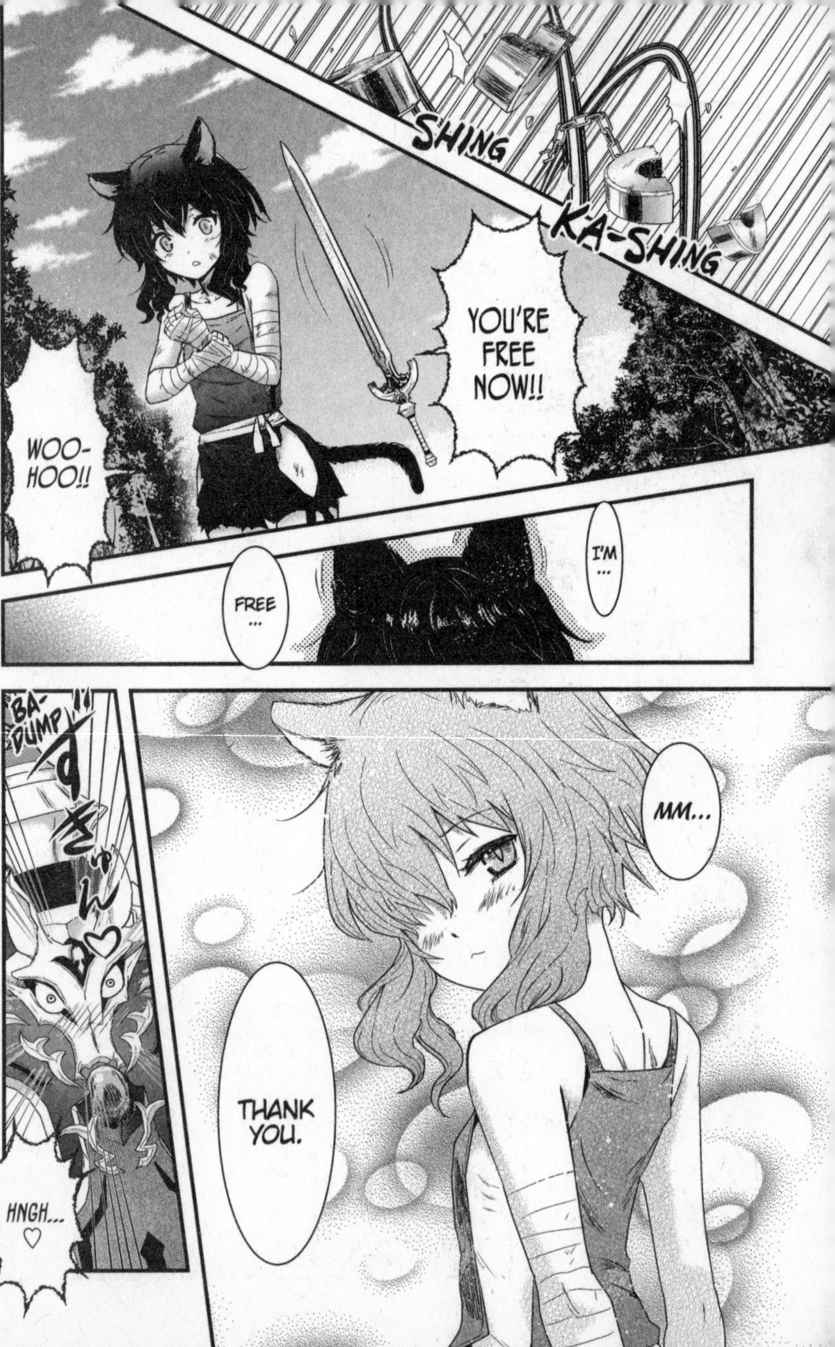
SHING
KA-SHING
YOU'RE FREE NOW!!
WOO-HOO!!
I'M ...
FREE ...
MM...
THANK YOU.
BA-DUMP
HNGH... ♡

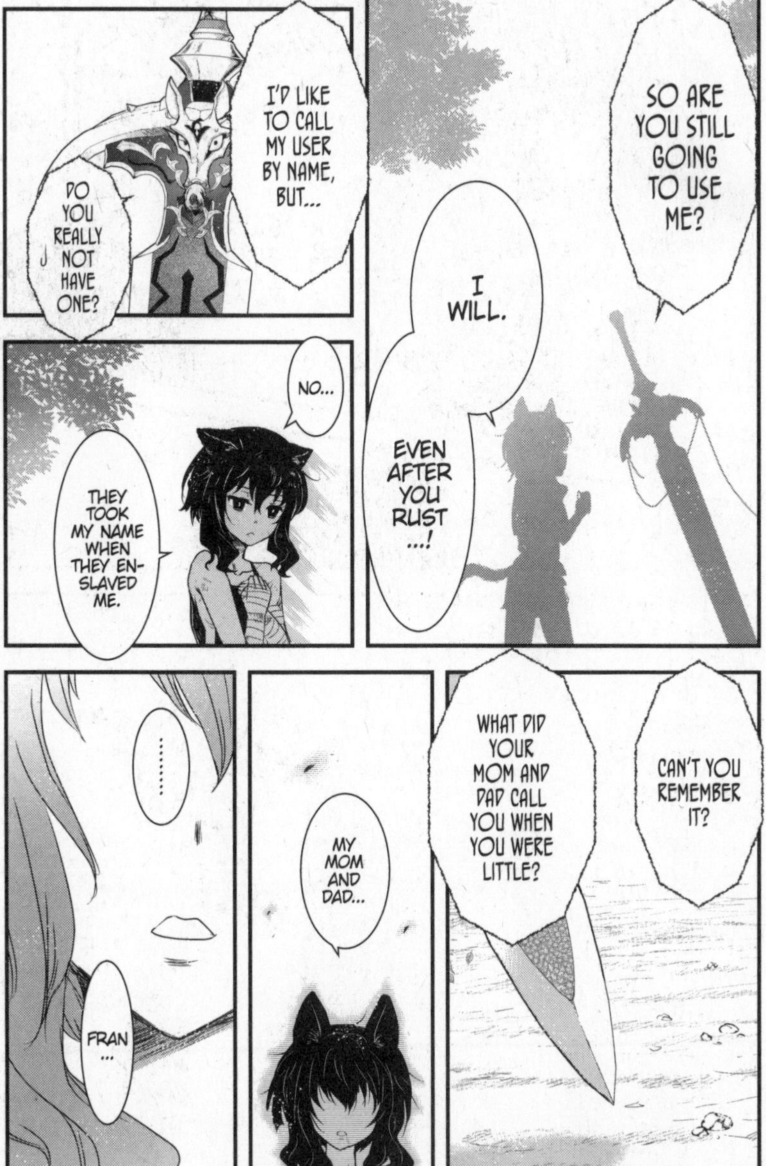

SO ARE YOU STILL GOING TO USE ME?
I WILL.
EVEN AFTER YOU RUST ...!
I'D LIKE TO CALL MY USER BY NAME, BUT...
DO YOU REALLY NOT HAVE ONE?
NO...
THEY TOOK MY NAME WHEN THEY EN-SLAVED ME.
CAN'T YOU REMEMBER IT?
WHAT DID YOUR MOM AND DAD CALL YOU WHEN YOU WERE LITTLE?
MY MOM AND DAD...
......
FRAN ...

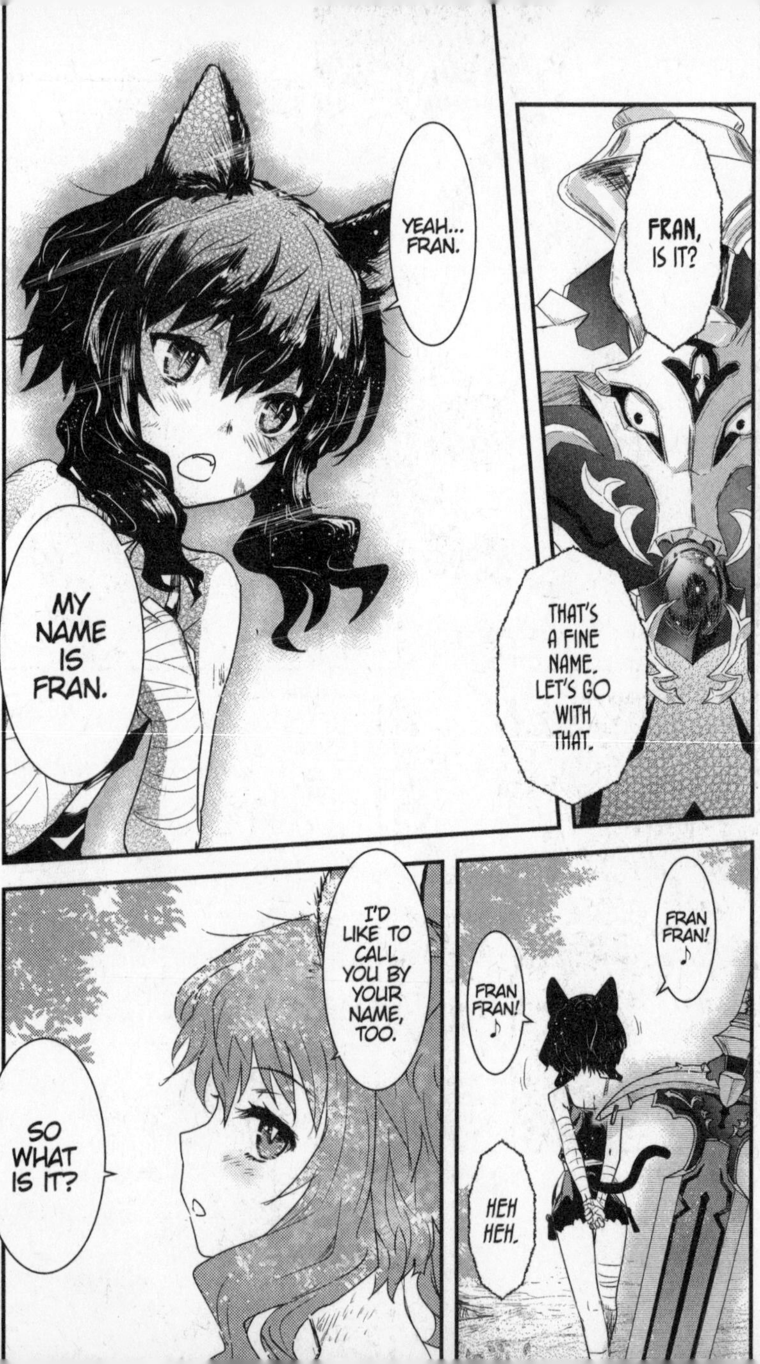
FRAN, IS IT?
THAT'S A FINE NAME. LET'S GO WITH THAT.
YEAH... FRAN.
MY NAME IS FRAN.
FRAN FRAN! ♪
FRAN FRAN! ♪
HEH HEH.
I'D LIKE TO CALL YOU BY YOUR NAME, TOO.
SO WHAT IS IT?

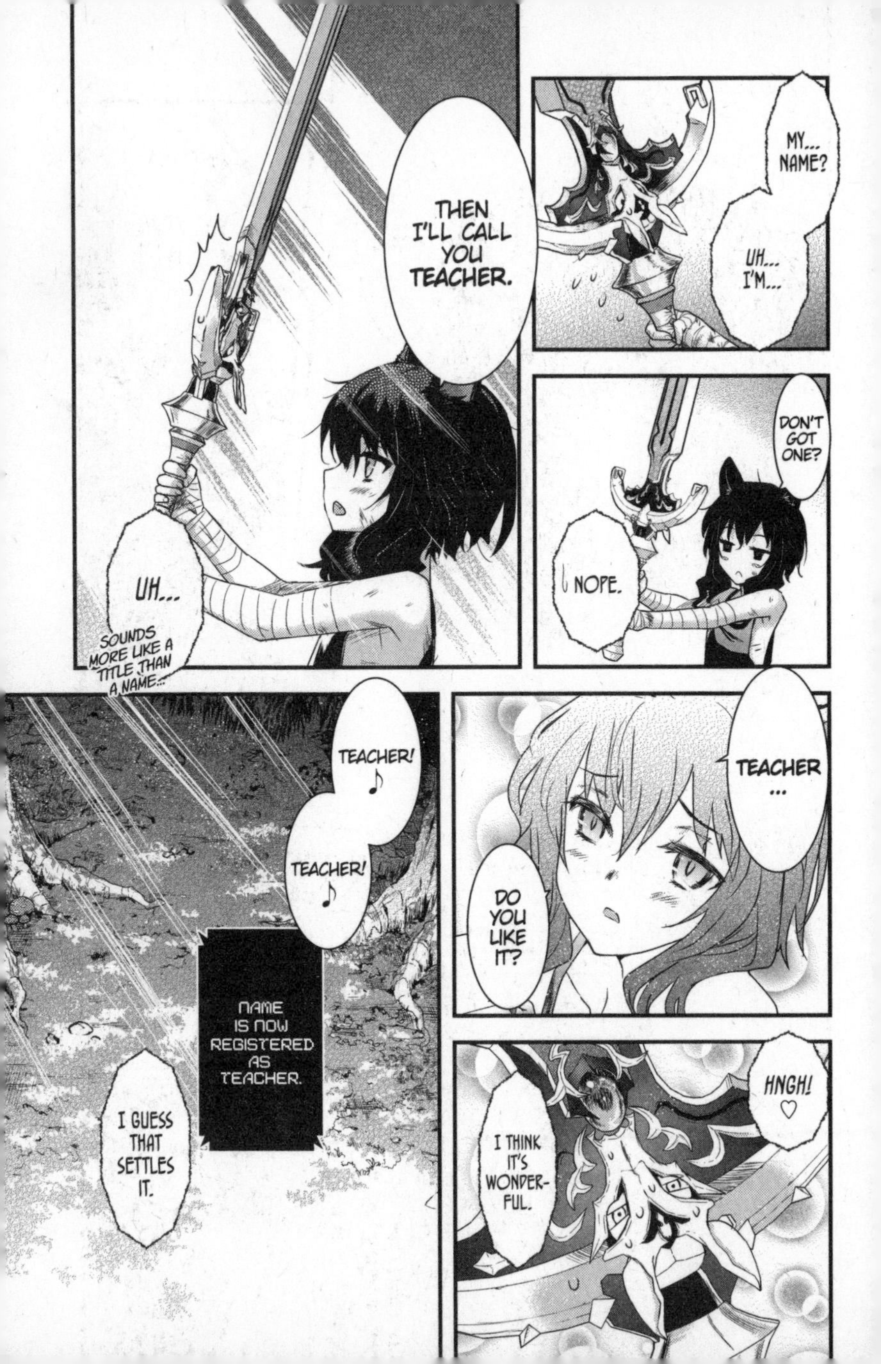
MY... NAME?
UH... I'M...
DON'T GOT ONE?
NOPE.
THEN I'LL CALL YOU TEACHER.
UH...
SOUNDS MORE LIKE A TITLE THAN A NAME...
TEACHER...
DO YOU LIKE IT?
HNGH! ♡
I THINK IT'S WONDER-FUL.
TEACHER! ♪
TEACHER! ♪
NAME IS NOW REGISTERED AS TEACHER.
I GUESS THAT SETTLES IT.

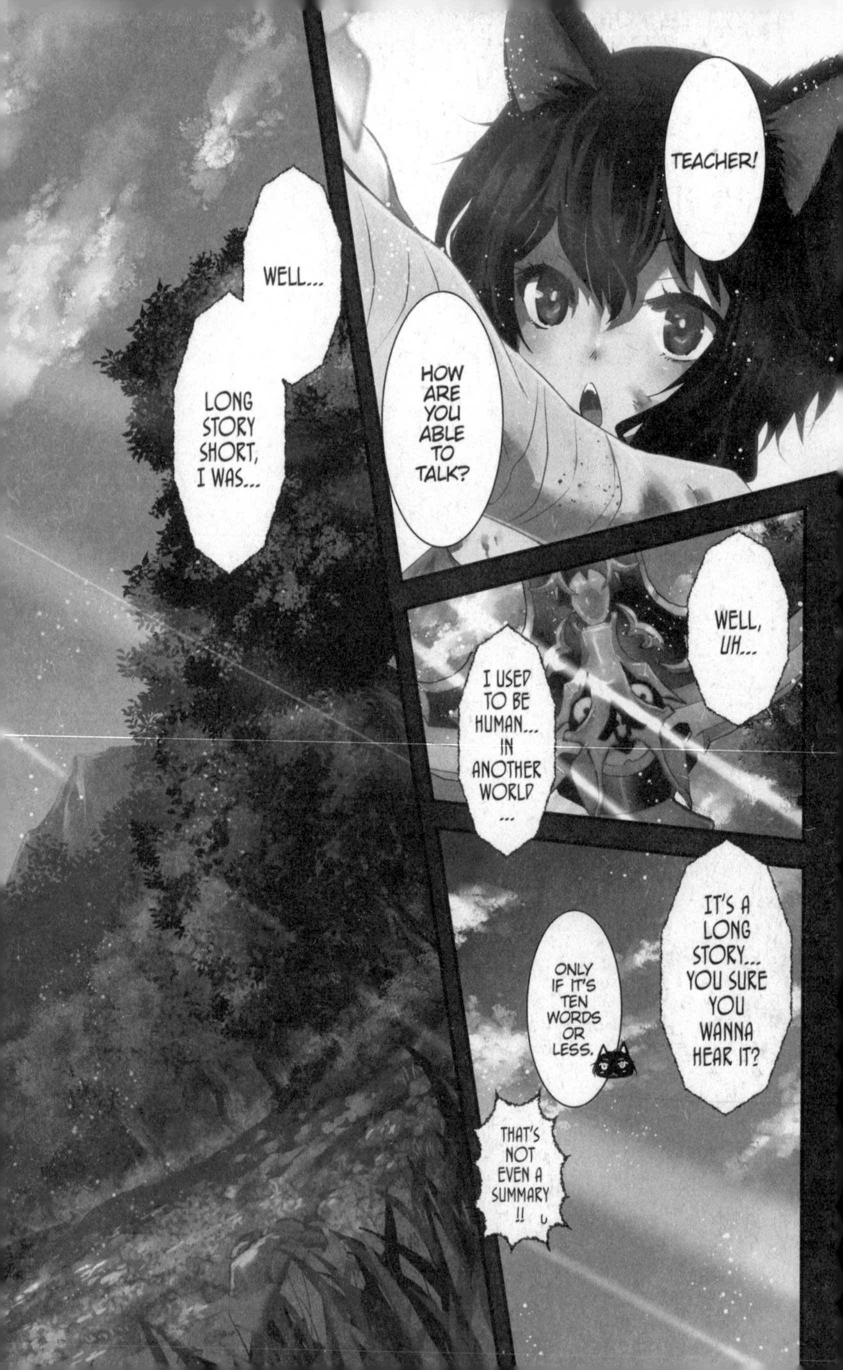
TEACHER!
HOW ARE YOU ABLE TO TALK?
WELL, UH...
I USED TO BE HUMAN... IN ANOTHER WORLD...
IT'S A LONG STORY... YOU SURE YOU WANNA HEAR IT?
ONLY IF IT'S TEN WORDS OR LESS.
THAT'S NOT EVEN A SUMMARY!!
WELL...
LONG STORY SHORT, I WAS...

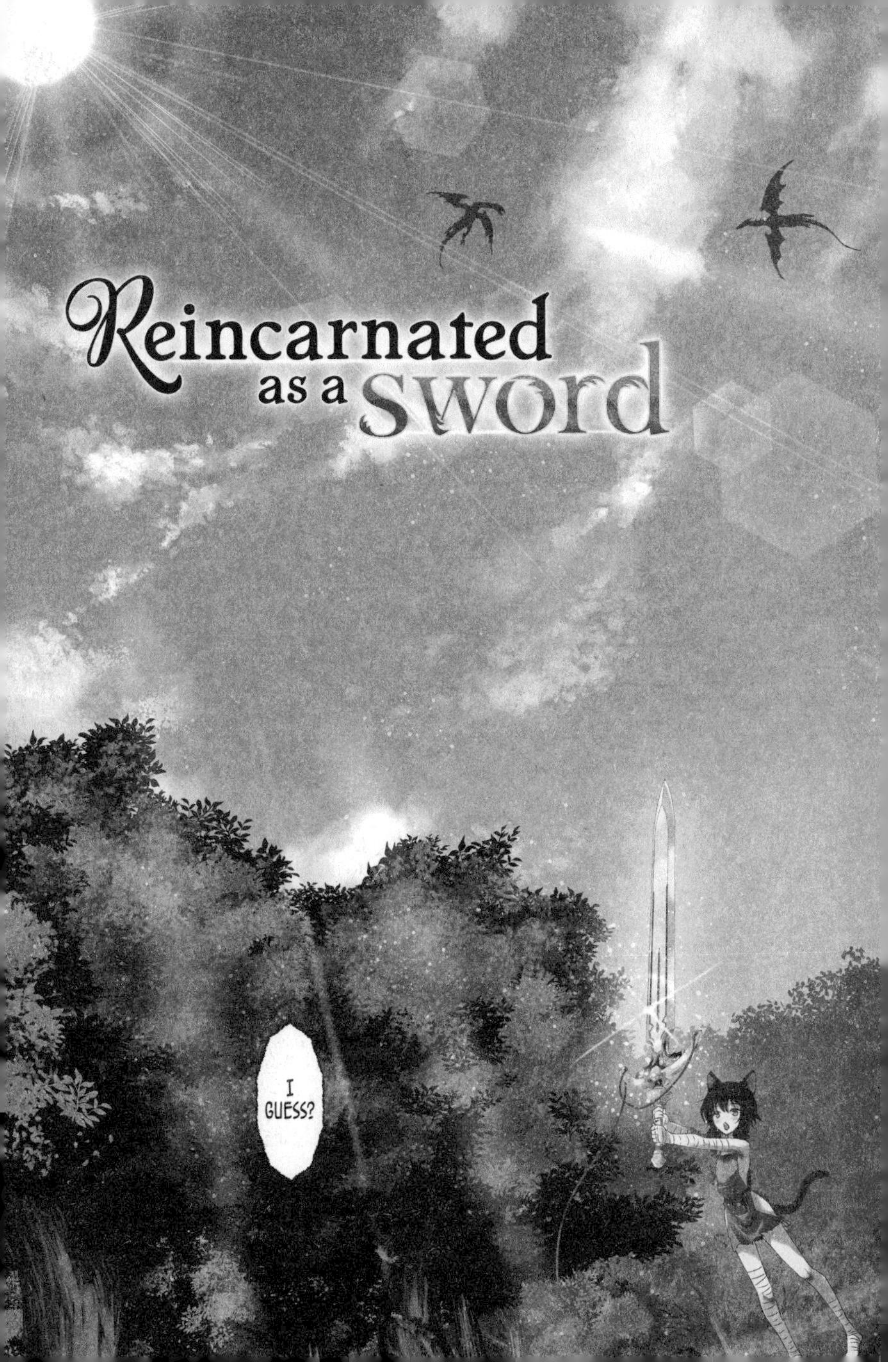
Reincarnated as a Sword
I GUESS?

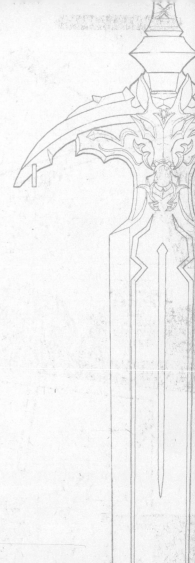

Reincarnated
as a sword

Chapter 2: I Was a Sword

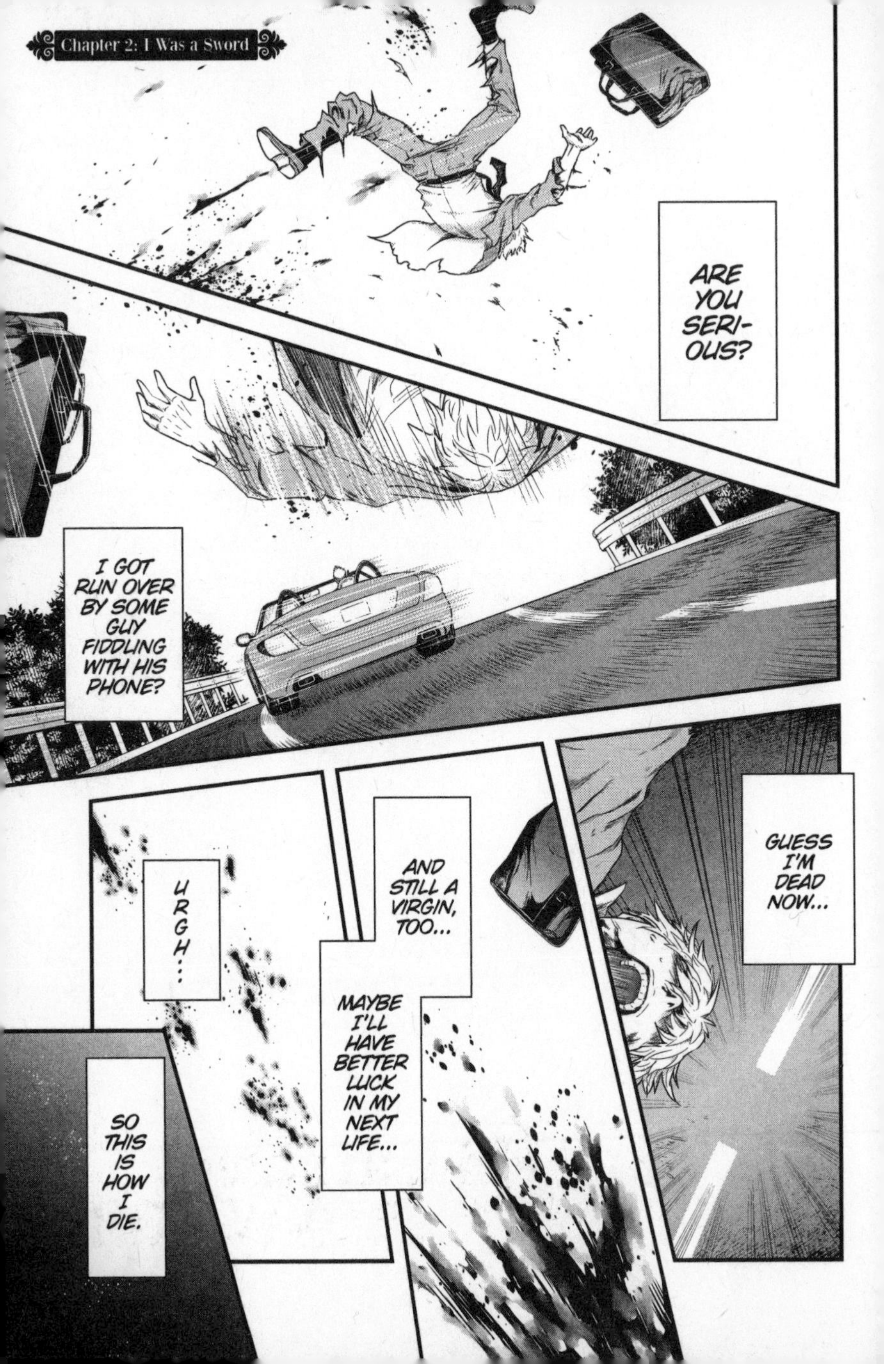
ARE YOU SERI-OUS?
I GOT RUN OVER BY SOME GUY FIDDLING WITH HIS PHONE?
GUESS I'M DEAD NOW...
AND STILL A VIRGIN, TOO...
MAYBE I'LL HAVE BETTER LUCK IN MY NEXT LIFE...
URGH...
SO THIS IS HOW I DIE.

Chapter 2: I Was a Sword

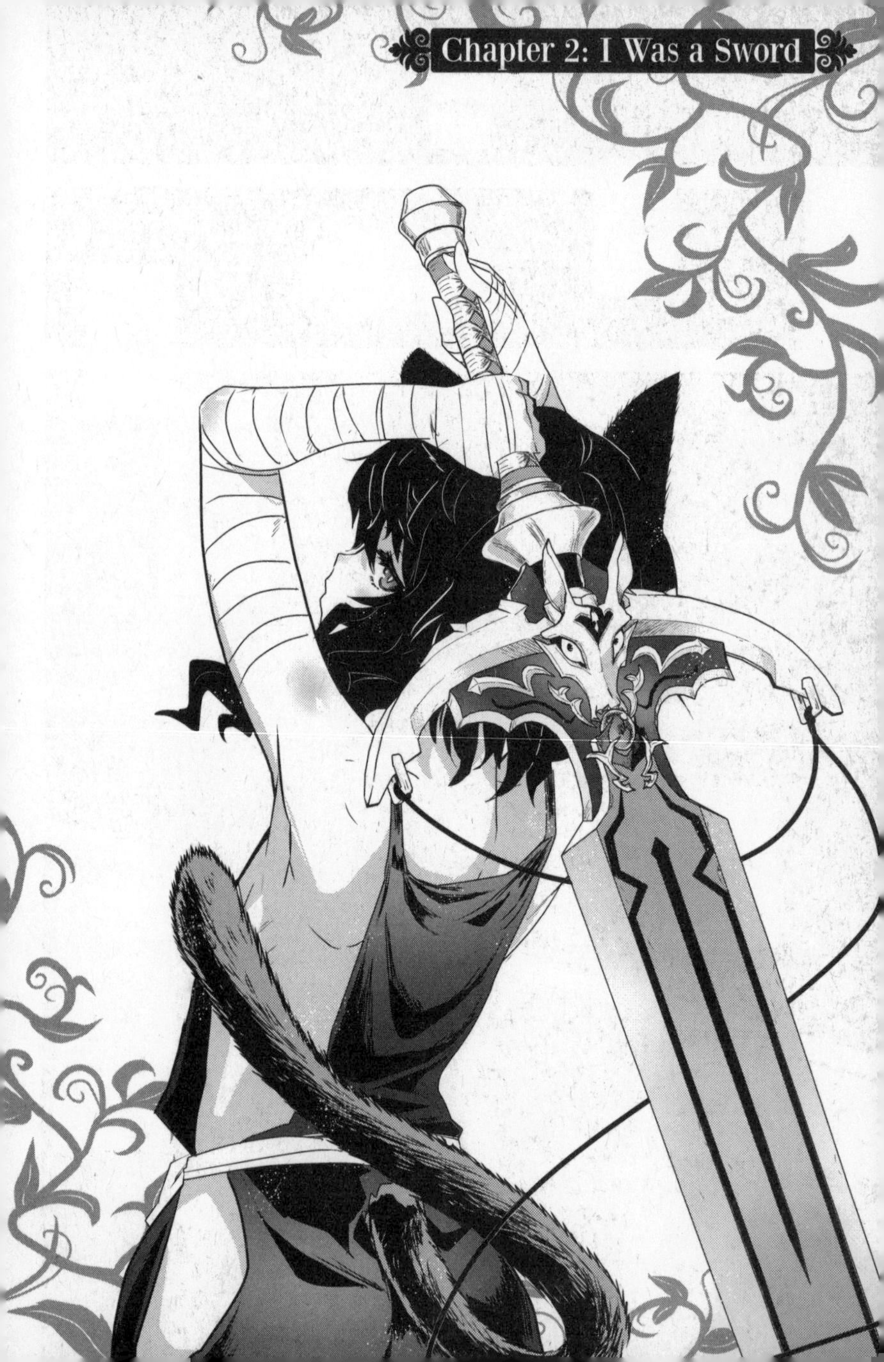

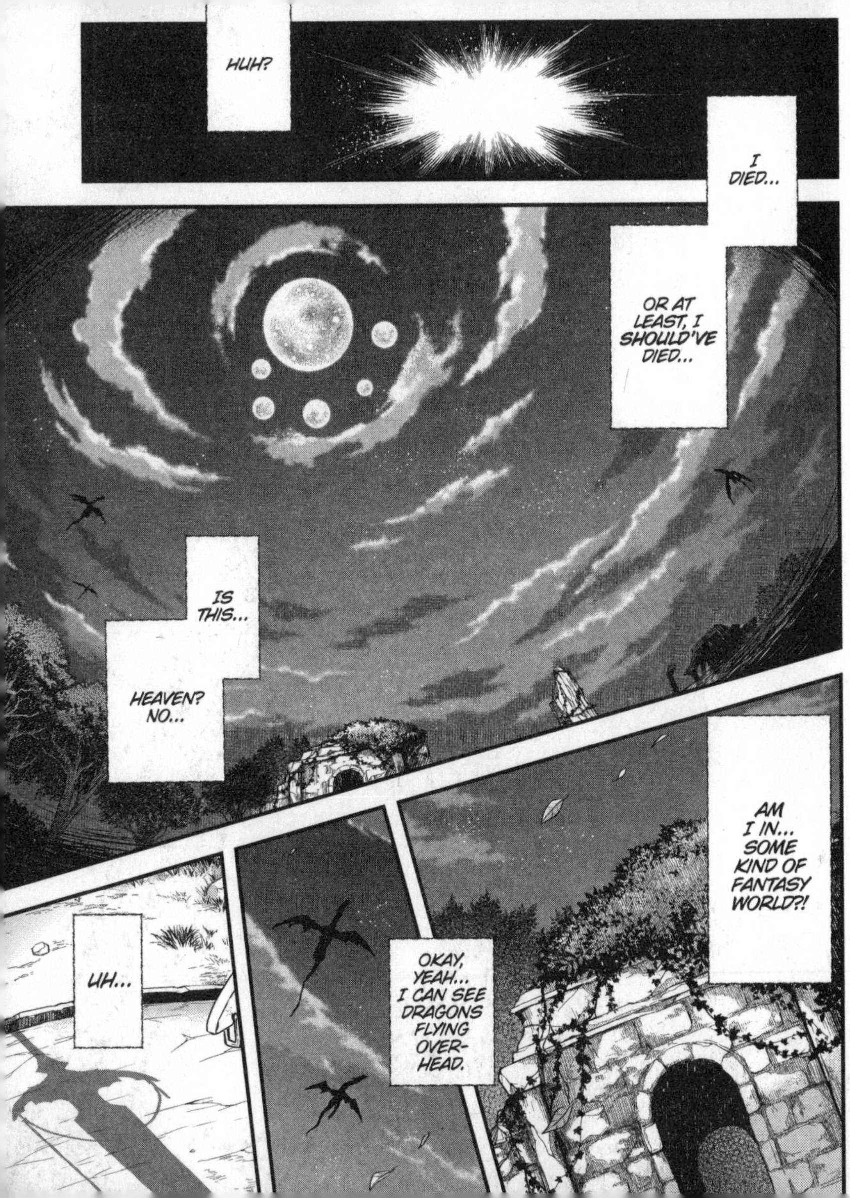
HUH?
I DIED...
OR AT LEAST, I SHOULD'VE DIED...
IS THIS...
HEAVEN? NO...
AM I IN... SOME KIND OF FANTASY WORLD?!
OKAY, YEAH... I CAN SEE DRAGONS FLYING OVER-HEAD.
UH...

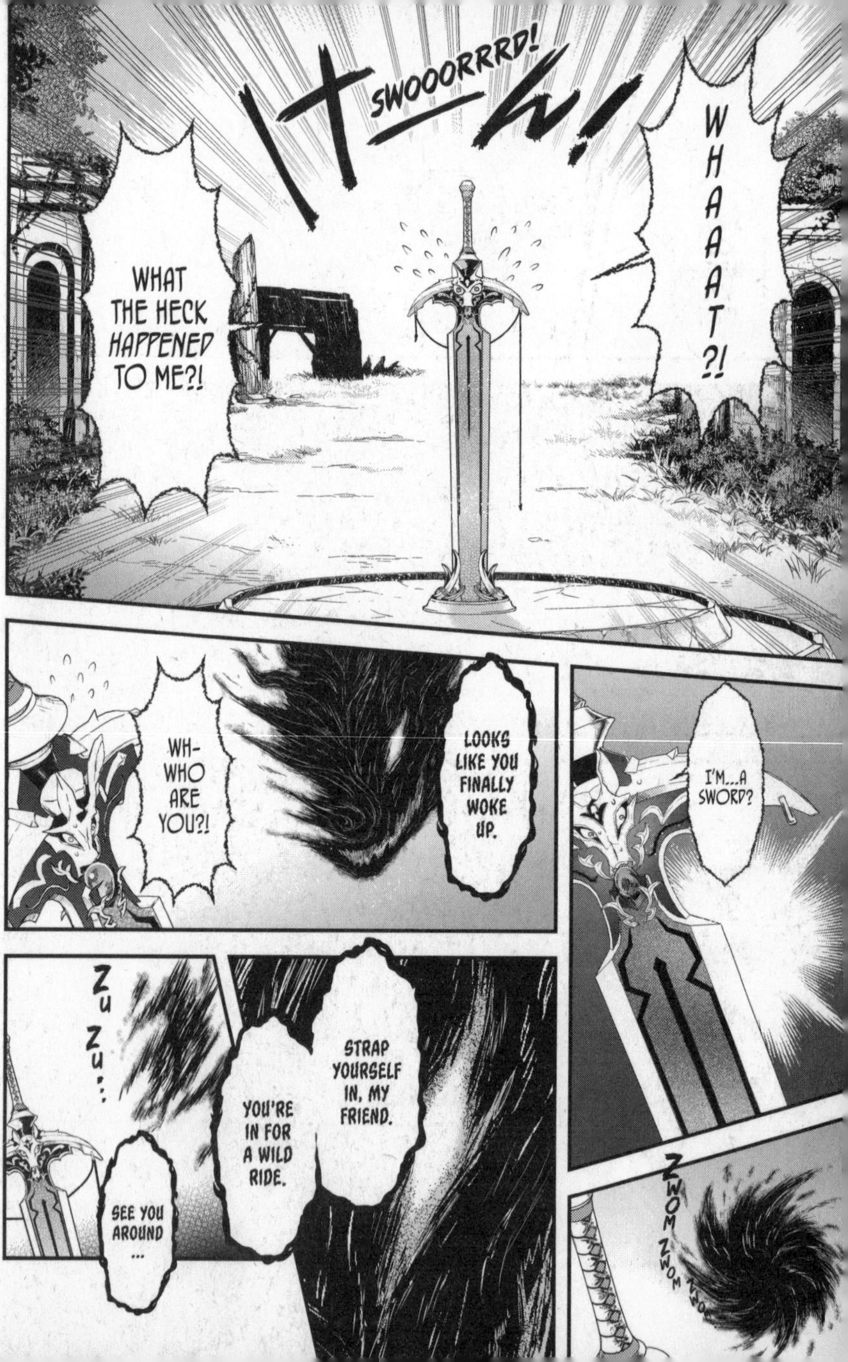
SWOOORRRD!
WHAAAAT?!
WHAT THE HECK HAPPENED TO ME?!
I'M...A SWORD?
ZWOM ZWOM ZWOM
LOOKS LIKE YOU FINALLY WOKE UP.
WH-WHO ARE YOU?!
STRAP YOURSELF IN, MY FRIEND.
YOU'RE IN FOR A WILD RIDE.
SEE YOU AROUND...
ZU ZU...

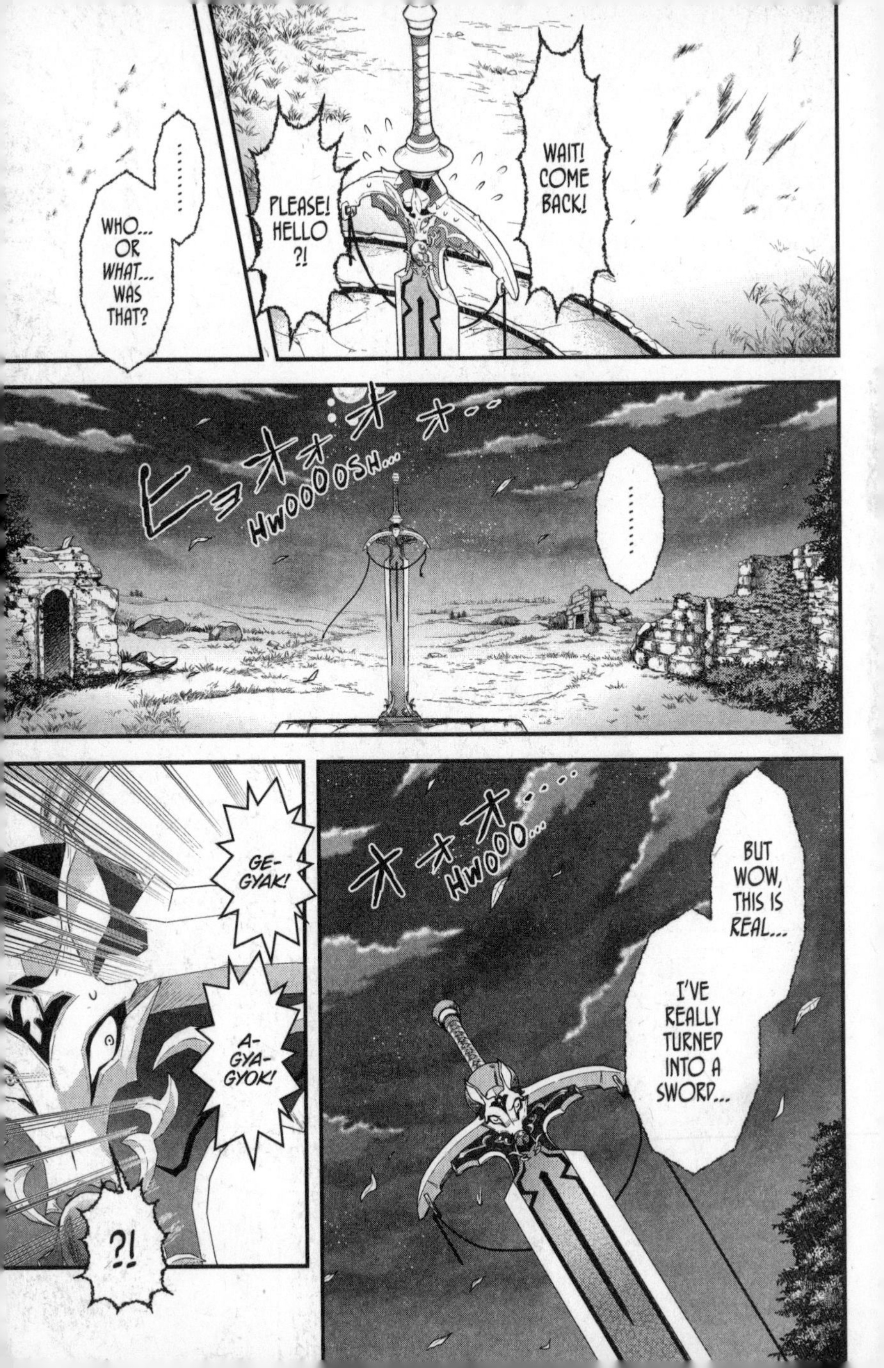
WAIT! COME BACK!
PLEASE! HELLO ?!
......
WHO... OR WHAT... WAS THAT?
ヒョオオオ…
HWOOOOSH...
......
オオオ...
HWOOO...
BUT WOW, THIS IS REAL...
I'VE REALLY TURNED INTO A SWORD...
GE-GYAK!
A-GYA-GYOK!
?!

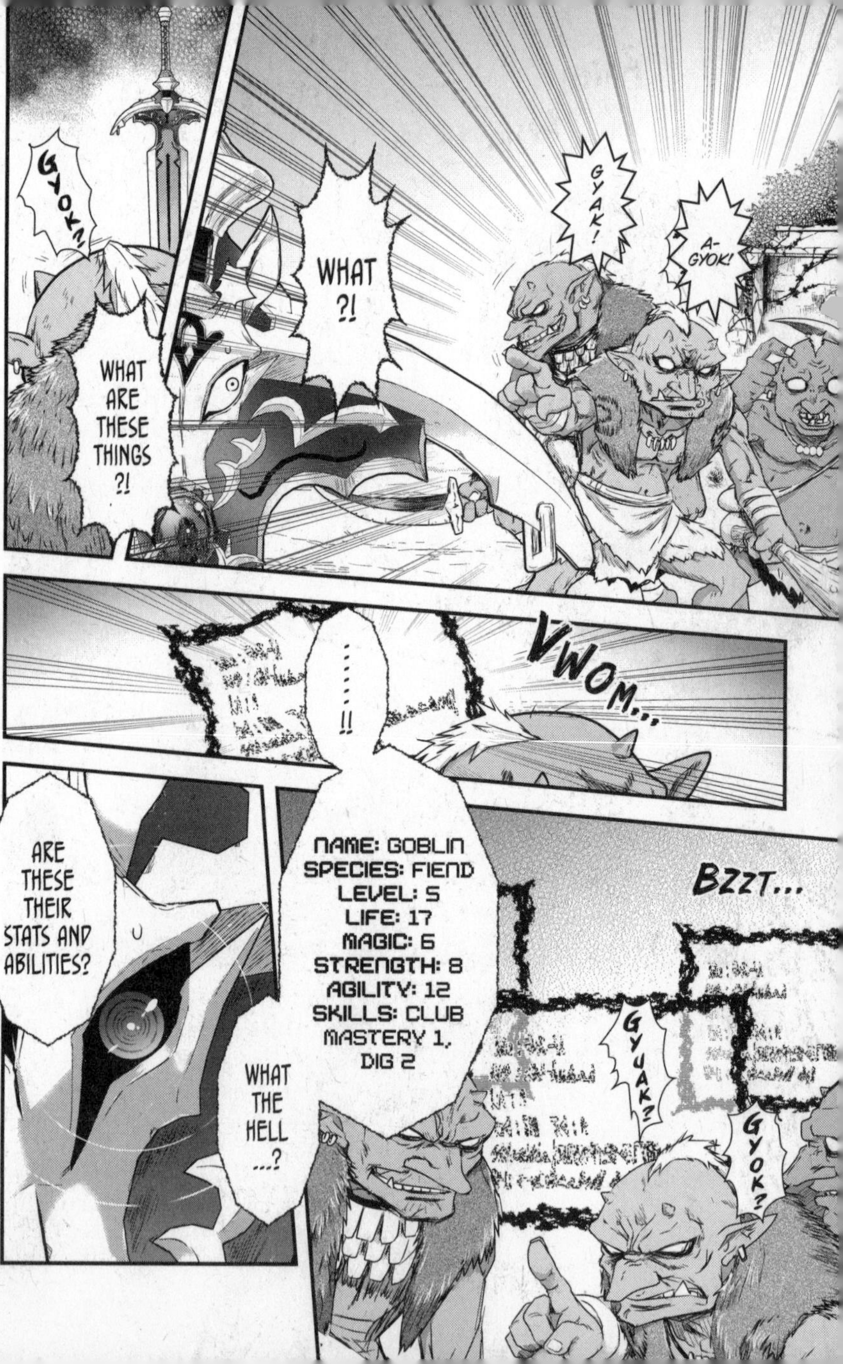
A-GYOK!
GYAK!
WHAT ?!
GYOK?!
WHAT ARE THESE THINGS ?!
VWOM...
......!!
BZZT...
GYOK?
GYUAK?
NAME: GOBLIN
SPECIES: FIEND
LEVEL: 5
LIFE: 17
MAGIC: 6
STRENGTH: 8
AGILITY: 12
SKILLS: CLUB MASTERY 1, DIG 2
ARE THESE THEIR STATS AND ABILITIES?
WHAT THE HELL ...?

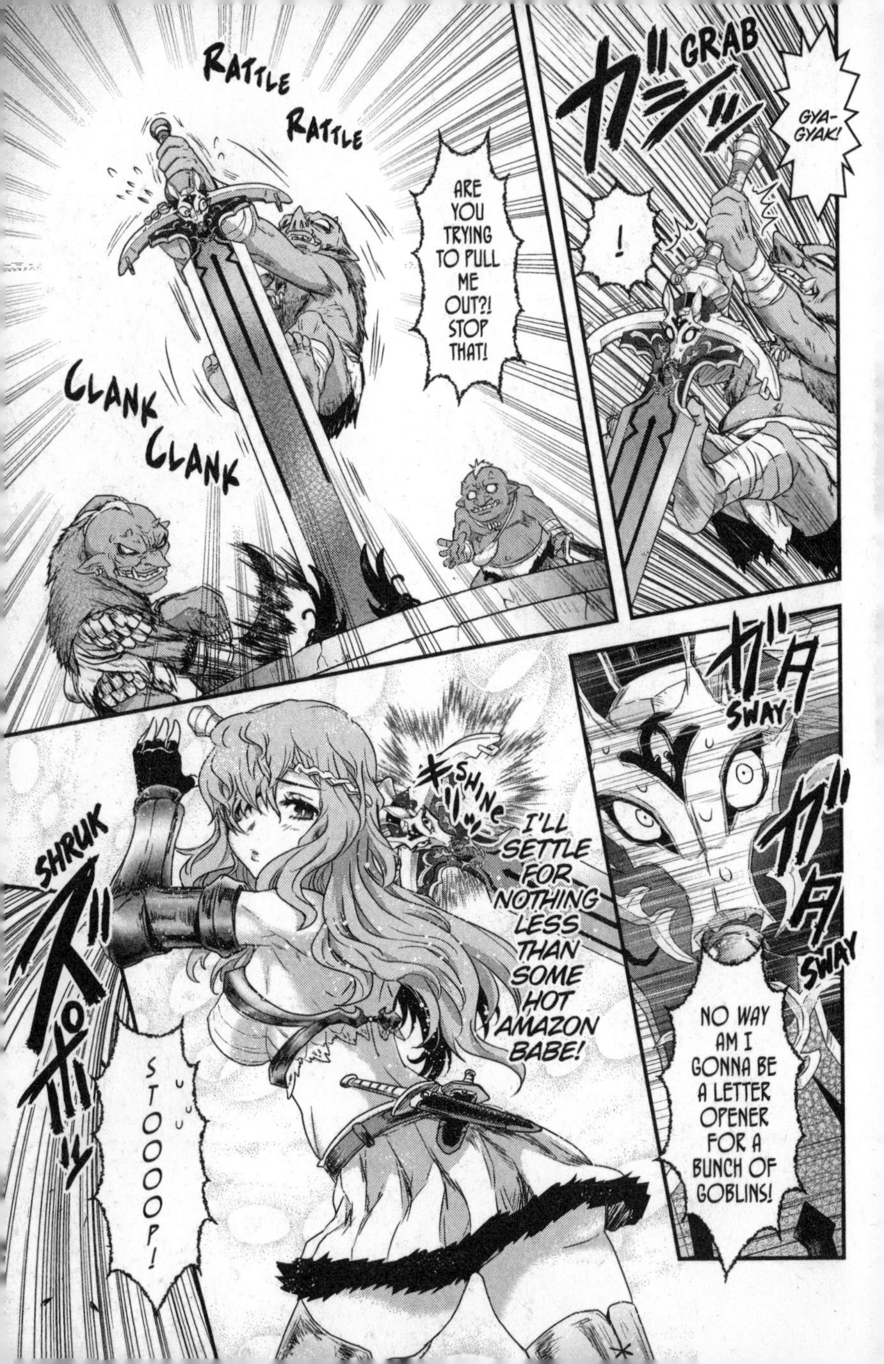
GRAB
GYA-GYAK!
!
RATTLE RATTLE
ARE YOU TRYING TO PULL ME OUT?! STOP THAT!
CLANK CLANK
SWAY
SWAY
NO WAY AM I GONNA BE A LETTER OPENER FOR A BUNCH OF GOBLINS!
SHINE
I'LL SETTLE FOR NOTHING LESS THAN SOME HOT AMAZON BABE!
SHRUK
STOOOOOP!

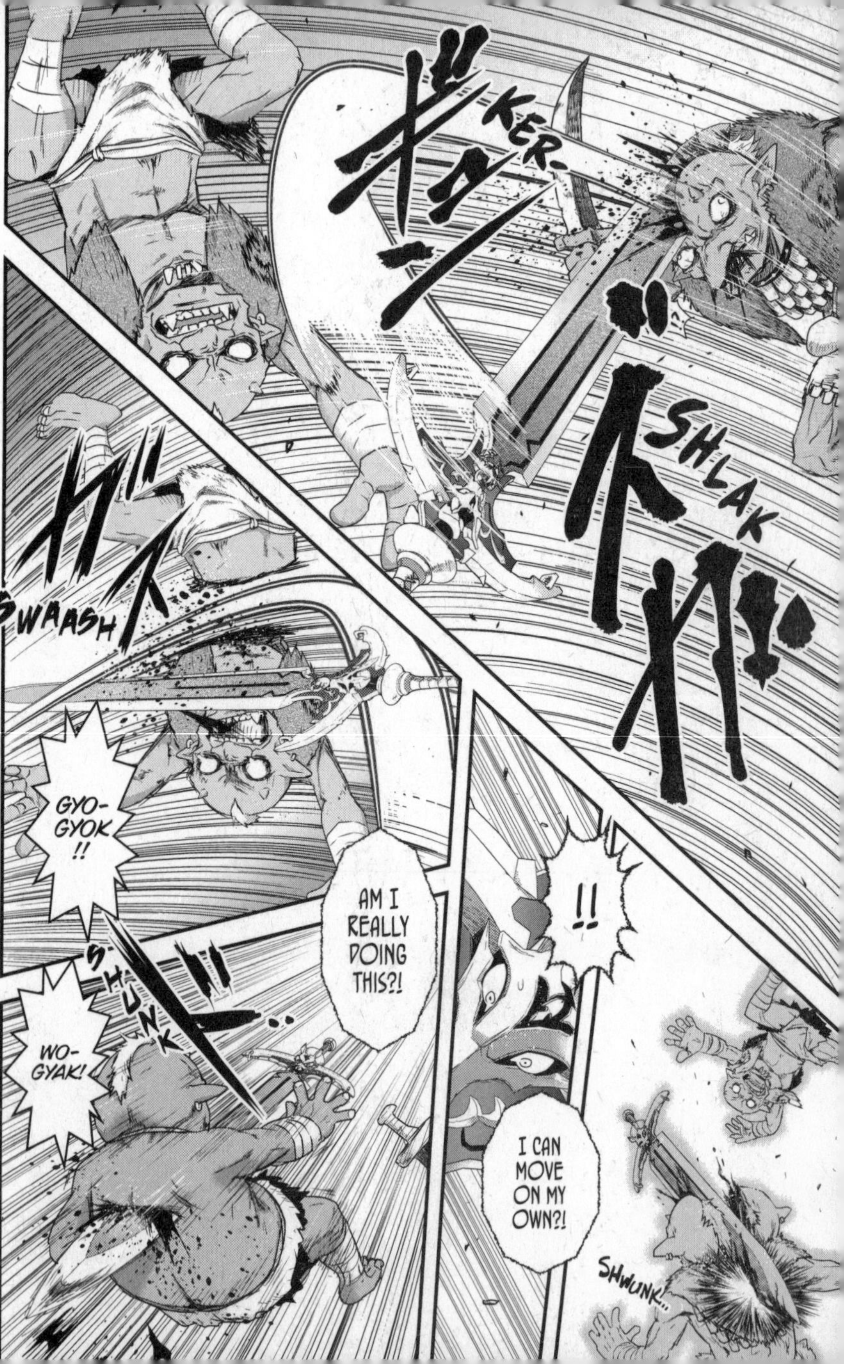
KER-
SHLAK
SWAASH
!!
I CAN MOVE ON MY OWN?!
SHWUNK...
GYO-GYOK!!
AM I REALLY DOING THIS?!
SHUNK
WO-GYAK!

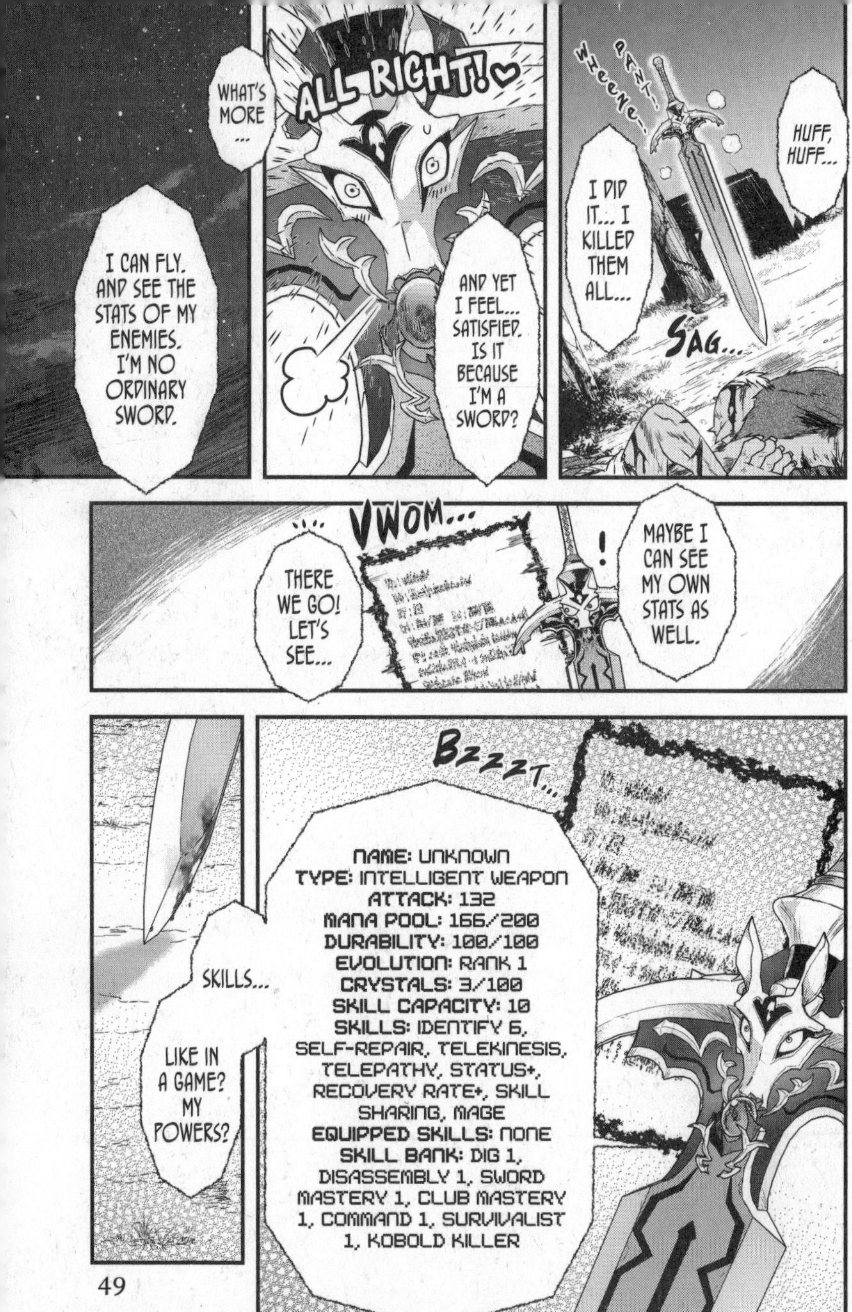
HUFF, HUFF...
PANT, WHEEZE...
I DID IT... I KILLED THEM ALL...
SAG...
ALL RIGHT!♥
AND YET I FEEL... SATISFIED. IS IT BECAUSE I'M A SWORD?
WHAT'S MORE ...
I CAN FLY. AND SEE THE STATS OF MY ENEMIES. I'M NO ORDINARY SWORD.
MAYBE I CAN SEE MY OWN STATS AS WELL.
!
VWOM...
THERE WE GO! LET'S SEE...
BZZZT...
NAME: UNKNOWN
TYPE: INTELLIGENT WEAPON
ATTACK: 132
MANA POOL: 166/200
DURABILITY: 100/100
EVOLUTION: RANK 1
CRYSTALS: 3/100
SKILL CAPACITY: 10
SKILLS: IDENTIFY 6, SELF-REPAIR, TELEKINESIS, TELEPATHY, STATUS+, RECOVERY RATE+, SKILL SHARING, MAGE
EQUIPPED SKILLS: NONE
SKILL BANK: DIG 1, DISASSEMBLY 1, SWORD MASTERY 1, CLUB MASTERY 1, COMMAND 1, SURVIVALIST 1, KOBOLD KILLER
SKILLS...
LIKE IN A GAME? MY POWERS?

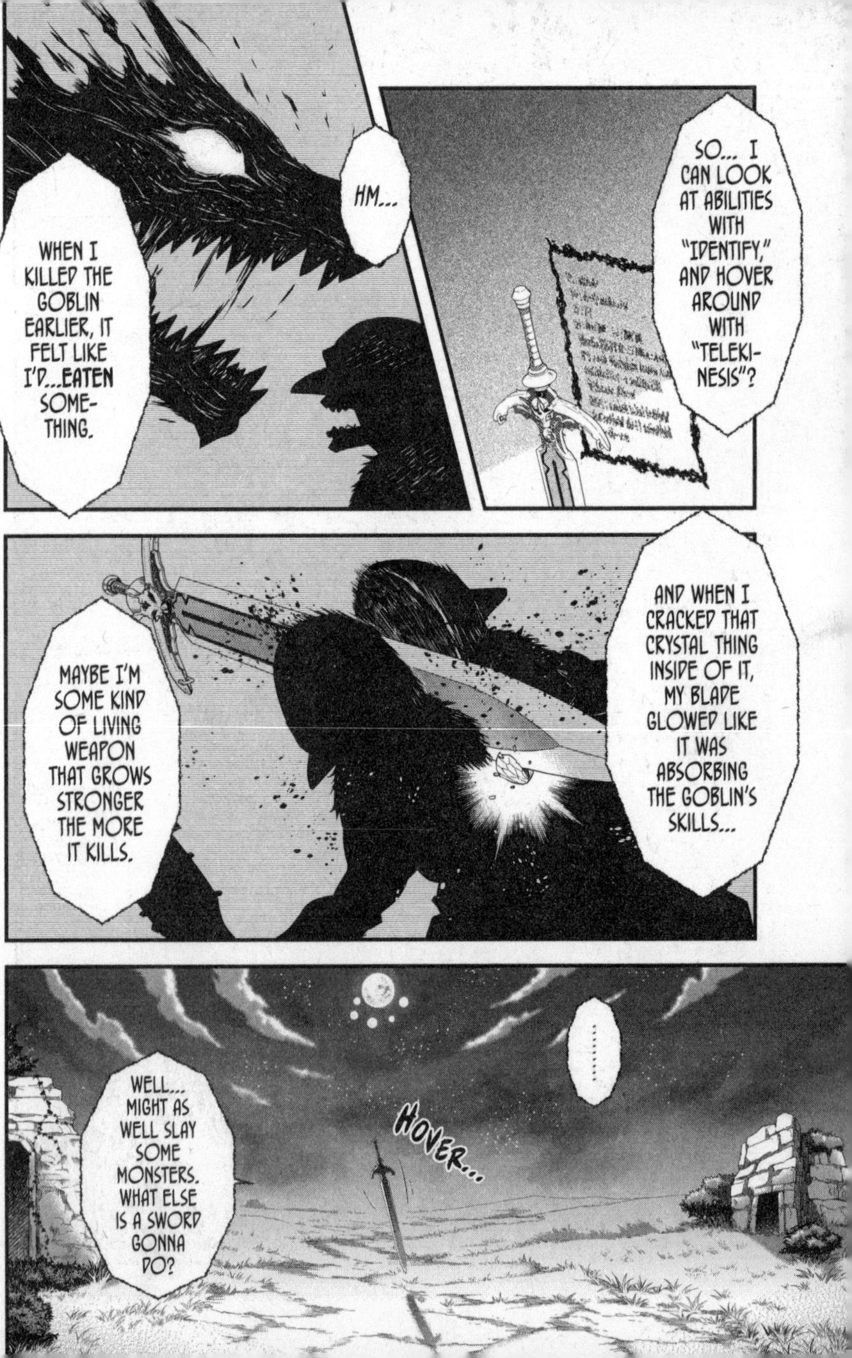
SO... I CAN LOOK AT ABILITIES WITH "IDENTIFY," AND HOVER AROUND WITH "TELEKINESIS"?
HM...
WHEN I KILLED THE GOBLIN EARLIER, IT FELT LIKE I'D...EATEN SOMETHING.
AND WHEN I CRACKED THAT CRYSTAL THING INSIDE OF IT, MY BLADE GLOWED LIKE IT WAS ABSORBING THE GOBLIN'S SKILLS...
MAYBE I'M SOME KIND OF LIVING WEAPON THAT GROWS STRONGER THE MORE IT KILLS.
......
HOVER...
WELL... MIGHT AS WELL SLAY SOME MONSTERS. WHAT ELSE IS A SWORD GONNA DO?

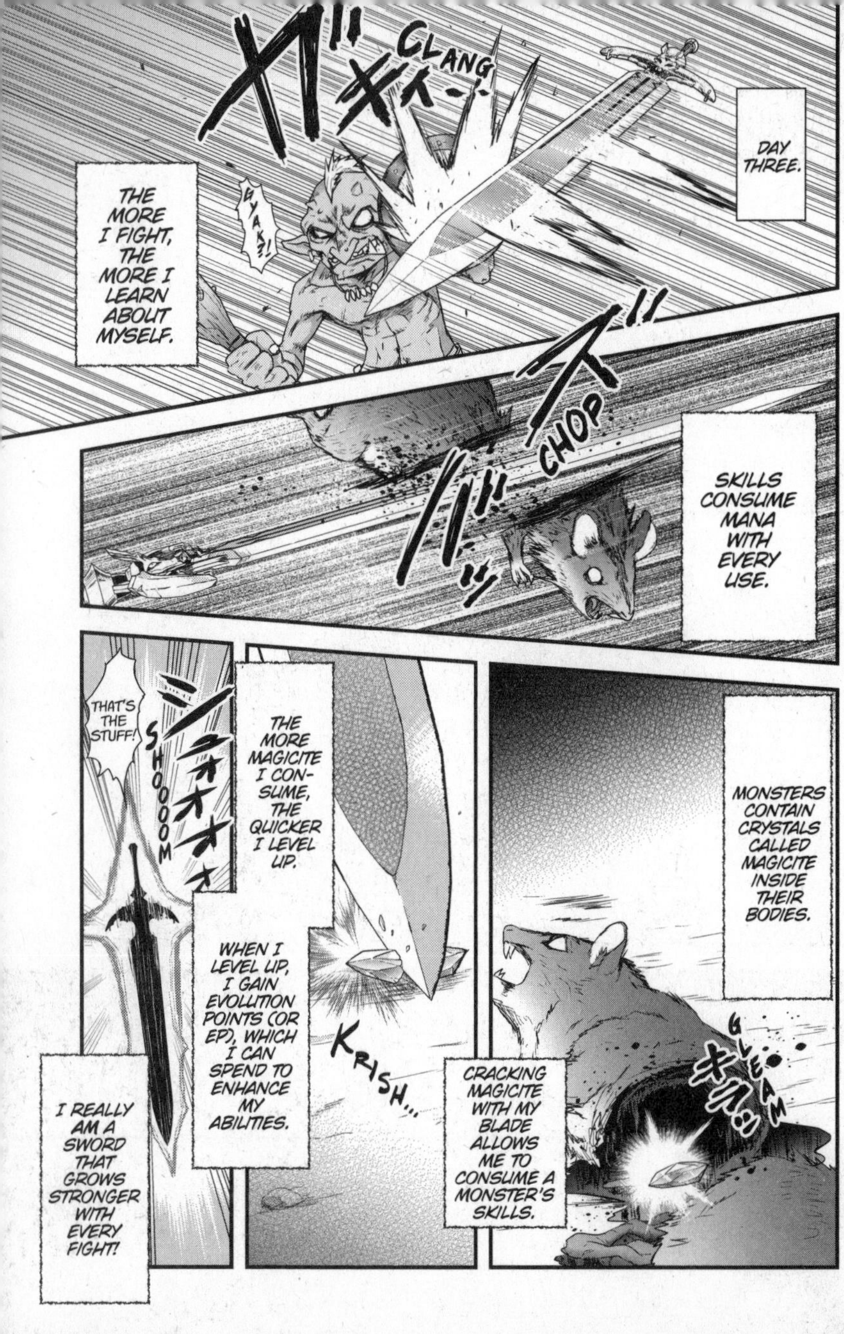
DAY THREE.
CLANG
GYAK?!
THE MORE I FIGHT, THE MORE I LEARN ABOUT MYSELF.
SKILLS CONSUME MANA WITH EVERY USE.
CHOP
MONSTERS CONTAIN CRYSTALS CALLED MAGICITE INSIDE THEIR BODIES.
GLEAM
CRACKING MAGICITE WITH MY BLADE ALLOWS ME TO CONSUME A MONSTER'S SKILLS.
THE MORE MAGICITE I CONSUME, THE QUICKER I LEVEL UP.
KRISH...
WHEN I LEVEL UP, I GAIN EVOLUTION POINTS (OR EP), WHICH I CAN SPEND TO ENHANCE MY ABILITIES.
THAT'S THE STUFF!
SHOOOOOM
I REALLY AM A SWORD THAT GROWS STRONGER WITH EVERY FIGHT!

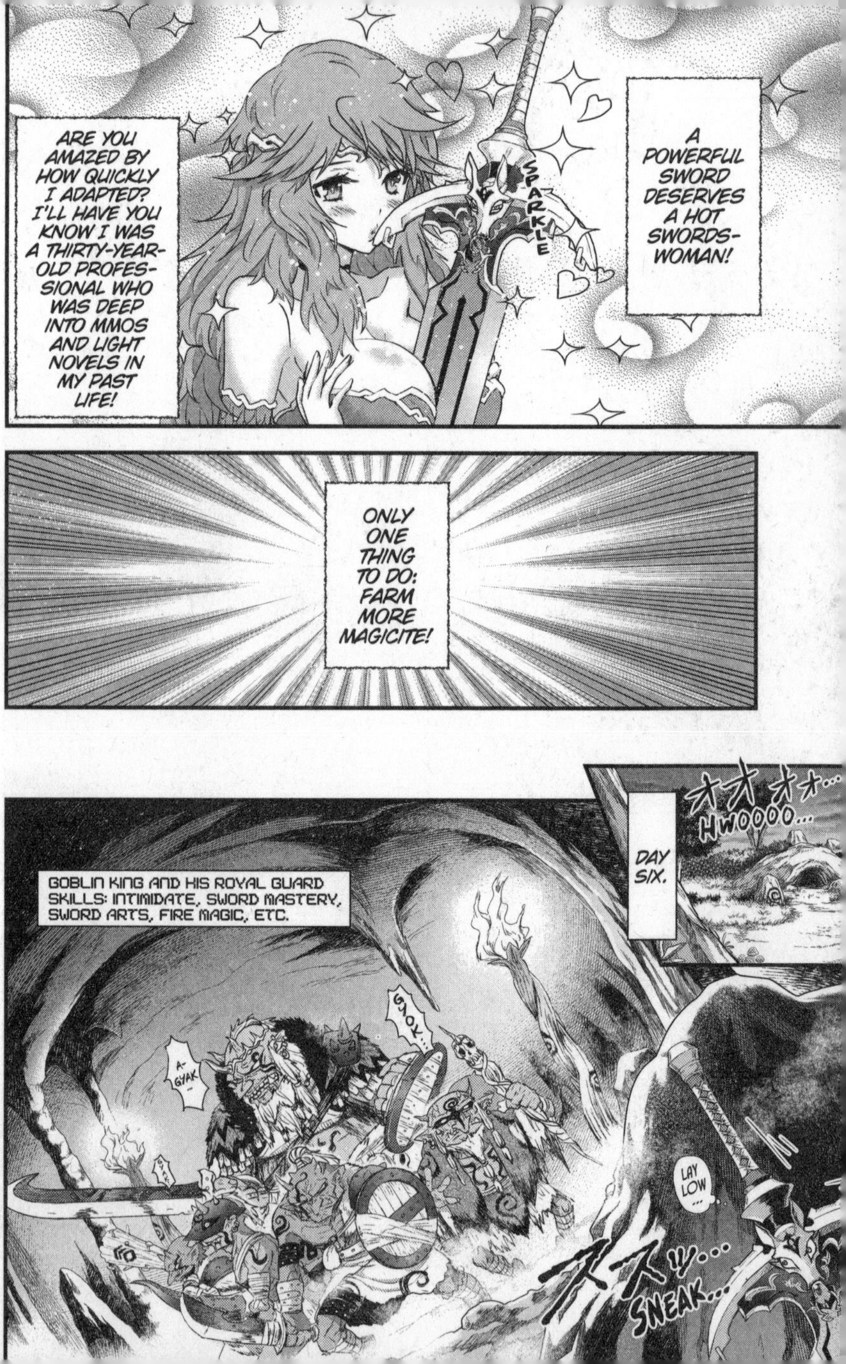
A POWERFUL SWORD DESERVES A HOT SWORDS-WOMAN!
SPARKLE
ARE YOU AMAZED BY HOW QUICKLY I ADAPTED? I'LL HAVE YOU KNOW I WAS A THIRTY-YEAR-OLD PROFES-SIONAL WHO WAS DEEP INTO MMOS AND LIGHT NOVELS IN MY PAST LIFE!
ONLY ONE THING TO DO: FARM MORE MAGICITE!
HWOOOO...
DAY SIX.
GOBLIN KING AND HIS ROYAL GUARD
SKILLS: INTIMIDATE, SWORD MASTERY, SWORD ARTS, FIRE MAGIC, ETC.
GYOK...
A-GYAK...
LAY LOW...
SNEAK...

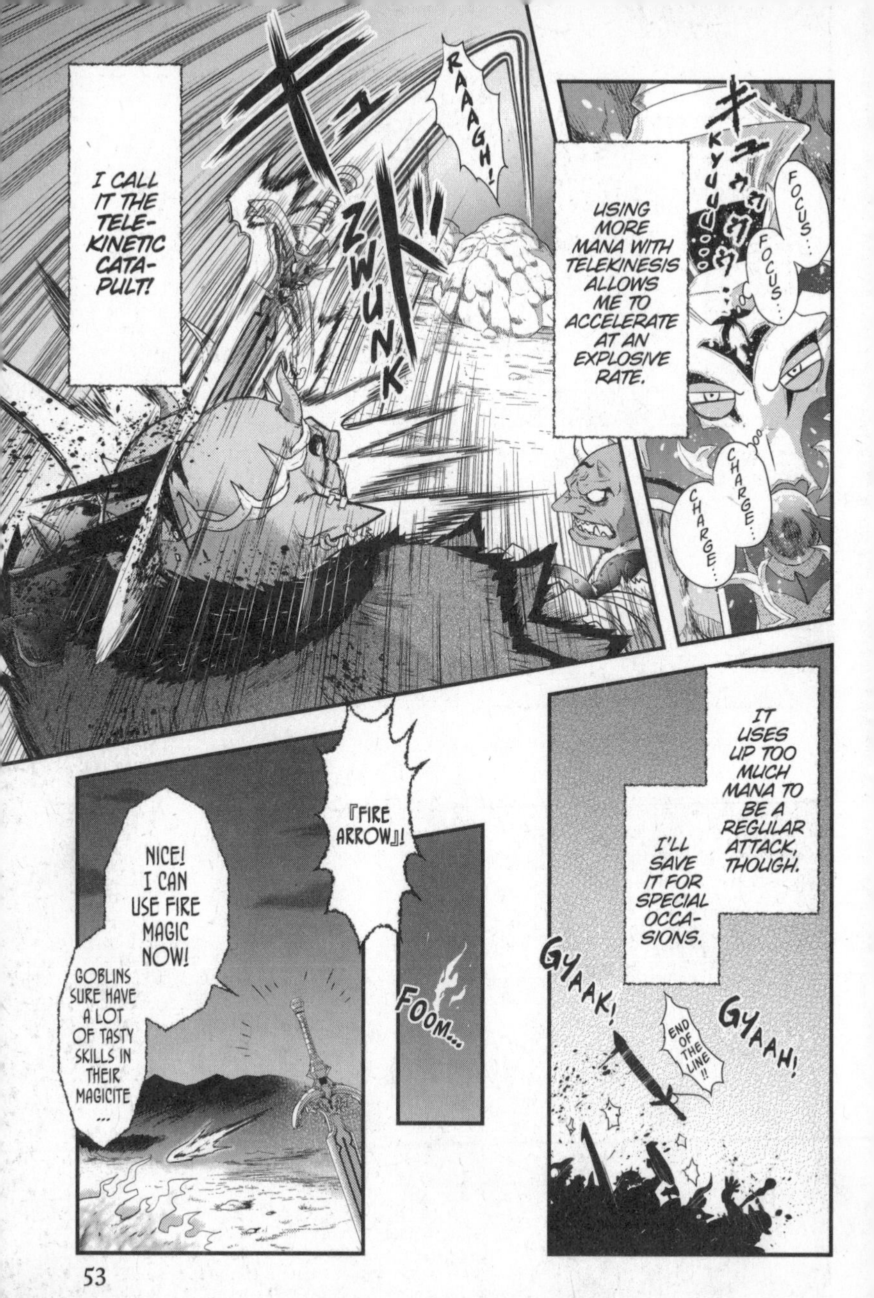
KYUUUU...
FOCUS...
FOCUS...
USING MORE MANA WITH TELEKINESIS ALLOWS ME TO ACCELERATE AT AN EXPLOSIVE RATE.
CHARGE...
CHARGE...
ZWUNK
RAAAGH!
I CALL IT THE TELE-KINETIC CATA-PULT!
IT USES UP TOO MUCH MANA TO BE A REGULAR ATTACK, THOUGH.
I'LL SAVE IT FOR SPECIAL OCCA-SIONS.
GYAAK!
GYAAH!
END OF THE LINE!!
『FIRE ARROW』!
FOOM...
NICE! I CAN USE FIRE MAGIC NOW!
GOBLINS SURE HAVE A LOT OF TASTY SKILLS IN THEIR MAGICITE...

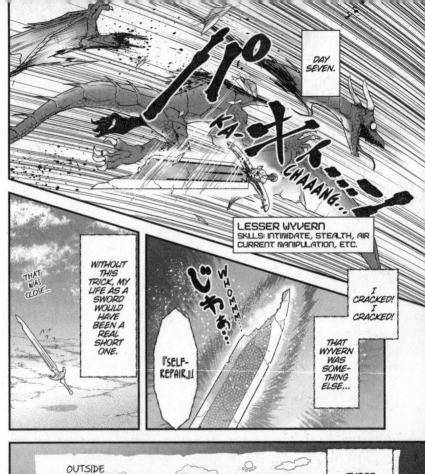

DAY SEVEN.
パ
KA-
CHAAAANG...
LESSER WYVERN
SKILLS: INTIMIDATE, STEALTH, AIR CURRENT MANIPULATION, ETC.
I CRACKED! I CRACKED!
THAT WYVERN WAS SOME-THING ELSE...
じゃぁ…
WHOMMM...
『SELF-REPAIR』!
WITHOUT THIS TRICK, MY LIFE AS A SWORD WOULD HAVE BEEN A REAL SHORT ONE.
THAT WAS CLOSE...
THESE GRASS-LANDS APPEAR TO BE SURROUND-ED BY FOREST.
OUTSIDE
UNKNOWN
UNKNOWN FOREST BELT
SWORD PEDESTAL.
GOBLIN KING NEST.
LESSER WYVERN.
WEAK MONSTERS.
弱
BLAST TORTOISE.
GLUTTONY SLIMELORD.
GRASSLANDS.
強
STRONG MONSTERS.
MY PEDESTAL IS AT THE CENTER, AND THE FARTHER AWAY I GET, THE STRONGER THE MONSTERS ARE.

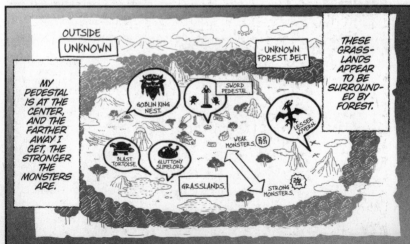

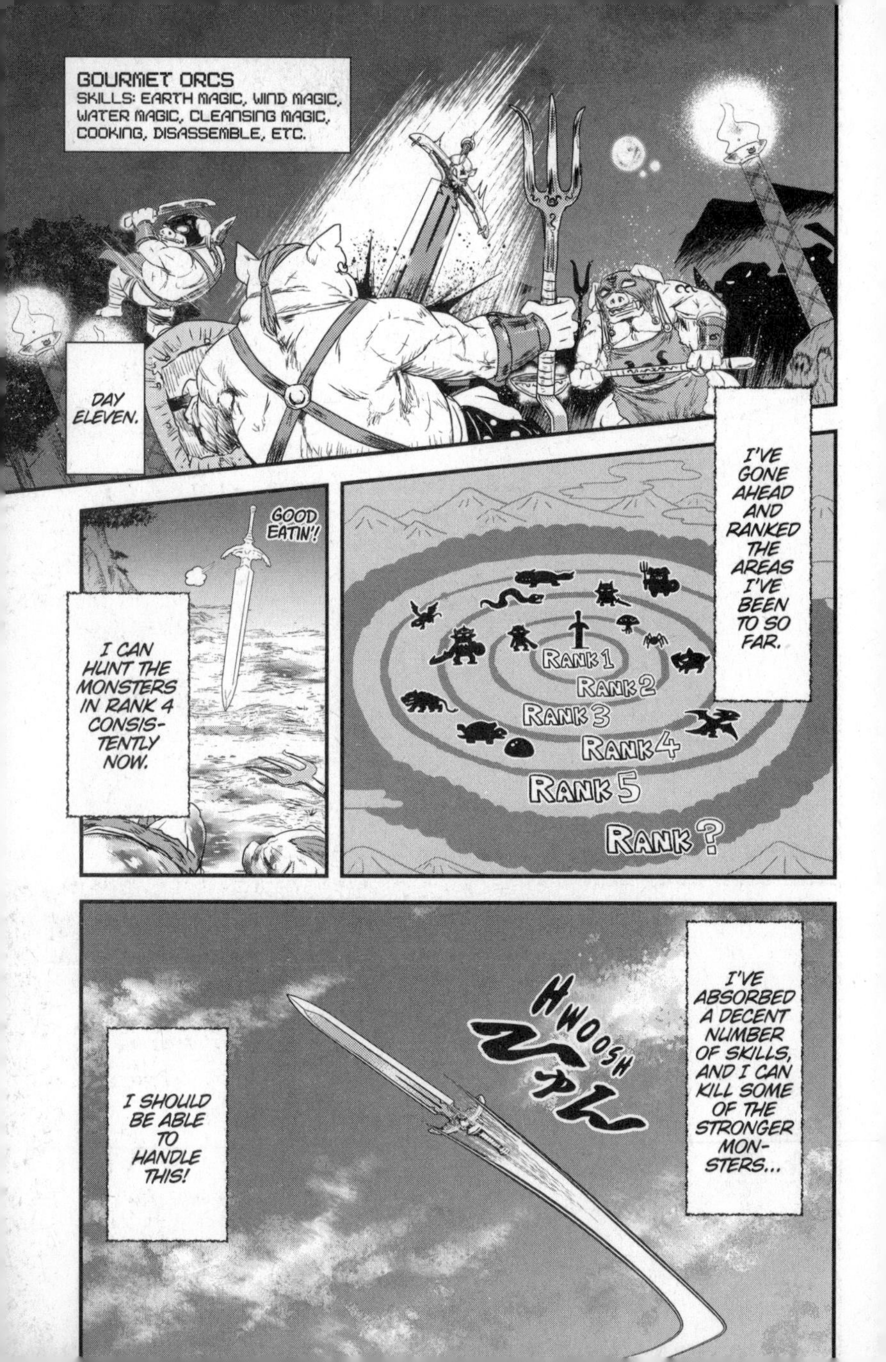
GOURMET ORCS
SKILLS: EARTH MAGIC, WIND MAGIC, WATER MAGIC, CLEANSING MAGIC, COOKING, DISASSEMBLE, ETC.
DAY ELEVEN.
I'VE GONE AHEAD AND RANKED THE AREAS I'VE BEEN TO SO FAR.
RANK 1
RANK 2
RANK 3
RANK 4
RANK 5
RANK ?
GOOD EATIN'!
I CAN HUNT THE MONSTERS IN RANK 4 CONSISTENTLY NOW.
I'VE ABSORBED A DECENT NUMBER OF SKILLS, AND I CAN KILL SOME OF THE STRONGER MONSTERS...
HWOOSH
I SHOULD BE ABLE TO HANDLE THIS!

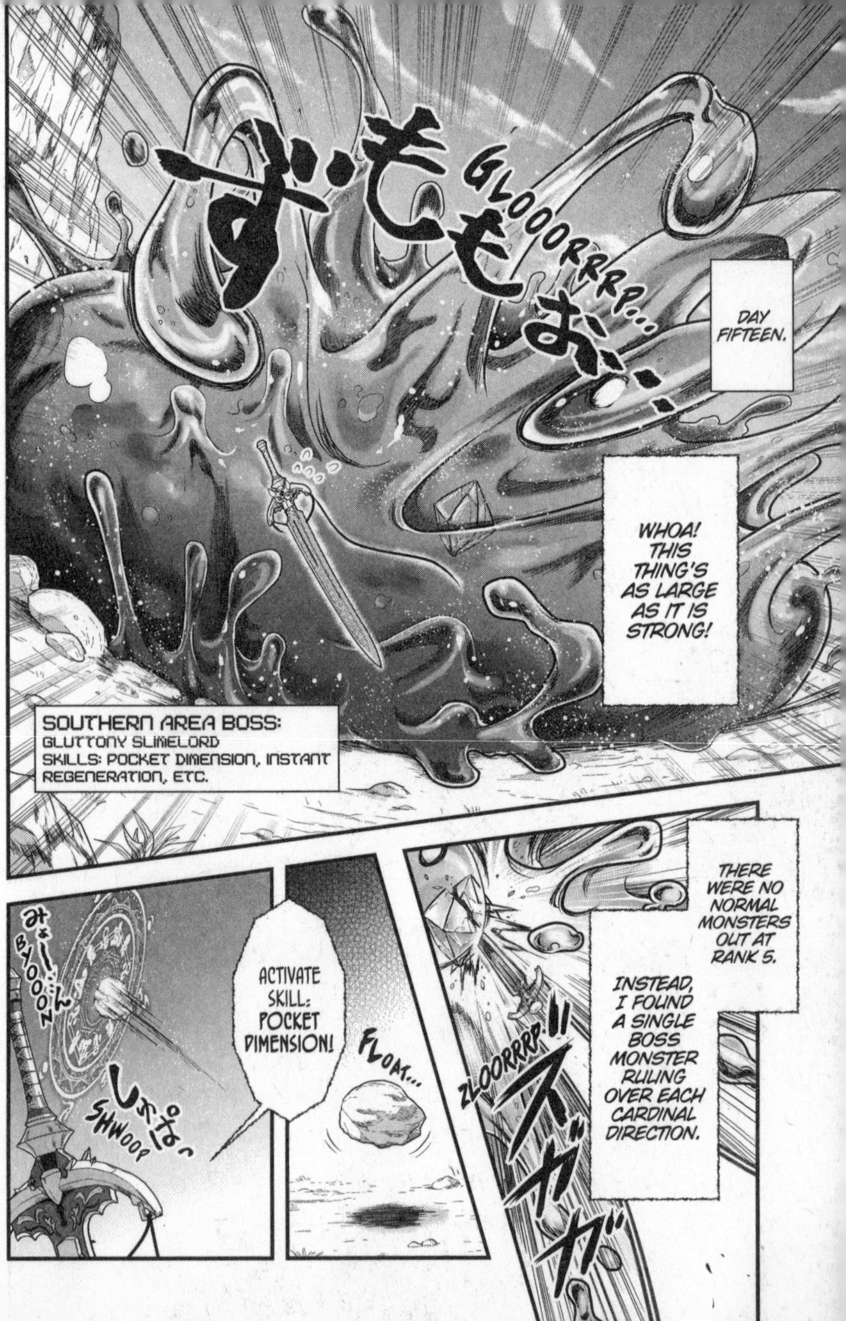
GLOOOORRRRP...
DAY FIFTEEN.
WHOA! THIS THING'S AS LARGE AS IT IS STRONG!
SOUTHERN AREA BOSS:
GLUTTONY SLIMELORD
SKILLS: POCKET DIMENSION, INSTANT REGENERATION, ETC.
THERE WERE NO NORMAL MONSTERS OUT AT RANK 5.
INSTEAD, I FOUND A SINGLE BOSS MONSTER RULING OVER EACH CARDINAL DIRECTION.
ZLOORRRP!!
FLOAT...
ACTIVATE SKILL: POCKET DIMENSION!
BYOOOON
SHWOOP

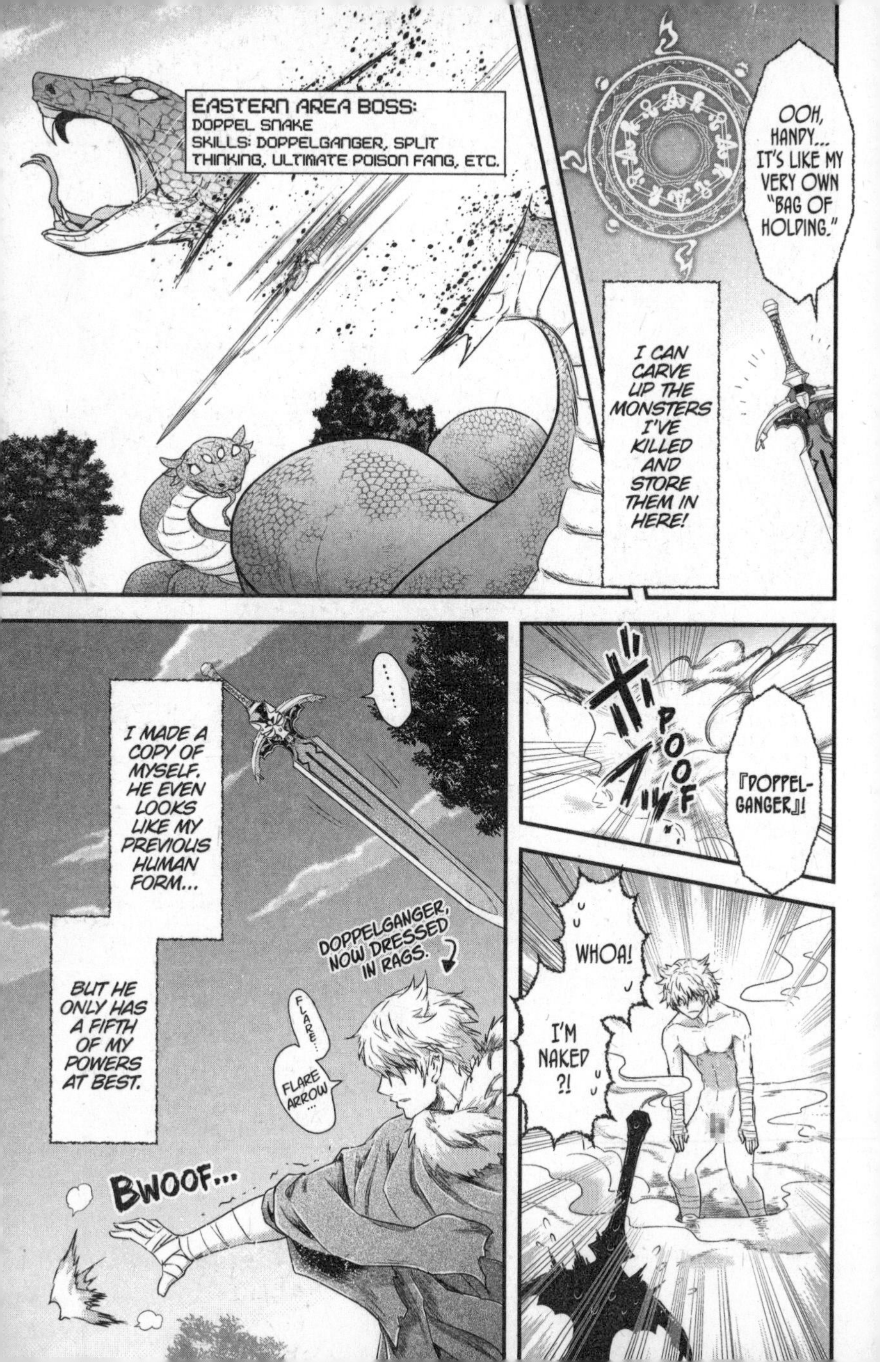
OOH, HANDY... IT'S LIKE MY VERY OWN "BAG OF HOLDING."
I CAN CARVE UP THE MONSTERS I'VE KILLED AND STORE THEM IN HERE!
EASTERN AREA BOSS:
DOPPEL SNAKE
SKILLS: DOPPELGANGER, SPLIT THINKING, ULTIMATE POISON FANG, ETC.
『DOPPEL-GANGER』!
POOF
WHOA!
I'M NAKED?!
......
I MADE A COPY OF MYSELF. HE EVEN LOOKS LIKE MY PREVIOUS HUMAN FORM...
BUT HE ONLY HAS A FIFTH OF MY POWERS AT BEST.
DOPPELGANGER, NOW DRESSED IN RAGS.
FLARE...
FLARE ARROW...
BWOOF...

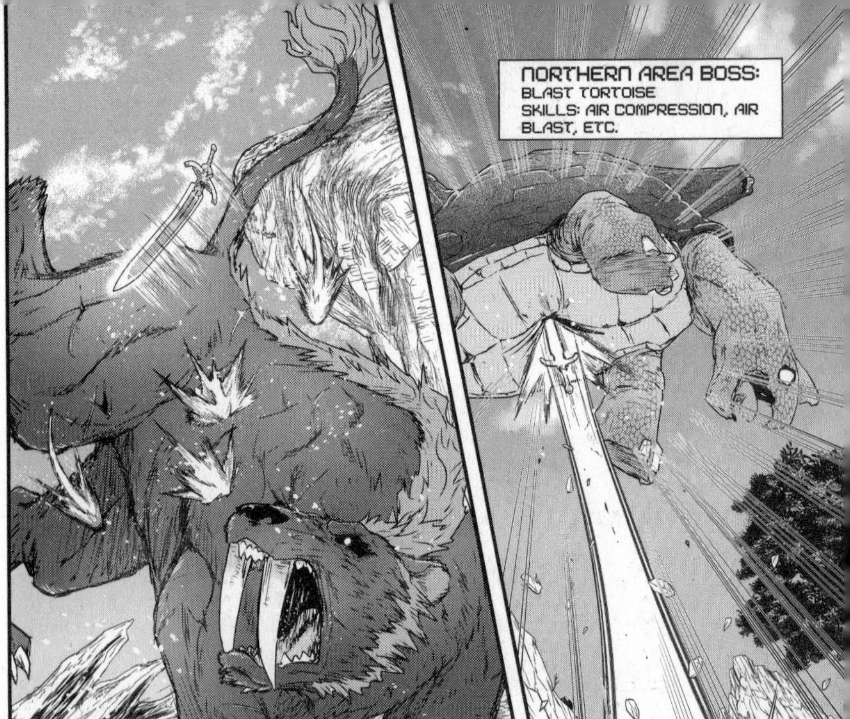
NORTHERN AREA BOSS:
BLAST TORTOISE
SKILLS: AIR COMPRESSION, AIR BLAST, ETC.
WESTERN AREA BOSS:
TYRANT SABRETOOTH
SKILLS: OSCILLATION, VIBROFANG, ETC.

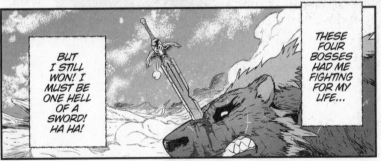

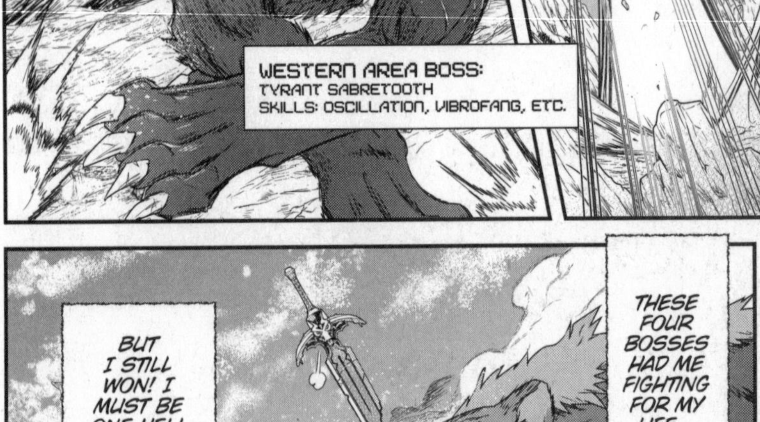
THESE FOUR BOSSES HAD ME FIGHTING FOR MY LIFE...
BUT I STILL WON! I MUST BE ONE HELL OF A SWORD! HA HA!

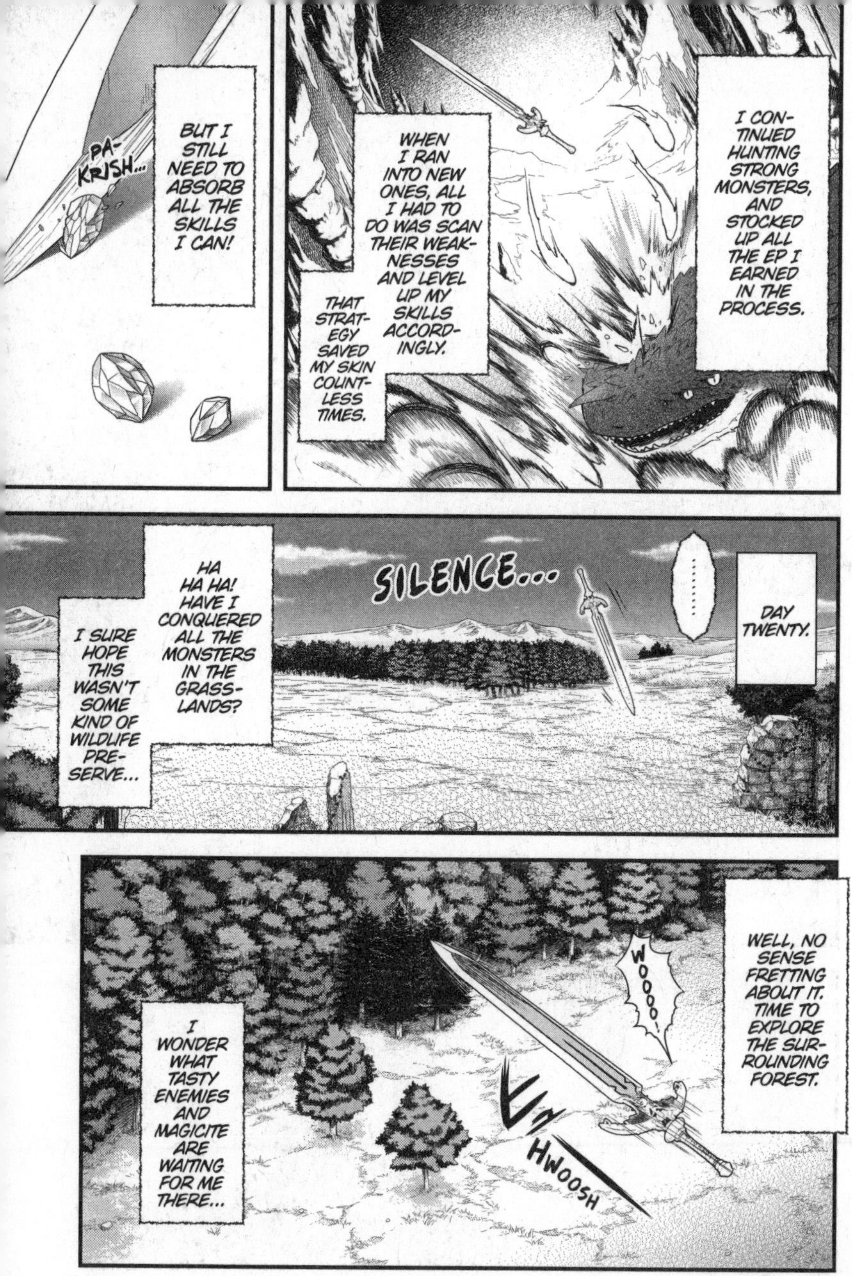
I CONTINUED HUNTING STRONG MONSTERS, AND STOCKED UP ALL THE EP I EARNED IN THE PROCESS.
WHEN I RAN INTO NEW ONES, ALL I HAD TO DO WAS SCAN THEIR WEAKNESSES AND LEVEL UP MY SKILLS ACCORDINGLY.
THAT STRATEGY SAVED MY SKIN COUNTLESS TIMES.
BUT I STILL NEED TO ABSORB ALL THE SKILLS I CAN!
PA-KRISH...
DAY TWENTY.
......
SILENCE...
HA HA HA! HAVE I CONQUERED ALL THE MONSTERS IN THE GRASSLANDS?
I SURE HOPE THIS WASN'T SOME KIND OF WILDLIFE PRESERVE...
WELL, NO SENSE FRETTING ABOUT IT. TIME TO EXPLORE THE SURROUNDING FOREST.
WOOOO!
HWOOSH
I WONDER WHAT TASTY ENEMIES AND MAGICITE ARE WAITING FOR ME THERE...

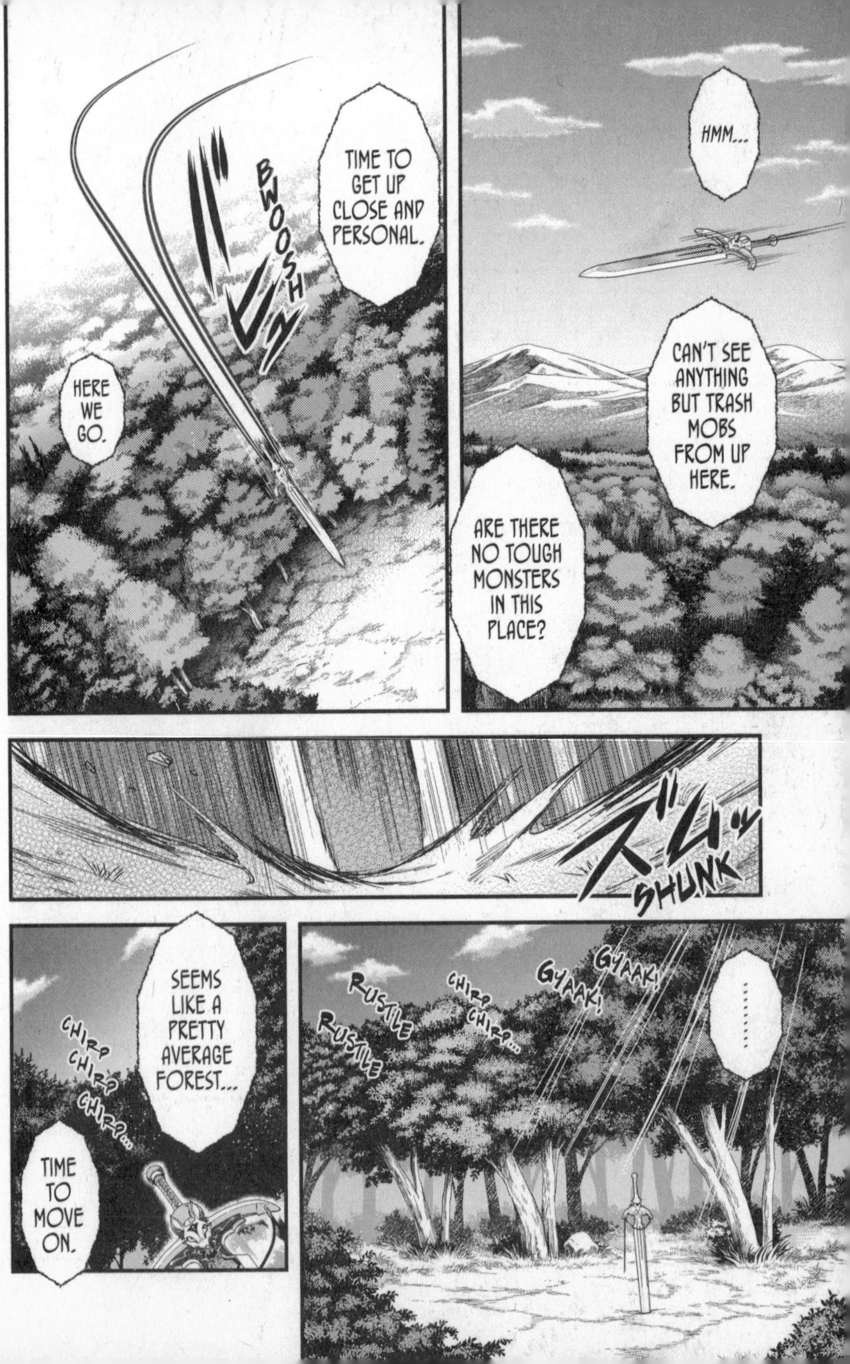
HMM...
CAN'T SEE ANYTHING BUT TRASH MOBS FROM UP HERE.
ARE THERE NO TOUGH MONSTERS IN THIS PLACE?
TIME TO GET UP CLOSE AND PERSONAL.
BWOOSH
HERE WE GO.
SHUNK
......
GYAAK! GYAAK!
CHIRP CHIRP CHIRP...
RUSTLE RUSTLE
SEEMS LIKE A PRETTY AVERAGE FOREST...
CHIRP CHIRP CHIRP...
TIME TO MOVE ON.

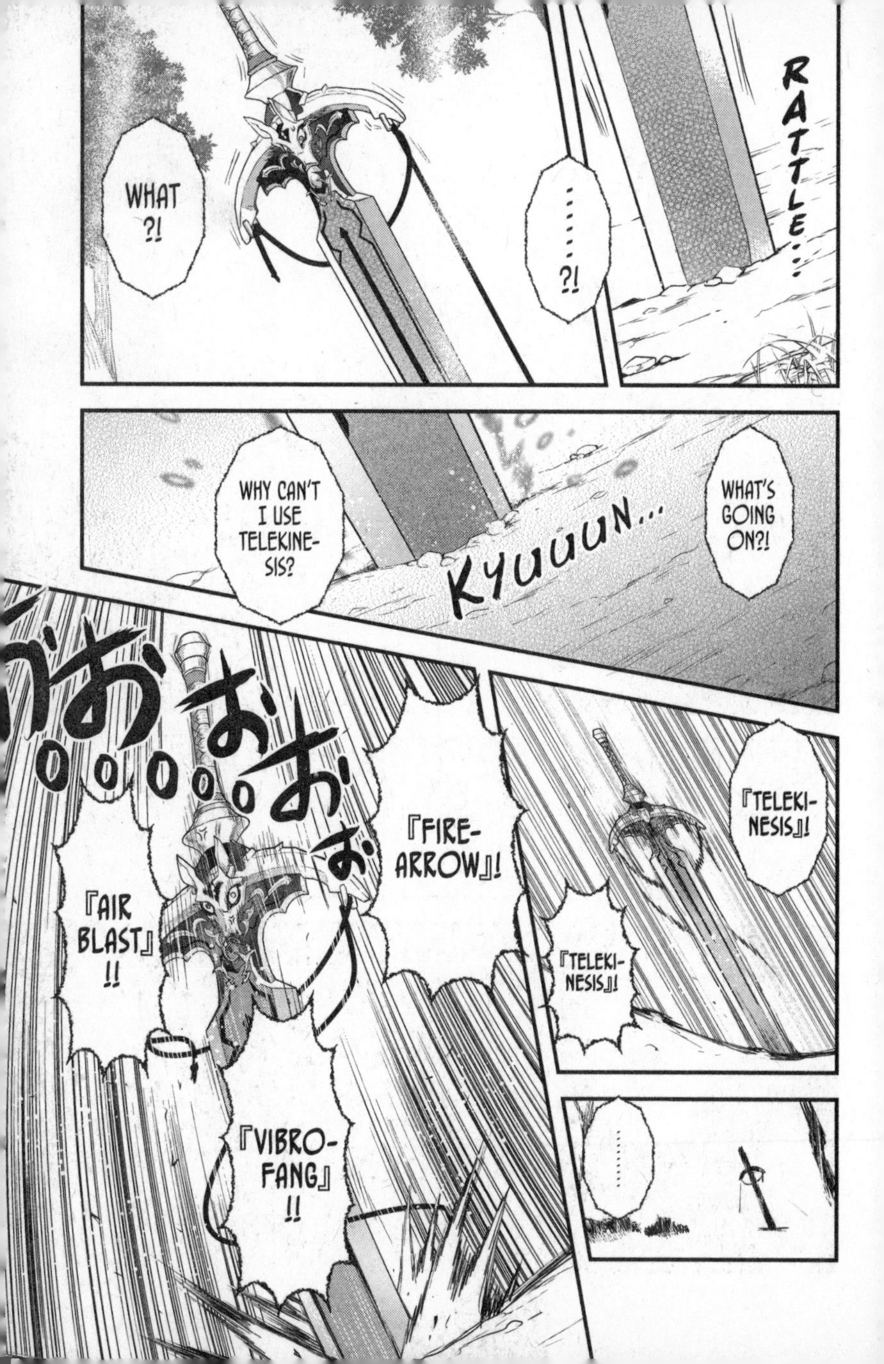

RATTLE...
......?!
WHAT ?!
WHAT'S GOING ON?!
KYUUUN...
WHY CAN'T I USE TELEKINESIS?
『TELEKINESIS』!
『TELEKINESIS』!
......
がおおおおお
OOOOO
『FIRE-ARROW』!
『AIR BLAST』!!
『VIBRO-FANG』!!

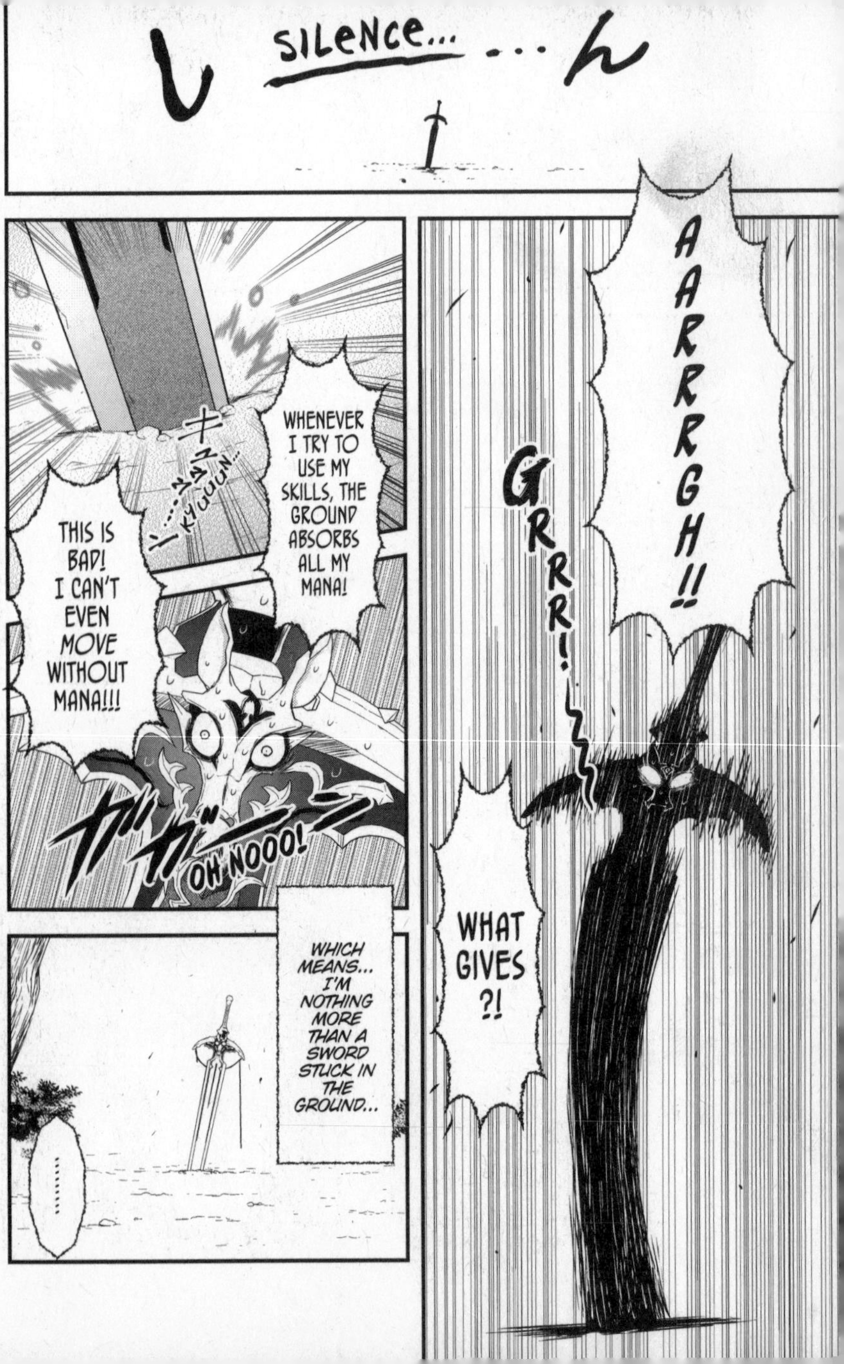
SILENCE...
AARRRGH!!
GRRRR!
WHAT GIVES?!
KYUUUN...
WHENEVER I TRY TO USE MY SKILLS, THE GROUND ABSORBS ALL MY MANA!
THIS IS BAD! I CAN'T EVEN MOVE WITHOUT MANA!!!
OH NOOO!
WHICH MEANS... I'M NOTHING MORE THAN A SWORD STUCK IN THE GROUND...
......

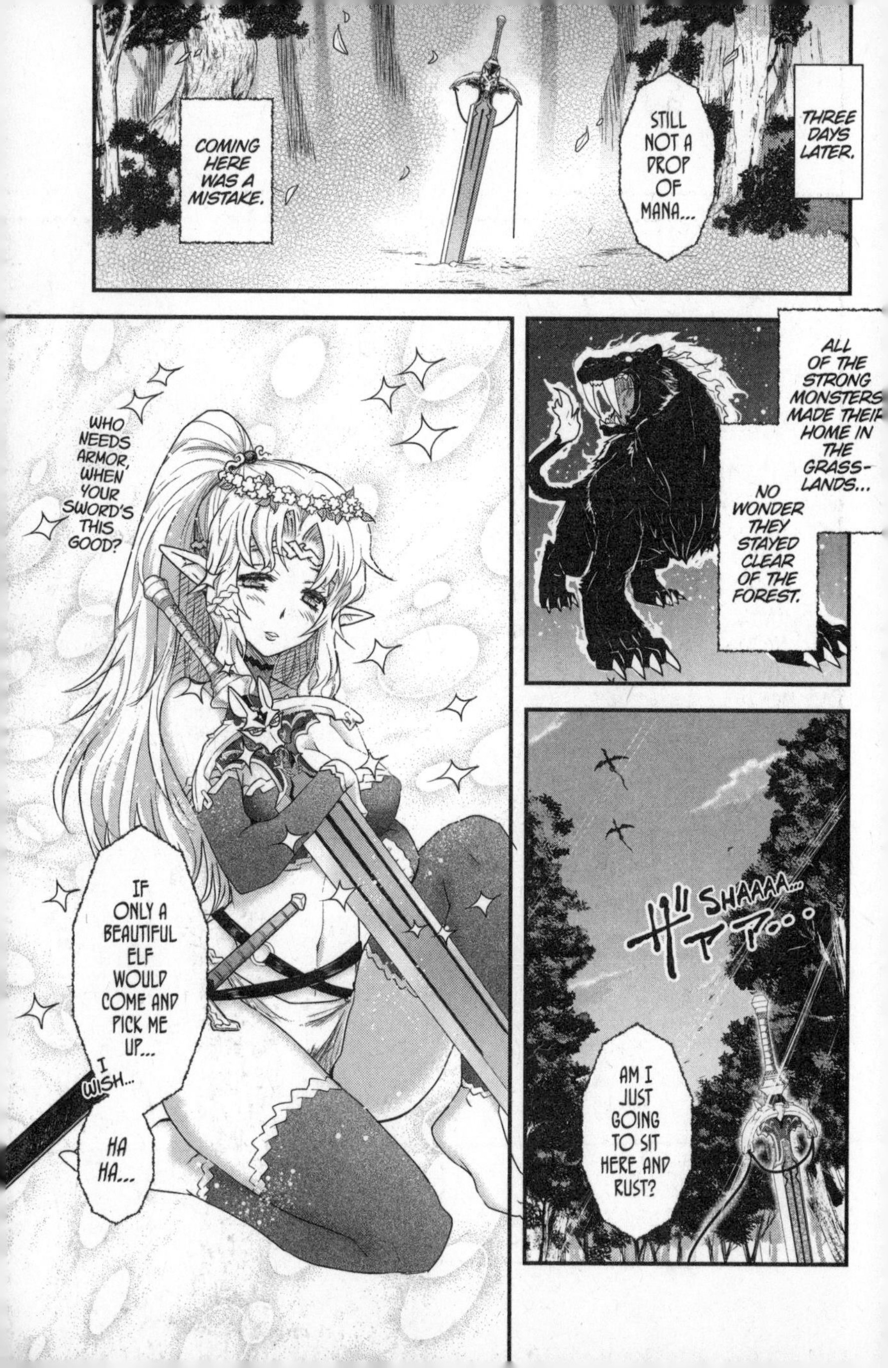
THREE DAYS LATER.
STILL NOT A DROP OF MANA...
COMING HERE WAS A MISTAKE.
ALL OF THE STRONG MONSTERS MADE THEIR HOME IN THE GRASSLANDS...
NO WONDER THEY STAYED CLEAR OF THE FOREST.
SHAAAA...
AM I JUST GOING TO SIT HERE AND RUST?
WHO NEEDS ARMOR, WHEN YOUR SWORD'S THIS GOOD?
IF ONLY A BEAUTIFUL ELF WOULD COME AND PICK ME UP...
I WISH...
HA HA...

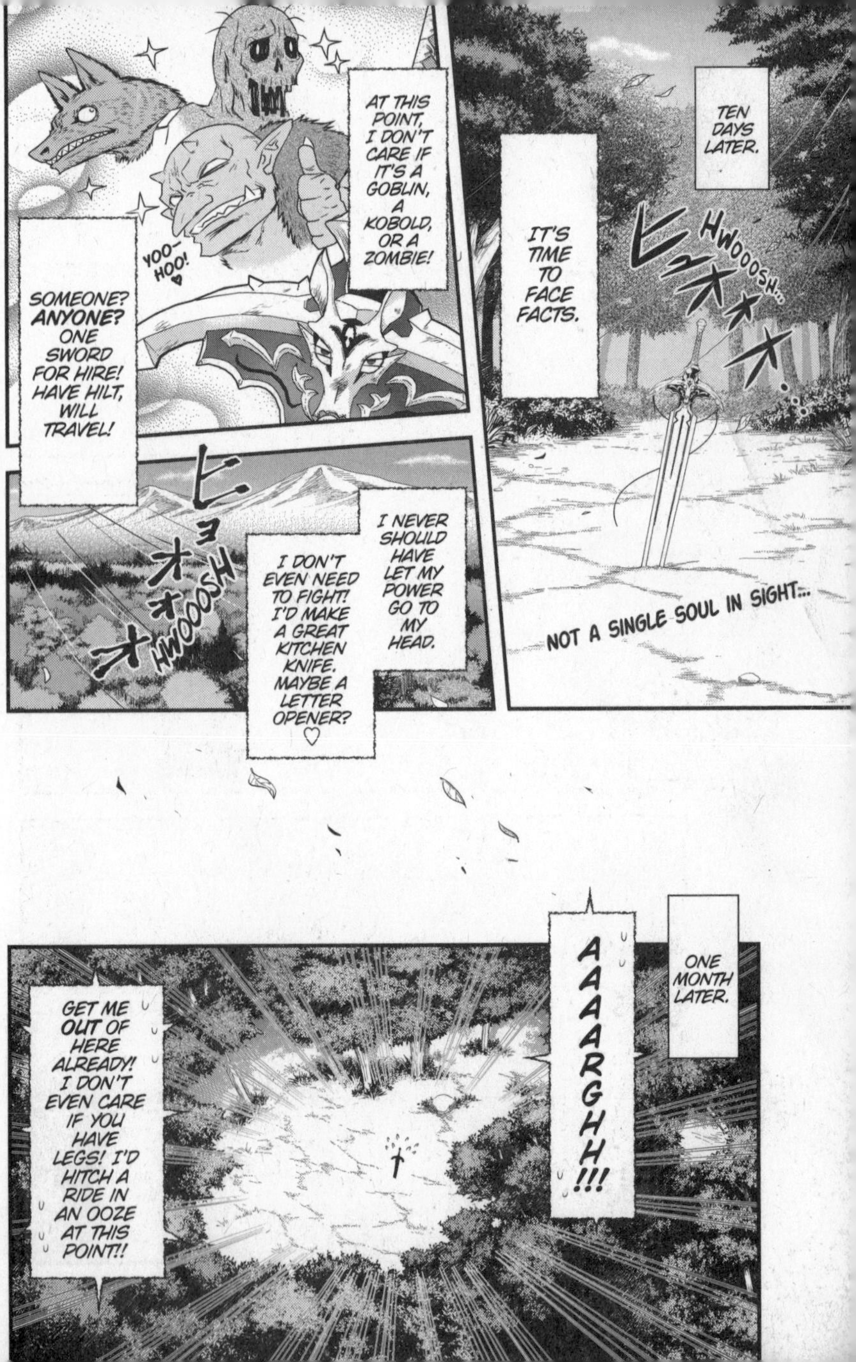

TEN DAYS LATER.
IT'S TIME TO FACE FACTS.
HWOOOSH...
NOT A SINGLE SOUL IN SIGHT...
AT THIS POINT, I DON'T CARE IF IT'S A GOBLIN, A KOBOLD, OR A ZOMBIE!
YOO-HOO! ♥
SOMEONE? **ANYONE?** ONE SWORD FOR HIRE! HAVE HILT, WILL TRAVEL!
I NEVER SHOULD HAVE LET MY POWER GO TO MY HEAD.
I DON'T EVEN NEED TO FIGHT! I'D MAKE A GREAT KITCHEN KNIFE. MAYBE A LETTER OPENER? ♡
HWOOOSH
ONE MONTH LATER.
AAAARGHH!!!
GET ME **OUT** OF HERE ALREADY! I DON'T EVEN CARE IF YOU HAVE LEGS! I'D HITCH A RIDE IN AN OOZE AT THIS POINT!!

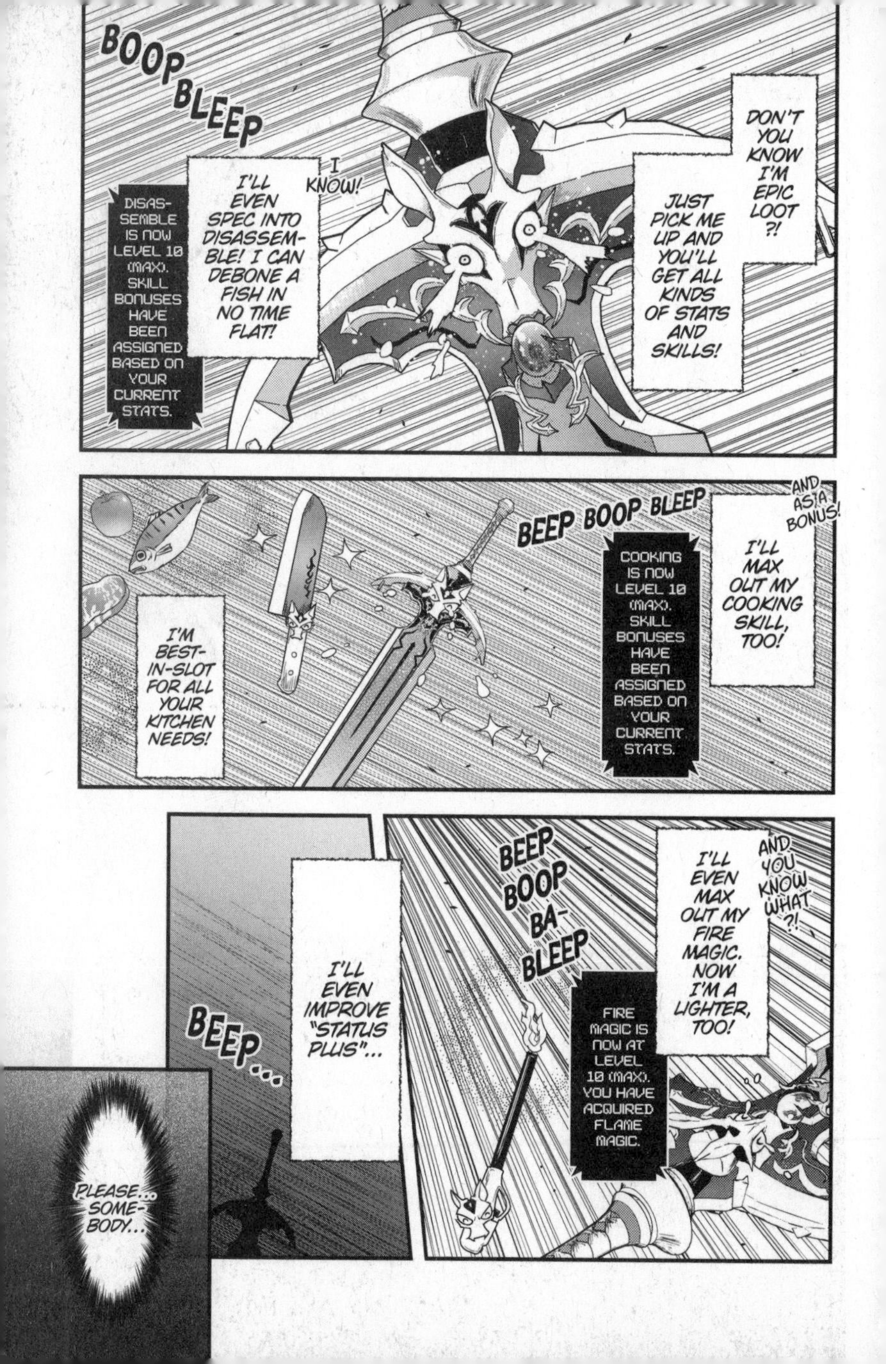
DON'T YOU KNOW I'M EPIC LOOT ?!
JUST PICK ME UP AND YOU'LL GET ALL KINDS OF STATS AND SKILLS!
I KNOW!
I'LL EVEN SPEC INTO DISASSEMBLE! I CAN DEBONE A FISH IN NO TIME FLAT!
DISASSEMBLE IS NOW LEVEL 10 (MAX). SKILL BONUSES HAVE BEEN ASSIGNED BASED ON YOUR CURRENT STATS.
BOOP BLEEP
AND AS A BONUS!
I'LL MAX OUT MY COOKING SKILL, TOO!
BEEP BOOP BLEEP
COOKING IS NOW LEVEL 10 (MAX). SKILL BONUSES HAVE BEEN ASSIGNED BASED ON YOUR CURRENT STATS.
I'M BEST-IN-SLOT FOR ALL YOUR KITCHEN NEEDS!
AND YOU KNOW WHAT ?!
I'LL EVEN MAX OUT MY FIRE MAGIC. NOW I'M A LIGHTER, TOO!
BEEP BOOP BA-BLEEP
FIRE MAGIC IS NOW AT LEVEL 10 (MAX). YOU HAVE ACQUIRED FLAME MAGIC.
I'LL EVEN IMPROVE "STATUS PLUS"...
BEEP...
PLEASE... SOMEBODY...

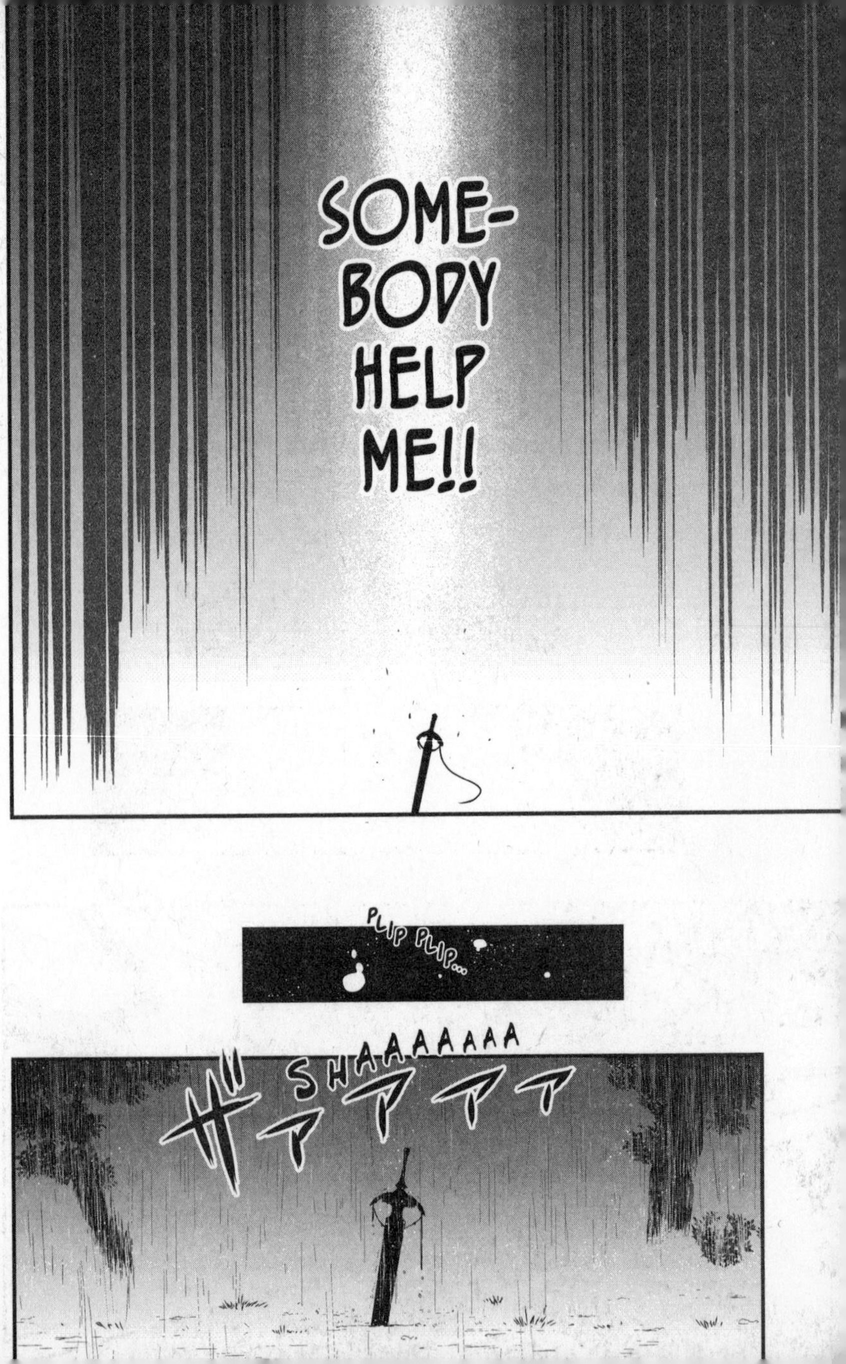
SOME-BODY HELP ME!!
PLIP PLIP...
SHAAAAAAA

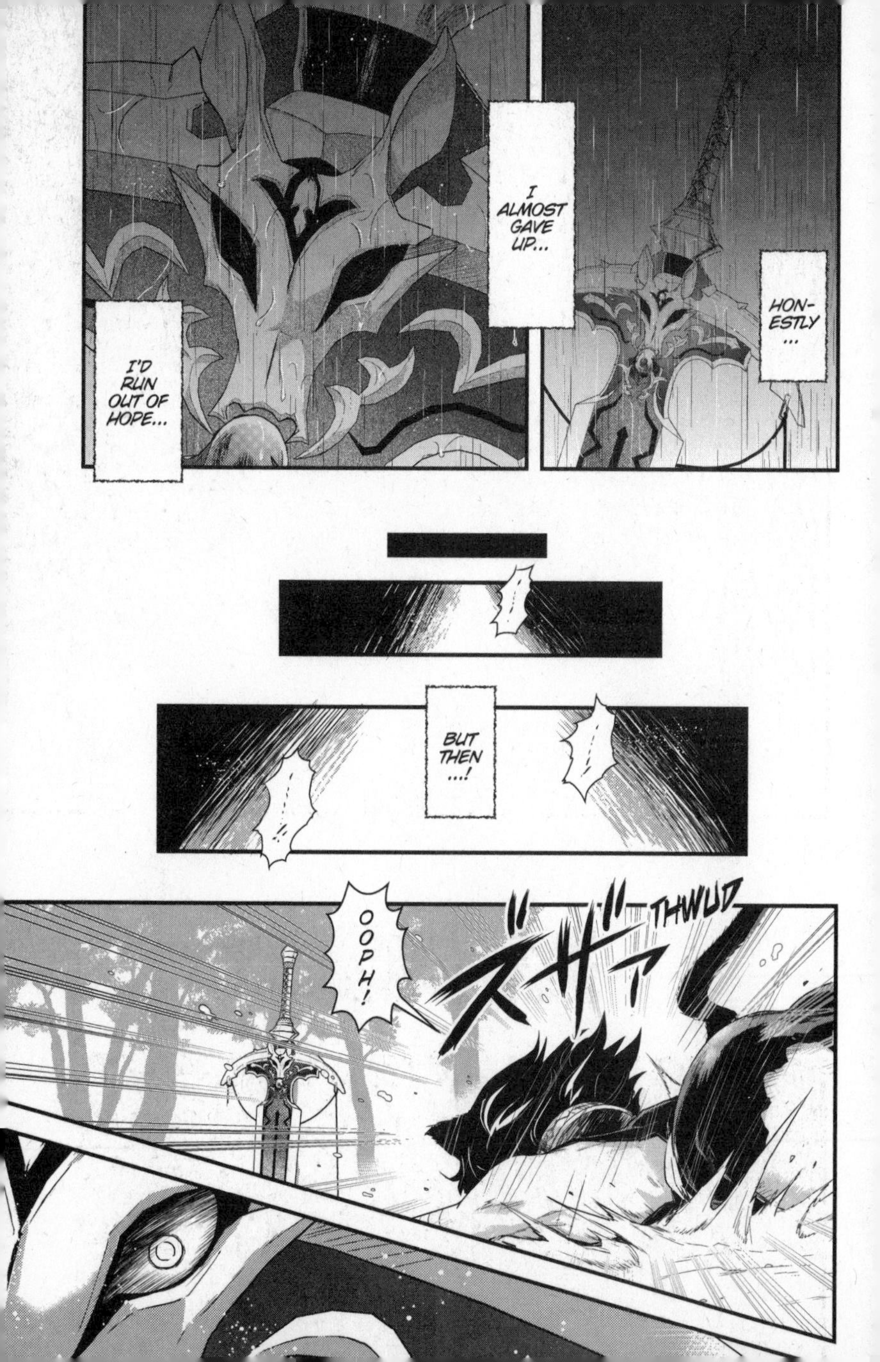
HON-ESTLY ...
I ALMOST GAVE UP...
I'D RUN OUT OF HOPE...
BUT THEN ...!
THWUD
OOPH!

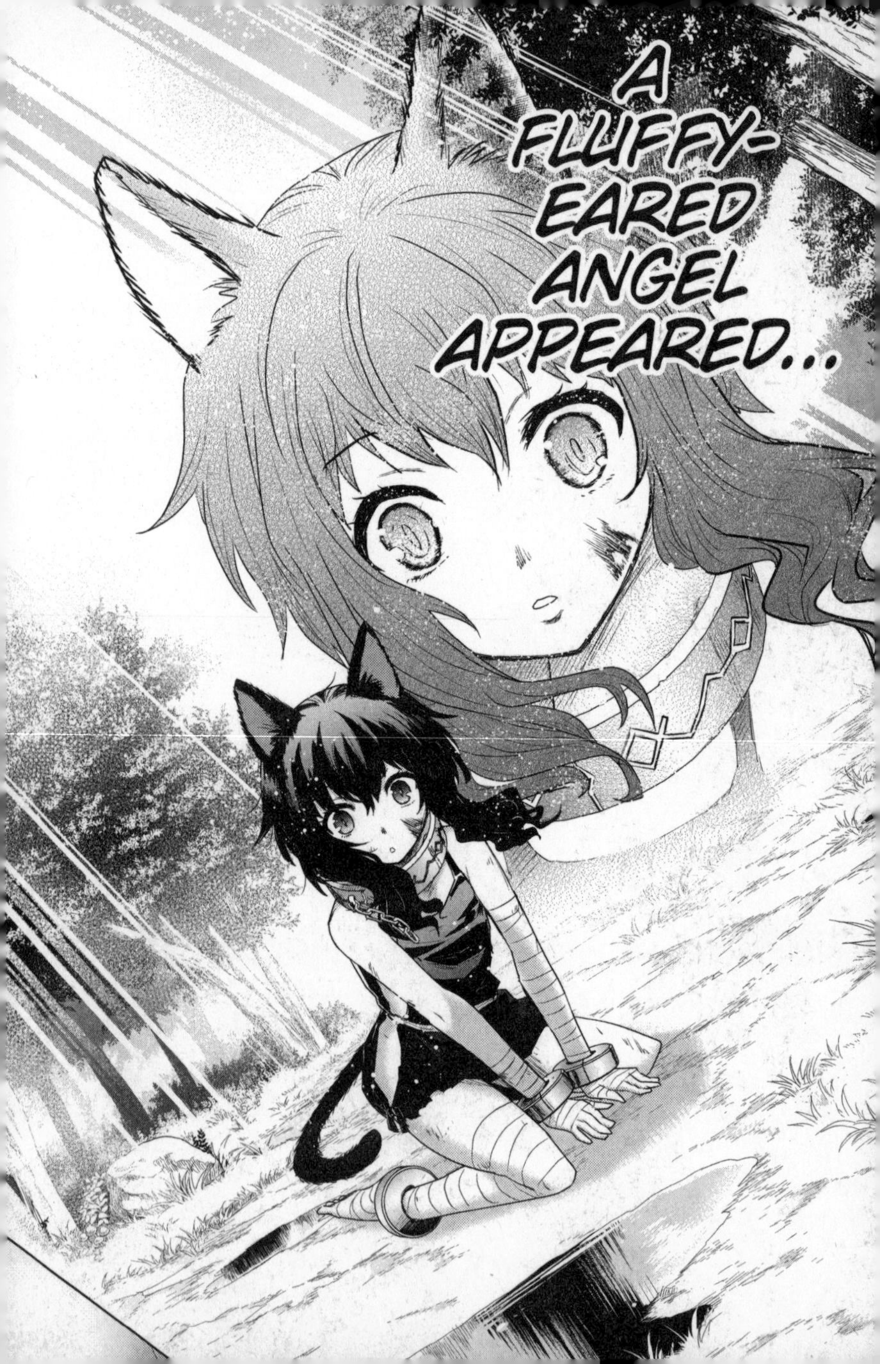
A FLUFFY-EARED ANGEL APPEARED...

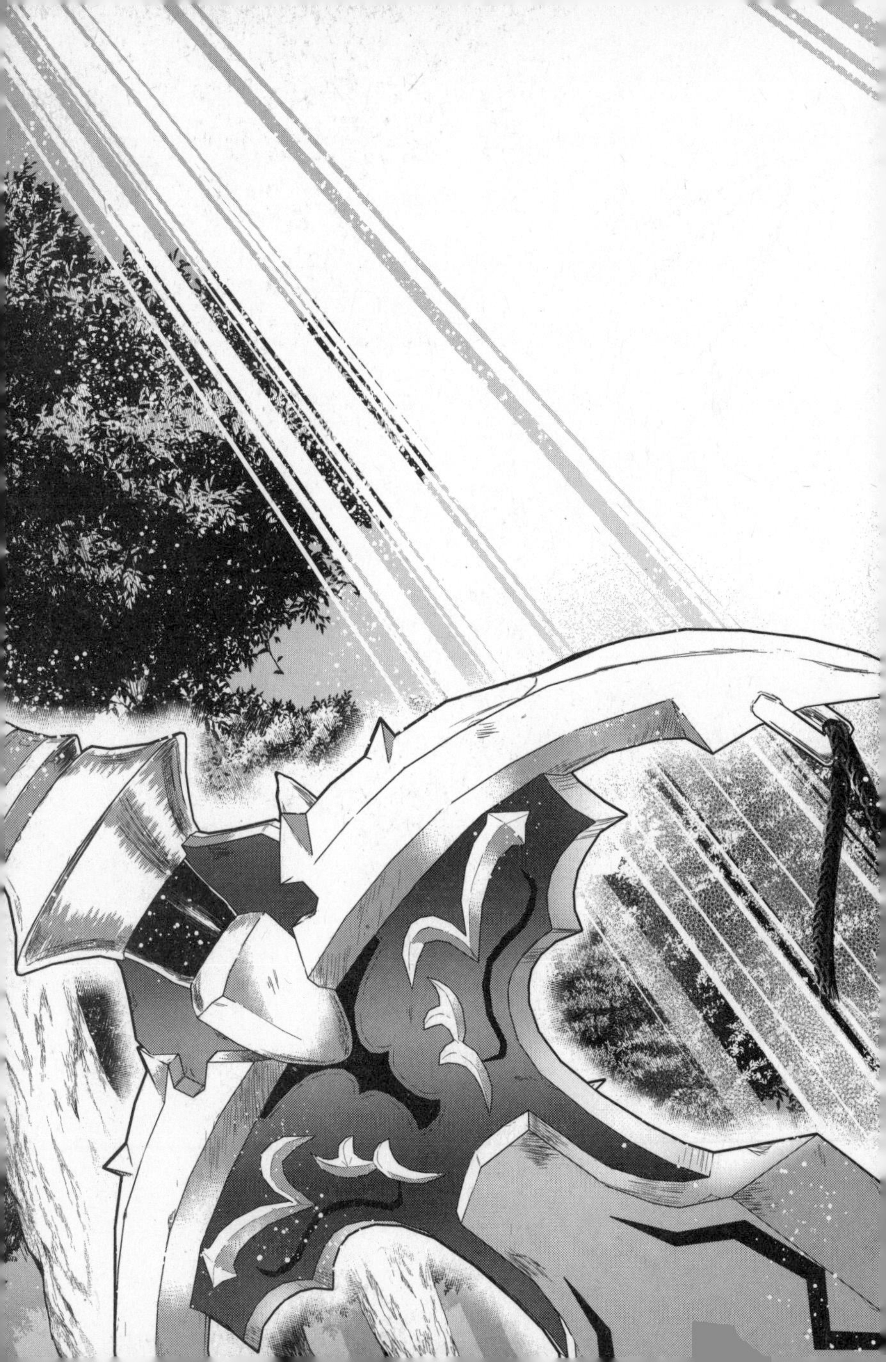

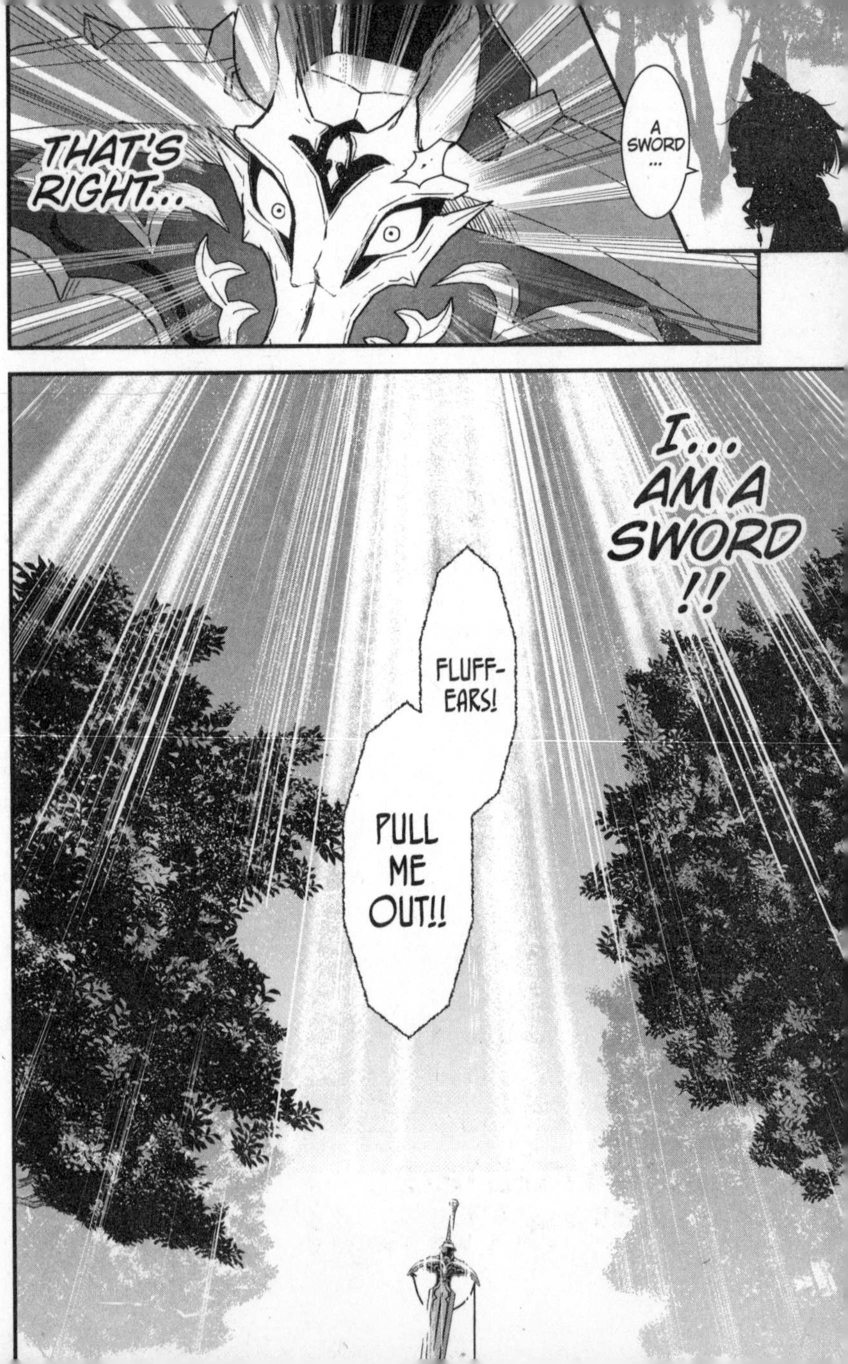
A SWORD ...
THAT'S RIGHT...
I... AM A SWORD!!
FLUFF-EARS!
PULL ME OUT!!

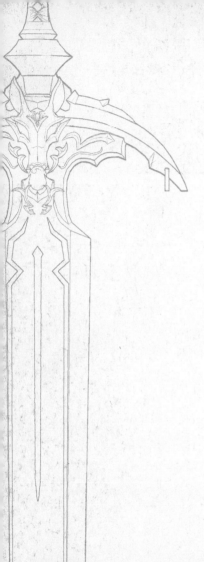

Reincarnated
as a sword

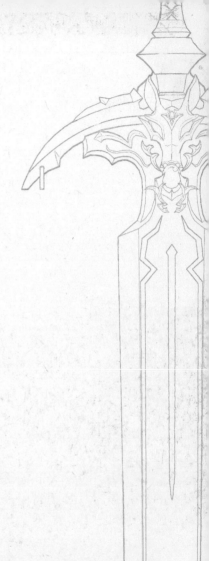

Reincarnated
as a sword

Chapter 3: Citybound

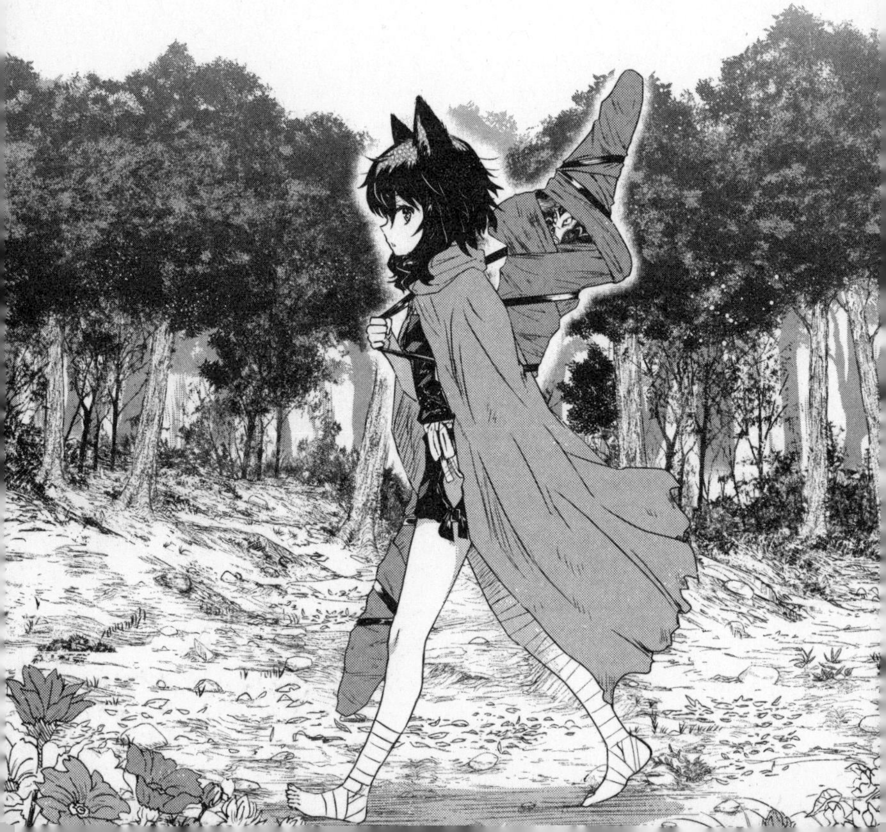

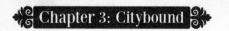

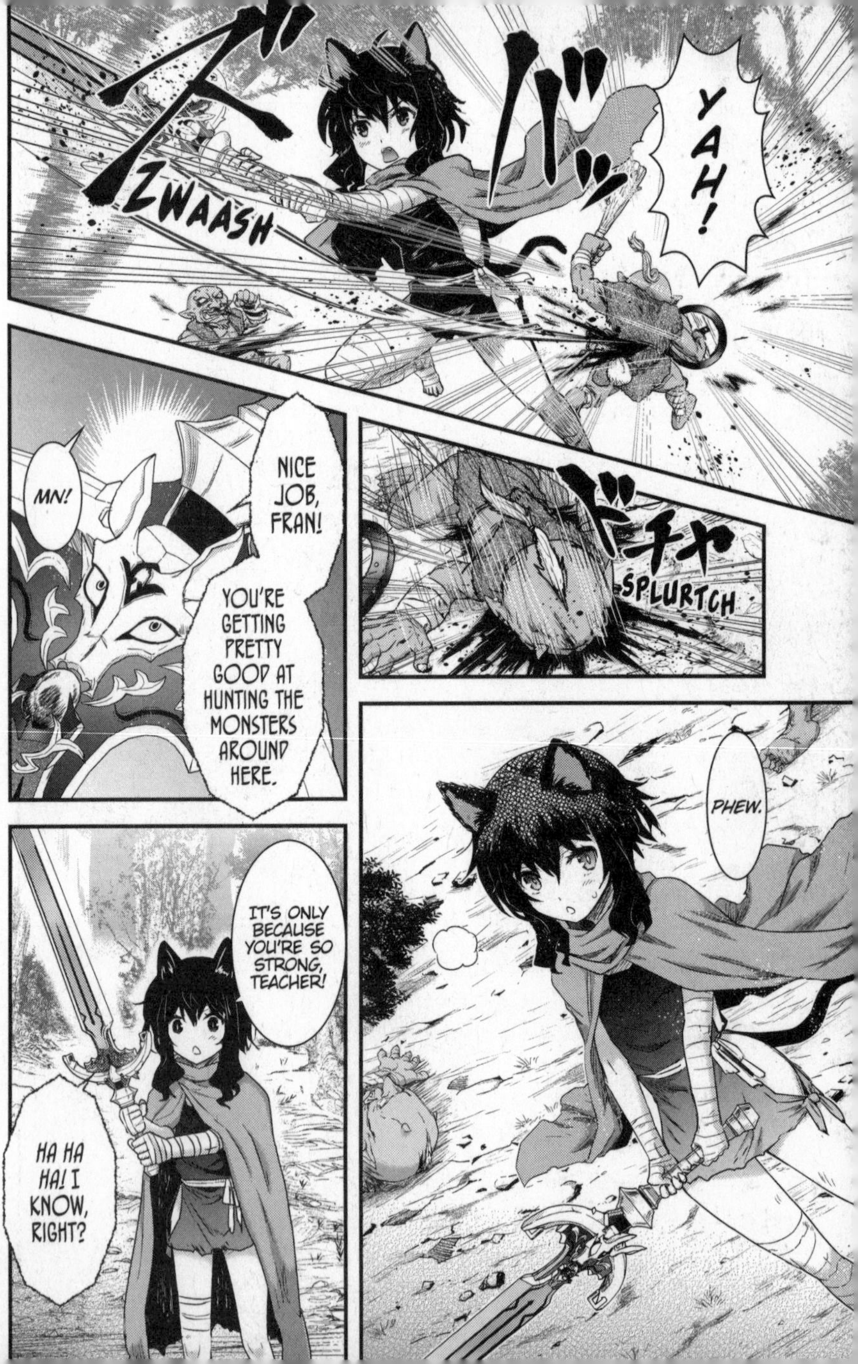
YAH!
ズバッ
ZWAASH
ドチャ
SPLURTCH
NICE JOB, FRAN!
YOU'RE GETTING PRETTY GOOD AT HUNTING THE MONSTERS AROUND HERE.
MN!
PHEW.
IT'S ONLY BECAUSE YOU'RE SO STRONG, TEACHER!
HA HA HA! I KNOW, RIGHT?

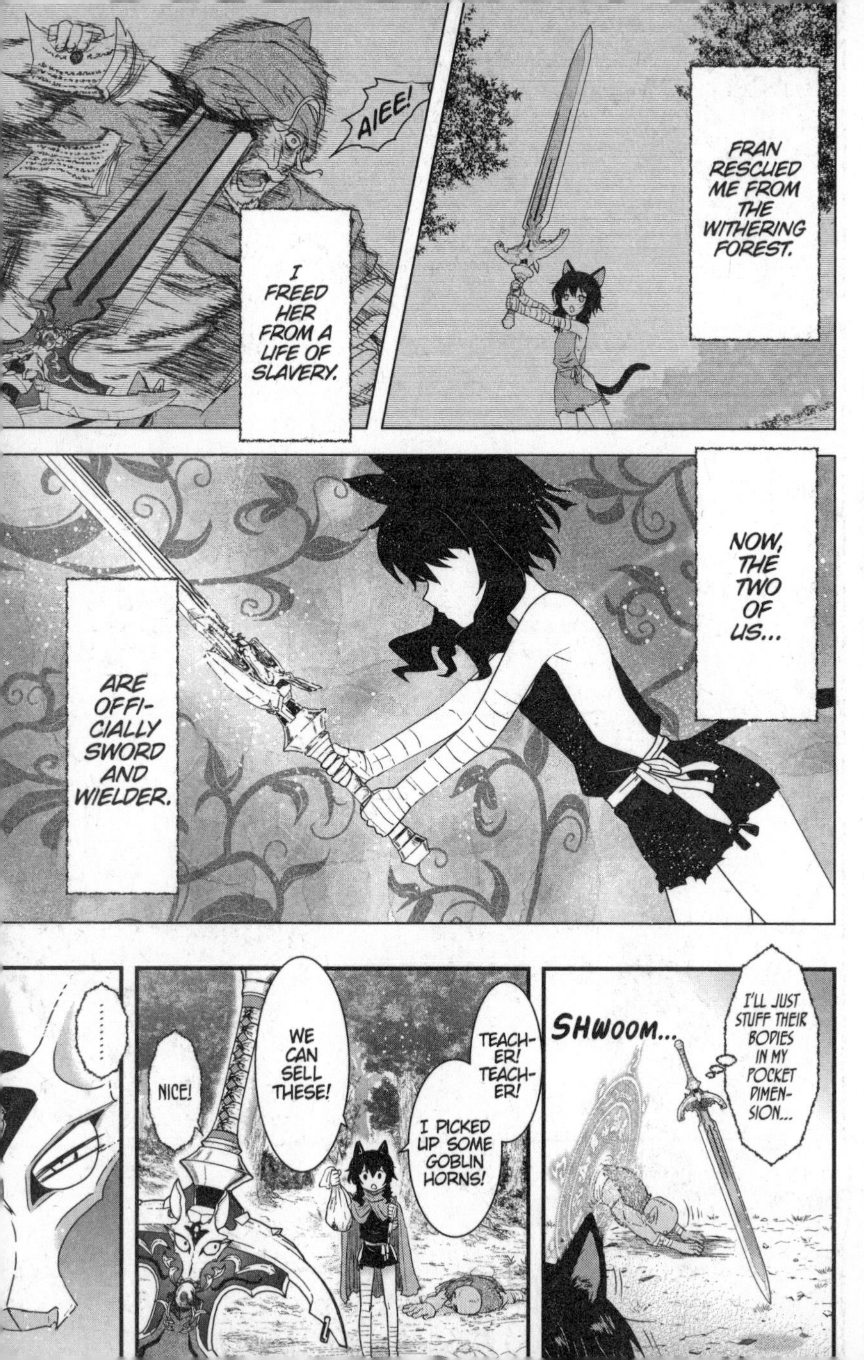
FRAN RESCUED ME FROM THE WITHERING FOREST.
AIEE!
I FREED HER FROM A LIFE OF SLAVERY.
NOW, THE TWO OF US...
ARE OFFICIALLY SWORD AND WIELDER.
I'LL JUST STUFF THEIR BODIES IN MY POCKET DIMENSION...
SHWOOM...
TEACHER! TEACHER!
I PICKED UP SOME GOBLIN HORNS!
WE CAN SELL THESE!
NICE!
......

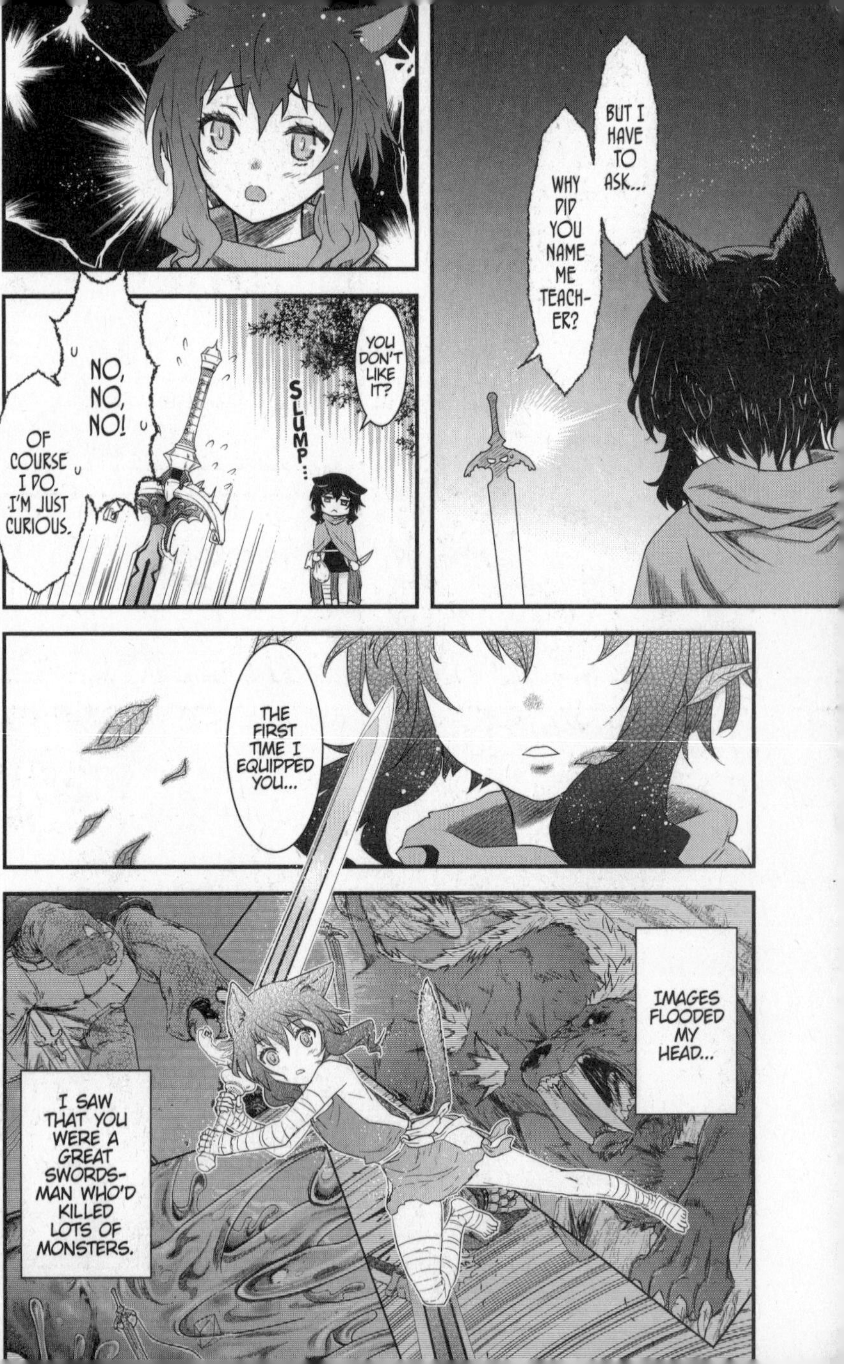
BUT I HAVE TO ASK...
WHY DID YOU NAME ME TEACHER?
YOU DON'T LIKE IT?
SLUMP...
NO, NO, NO!
OF COURSE I DO. I'M JUST CURIOUS.
THE FIRST TIME I EQUIPPED YOU...
IMAGES FLOODED MY HEAD...
I SAW THAT YOU WERE A GREAT SWORDSMAN WHO'D KILLED LOTS OF MONSTERS.

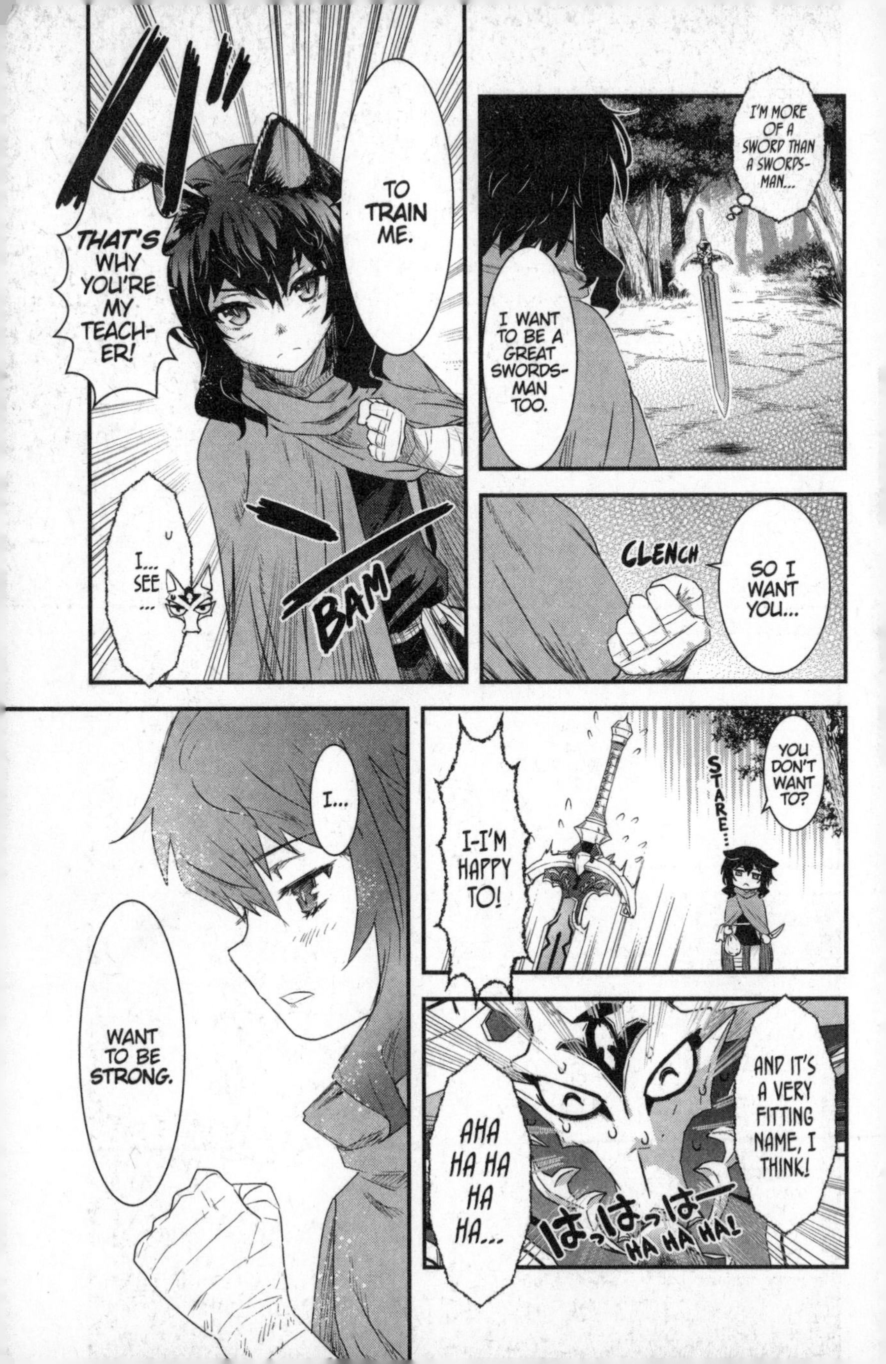
I'M MORE OF A SWORD THAN A SWORDS-MAN...
I WANT TO BE A GREAT SWORDS-MAN TOO.
CLENCH
SO I WANT YOU...
TO TRAIN ME.
THAT'S WHY YOU'RE MY TEACH-ER!
BAM
I... SEE ...
YOU DON'T WANT TO?
STARE...
I-I'M HAPPY TO!
AND IT'S A VERY FITTING NAME, I THINK!
AHA HA HA HA HA...
はっはっはー
HA HA HA!
I...
WANT TO BE STRONG.

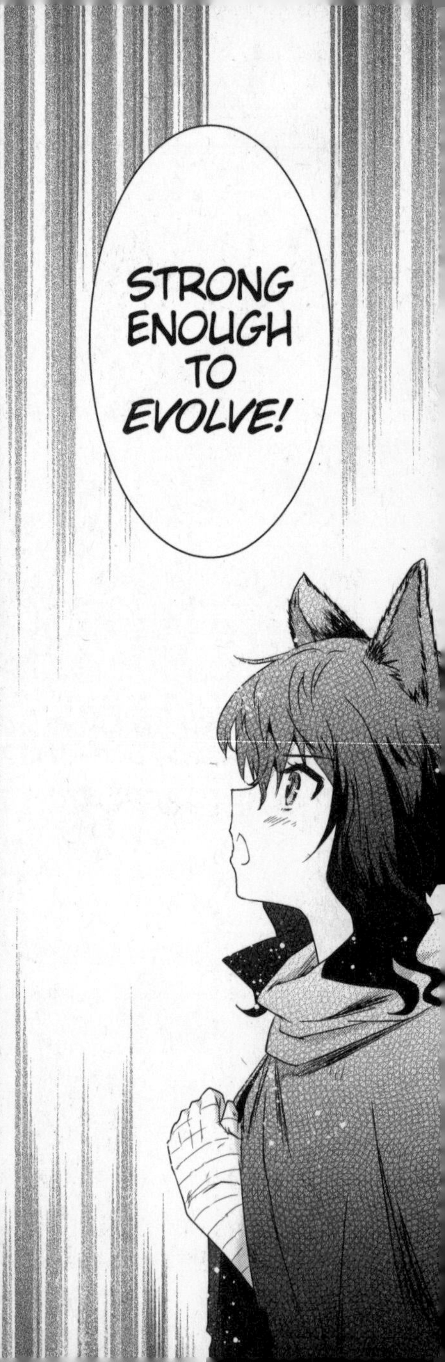
STRONG ENOUGH TO EVOLVE!

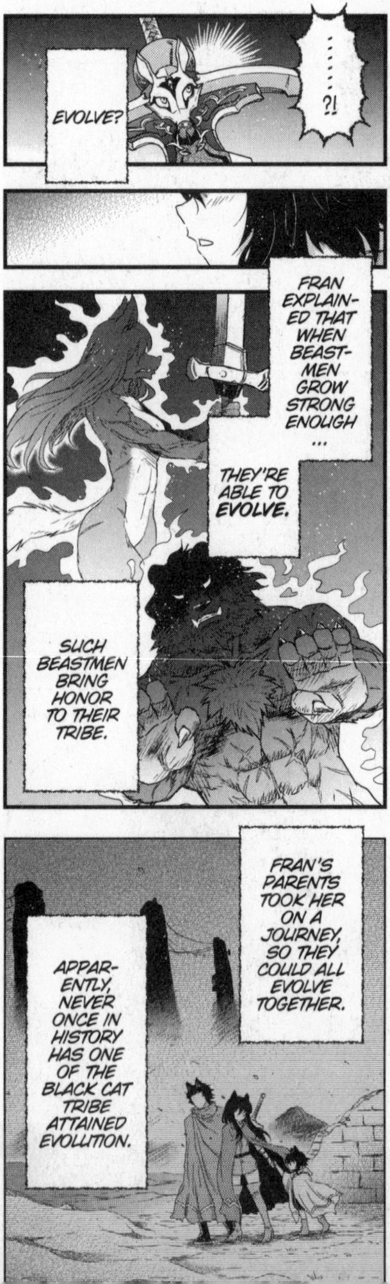
......?!
EVOLVE?
FRAN EXPLAINED THAT WHEN BEASTMEN GROW STRONG ENOUGH...
THEY'RE ABLE TO EVOLVE.
SUCH BEASTMEN BRING HONOR TO THEIR TRIBE.
FRAN'S PARENTS TOOK HER ON A JOURNEY, SO THEY COULD ALL EVOLVE TOGETHER.
APPARENTLY, NEVER ONCE IN HISTORY HAS ONE OF THE BLACK CAT TRIBE ATTAINED EVOLUTION.

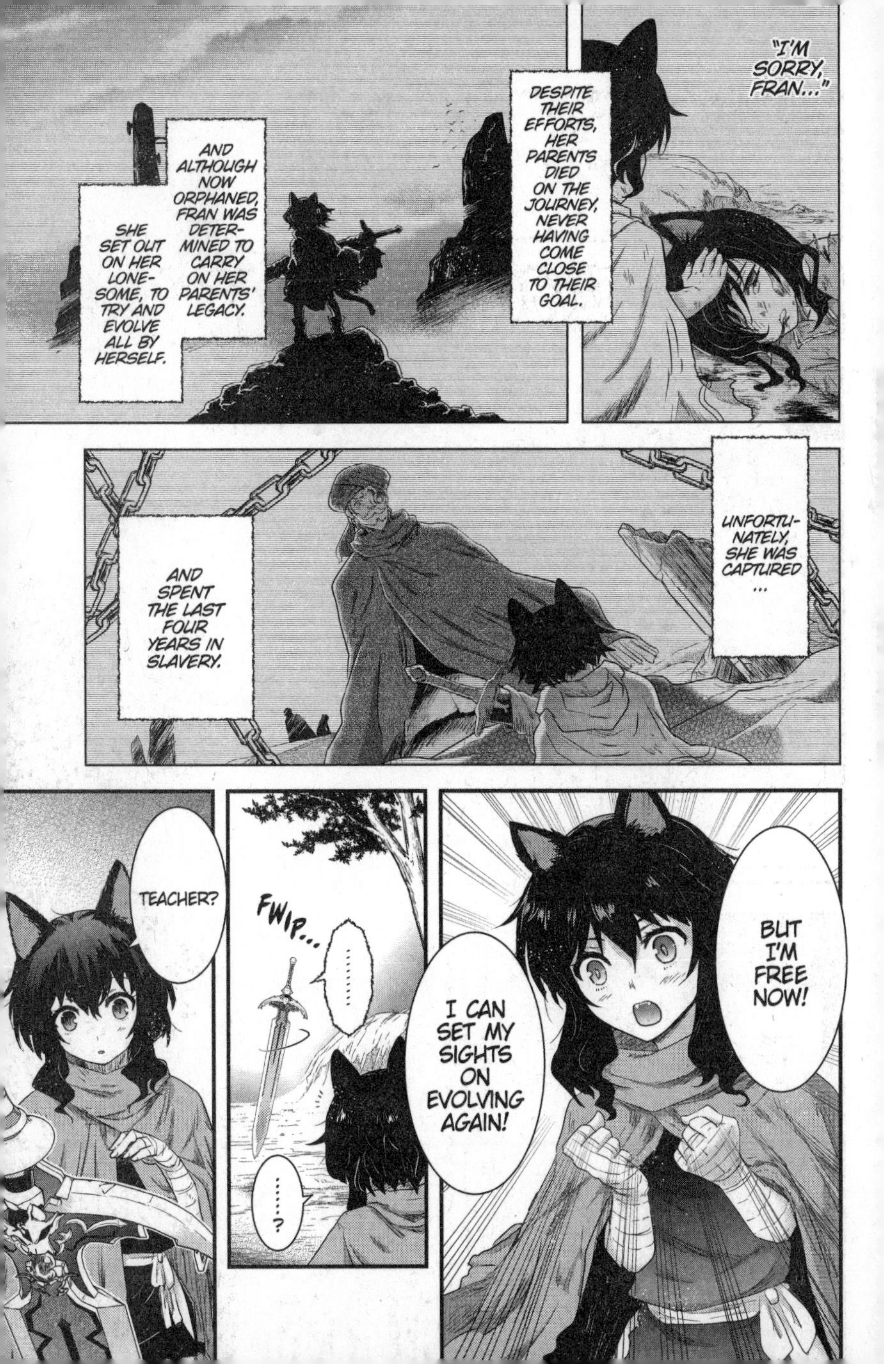
"I'M SORRY, FRAN..."
DESPITE THEIR EFFORTS, HER PARENTS DIED ON THE JOURNEY, NEVER HAVING COME CLOSE TO THEIR GOAL.
AND ALTHOUGH NOW ORPHANED, FRAN WAS DETER-MINED TO CARRY ON HER PARENTS' LEGACY.
SHE SET OUT ON HER LONE-SOME, TO TRY AND EVOLVE ALL BY HERSELF.
UNFORTU-NATELY, SHE WAS CAPTURED ...
AND SPENT THE LAST FOUR YEARS IN SLAVERY.
BUT I'M FREE NOW!
I CAN SET MY SIGHTS ON EVOLVING AGAIN!
......
FWIP...
......?
TEACHER?

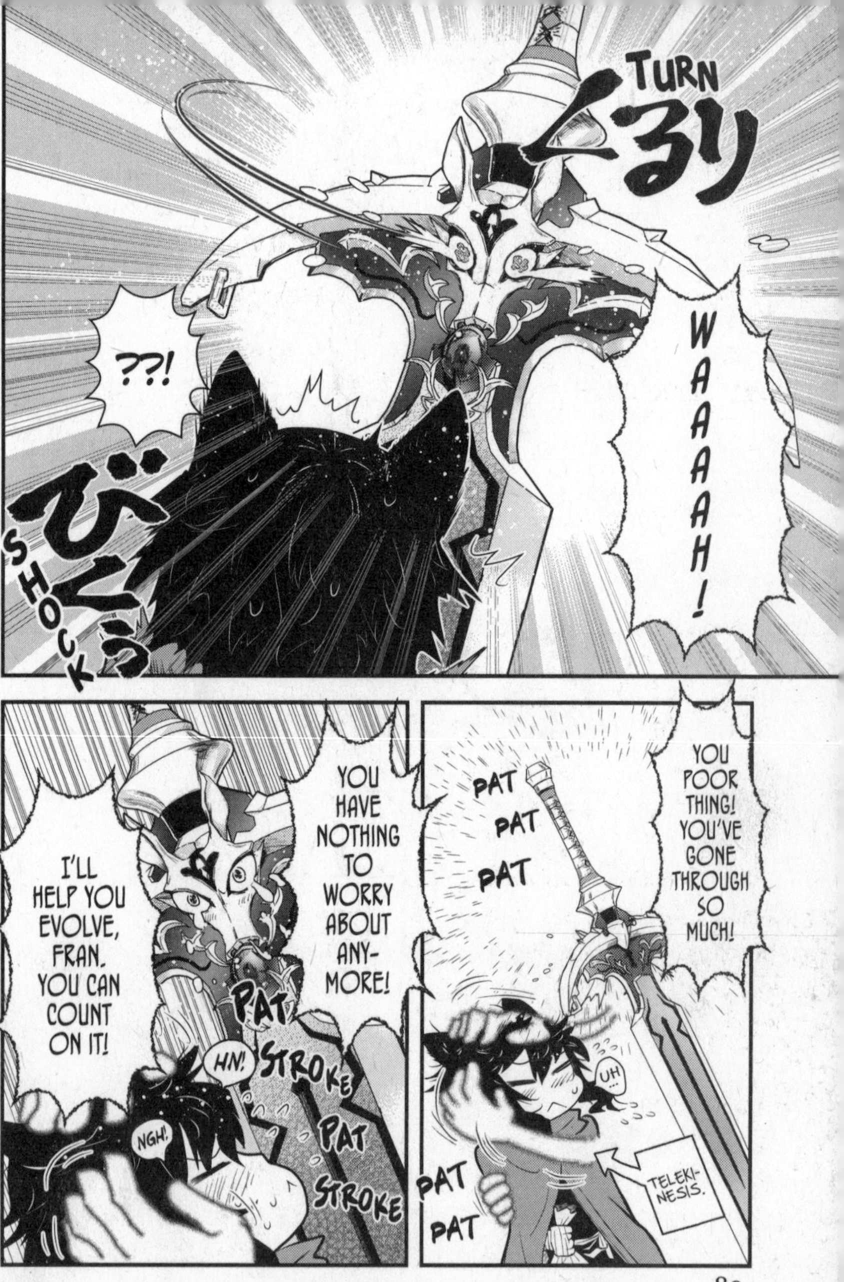
TURN
くるり
WAAAAAH!
??!
びくっ
SHOCK
YOU POOR THING! YOU'VE GONE THROUGH SO MUCH!
PAT
PAT
PAT
UH...
TELEKINESIS.
PAT
PAT
YOU HAVE NOTHING TO WORRY ABOUT ANYMORE!
I'LL HELP YOU EVOLVE, FRAN. YOU CAN COUNT ON IT!
PAT
HN!
STROKE
PAT
STROKE
NGH!

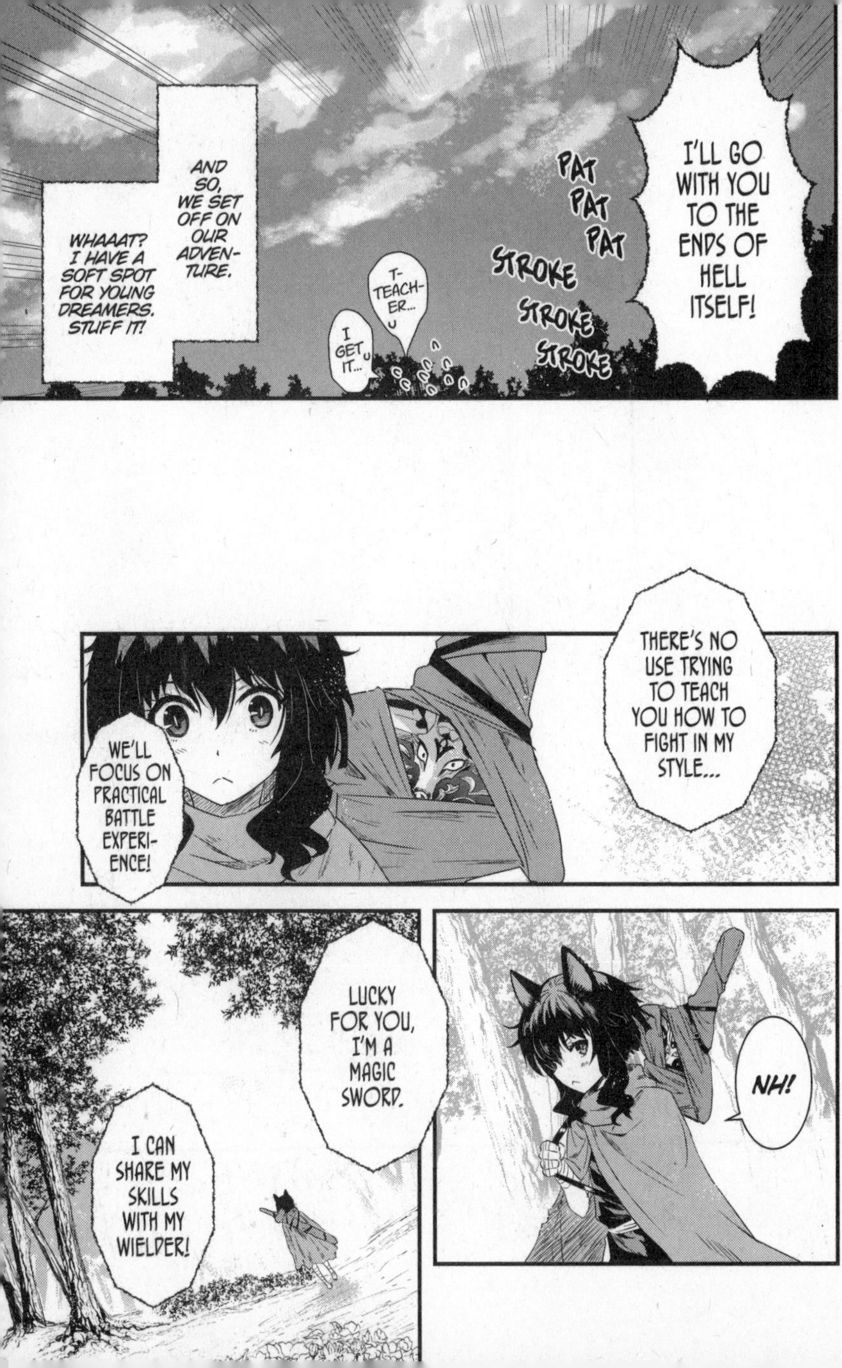
I'LL GO WITH YOU TO THE ENDS OF HELL ITSELF!
PAT PAT PAT
STROKE STROKE STROKE
T-TEACHER...
I GET IT...
AND SO, WE SET OFF ON OUR ADVENTURE.
WHAAAT? I HAVE A SOFT SPOT FOR YOUNG DREAMERS. STUFF IT!
THERE'S NO USE TRYING TO TEACH YOU HOW TO FIGHT IN MY STYLE...
WE'LL FOCUS ON PRACTICAL BATTLE EXPERIENCE!
NH!
LUCKY FOR YOU, I'M A MAGIC SWORD.
I CAN SHARE MY SKILLS WITH MY WIELDER!

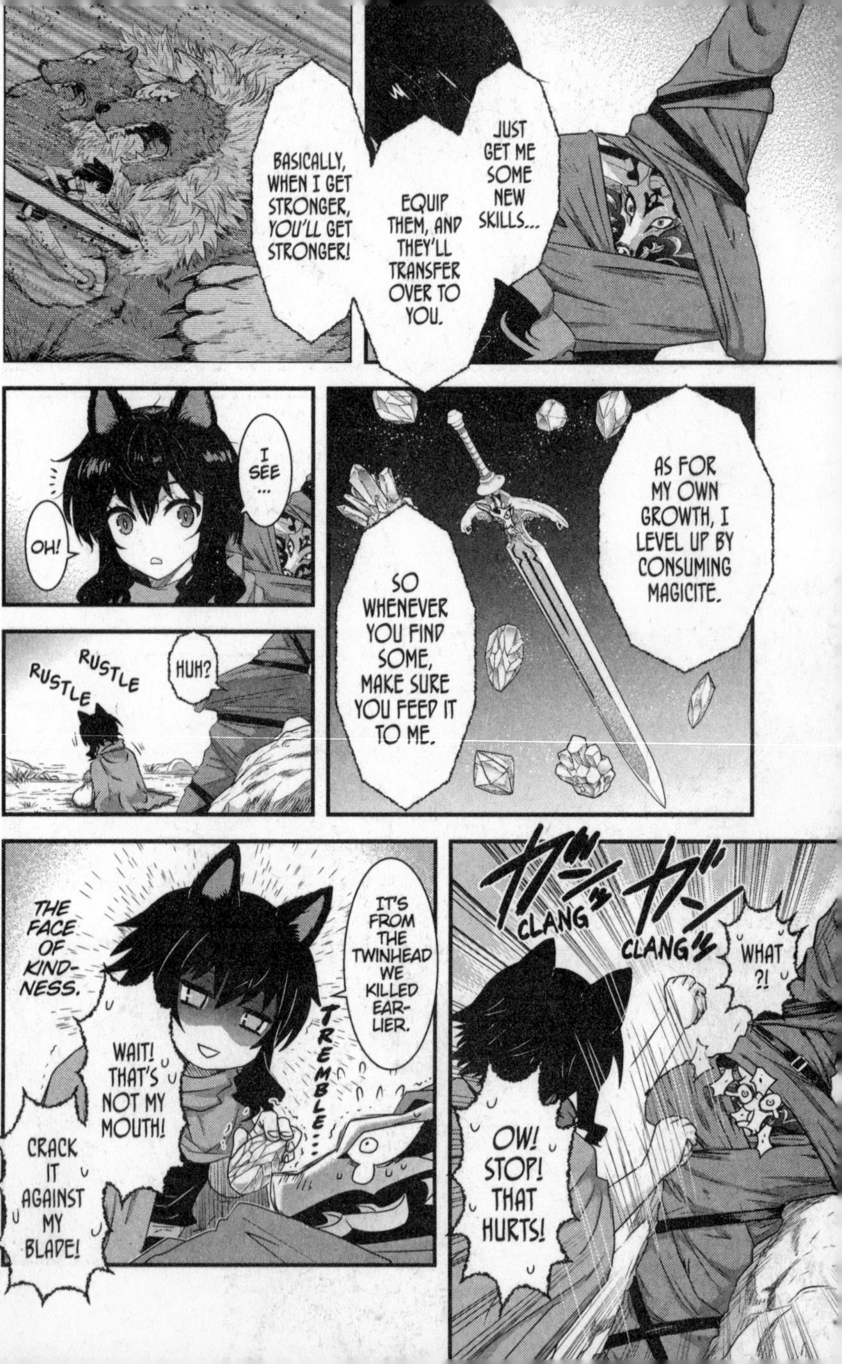
JUST GET ME SOME NEW SKILLS...
EQUIP THEM, AND THEY'LL TRANSFER OVER TO YOU.
BASICALLY, WHEN I GET STRONGER, *YOU'LL* GET STRONGER!
AS FOR MY OWN GROWTH, I LEVEL UP BY CONSUMING MAGICITE.
SO WHENEVER YOU FIND SOME, MAKE SURE YOU FEED IT TO ME.
I SEE...
OH!
HUH?
RUSTLE
RUSTLE
CLANG
CLANG
WHAT?!
OW! STOP! THAT HURTS!
IT'S FROM THE TWINHEAD WE KILLED EARLIER.
TREMBLE...
THE FACE OF KINDNESS.
WAIT! THAT'S NOT MY MOUTH!
CRACK IT AGAINST MY BLADE!

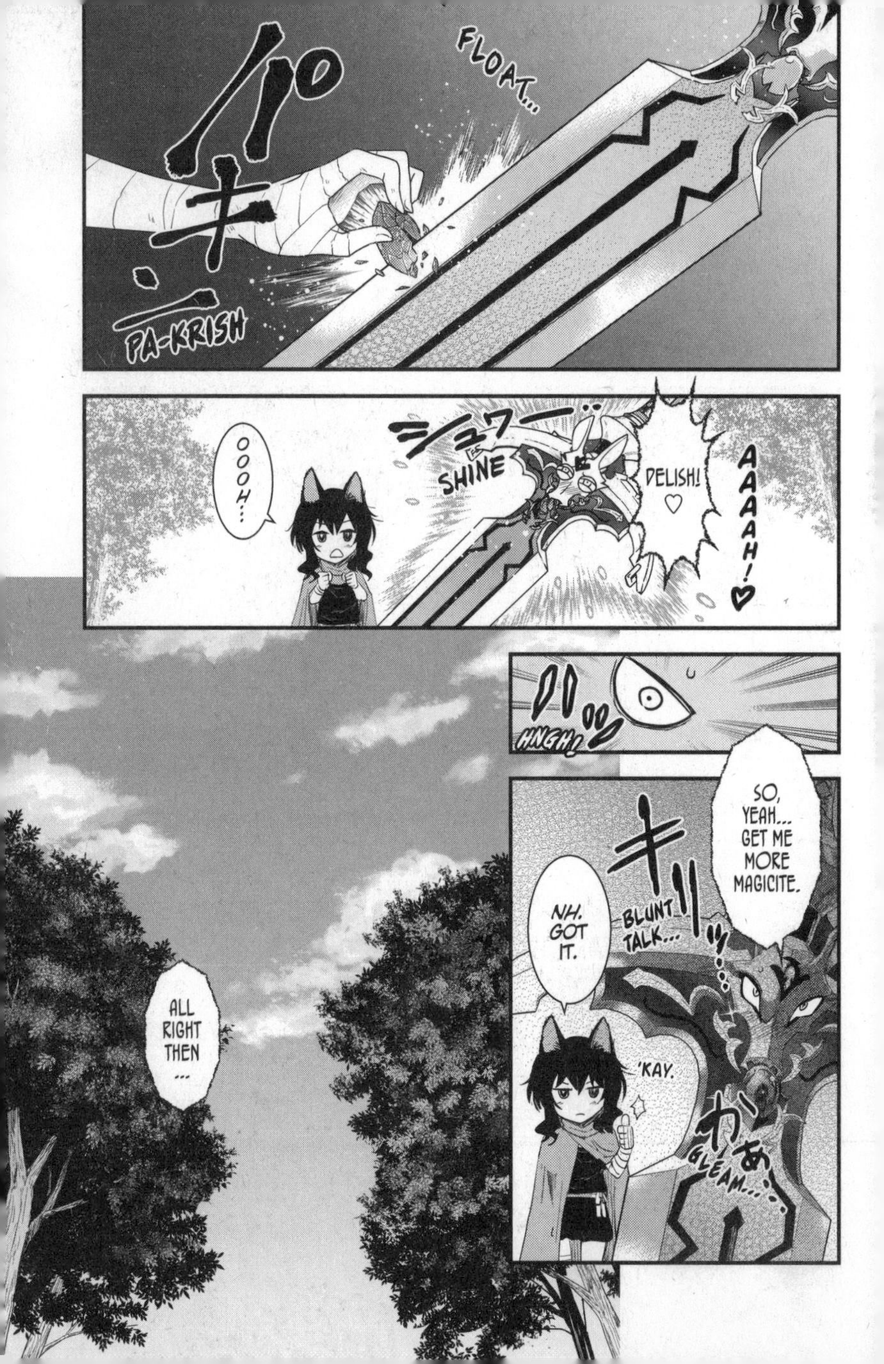
FLOAT...
パキ
PA-KRISH
AAAAH!♡
DELISH! ♡
シュワー
SHINE
OOOH...
HNGH!
SO, YEAH... GET ME MORE MAGICITE.
キリッ
BLUNT TALK...
NH. GOT IT.
'KAY.
GLEAM...
ALL RIGHT THEN ...

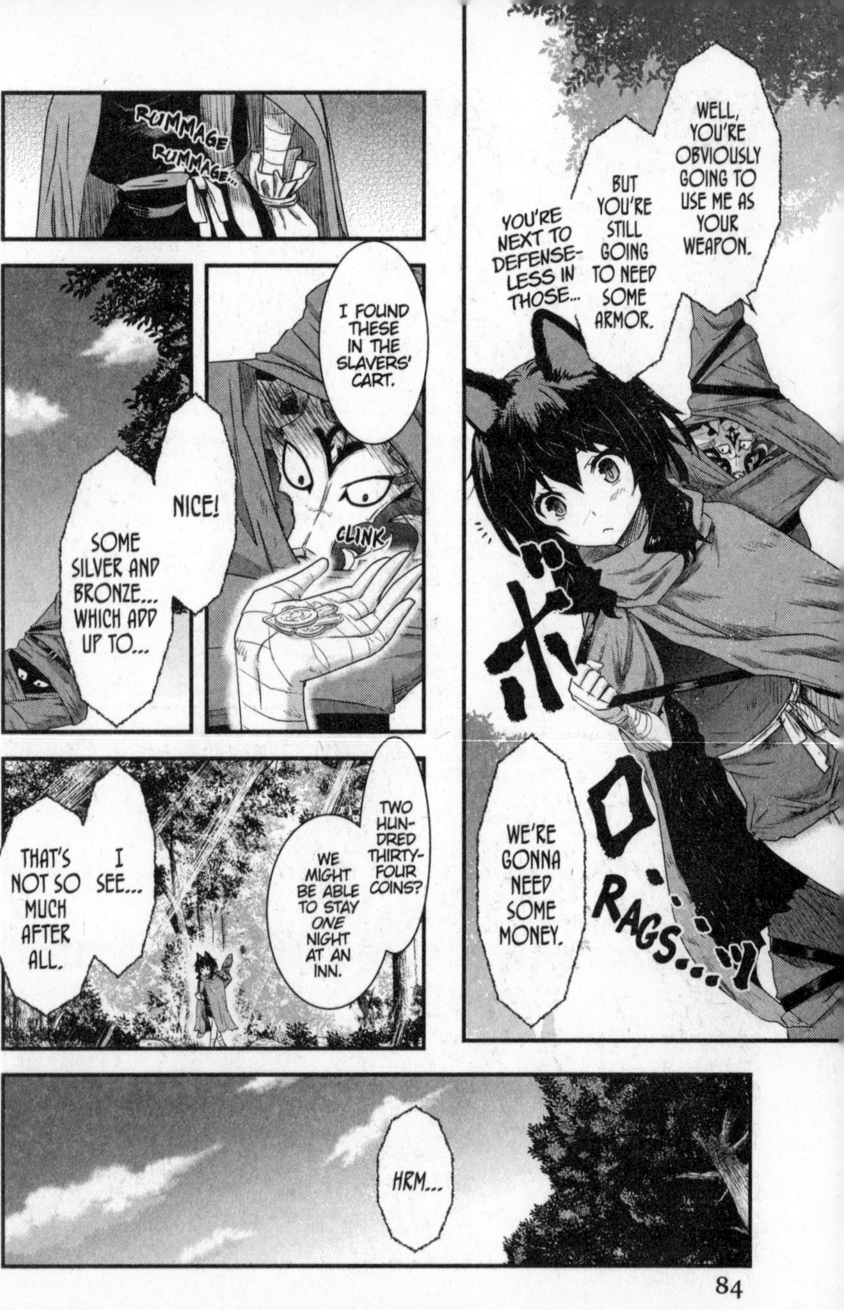
WELL, YOU'RE OBVIOUSLY GOING TO USE ME AS YOUR WEAPON.
BUT YOU'RE STILL GOING TO NEED SOME ARMOR.
YOU'RE NEXT TO DEFENSE-LESS IN THOSE...
ボロ
RAGS...!!
WE'RE GONNA NEED SOME MONEY.
RUMMAGE RUMMAGE...
I FOUND THESE IN THE SLAVERS' CART.
CLINK
NICE!
SOME SILVER AND BRONZE... WHICH ADD UP TO...
TWO HUN-DRED THIRTY-FOUR COINS?
WE MIGHT BE ABLE TO STAY *ONE* NIGHT AT AN INN.
I SEE...
THAT'S NOT SO MUCH AFTER ALL.
HRM...

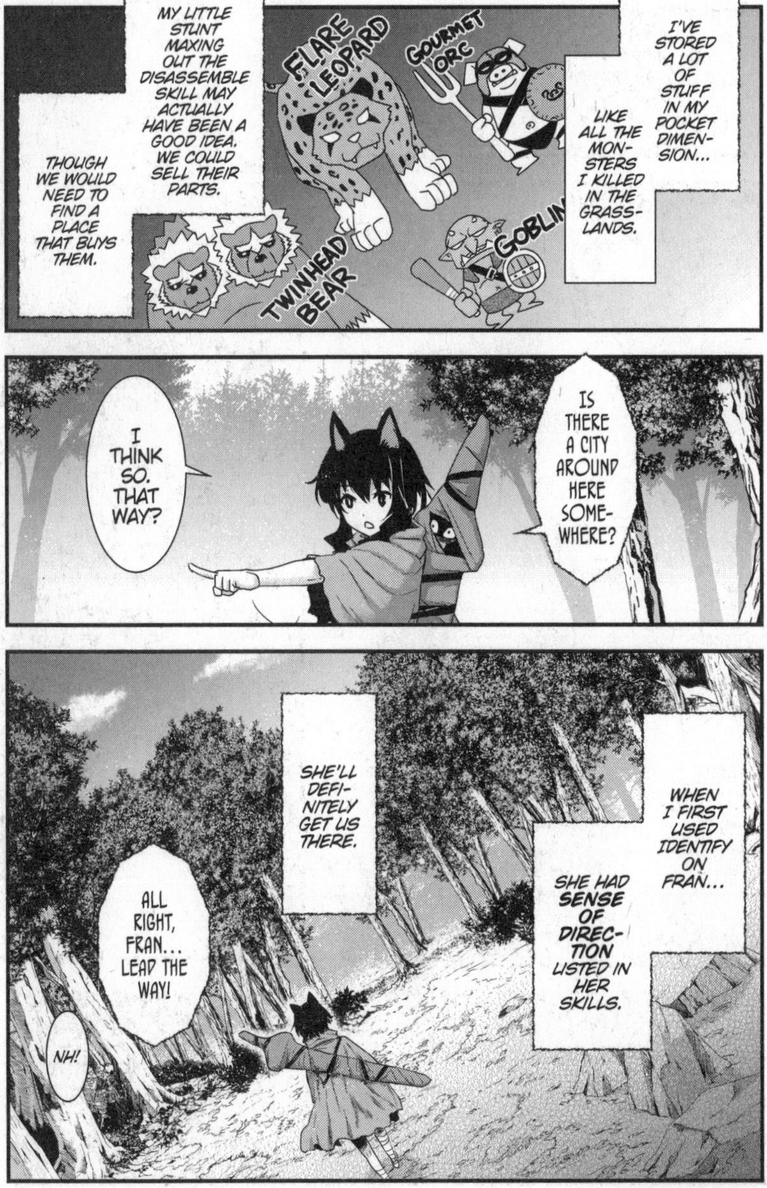
I'VE STORED A LOT OF STUFF IN MY POCKET DIMENSION...
LIKE ALL THE MONSTERS I KILLED IN THE GRASSLANDS.
GOURMET ORC
FLARE LEOPARD
GOBLIN
TWINHEAD BEAR
MY LITTLE STUNT MAXING OUT THE DISASSEMBLE SKILL MAY ACTUALLY HAVE BEEN A GOOD IDEA. WE COULD SELL THEIR PARTS.
THOUGH WE WOULD NEED TO FIND A PLACE THAT BUYS THEM.
IS THERE A CITY AROUND HERE SOMEWHERE?
I THINK SO. THAT WAY?
WHEN I FIRST USED IDENTIFY ON FRAN...
SHE HAD **SENSE OF DIRECTION** LISTED IN HER SKILLS.
SHE'LL DEFINITELY GET US THERE.
ALL RIGHT, FRAN... LEAD THE WAY!
NH!

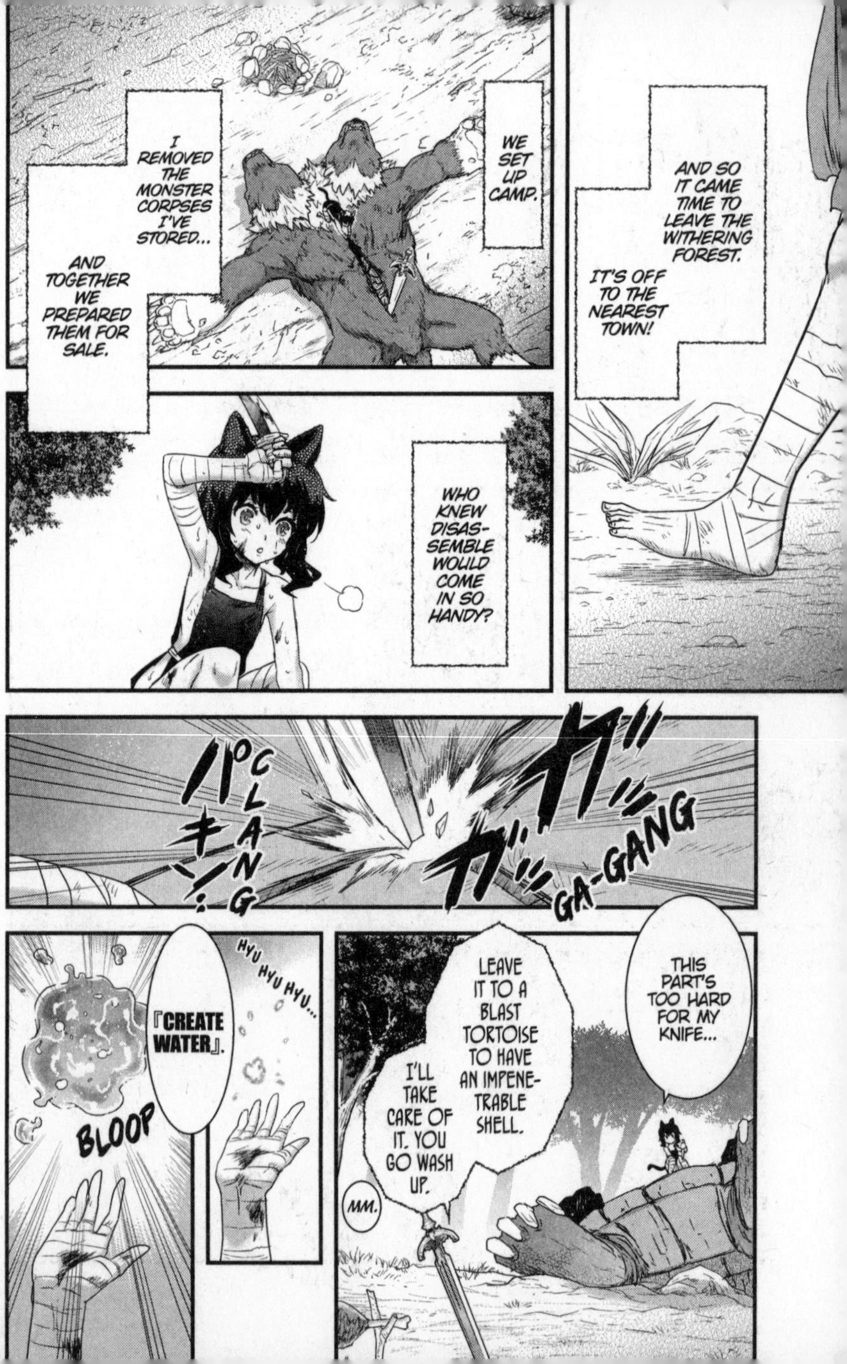
AND SO IT CAME TIME TO LEAVE THE WITHERING FOREST.
IT'S OFF TO THE NEAREST TOWN!
WE SET UP CAMP.
I REMOVED THE MONSTER CORPSES I'VE STORED...
AND TOGETHER WE PREPARED THEM FOR SALE.
WHO KNEW DISASSEMBLE WOULD COME IN SO HANDY?
GA-GANG
CLANG
THIS PART'S TOO HARD FOR MY KNIFE...
LEAVE IT TO A BLAST TORTOISE TO HAVE AN IMPENETRABLE SHELL.
I'LL TAKE CARE OF IT. YOU GO WASH UP.
MM.
HYU HYU HYU...
『CREATE WATER』.
BLOOP

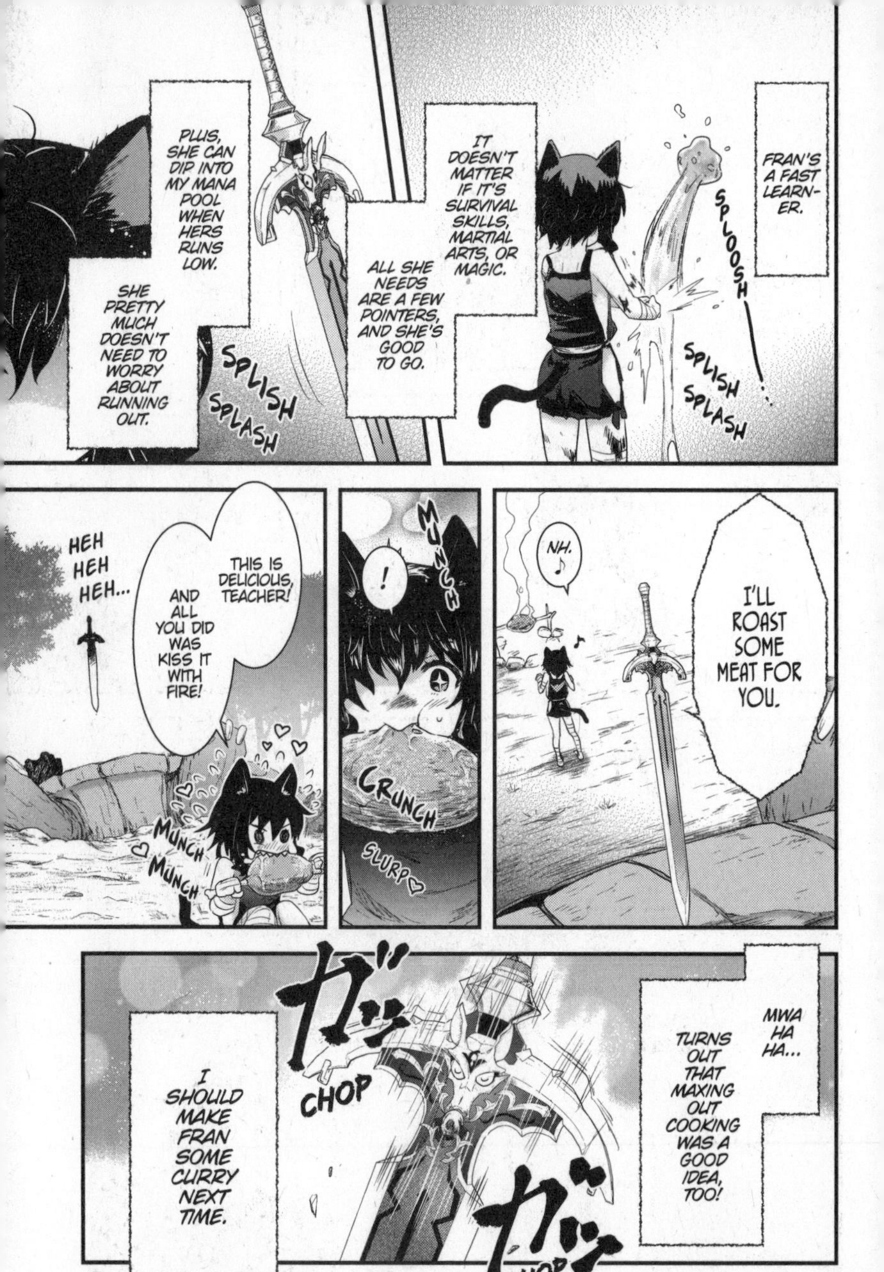
FRAN'S A FAST LEARNER.
SPLOOSH...
SPLISH SPLASH
IT DOESN'T MATTER IF IT'S SURVIVAL SKILLS, MARTIAL ARTS, OR MAGIC.
ALL SHE NEEDS ARE A FEW POINTERS, AND SHE'S GOOD TO GO.
PLUS, SHE CAN DIP INTO MY MANA POOL WHEN HERS RUNS LOW.
SHE PRETTY MUCH DOESN'T NEED TO WORRY ABOUT RUNNING OUT.
SPLISH SPLASH
I'LL ROAST SOME MEAT FOR YOU.
NH. ♪
MUNCH
!
CRUNCH
SLURP♡
THIS IS DELICIOUS, TEACHER!
AND ALL YOU DID WAS KISS IT WITH FIRE!
HEH HEH HEH...
MUNCH MUNCH
MWA HA HA...
TURNS OUT THAT MAXING OUT COOKING WAS A GOOD IDEA, TOO!
ガッ
CHOP
ガッ
CHOP
I SHOULD MAKE FRAN SOME CURRY NEXT TIME.

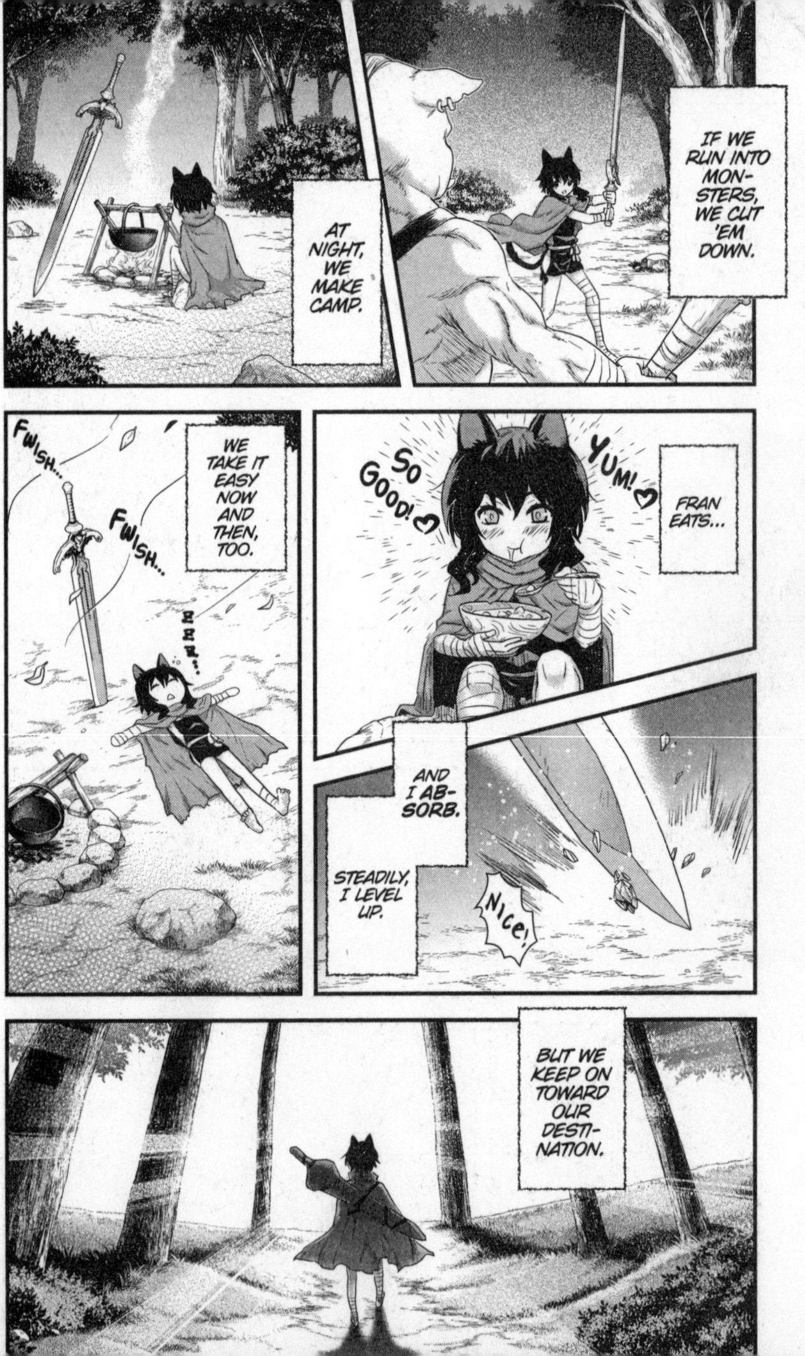
IF WE RUN INTO MONSTERS, WE CUT 'EM DOWN.
AT NIGHT, WE MAKE CAMP.
FRAN EATS...
YUM!♡
SO GOOD!♡
AND I ABSORB.
STEADILY, I LEVEL UP.
Nice!
WE TAKE IT EASY NOW AND THEN, TOO.
FWISH...
FWISH...
ZZZ...
BUT WE KEEP ON TOWARD OUR DESTINATION.

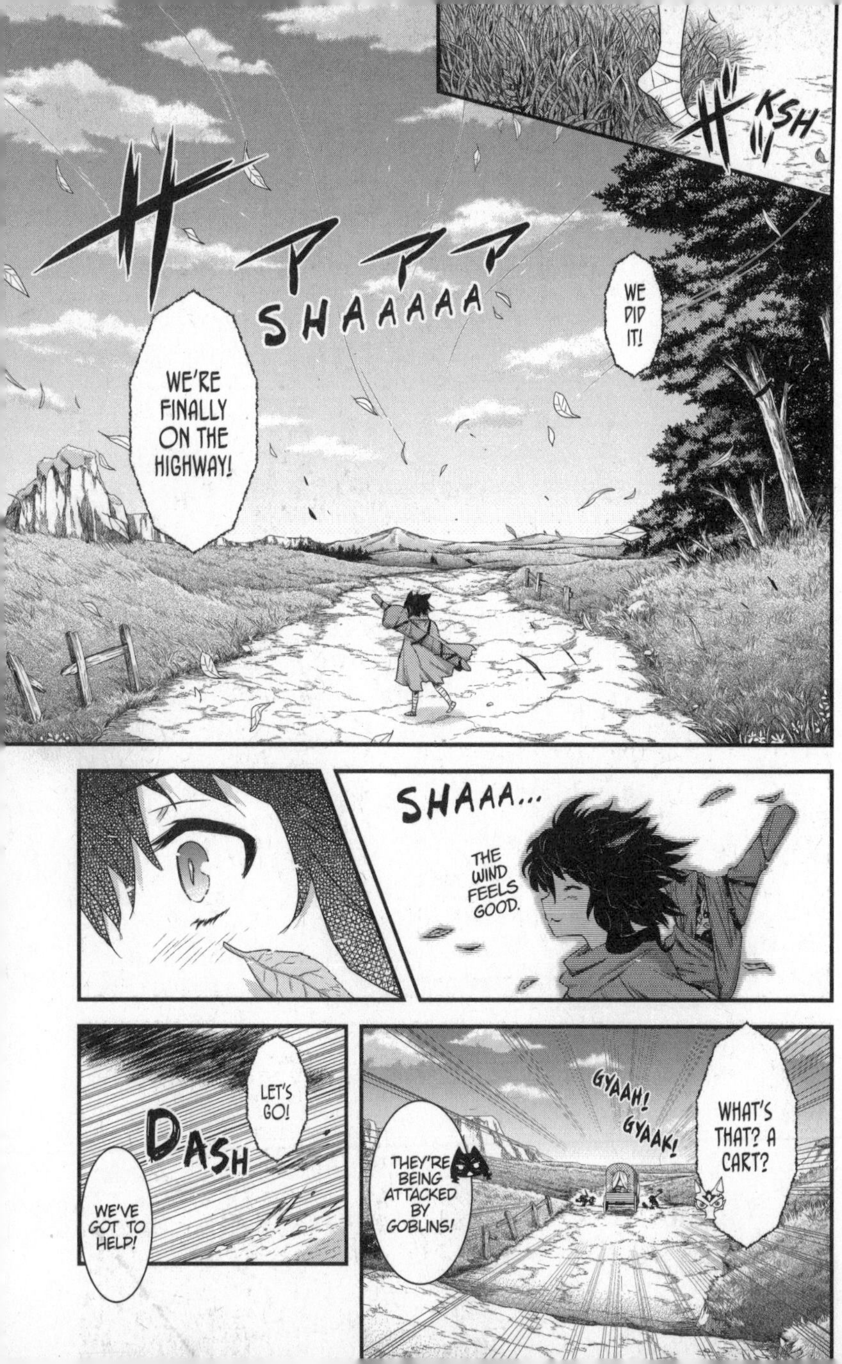
KSH
SHAAAAA
WE DID IT!
WE'RE FINALLY ON THE HIGHWAY!
SHAAA...
THE WIND FEELS GOOD.
WHAT'S THAT? A CART?
GYAAH! GYAAK!
THEY'RE BEING ATTACKED BY GOBLINS!
LET'S GO!
DASH
WE'VE GOT TO HELP!

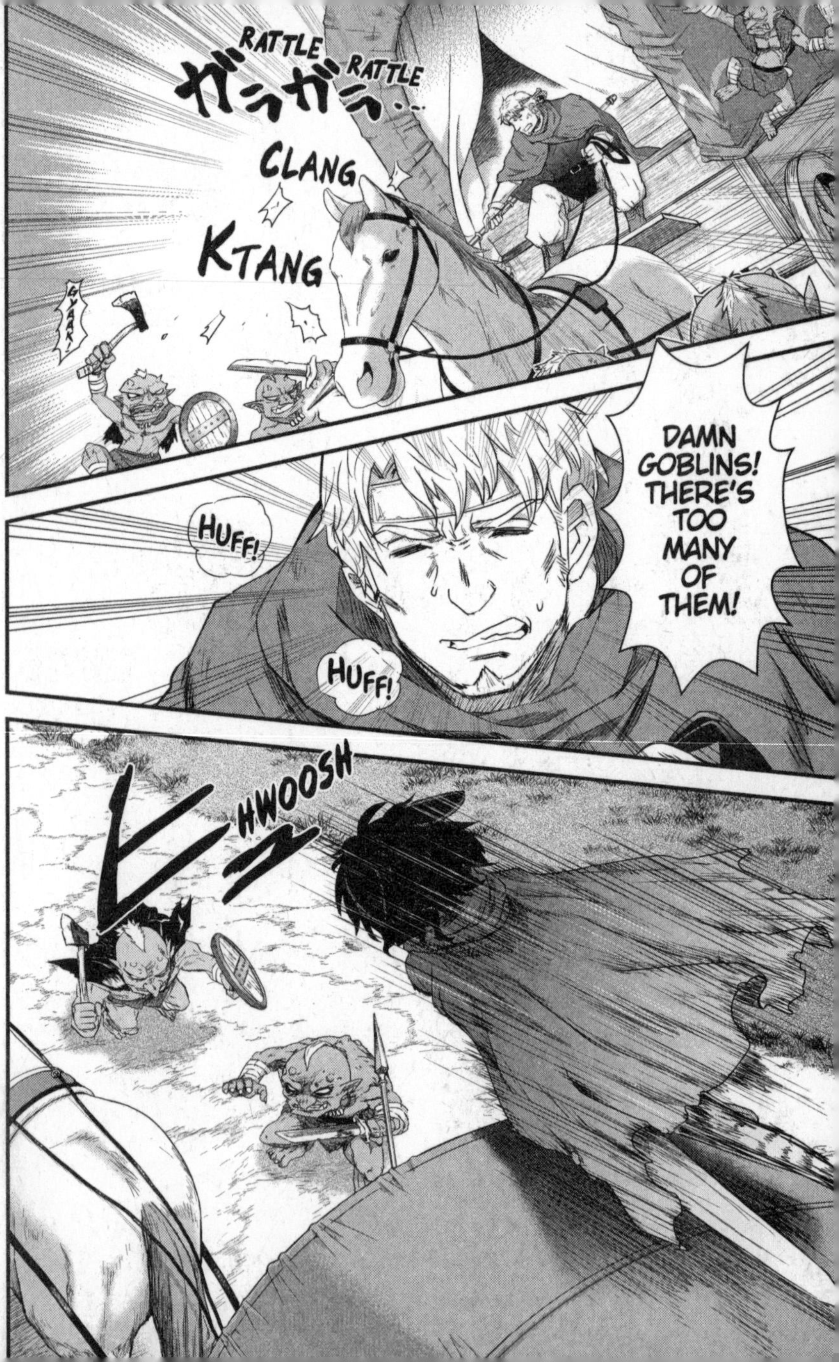

RATTLE RATTLE
ガラガラ…
CLANG
KTANG
GYAAK!
DAMN GOBLINS! THERE'S TOO MANY OF THEM!
HUFF!
HUFF!
HWOOSH
ビュ

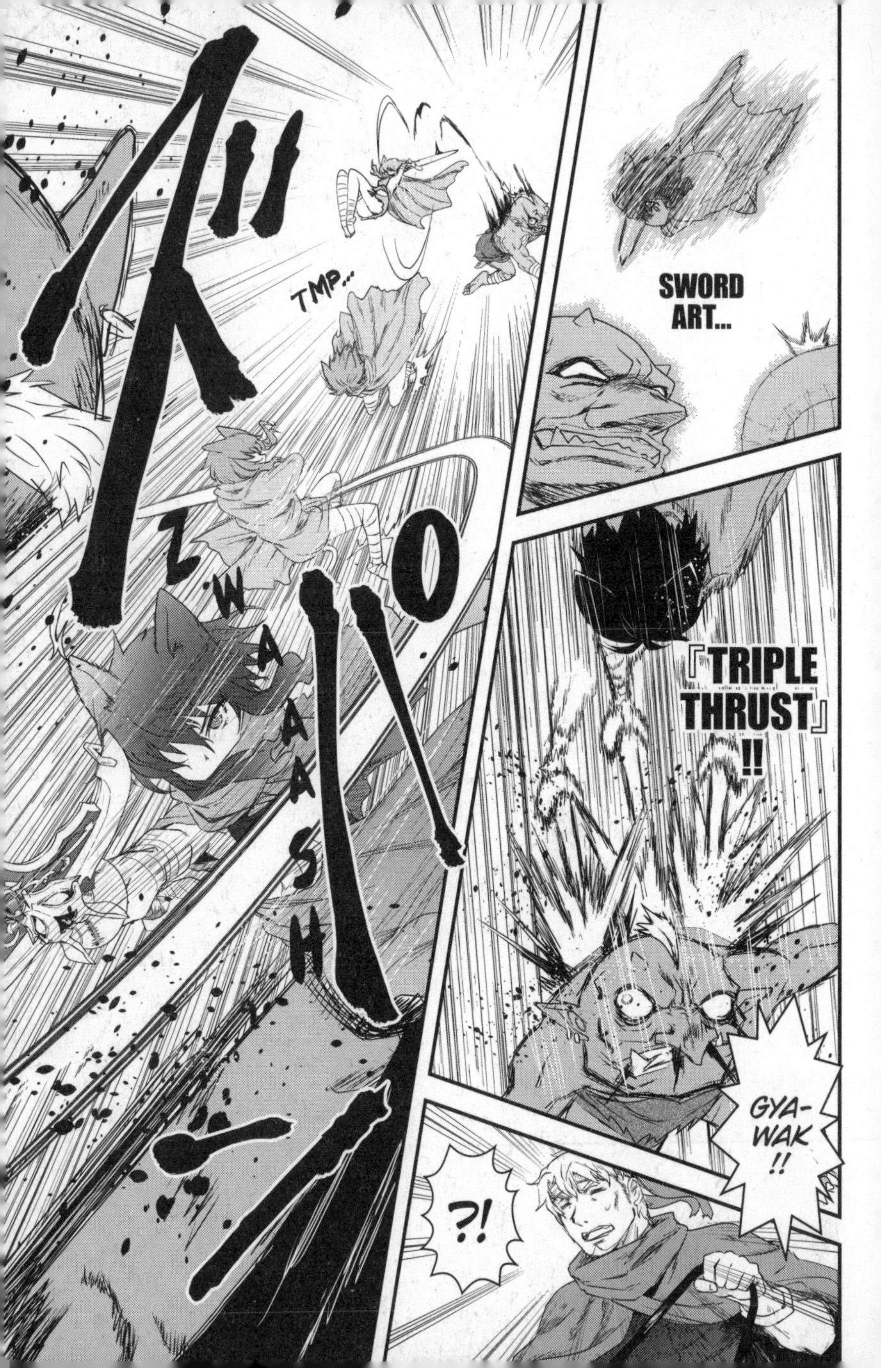

SWORD ART...
『TRIPLE THRUST』!!
GYA-WAK!!
?!
TMP...
ZWAAASH

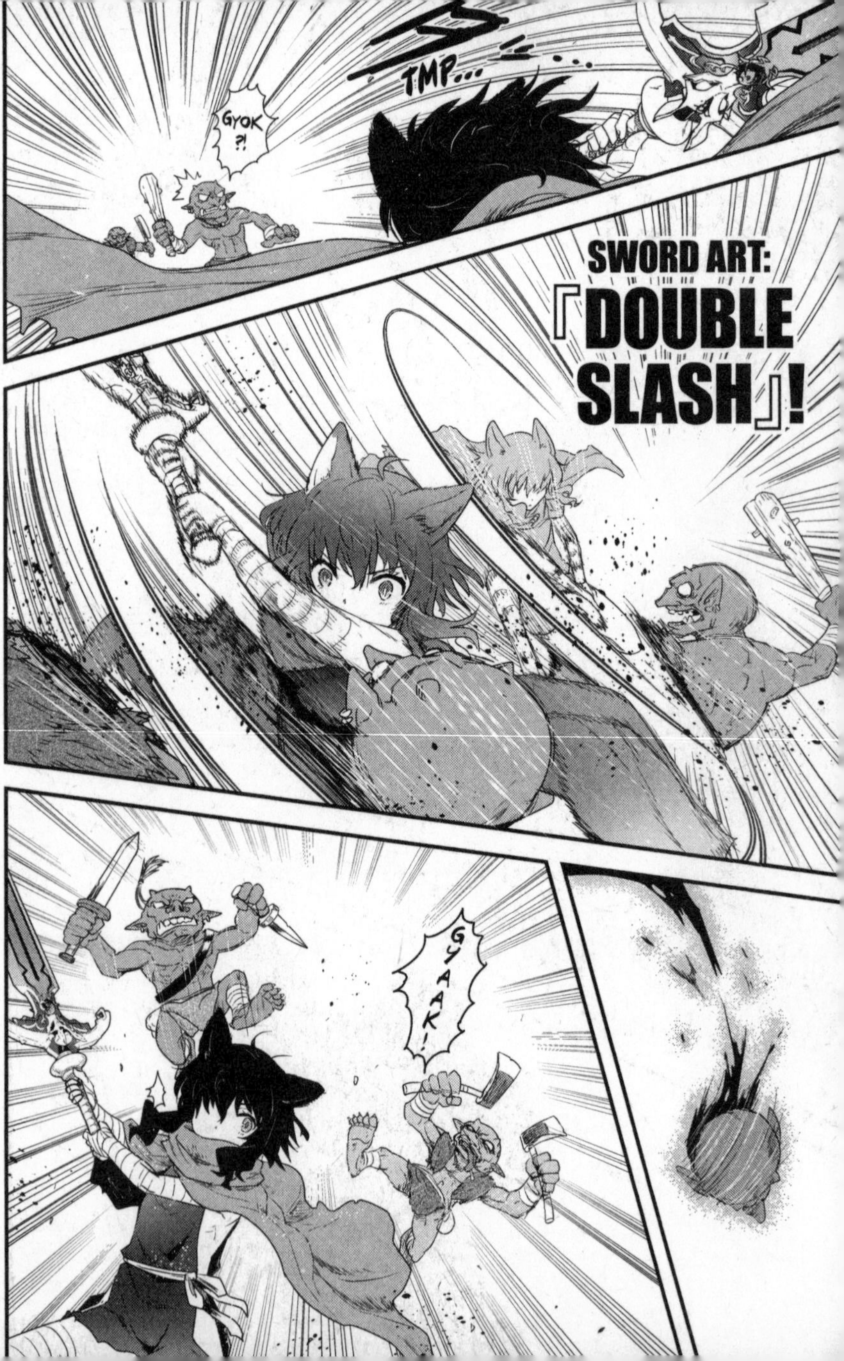
TMP...
GYOK ?!
SWORD ART: 『DOUBLE SLASH』!
GYAAAK!

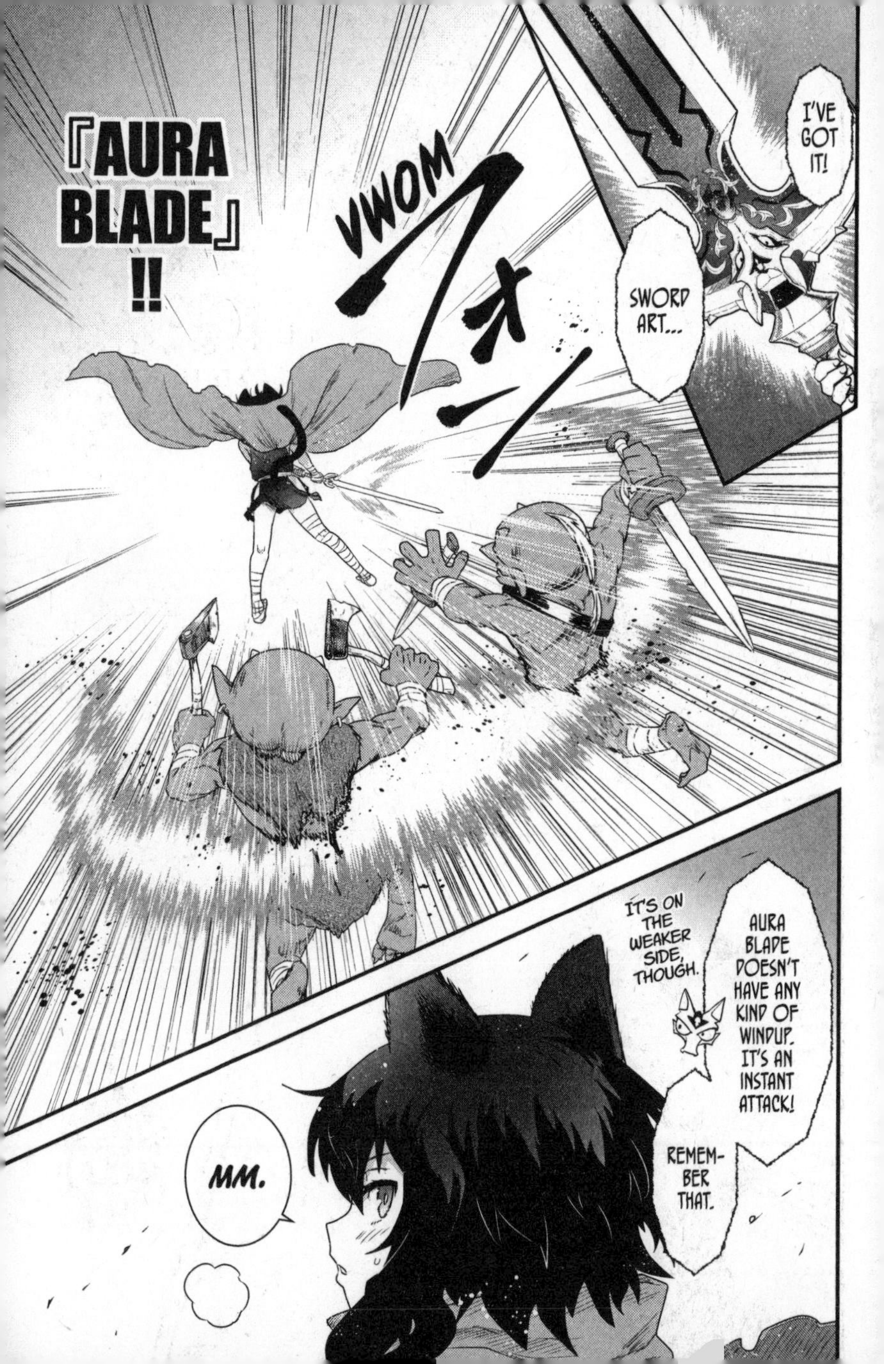
I'VE GOT IT!
SWORD ART...
VWOM
『AURA BLADE』!!
AURA BLADE DOESN'T HAVE ANY KIND OF WINDUP. IT'S AN INSTANT ATTACK!
IT'S ON THE WEAKER SIDE, THOUGH.
REMEMBER THAT.
MM.

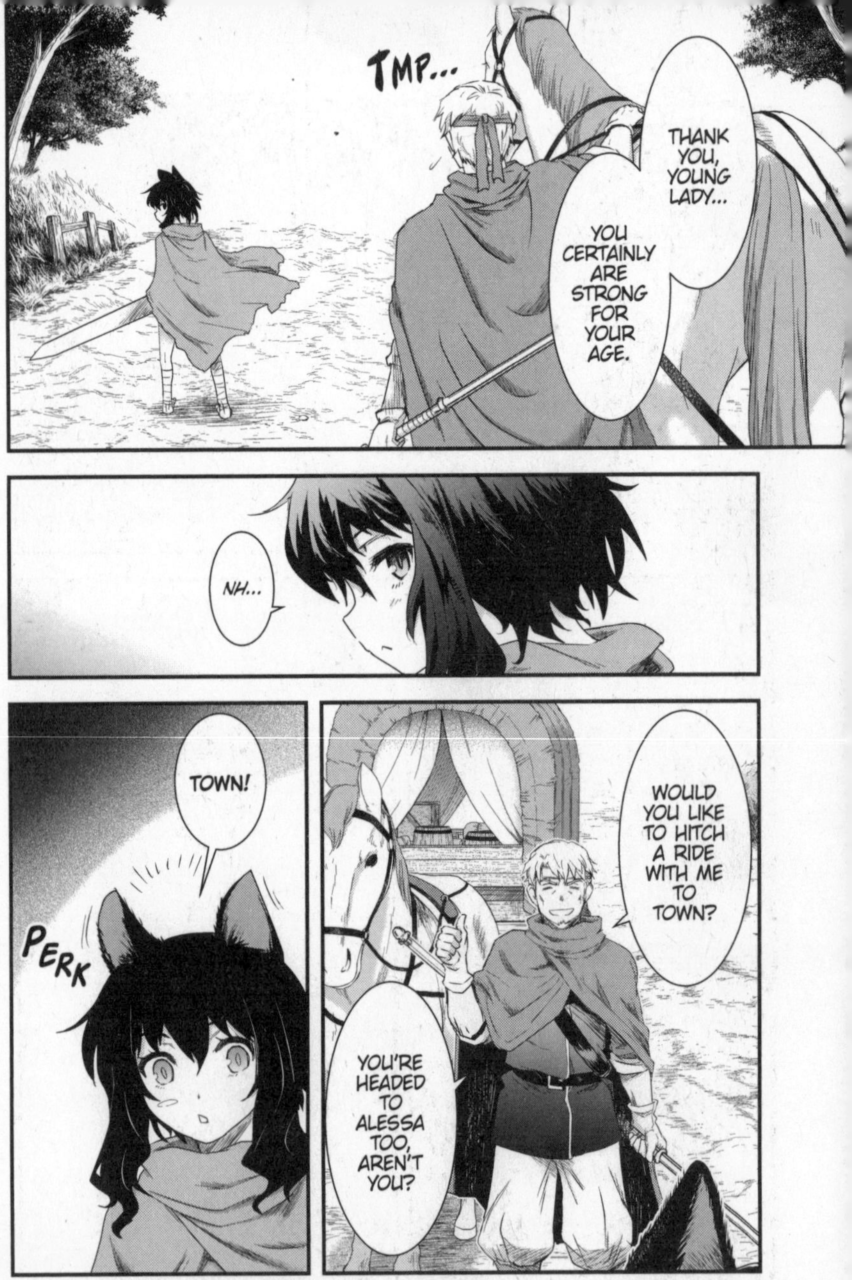

TMP...
THANK YOU, YOUNG LADY...
YOU CERTAINLY ARE STRONG FOR YOUR AGE.
NH...
WOULD YOU LIKE TO HITCH A RIDE WITH ME TO TOWN?
YOU'RE HEADED TO ALESSA TOO, AREN'T YOU?
TOWN!
PERK

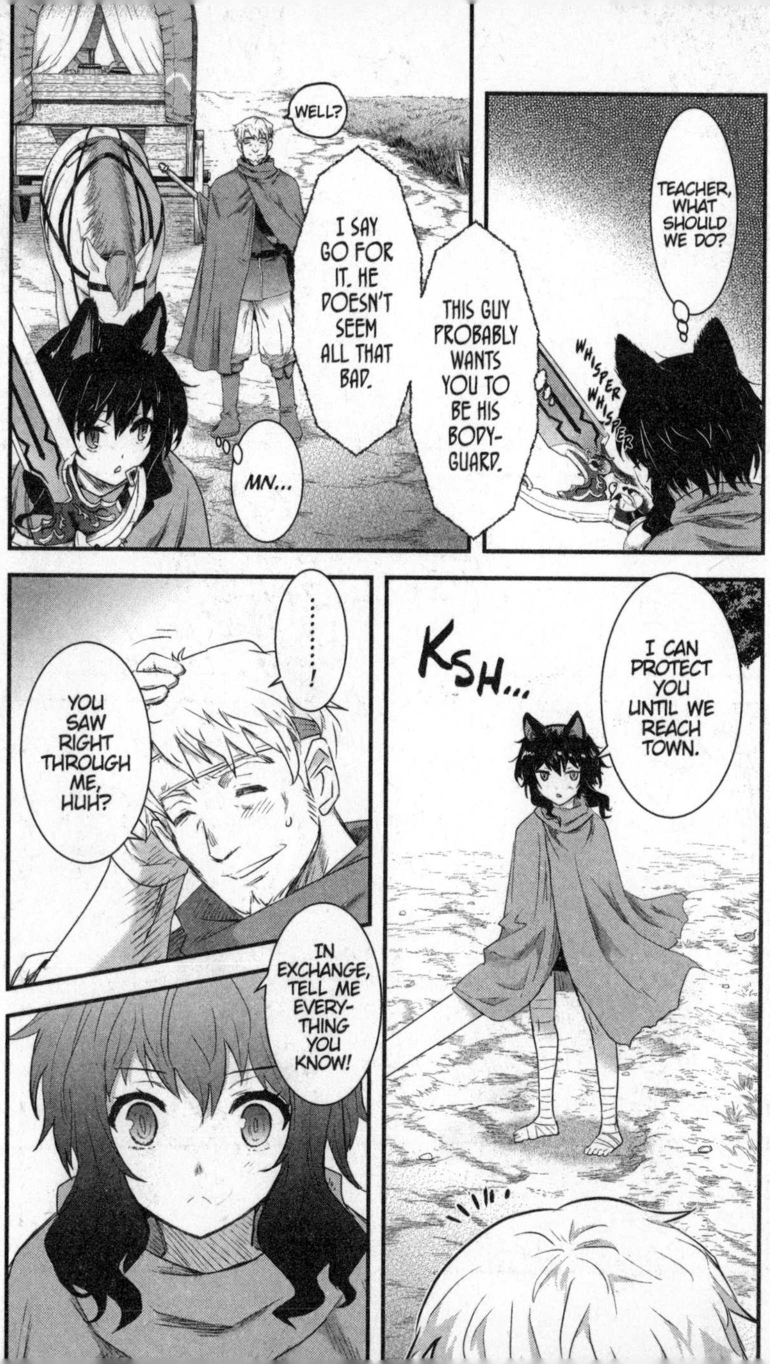
TEACHER, WHAT SHOULD WE DO?
WHISPER WHISPER
WELL?
THIS GUY PROBABLY WANTS YOU TO BE HIS BODY-GUARD.
I SAY GO FOR IT. HE DOESN'T SEEM ALL THAT BAD.
MN...
I CAN PROTECT YOU UNTIL WE REACH TOWN.
KSH...
......!
YOU SAW RIGHT THROUGH ME, HUH?
IN EXCHANGE, TELL ME EVERY-THING YOU KNOW!

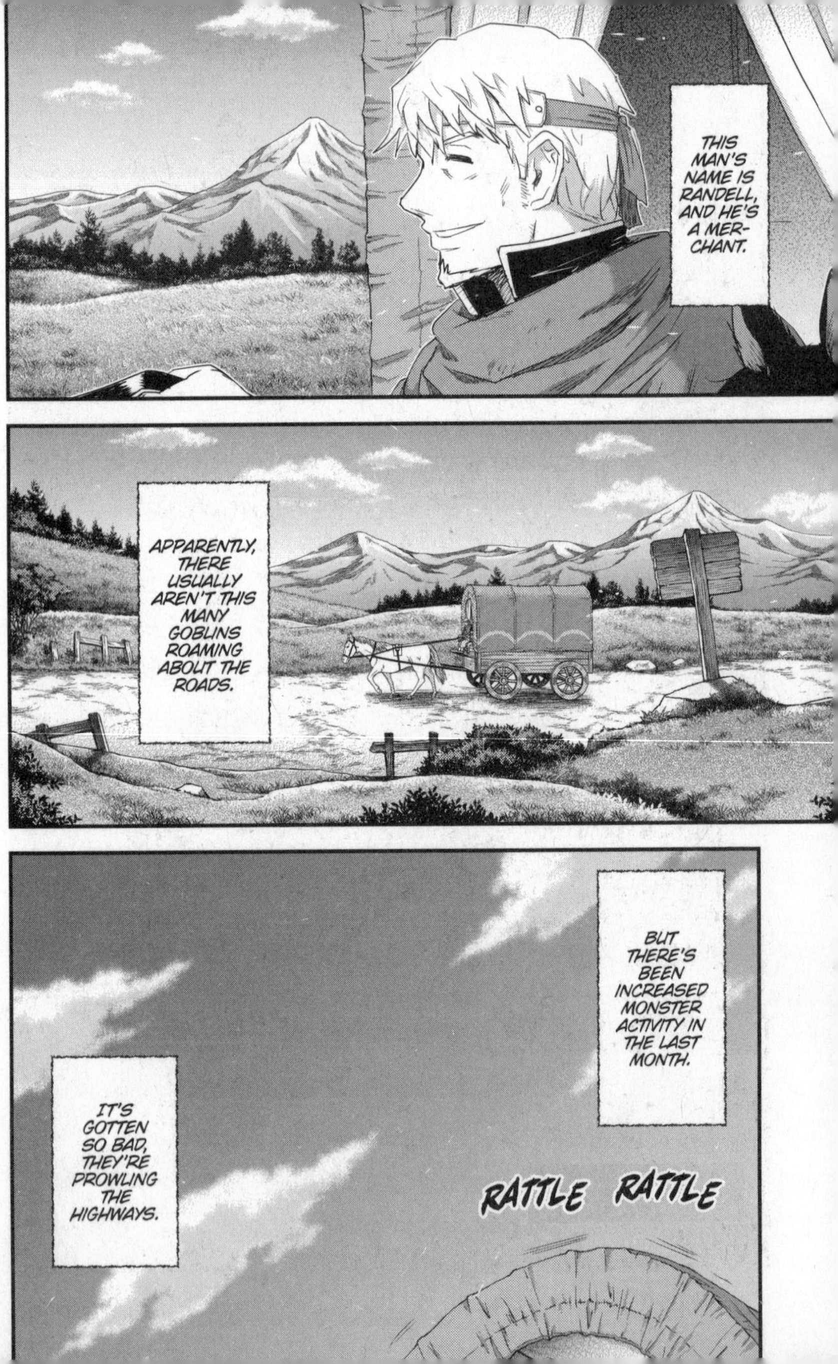
THIS MAN'S NAME IS RANDELL, AND HE'S A MER-CHANT.
APPARENTLY, THERE USUALLY AREN'T THIS MANY GOBLINS ROAMING ABOUT THE ROADS.
BUT THERE'S BEEN INCREASED MONSTER ACTIVITY IN THE LAST MONTH.
IT'S GOTTEN SO BAD, THEY'RE PROWLING THE HIGHWAYS.
RATTLE RATTLE

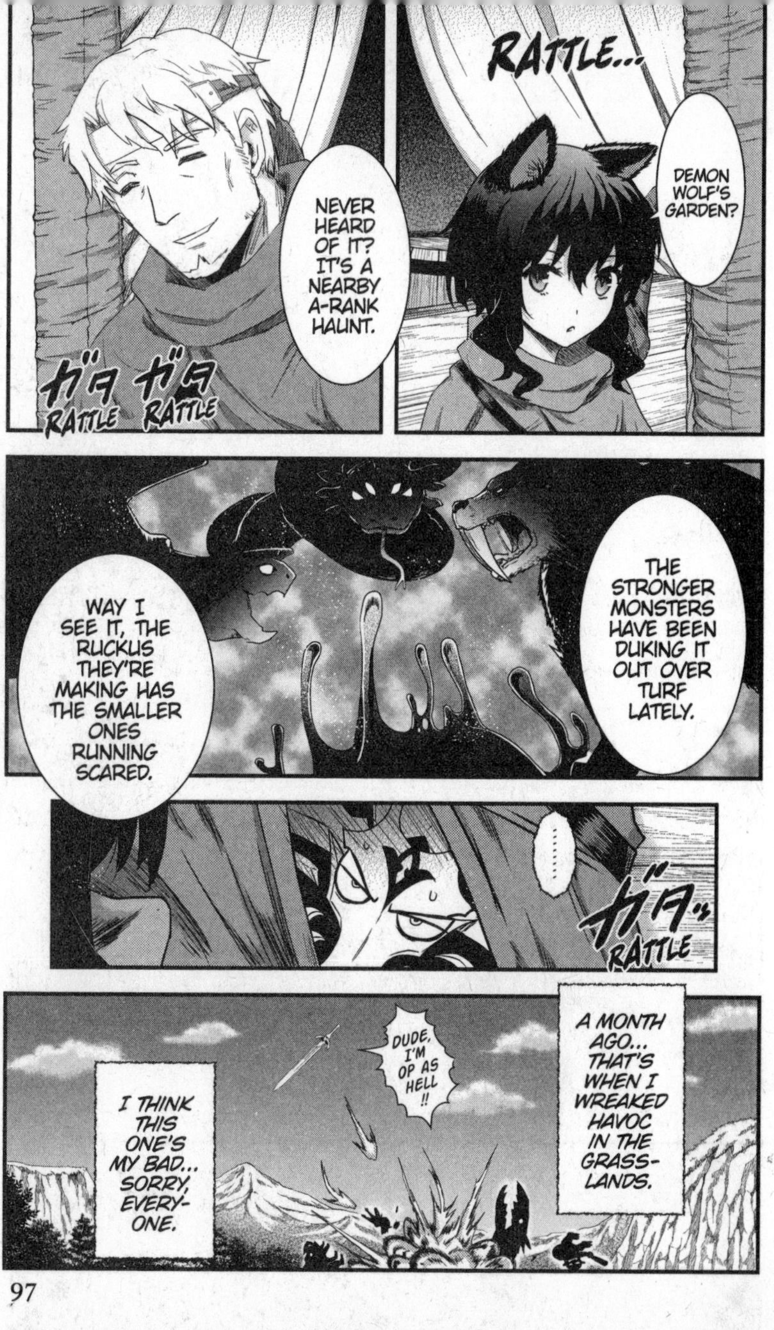
RATTLE...
DEMON WOLF'S GARDEN?
NEVER HEARD OF IT? IT'S A NEARBY A-RANK HAUNT.
ガタガタ
RATTLE RATTLE
THE STRONGER MONSTERS HAVE BEEN DUKING IT OUT OVER TURF LATELY.
WAY I SEE IT, THE RUCKUS THEY'RE MAKING HAS THE SMALLER ONES RUNNING SCARED.
......
ガタッ
RATTLE
A MONTH AGO... THAT'S WHEN I WREAKED HAVOC IN THE GRASS-LANDS.
DUDE, I'M OP AS HELL!!
I THINK THIS ONE'S MY BAD... SORRY, EVERY-ONE.

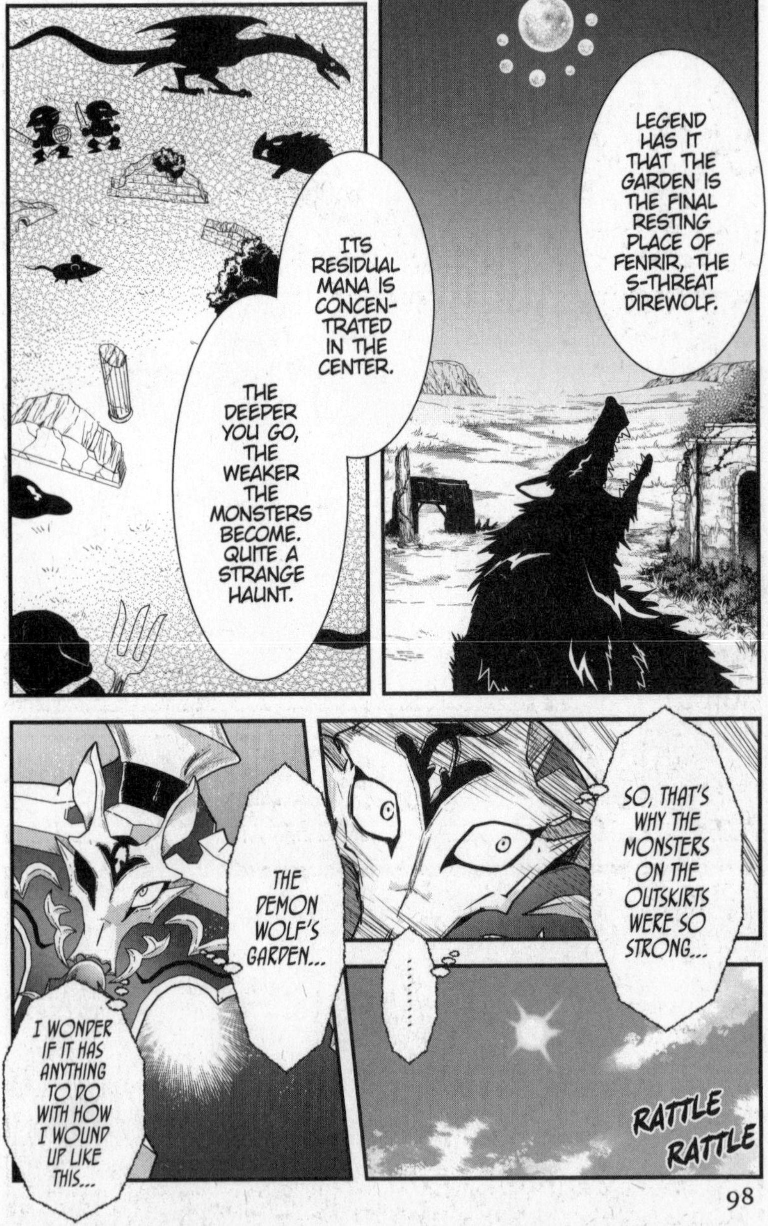
LEGEND HAS IT THAT THE GARDEN IS THE FINAL RESTING PLACE OF FENRIR, THE S-THREAT DIREWOLF.
ITS RESIDUAL MANA IS CONCENTRATED IN THE CENTER.
THE DEEPER YOU GO, THE WEAKER THE MONSTERS BECOME. QUITE A STRANGE HAUNT.
SO, THAT'S WHY THE MONSTERS ON THE OUTSKIRTS WERE SO STRONG...
......
RATTLE RATTLE
THE DEMON WOLF'S GARDEN...
I WONDER IF IT HAS ANYTHING TO DO WITH HOW I WOUND UP LIKE THIS...

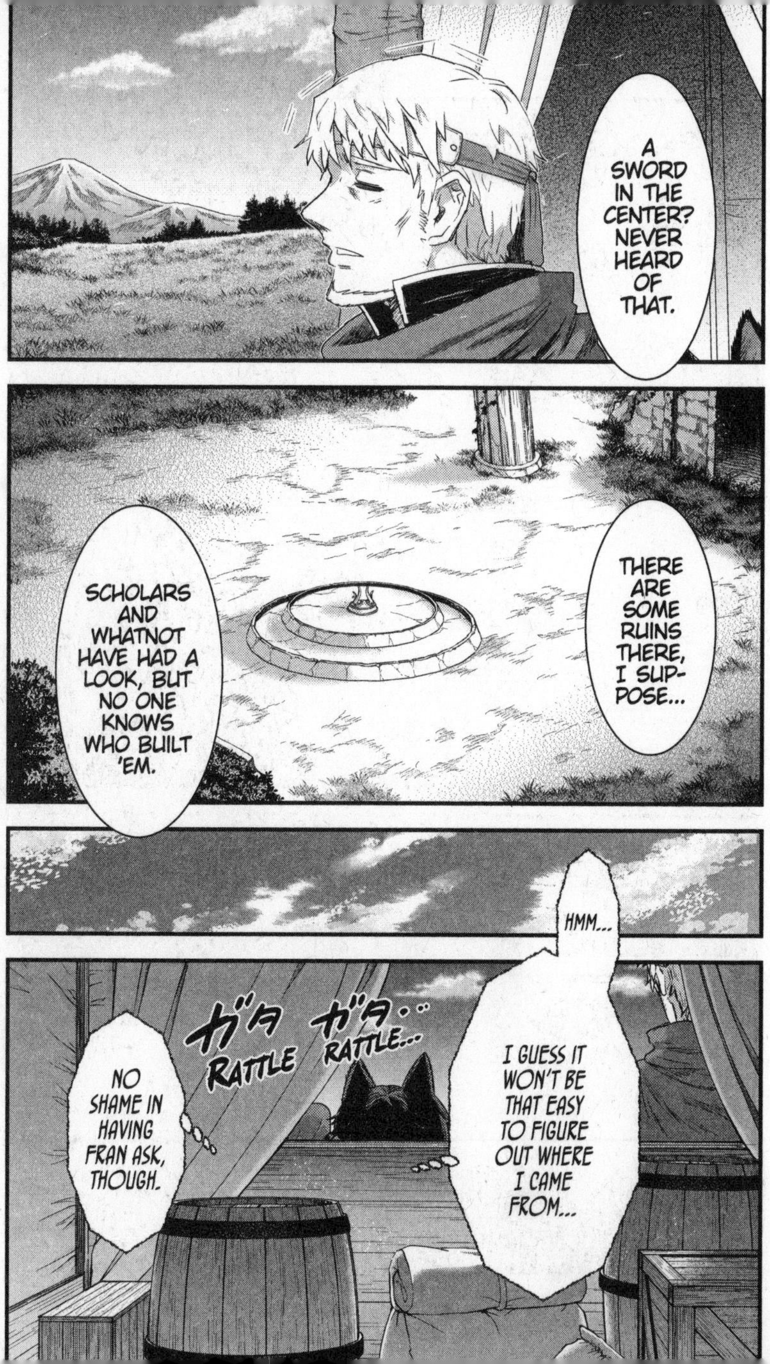
A SWORD IN THE CENTER? NEVER HEARD OF THAT.
THERE ARE SOME RUINS THERE, I SUPPOSE...
SCHOLARS AND WHATNOT HAVE HAD A LOOK, BUT NO ONE KNOWS WHO BUILT 'EM.
HMM...
I GUESS IT WON'T BE THAT EASY TO FIGURE OUT WHERE I CAME FROM...
ガタ ガタ…
RATTLE RATTLE...
NO SHAME IN HAVING FRAN ASK, THOUGH.

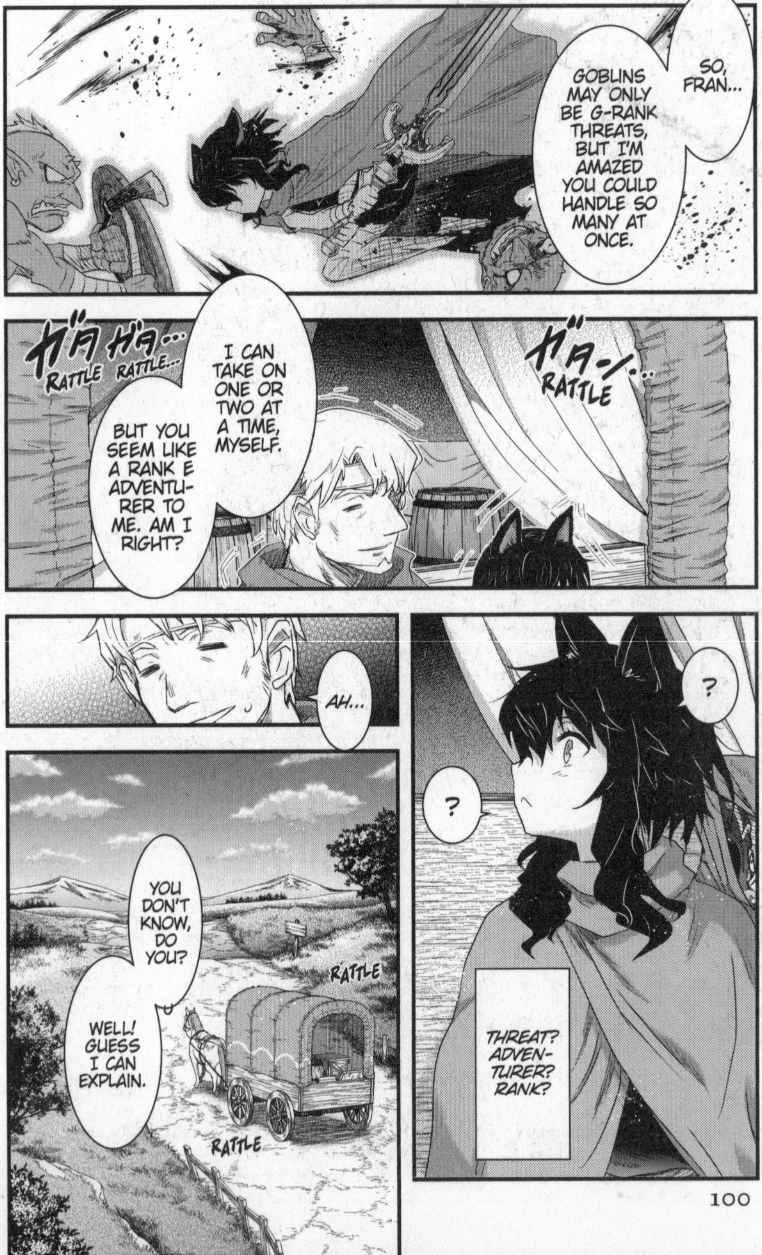
SO, FRAN...
GOBLINS MAY ONLY BE G-RANK THREATS, BUT I'M AMAZED YOU COULD HANDLE SO MANY AT ONCE.
ガタン…
RATTLE
I CAN TAKE ON ONE OR TWO AT A TIME, MYSELF.
BUT YOU SEEM LIKE A RANK E ADVENTURER TO ME. AM I RIGHT?
ガタガタ…
RATTLE RATTLE...
?
?
THREAT? ADVENTURER? RANK?
AH...
YOU DON'T KNOW, DO YOU?
WELL! GUESS I CAN EXPLAIN.
RATTLE
RATTLE

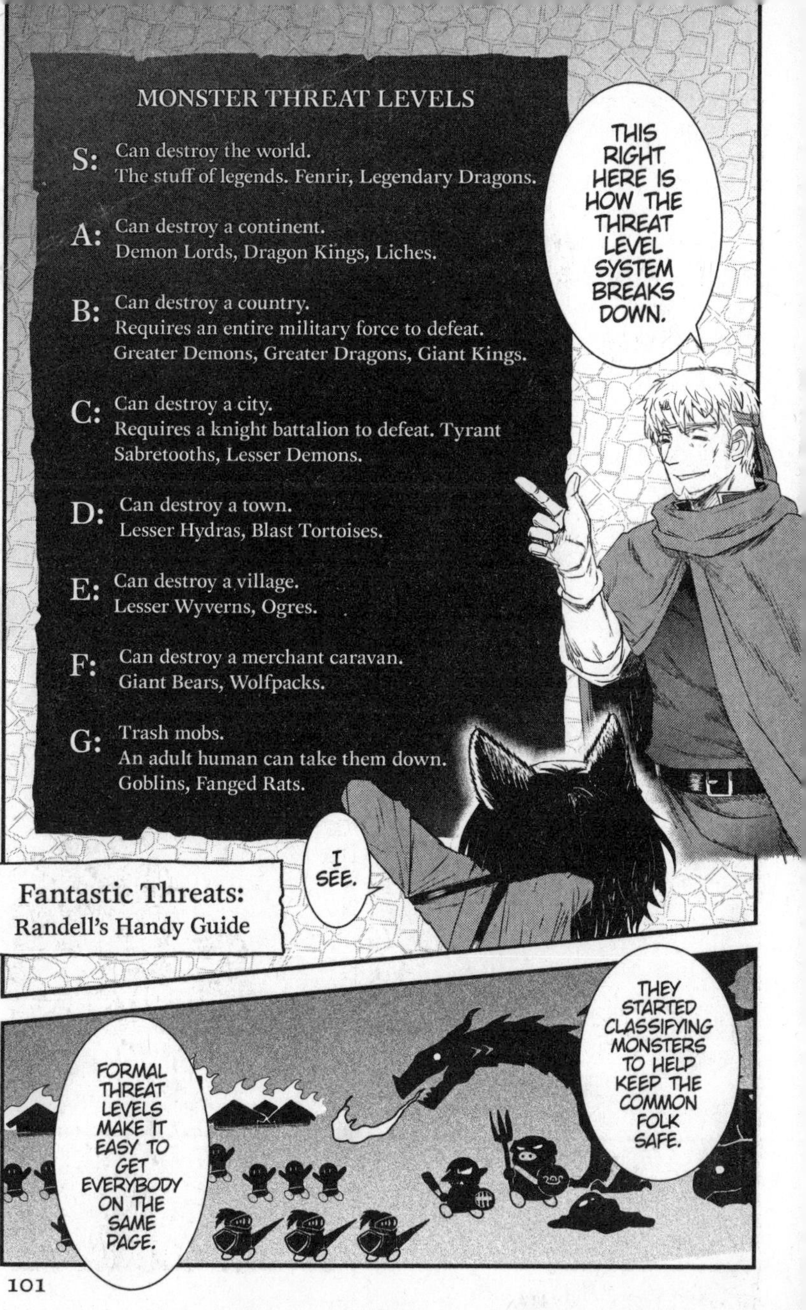
THIS RIGHT HERE IS HOW THE THREAT LEVEL SYSTEM BREAKS DOWN.
MONSTER THREAT LEVELS
S: Can destroy the world. The stuff of legends. Fenrir, Legendary Dragons.
A: Can destroy a continent. Demon Lords, Dragon Kings, Liches.
B: Can destroy a country. Requires an entire military force to defeat. Greater Demons, Greater Dragons, Giant Kings.
C: Can destroy a city. Requires a knight battalion to defeat. Tyrant Sabretooths, Lesser Demons.
D: Can destroy a town. Lesser Hydras, Blast Tortoises.
E: Can destroy a village. Lesser Wyverns, Ogres.
F: Can destroy a merchant caravan. Giant Bears, Wolfpacks.
G: Trash mobs. An adult human can take them down. Goblins, Fanged Rats.
I SEE.
Fantastic Threats: Randell's Handy Guide
THEY STARTED CLASSIFYING MONSTERS TO HELP KEEP THE COMMON FOLK SAFE.
FORMAL THREAT LEVELS MAKE IT EASY TO GET EVERYBODY ON THE SAME PAGE.

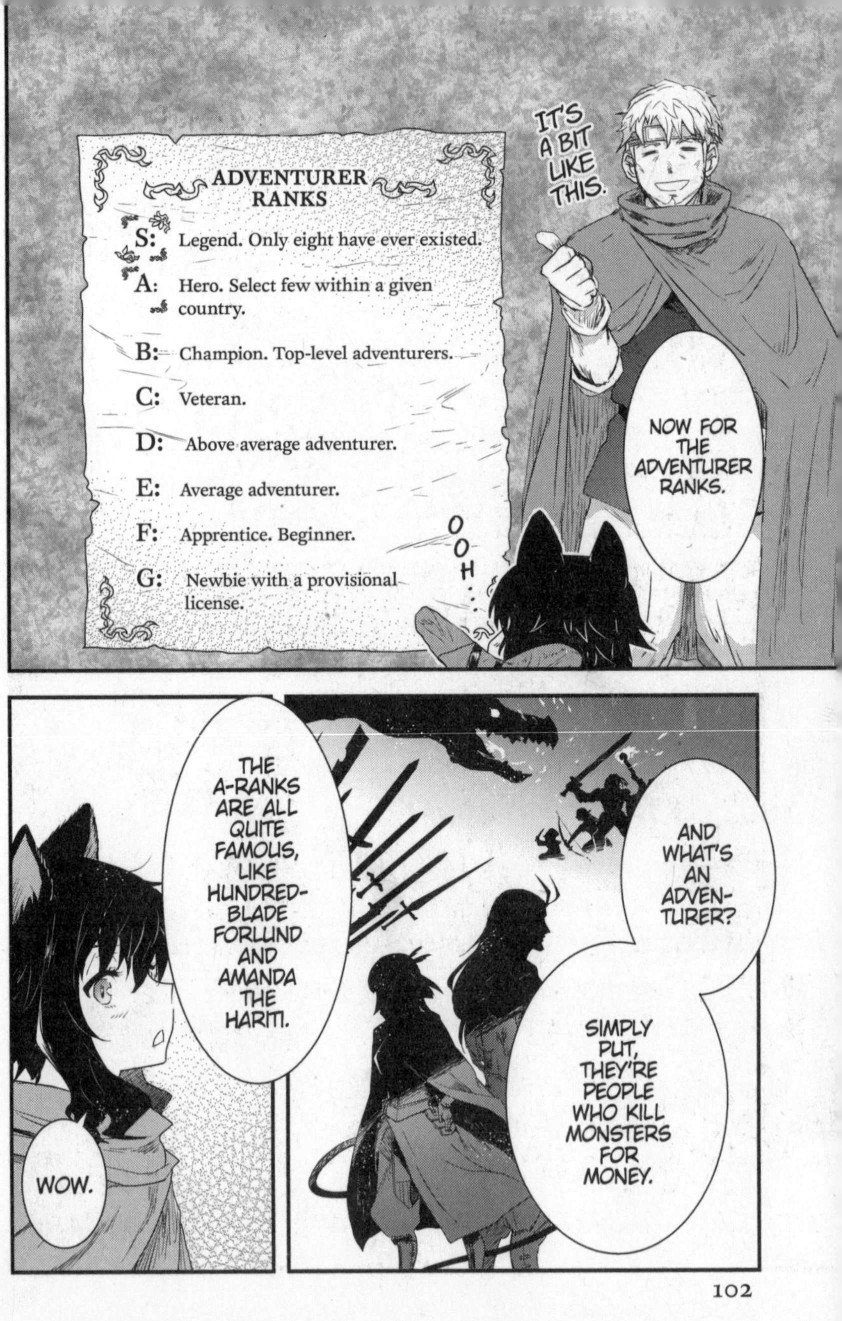
IT'S A BIT LIKE THIS.
NOW FOR THE ADVENTURER RANKS.
OOH...
ADVENTURER RANKS
S: Legend. Only eight have ever existed.
A: Hero. Select few within a given country.
B: Champion. Top-level adventurers.
C: Veteran.
D: Above average adventurer.
E: Average adventurer.
F: Apprentice. Beginner.
G: Newbie with a provisional license.
AND WHAT'S AN ADVENTURER?
SIMPLY PUT, THEY'RE PEOPLE WHO KILL MONSTERS FOR MONEY.
THE A-RANKS ARE ALL QUITE FAMOUS, LIKE HUNDRED-BLADE FORLUND AND AMANDA THE HARITI.
WOW.

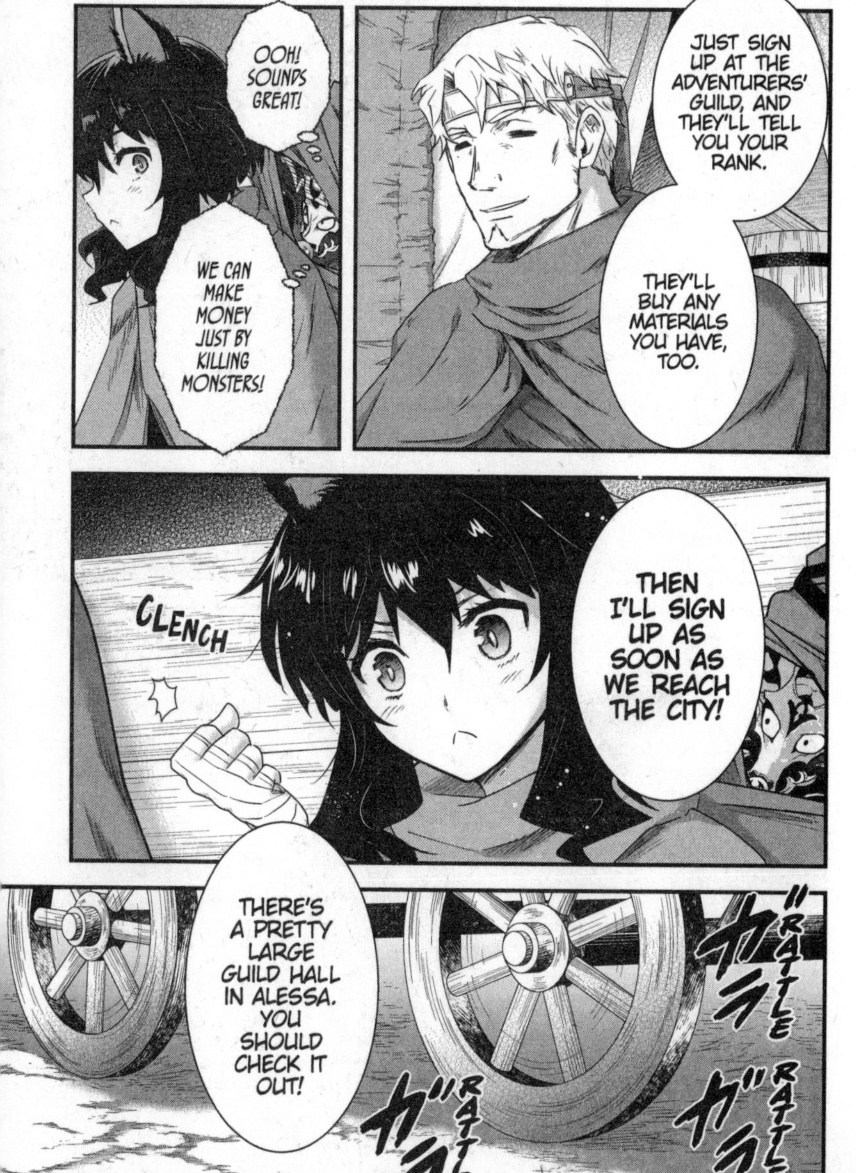
JUST SIGN UP AT THE ADVENTURERS' GUILD, AND THEY'LL TELL YOU YOUR RANK.
THEY'LL BUY ANY MATERIALS YOU HAVE, TOO.
OOH! SOUNDS GREAT!
WE CAN MAKE MONEY JUST BY KILLING MONSTERS!
THEN I'LL SIGN UP AS SOON AS WE REACH THE CITY!
CLENCH
THERE'S A PRETTY LARGE GUILD HALL IN ALESSA. YOU SHOULD CHECK IT OUT!
RATTLE
RATTLE
RATTLE

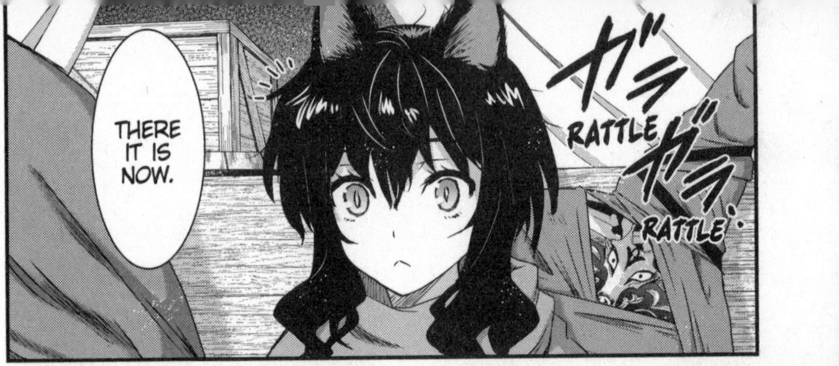
ガラ
RATTLE
ガラ
RATTLE
THERE IT IS NOW.
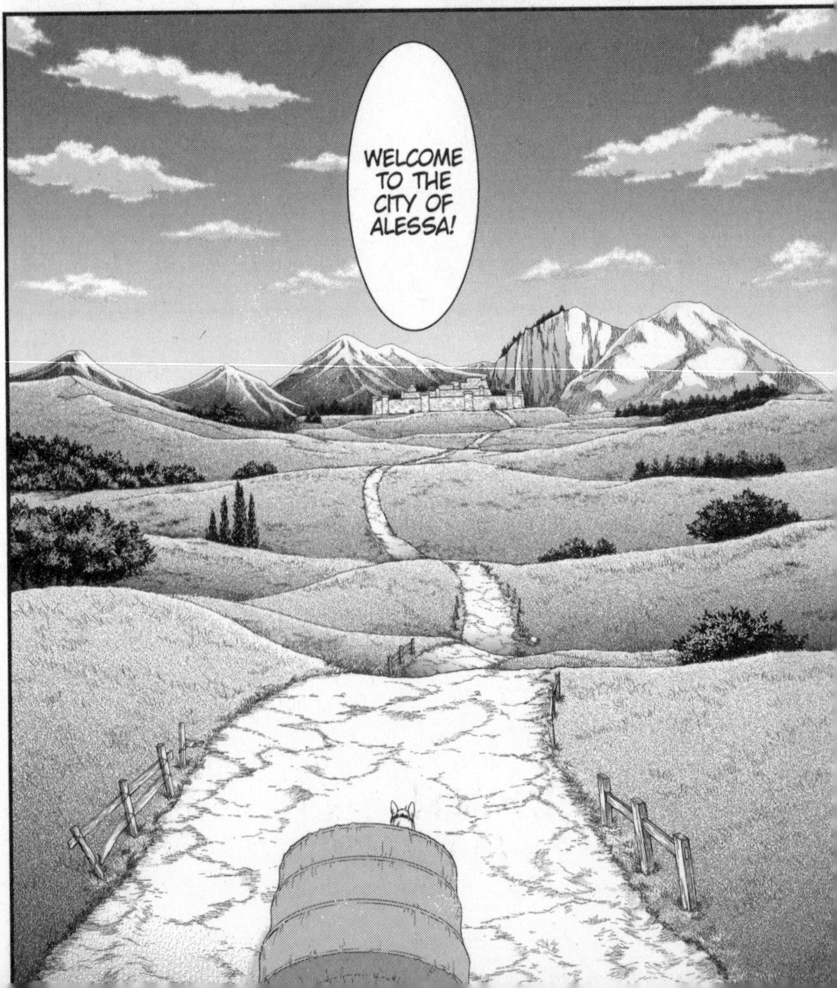
WELCOME TO THE CITY OF ALESSA!

Reincarnated
as a sword

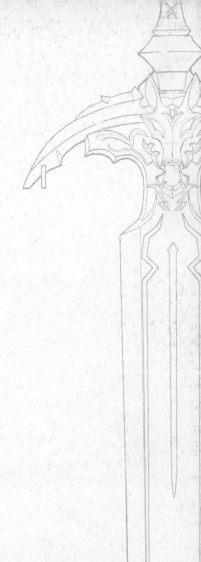

Reincarnated
as a sword

Chapter 4: Fran, Adventurer

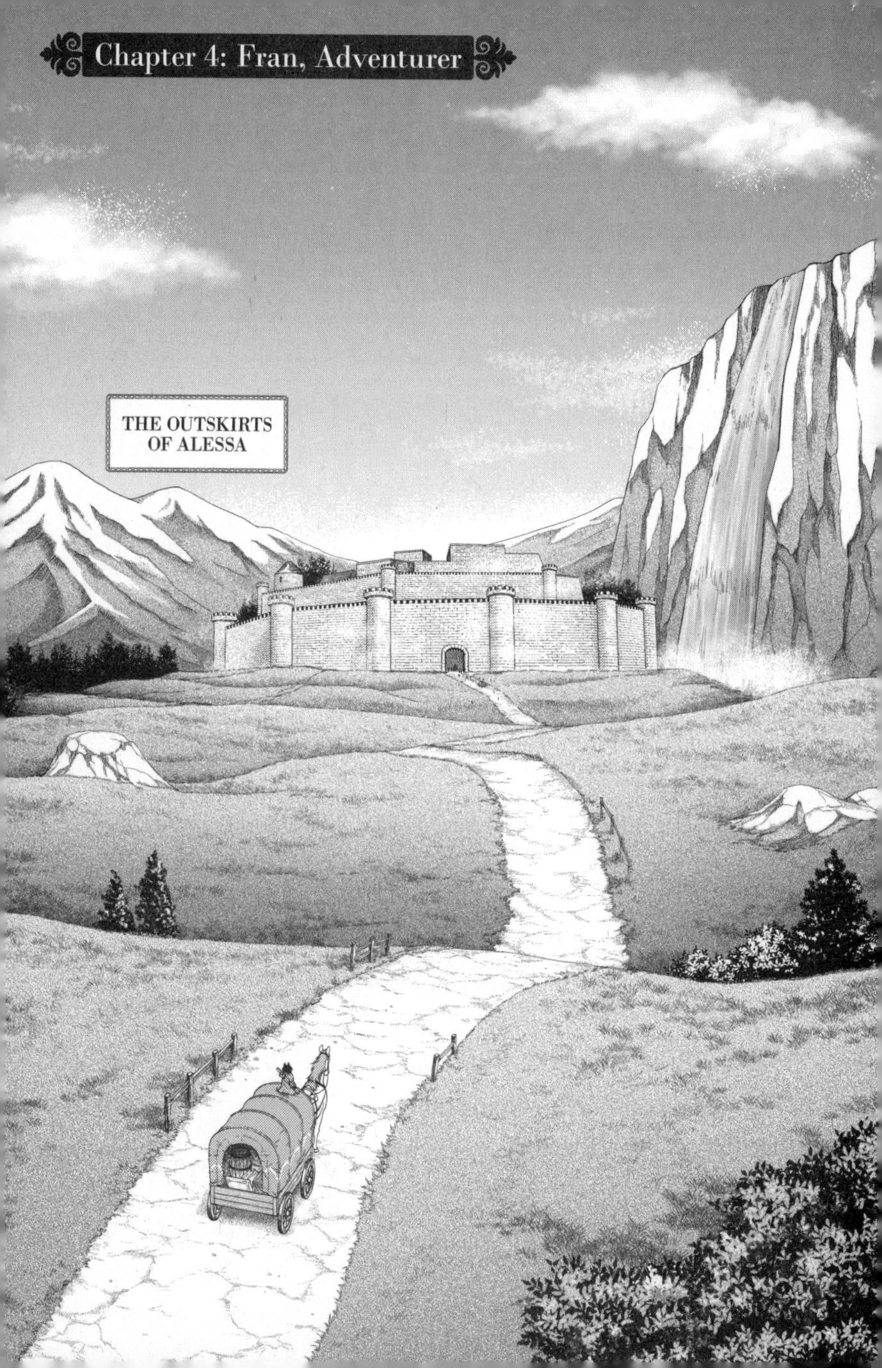
THE OUTSKIRTS OF ALESSA

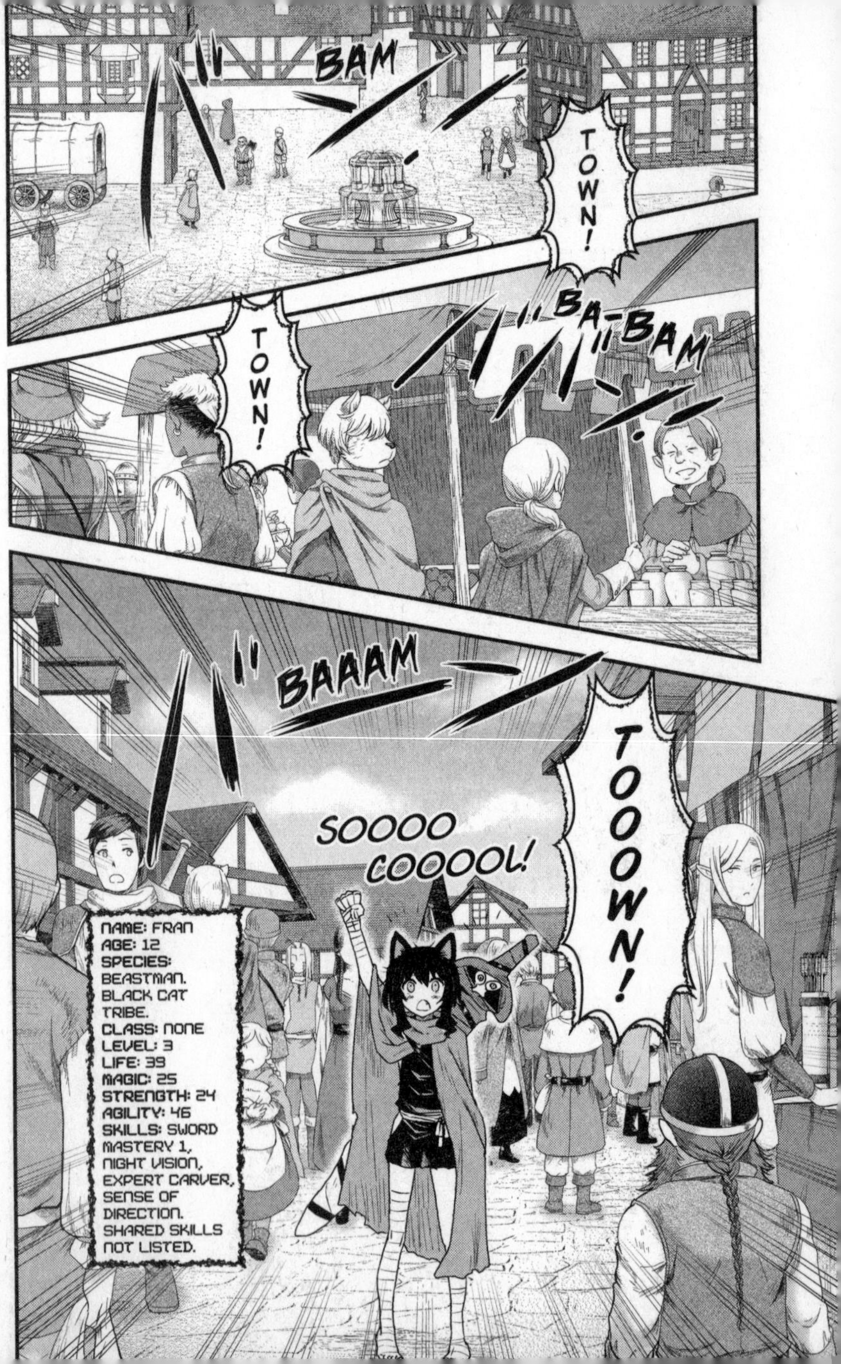
TOWN!
BAM
BA-BAM
TOWN!
TOOOOWN!
BAAAM
SOOOO COOOOL!
NAME: FRAN
AGE: 12
SPECIES: BEASTMAN. BLACK CAT TRIBE.
CLASS: NONE
LEVEL: 3
LIFE: 39
MAGIC: 25
STRENGTH: 24
AGILITY: 46
SKILLS: SWORD MASTERY 1, NIGHT VISION, EXPERT CARVER, SENSE OF DIRECTION. SHARED SKILLS NOT LISTED.

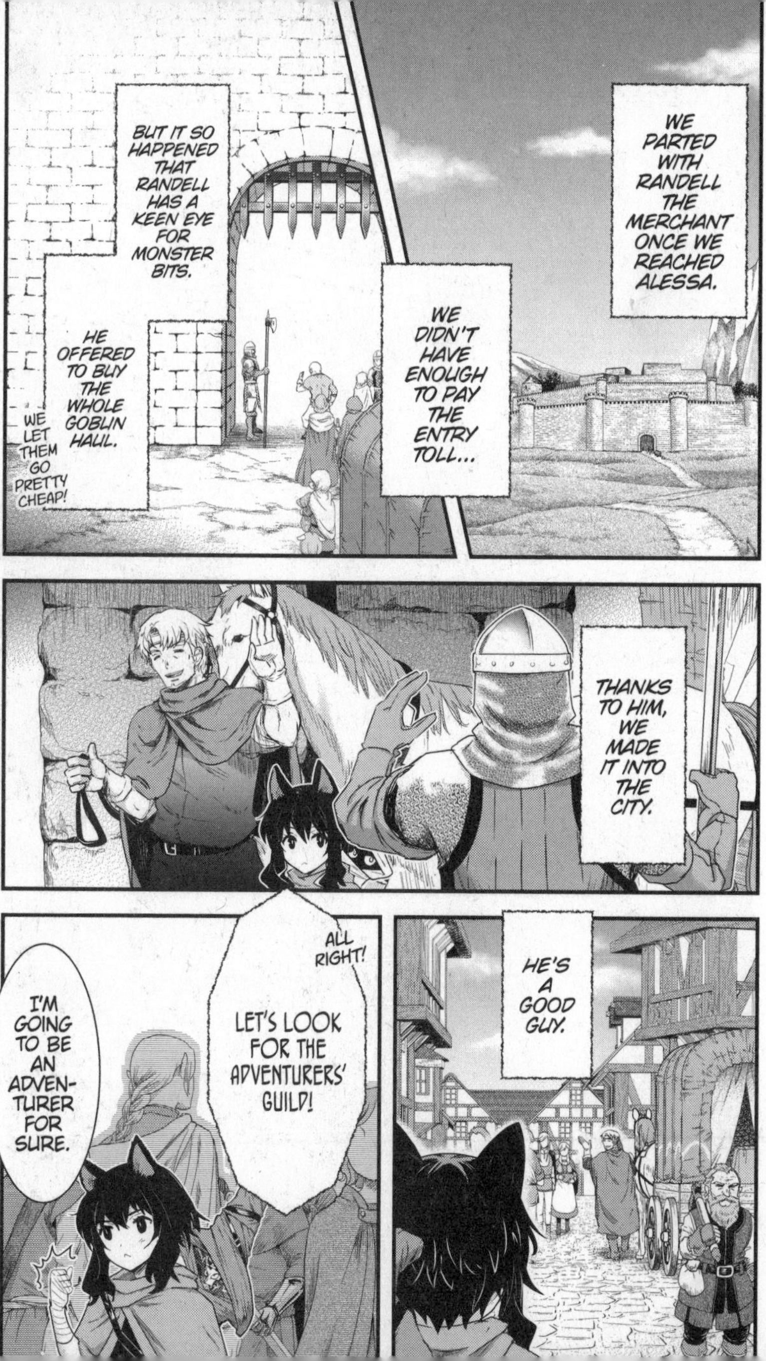
WE PARTED WITH RANDELL THE MERCHANT ONCE WE REACHED ALESSA.
WE DIDN'T HAVE ENOUGH TO PAY THE ENTRY TOLL...
BUT IT SO HAPPENED THAT RANDELL HAS A KEEN EYE FOR MONSTER BITS.
HE OFFERED TO BUY THE WHOLE GOBLIN HAUL.
WE LET THEM GO PRETTY CHEAP!
THANKS TO HIM, WE MADE IT INTO THE CITY.
HE'S A GOOD GUY.
ALL RIGHT!
LET'S LOOK FOR THE ADVENTURERS' GUILD!
I'M GOING TO BE AN ADVENTURER FOR SURE.

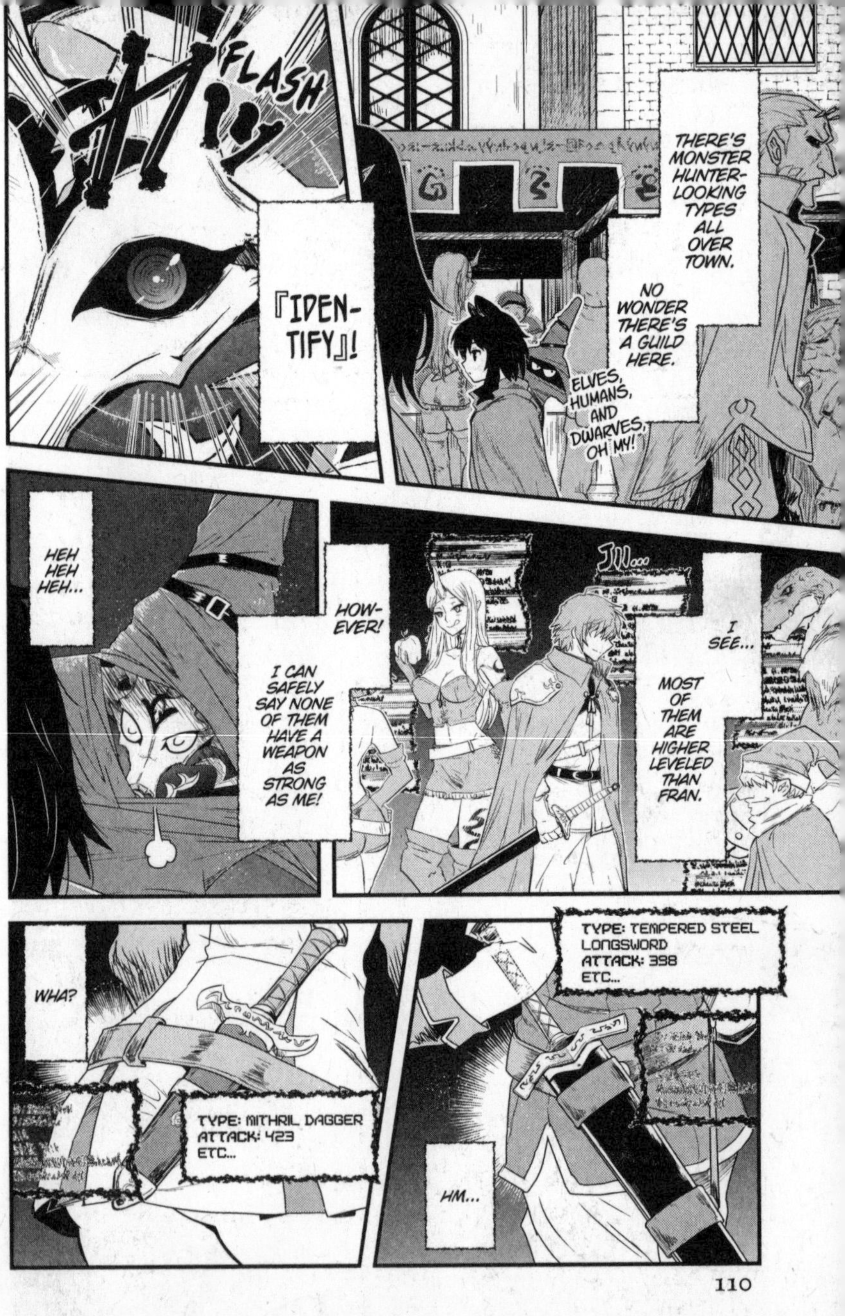
THERE'S MONSTER HUNTER-LOOKING TYPES ALL OVER TOWN.
NO WONDER THERE'S A GUILD HERE.
ELVES, HUMANS, AND DWARVES, OH MY!
FLASH
『IDEN-TIFY』!
JII...
I SEE...
MOST OF THEM ARE HIGHER LEVELED THAN FRAN.
HEH HEH HEH...
HOW-EVER!
I CAN SAFELY SAY NONE OF THEM HAVE A WEAPON AS STRONG AS ME!
TYPE: TEMPERED STEEL LONGSWORD
ATTACK: 398
ETC...
HM...
WHA?
TYPE: MITHRIL DAGGER
ATTACK: 423
ETC...

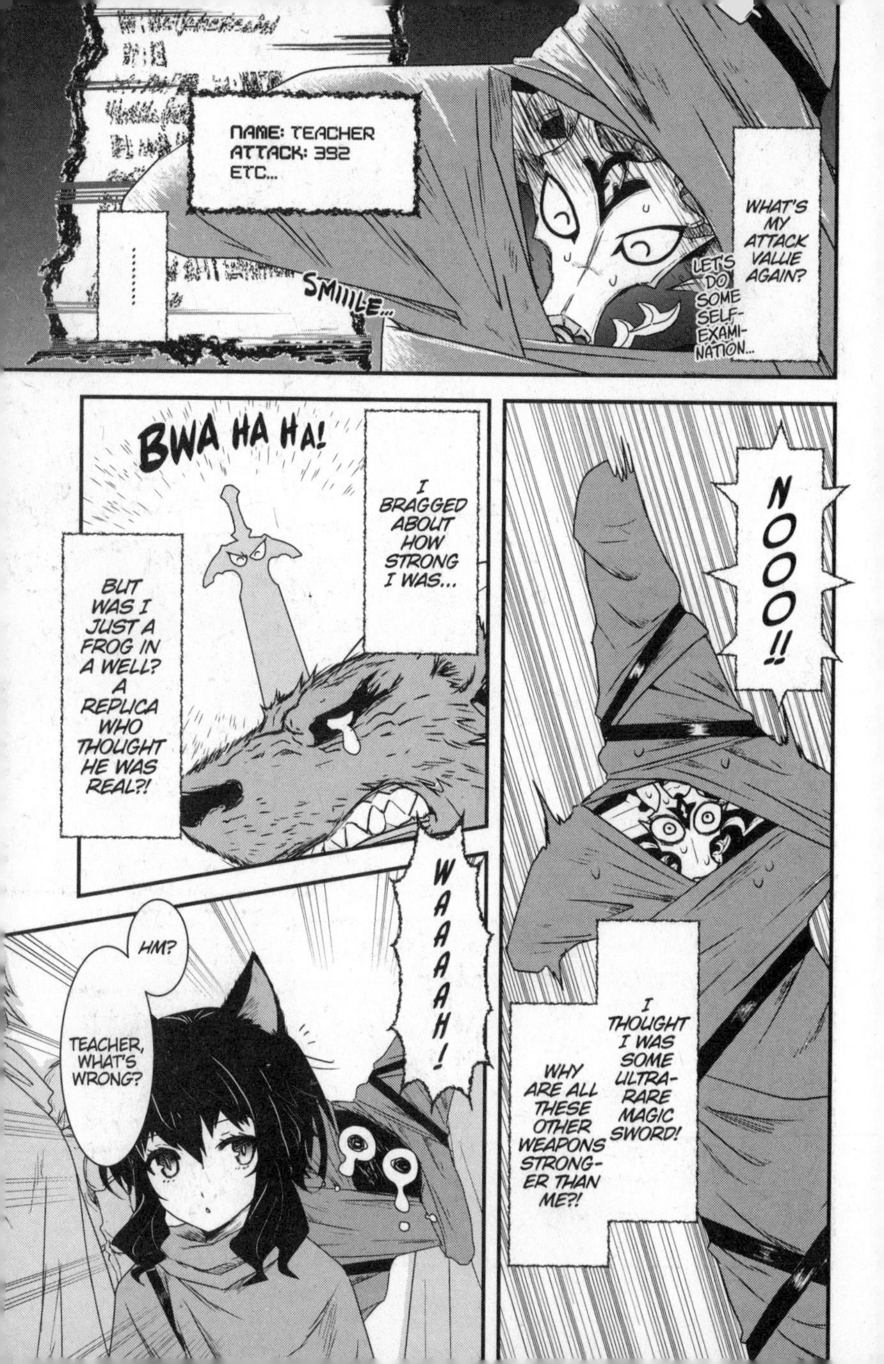
WHAT'S MY ATTACK VALUE AGAIN?
LET'S DO SOME SELF-EXAMINATION...
NAME: TEACHER
ATTACK: 392
ETC...
SMIIILE...
......
NOOOO!!
I THOUGHT I WAS SOME ULTRA-RARE MAGIC SWORD!
WHY ARE ALL THESE OTHER WEAPONS STRONGER THAN ME?!
I BRAGGED ABOUT HOW STRONG I WAS...
BWA HA HA!
BUT WAS I JUST A FROG IN A WELL? A REPLICA WHO THOUGHT HE WAS REAL?!
WAAAAAH!
HM?
TEACHER, WHAT'S WRONG?

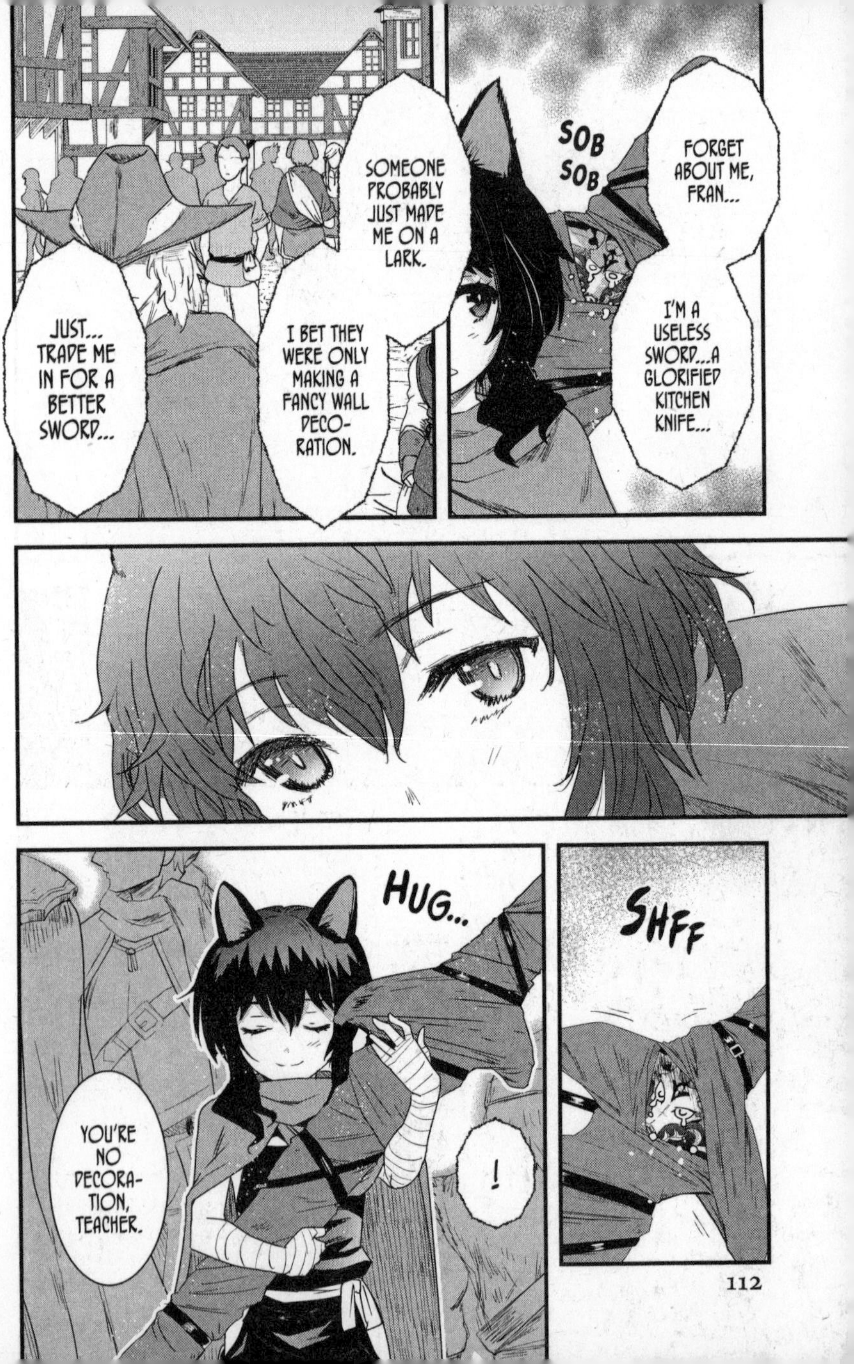
SOB SOB
FORGET ABOUT ME, FRAN...
I'M A USELESS SWORD...A GLORIFIED KITCHEN KNIFE...
SOMEONE PROBABLY JUST MADE ME ON A LARK.
I BET THEY WERE ONLY MAKING A FANCY WALL DECO-RATION.
JUST... TRADE ME IN FOR A BETTER SWORD...
SHFF
!
HUG...
YOU'RE NO DECORA-TION, TEACHER.

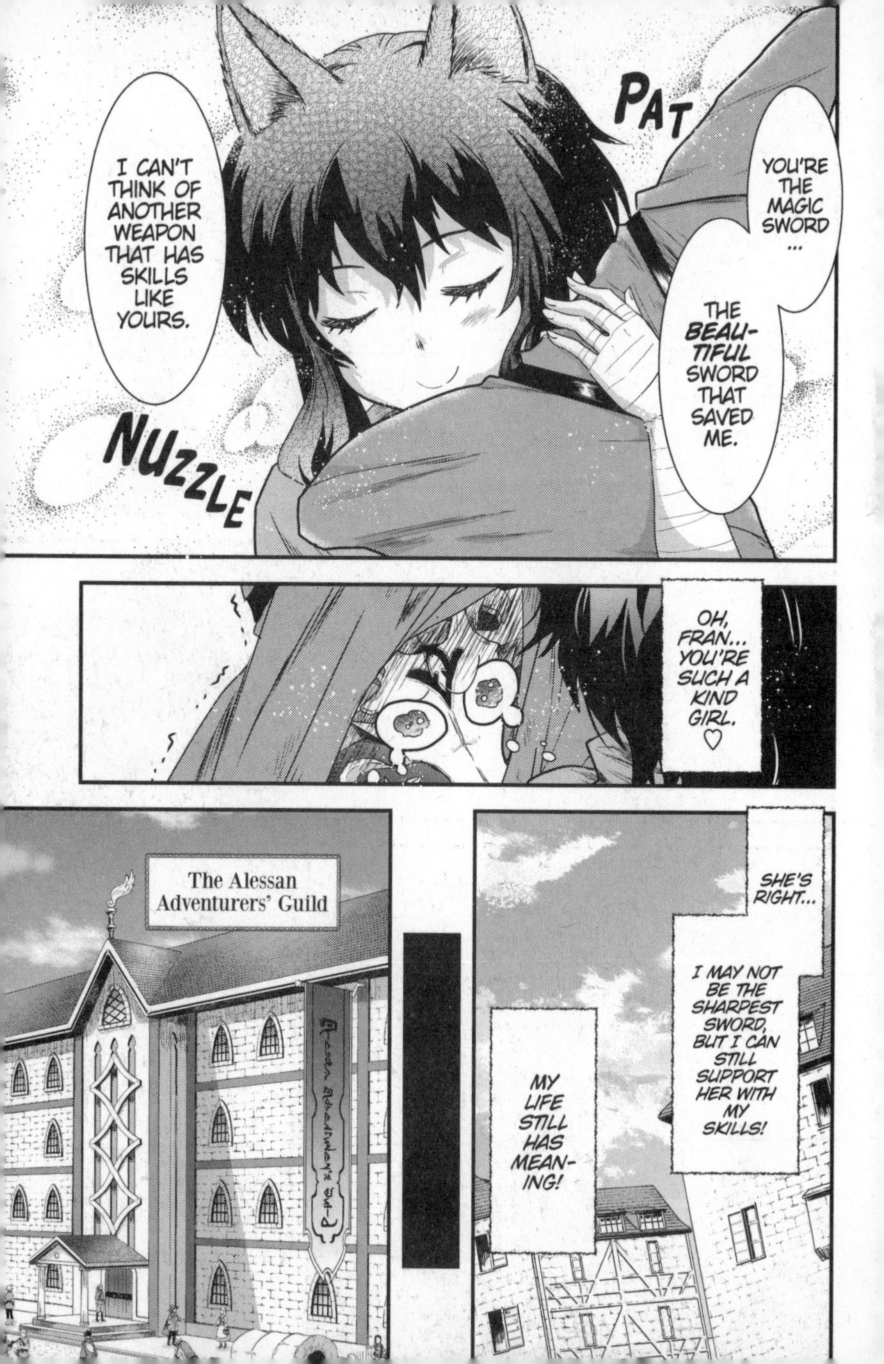
PAT
YOU'RE THE MAGIC SWORD...
THE BEAUTIFUL SWORD THAT SAVED ME.
I CAN'T THINK OF ANOTHER WEAPON THAT HAS SKILLS LIKE YOURS.
NUZZLE
OH, FRAN... YOU'RE SUCH A KIND GIRL. ♡
SHE'S RIGHT...
I MAY NOT BE THE SHARPEST SWORD, BUT I CAN STILL SUPPORT HER WITH MY SKILLS!
MY LIFE STILL HAS MEANING!
The Alessan Adventurers' Guild

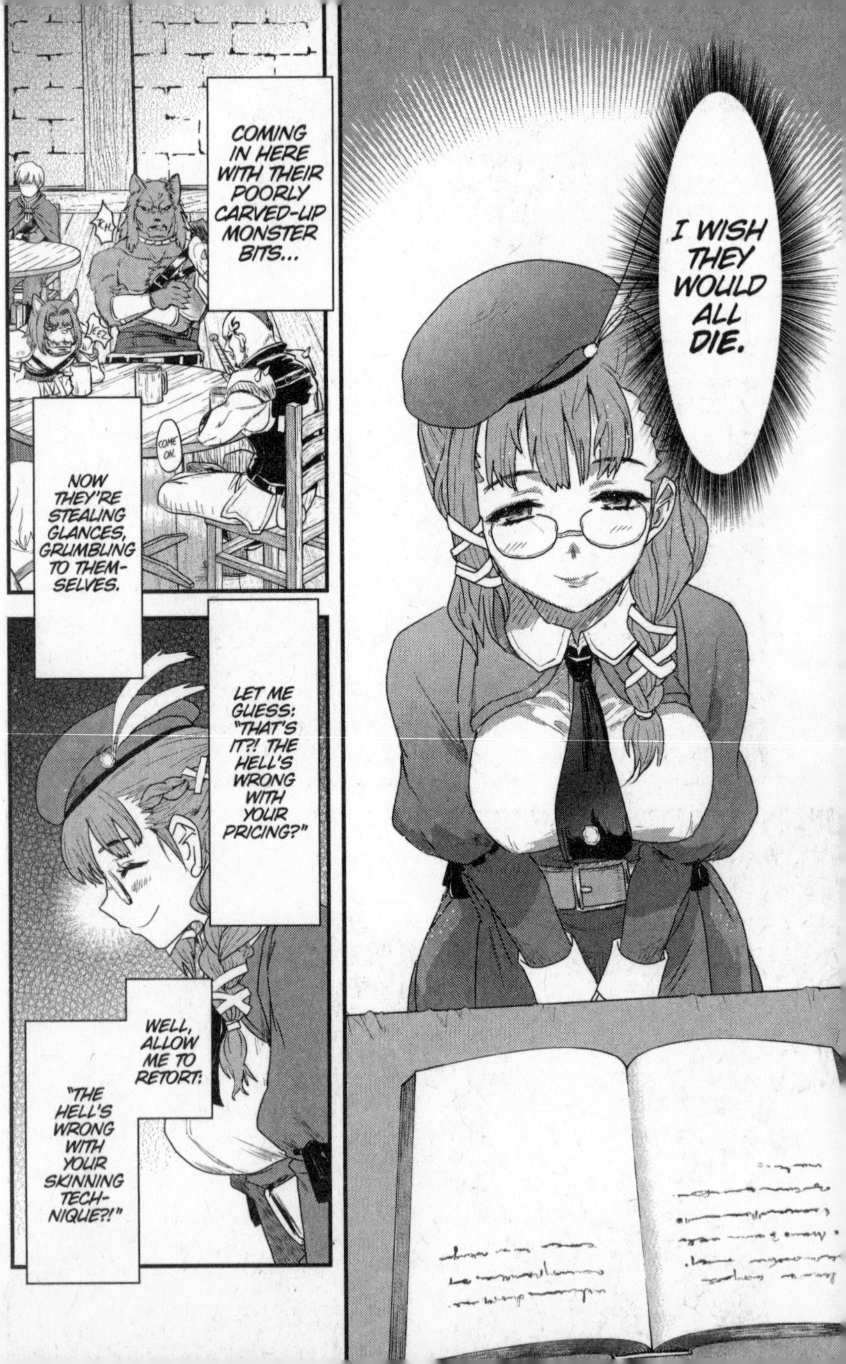
I WISH THEY WOULD ALL DIE.
COMING IN HERE WITH THEIR POORLY CARVED-UP MONSTER BITS...
COME ON.
NOW THEY'RE STEALING GLANCES, GRUMBLING TO THEM-SELVES.
LET ME GUESS: "THAT'S IT?! THE HELL'S WRONG WITH YOUR PRICING?"
WELL, ALLOW ME TO RETORT:
"THE HELL'S WRONG WITH YOUR SKINNING TECH-NIQUE?!"

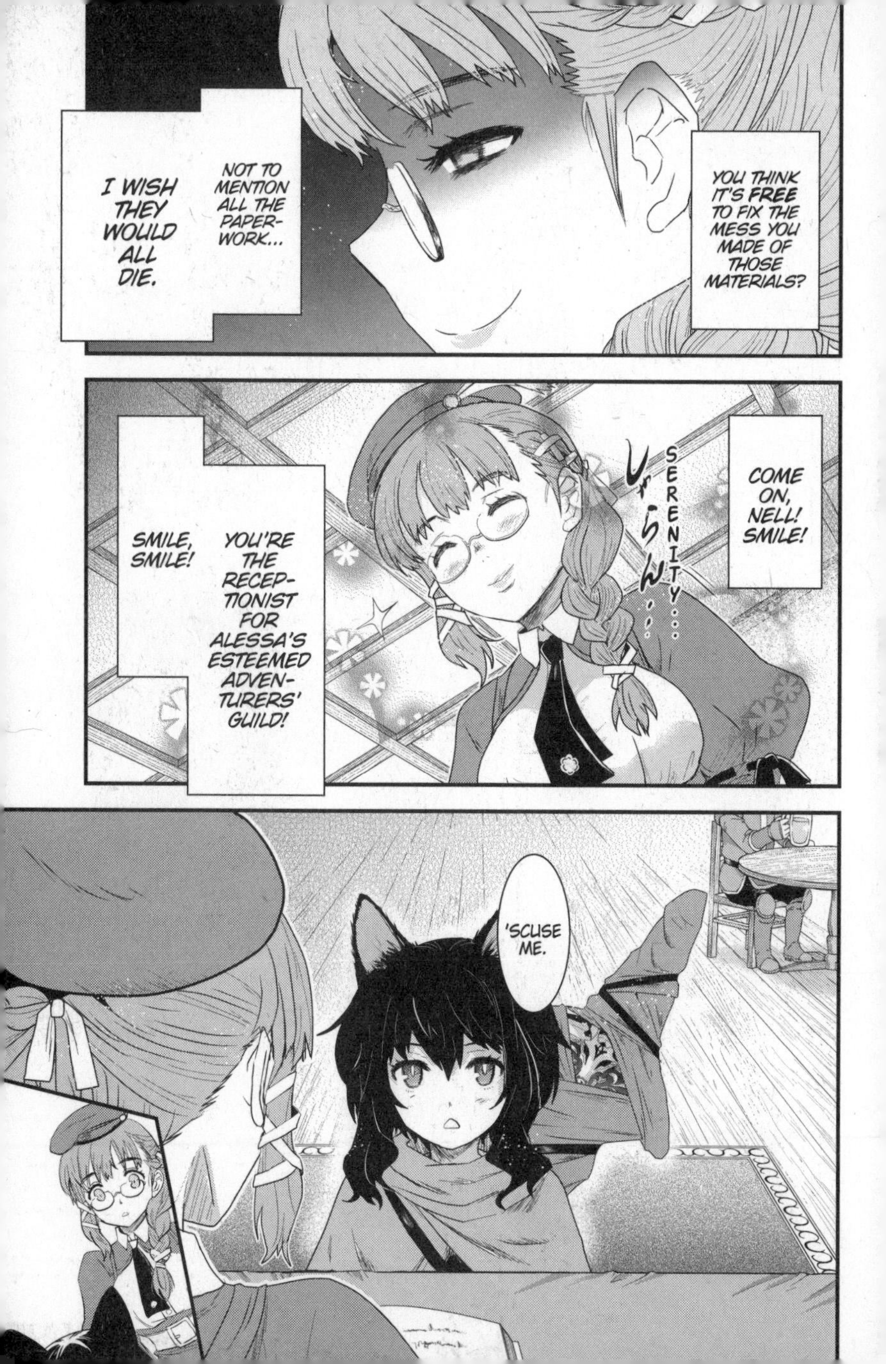
YOU THINK IT'S FREE TO FIX THE MESS YOU MADE OF THOSE MATERIALS?
NOT TO MENTION ALL THE PAPERWORK...
I WISH THEY WOULD ALL DIE.
COME ON, NELL! SMILE!
SERENITY...
YOU'RE THE RECEPTIONIST FOR ALESSA'S ESTEEMED ADVENTURERS' GUILD!
SMILE, SMILE!
'SCUSE ME.

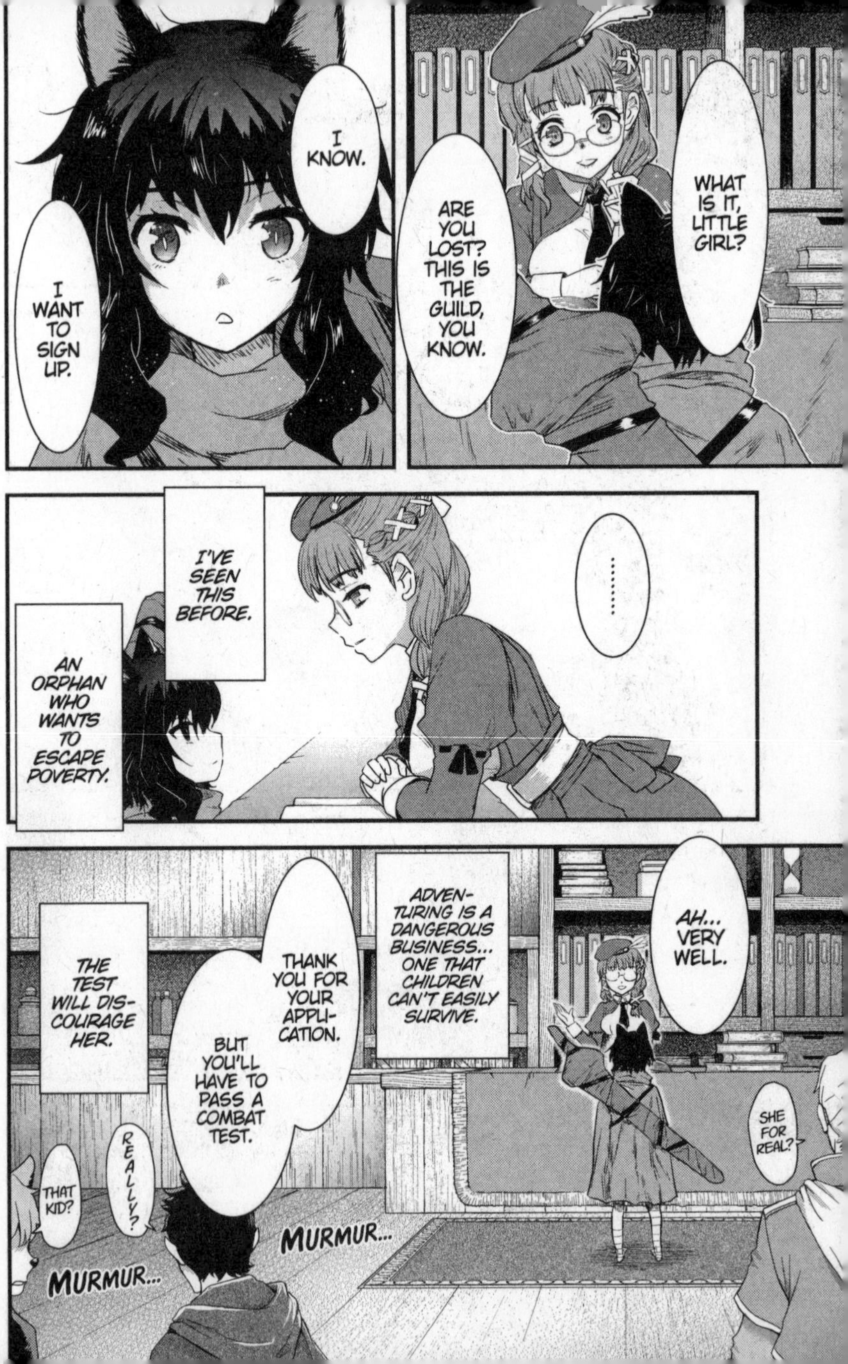
WHAT IS IT, LITTLE GIRL?
ARE YOU LOST? THIS IS THE GUILD, YOU KNOW.
I KNOW.
I WANT TO SIGN UP.
……
I'VE SEEN THIS BEFORE.
AN ORPHAN WHO WANTS TO ESCAPE POVERTY.
AH... VERY WELL.
ADVEN-TURING IS A DANGEROUS BUSINESS... ONE THAT CHILDREN CAN'T EASILY SURVIVE.
THANK YOU FOR YOUR APPLI-CATION.
BUT YOU'LL HAVE TO PASS A COMBAT TEST.
THE TEST WILL DIS-COURAGE HER.
SHE FOR REAL?
MURMUR...
REALLY?
THAT KID?
MURMUR...

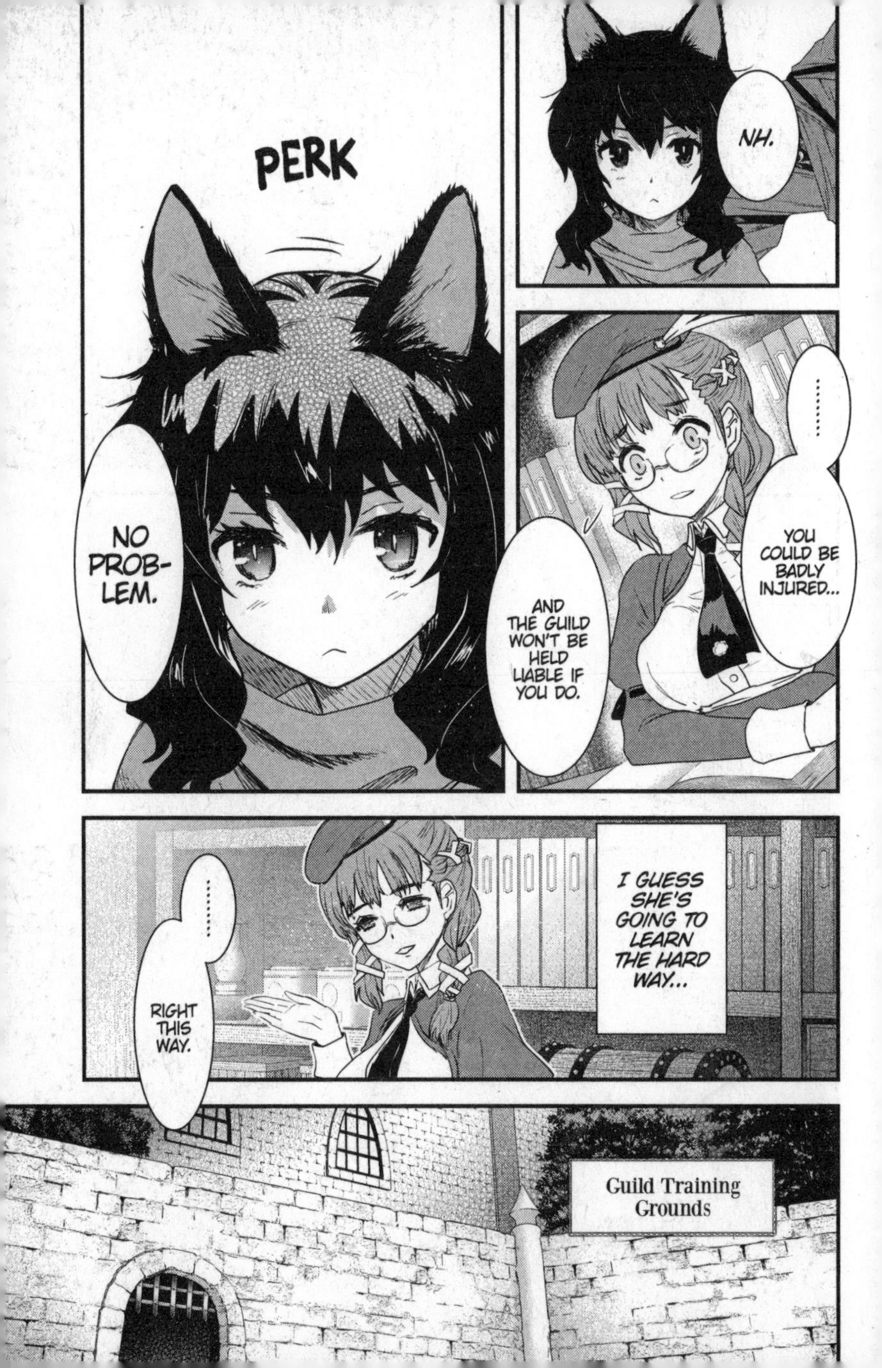
NH.
......
YOU COULD BE BADLY INJURED...
AND THE GUILD WON'T BE HELD LIABLE IF YOU DO.
PERK
NO PROBLEM.
I GUESS SHE'S GOING TO LEARN THE HARD WAY...
......
RIGHT THIS WAY.
Guild Training Grounds

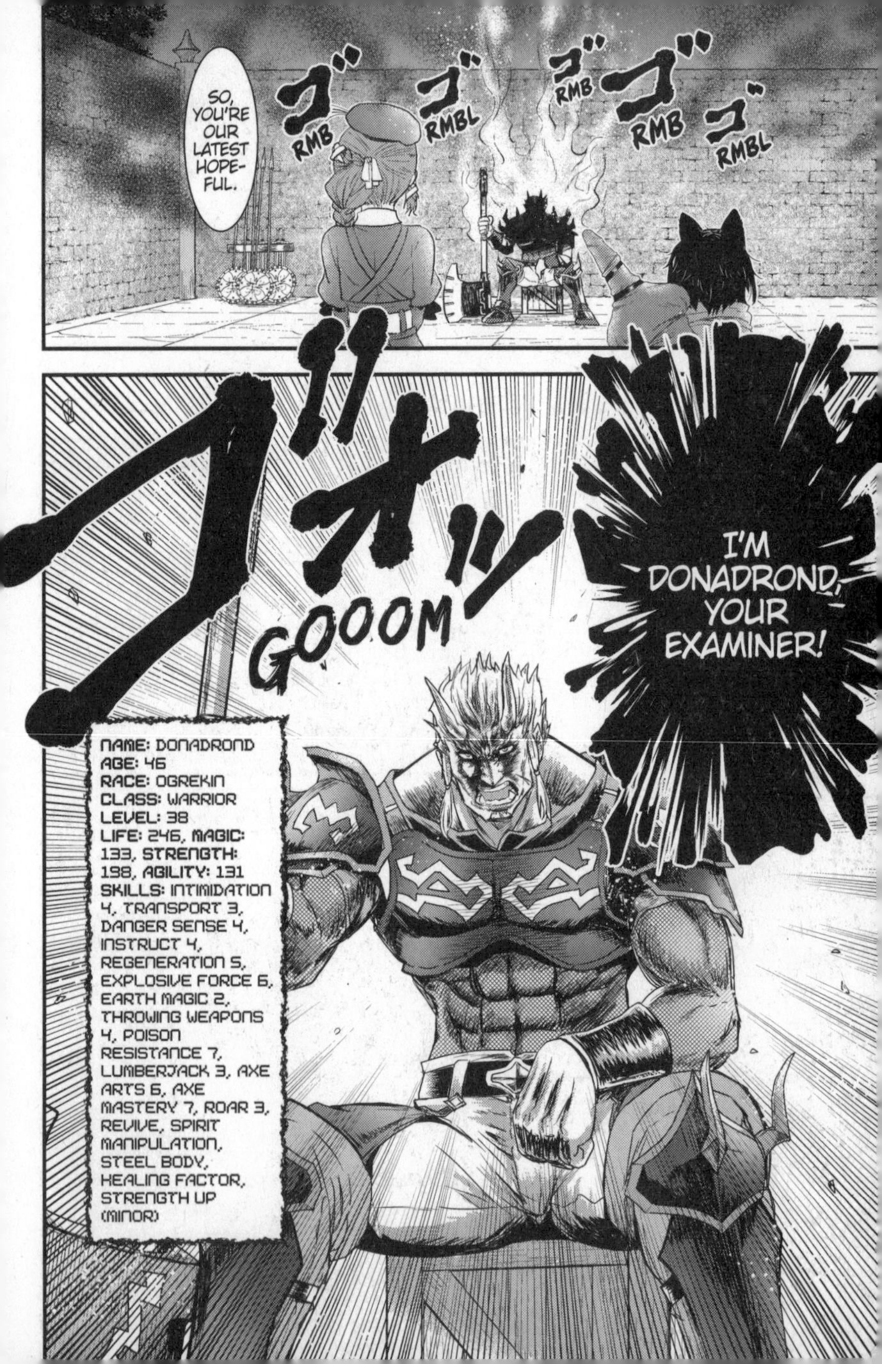
ゴ RMBL
ゴ RMB
ゴ RMB
ゴ RMBL
ゴ RMB
SO, YOU'RE OUR LATEST HOPE-FUL.
I'M DONADROND, YOUR EXAMINER!
ゴオッ GOOOM
NAME: DONADROND
AGE: 46
RACE: OGREKIN
CLASS: WARRIOR
LEVEL: 38
LIFE: 246, MAGIC: 133, STRENGTH: 198, AGILITY: 131
SKILLS: INTIMIDATION 4, TRANSPORT 3, DANGER SENSE 4, INSTRUCT 4, REGENERATION 5, EXPLOSIVE FORCE 6, EARTH MAGIC 2, THROWING WEAPONS 4, POISON RESISTANCE 7, LUMBERJACK 3, AXE ARTS 6, AXE MASTERY 7, ROAR 3, REVIVE, SPIRIT MANIPULATION, STEEL BODY, HEALING FACTOR, STRENGTH UP (MINOR)

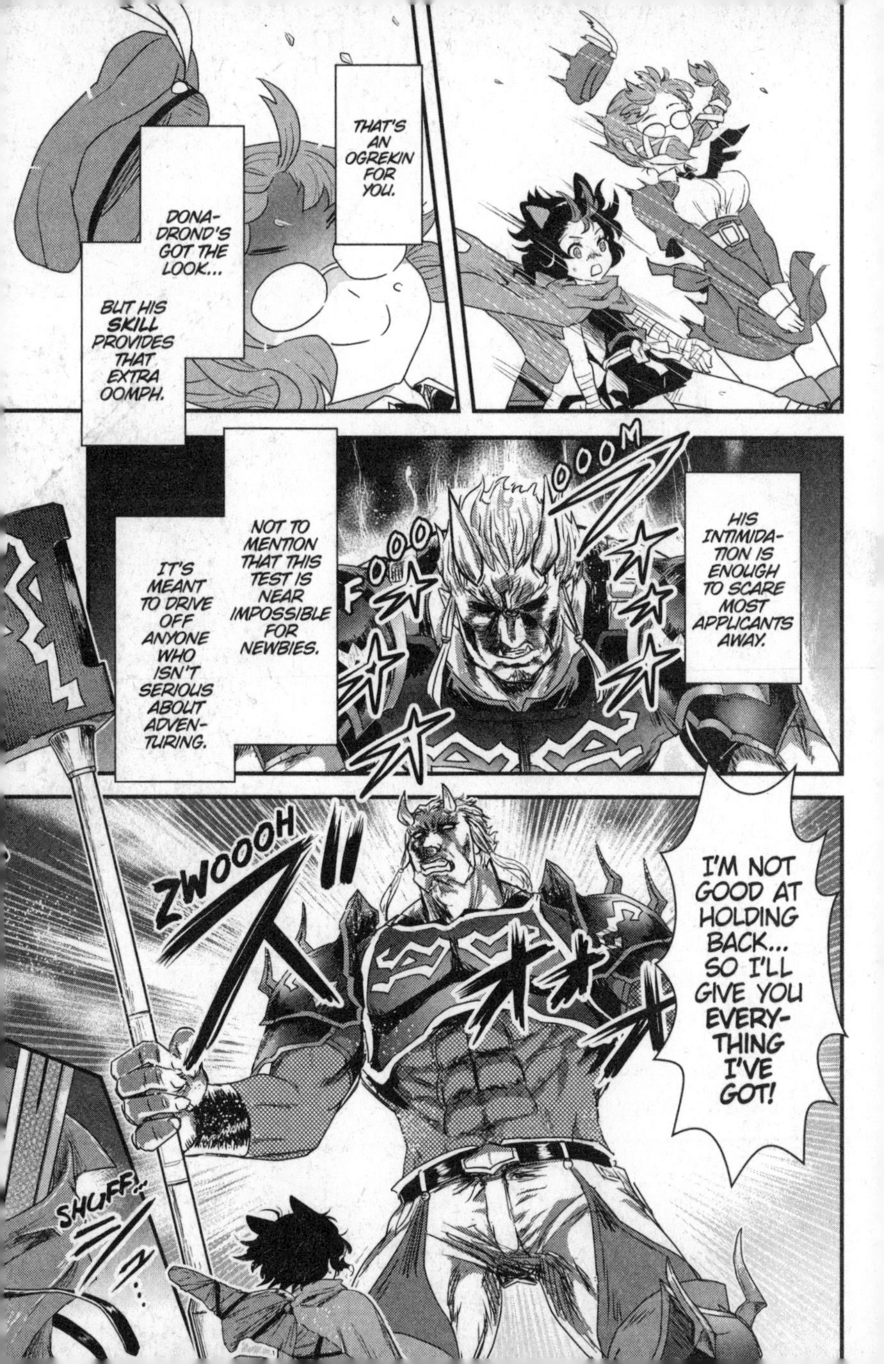
THAT'S AN OGREKIN FOR YOU.
DONA-DROND'S GOT THE LOOK...
BUT HIS SKILL PROVIDES THAT EXTRA OOMPH.
FOOOOOOM
HIS INTIMIDA-TION IS ENOUGH TO SCARE MOST APPLICANTS AWAY.
NOT TO MENTION THAT THIS TEST IS NEAR IMPOSSIBLE FOR NEWBIES.
IT'S MEANT TO DRIVE OFF ANYONE WHO ISN'T SERIOUS ABOUT ADVEN-TURING.
I'M NOT GOOD AT HOLDING BACK... SO I'LL GIVE YOU EVERY-THING I'VE GOT!
ZWOOOOH
SHUFF...

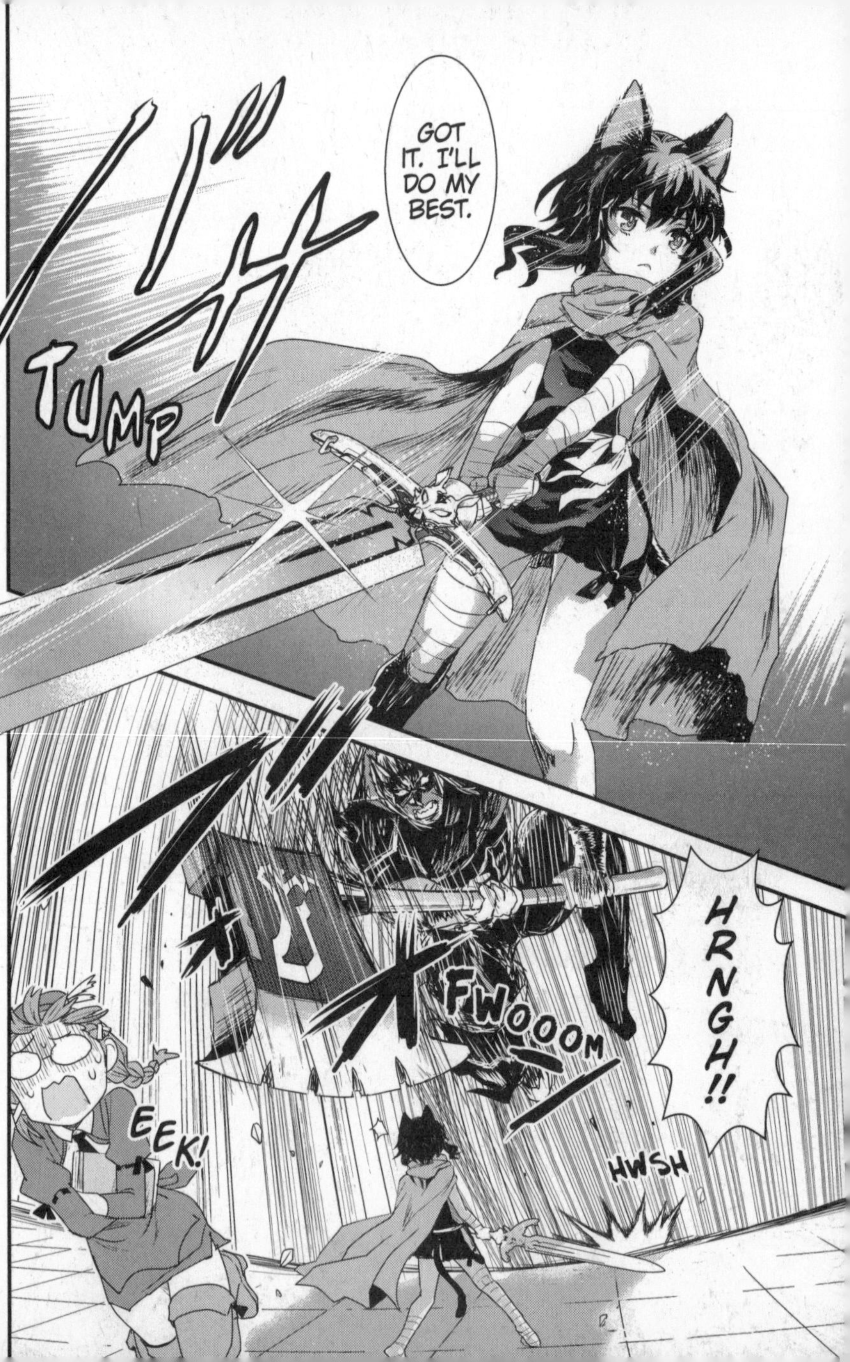
GOT IT. I'LL DO MY BEST.
TUMP
HRNGH!!
FWOOOM
HWSH
EEK!

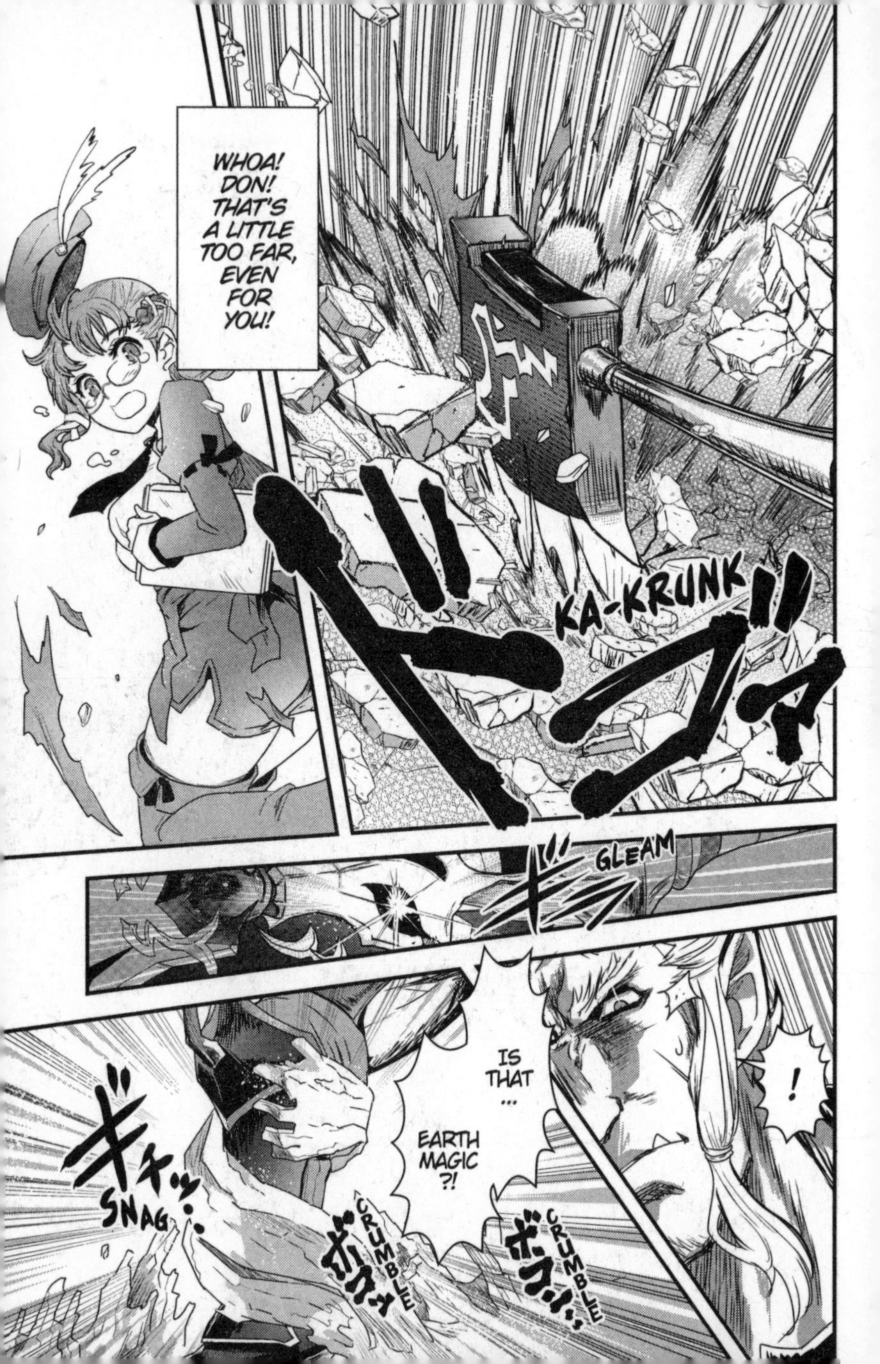
KA-KRUNK
WHOA! DON! THAT'S A LITTLE TOO FAR, EVEN FOR YOU!
GLEAM
!
IS THAT ... EARTH MAGIC?!
CRUMBLE
CRUMBLE
SNAG

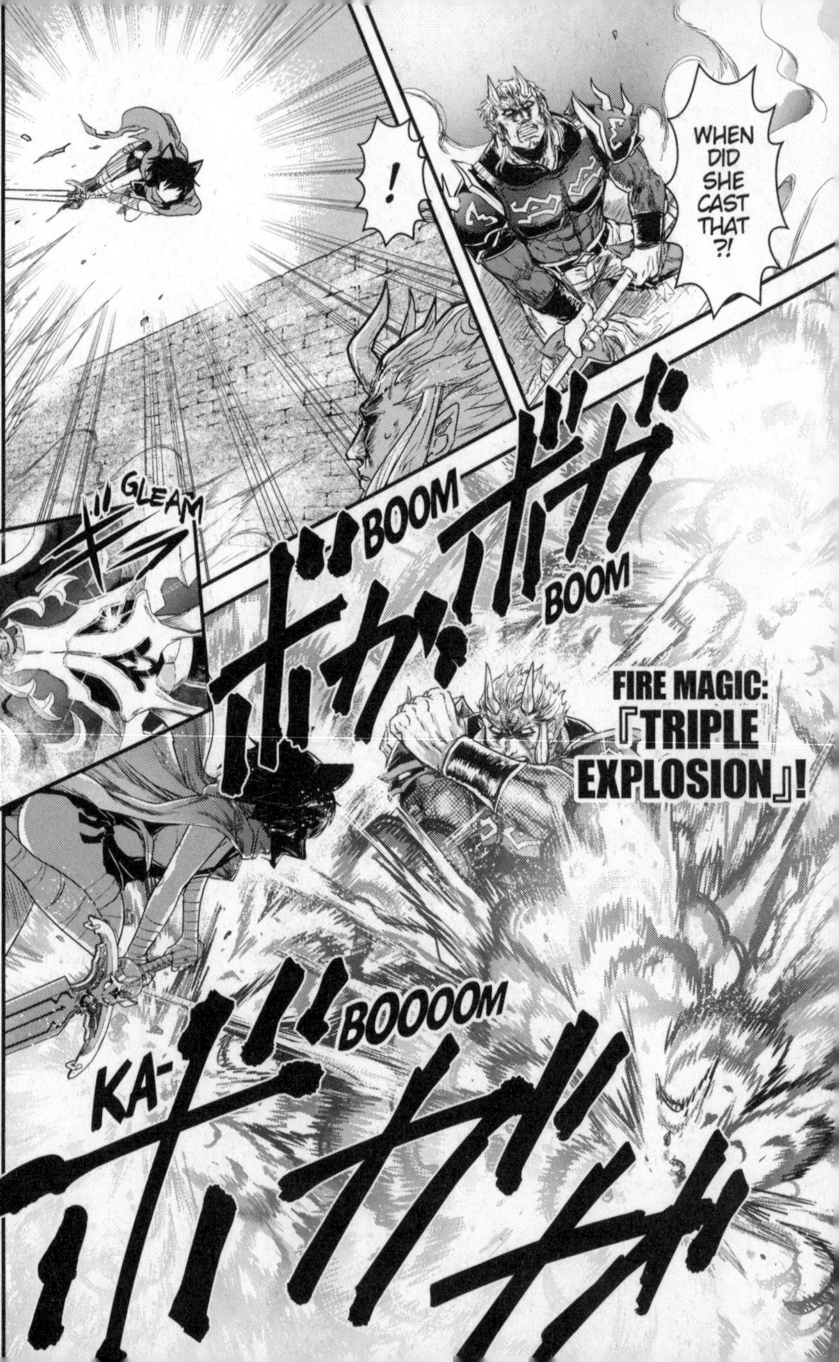
WHEN DID SHE CAST THAT?!
!
GLEAM
BOOM
BOOM
FIRE MAGIC: 『TRIPLE EXPLOSION』!
KA-
BOOOOM

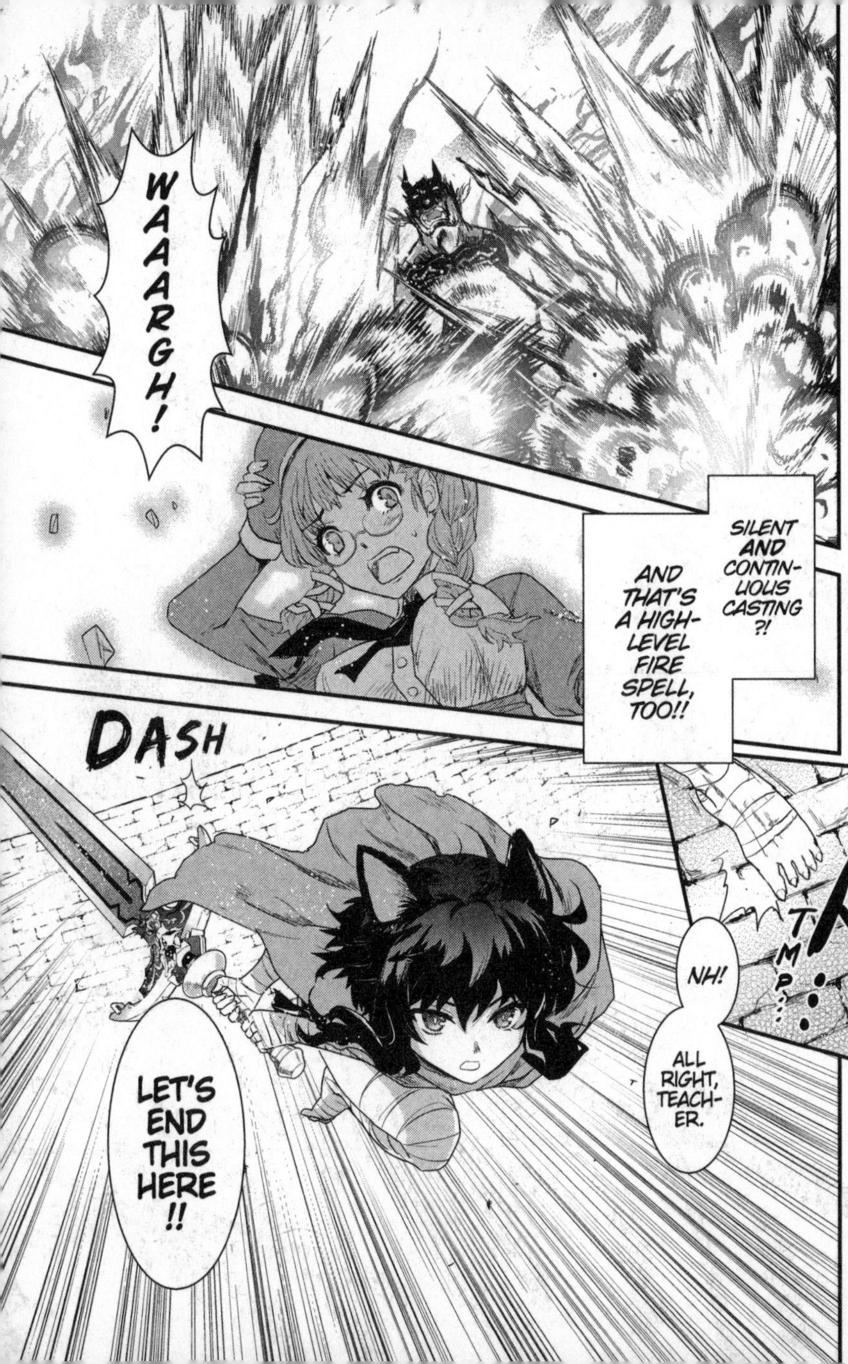
WAAAARGH!
SILENT AND CONTIN-UOUS CASTING?!
AND THAT'S A HIGH-LEVEL FIRE SPELL, TOO!!
TMP...
NH!
ALL RIGHT, TEACH-ER.
DASH
LET'S END THIS HERE!!

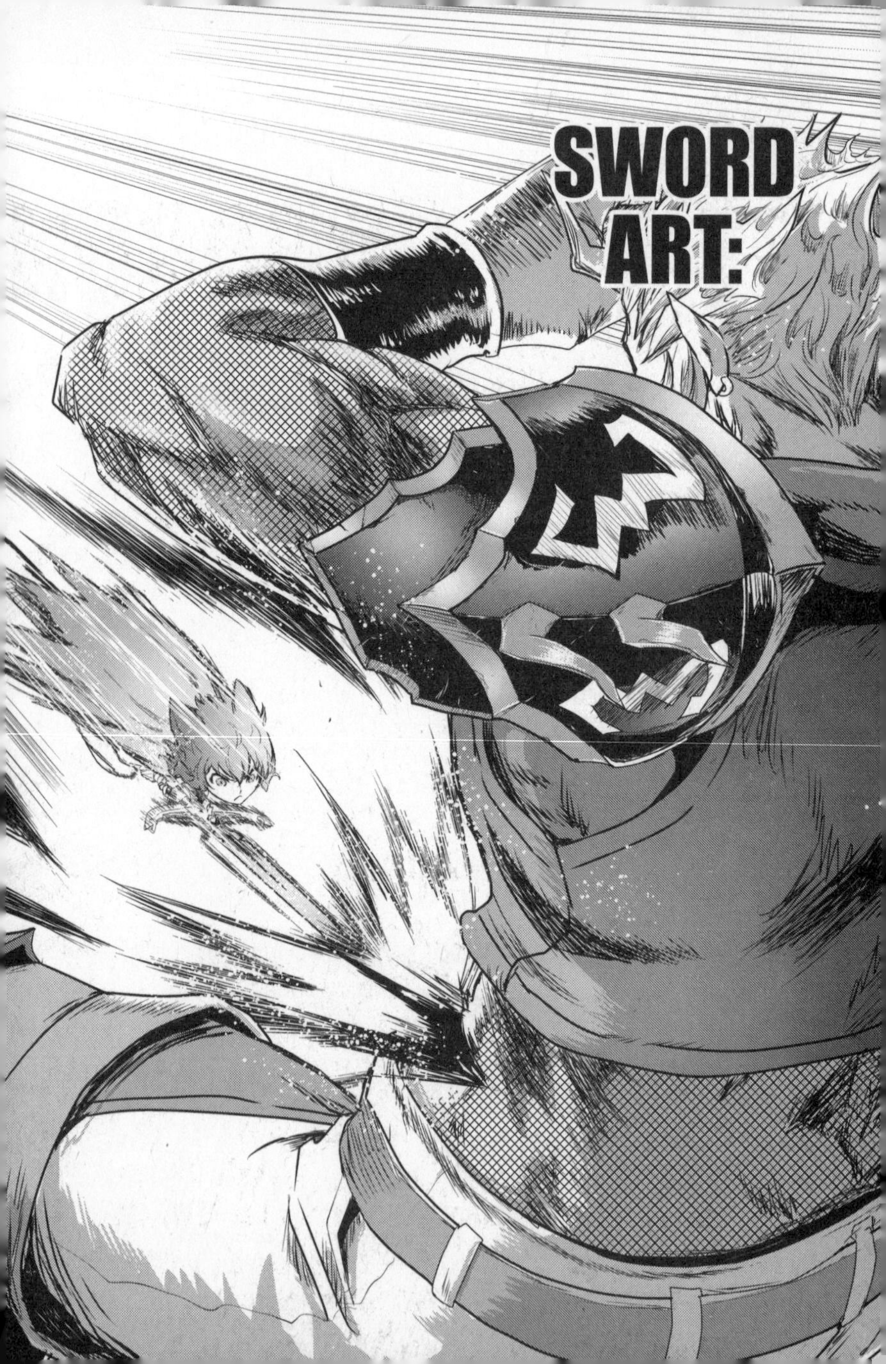
SWORD ART:

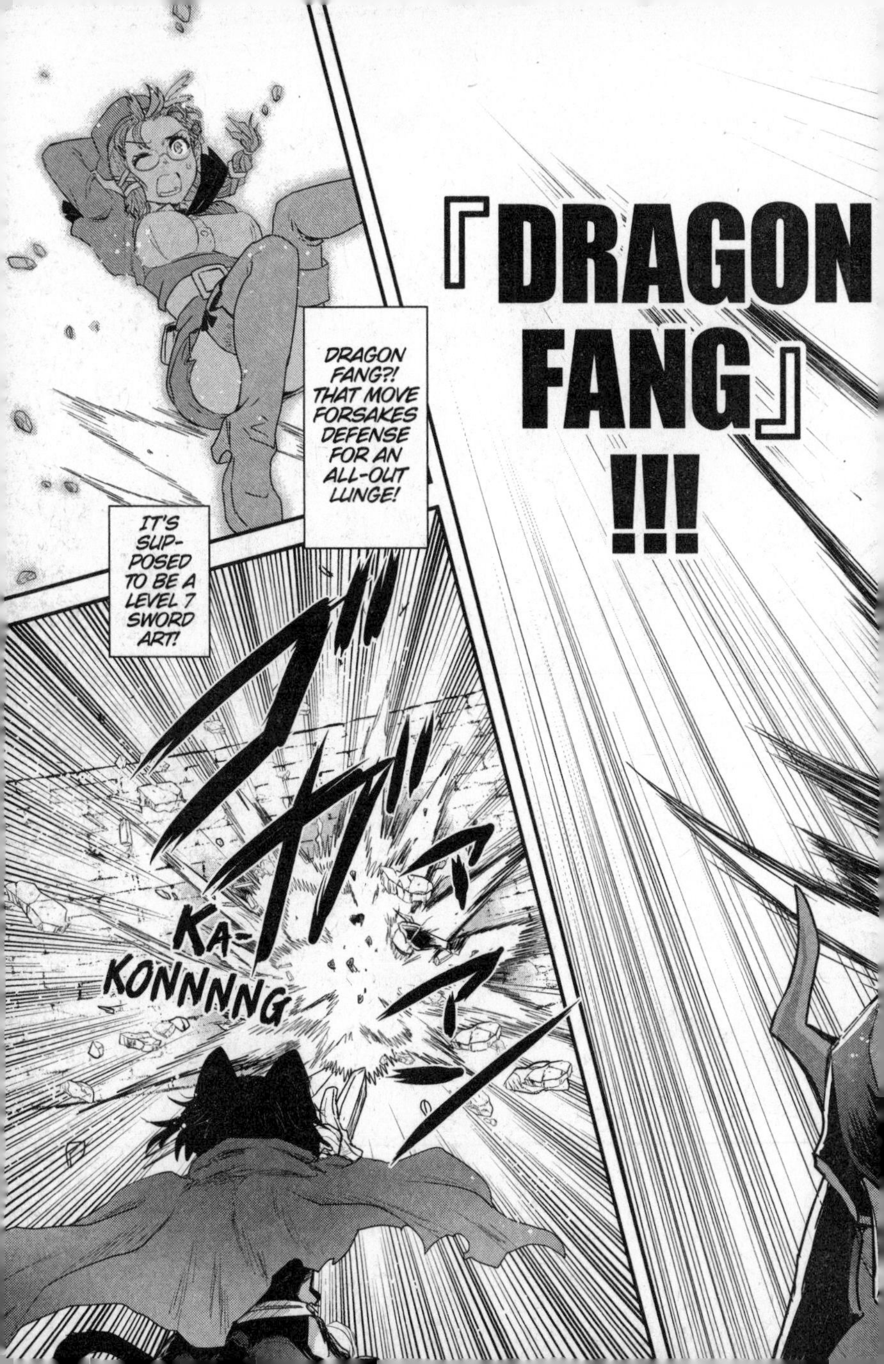
『DRAGON FANG』!!!
DRAGON FANG?! THAT MOVE FORSAKES DEFENSE FOR AN ALL-OUT LUNGE!
IT'S SUP-POSED TO BE A LEVEL 7 SWORD ART!
KA-KONNNNG

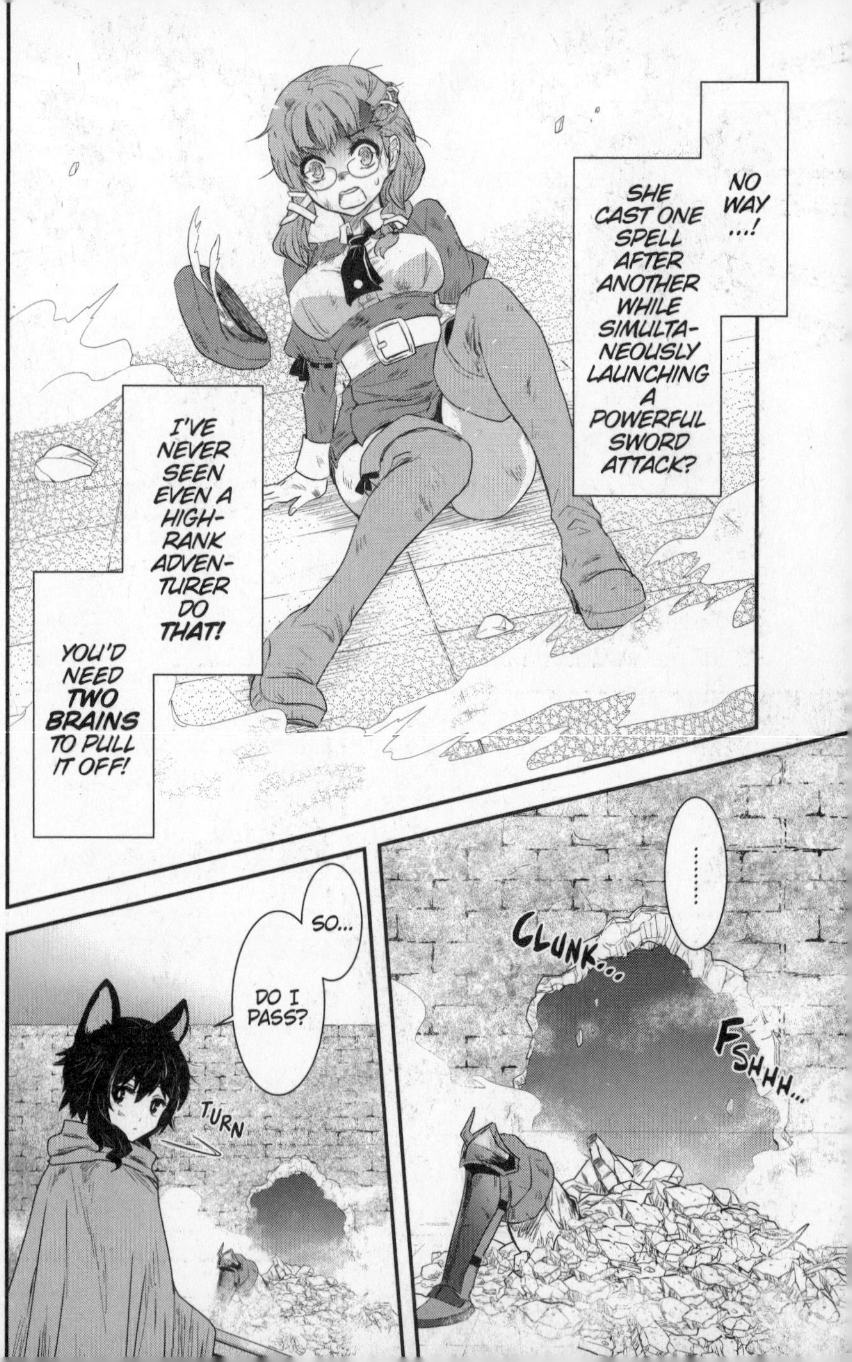
NO WAY ...!
SHE CAST ONE SPELL AFTER ANOTHER WHILE SIMULTA-NEOUSLY LAUNCHING A POWERFUL SWORD ATTACK?
I'VE NEVER SEEN EVEN A HIGH-RANK ADVEN-TURER DO THAT!
YOU'D NEED TWO BRAINS TO PULL IT OFF!
......
CLUNK...
FSHHH...
SO...
DO I PASS?
TURN

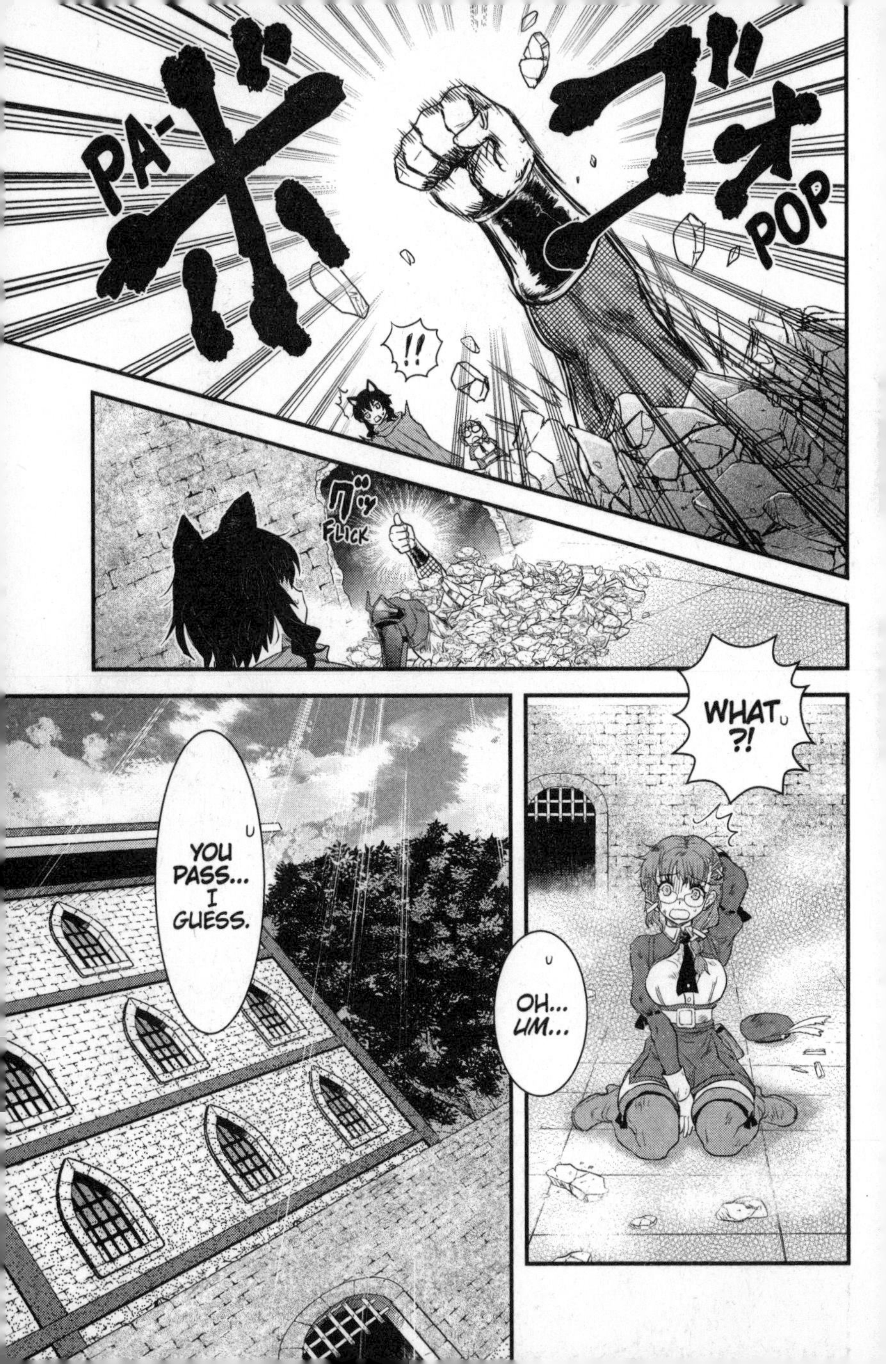
POP
PA-
!!
グッ
FLICK
WHAT?!
OH... UM...
YOU PASS... I GUESS.

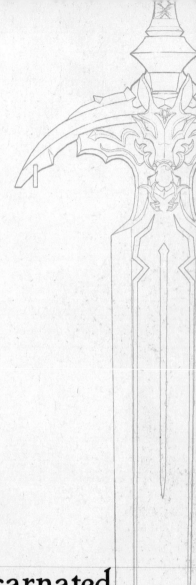

Reincarnated
as a sword

Chapter 5: The Guildmaster

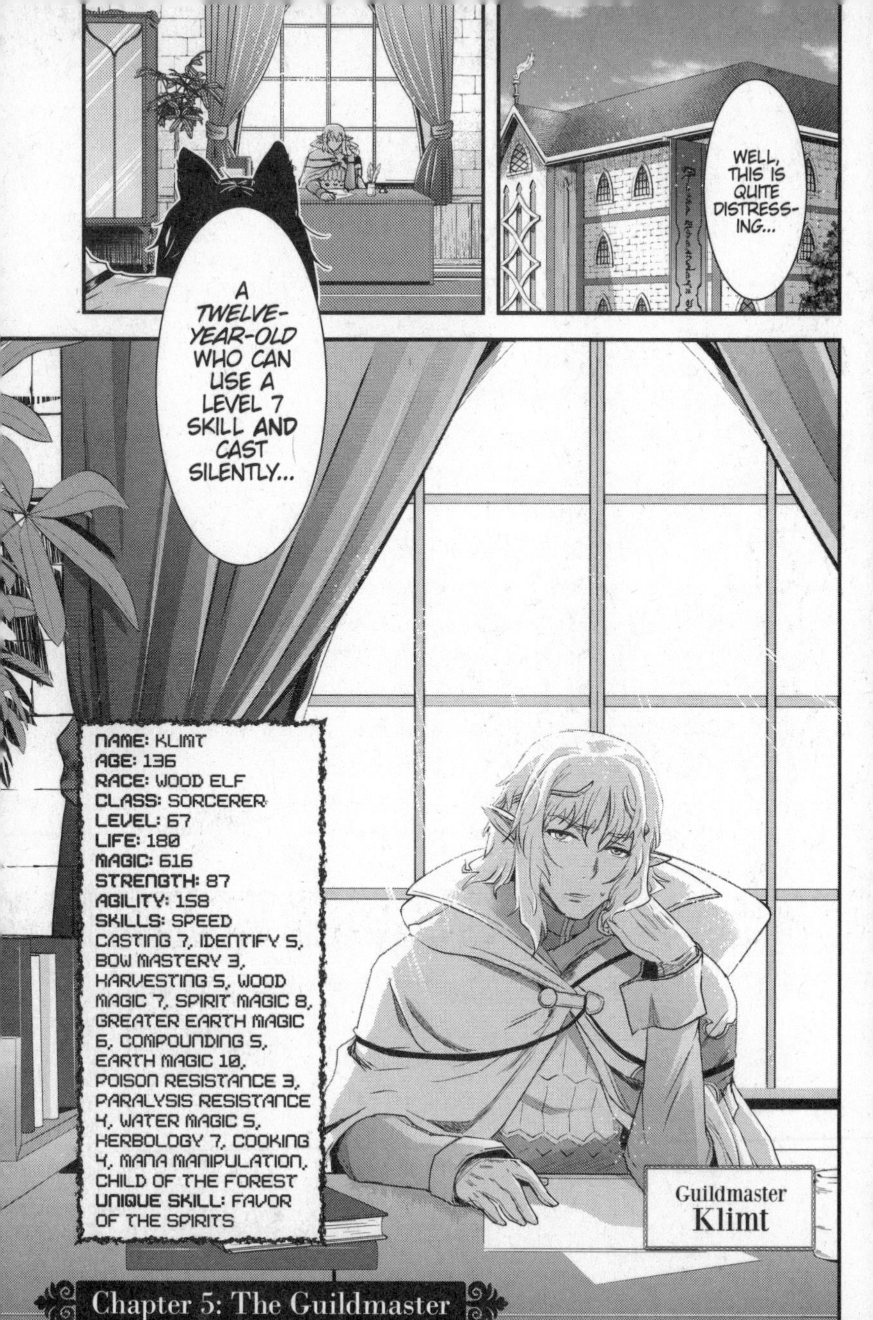

WELL, THIS IS QUITE DISTRESSING...
A TWELVE-YEAR-OLD WHO CAN USE A LEVEL 7 SKILL AND CAST SILENTLY...
NAME: KLIMT
AGE: 136
RACE: WOOD ELF
CLASS: SORCERER
LEVEL: 67
LIFE: 180
MAGIC: 616
STRENGTH: 87
ABILITY: 158
SKILLS: SPEED CASTING 7, IDENTIFY 5, BOW MASTERY 3, HARVESTING 5, WOOD MAGIC 7, SPIRIT MAGIC 8, GREATER EARTH MAGIC 6, COMPOUNDING 5, EARTH MAGIC 10, POISON RESISTANCE 3, PARALYSIS RESISTANCE 4, WATER MAGIC 5, HERBOLOGY 7, COOKING 4, MANA MANIPULATION, CHILD OF THE FOREST
UNIQUE SKILL: FAVOR OF THE SPIRITS
Guildmaster Klimt

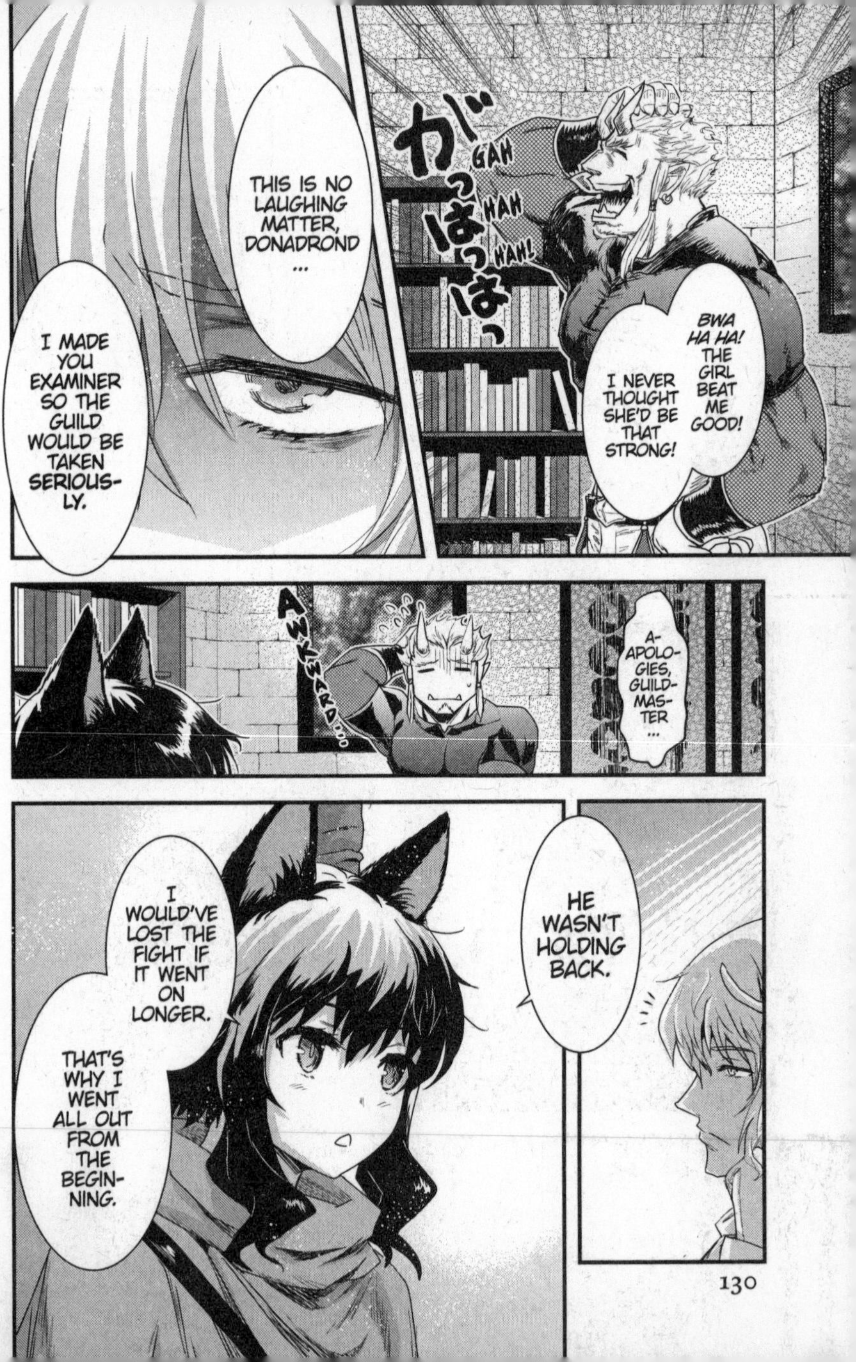
わっはっはっ
GAH HAH HAH!
BWA HA HA! THE GIRL BEAT ME GOOD!
I NEVER THOUGHT SHE'D BE THAT STRONG!
THIS IS NO LAUGHING MATTER, DONADROND ...
I MADE YOU EXAMINER SO THE GUILD WOULD BE TAKEN SERIOUS-LY.
A-APOLO-GIES, GUILD-MAS-TER ...
AWKWARD...
HE WASN'T HOLDING BACK.
I WOULD'VE LOST THE FIGHT IF IT WENT ON LONGER.
THAT'S WHY I WENT ALL OUT FROM THE BEGIN-NING.

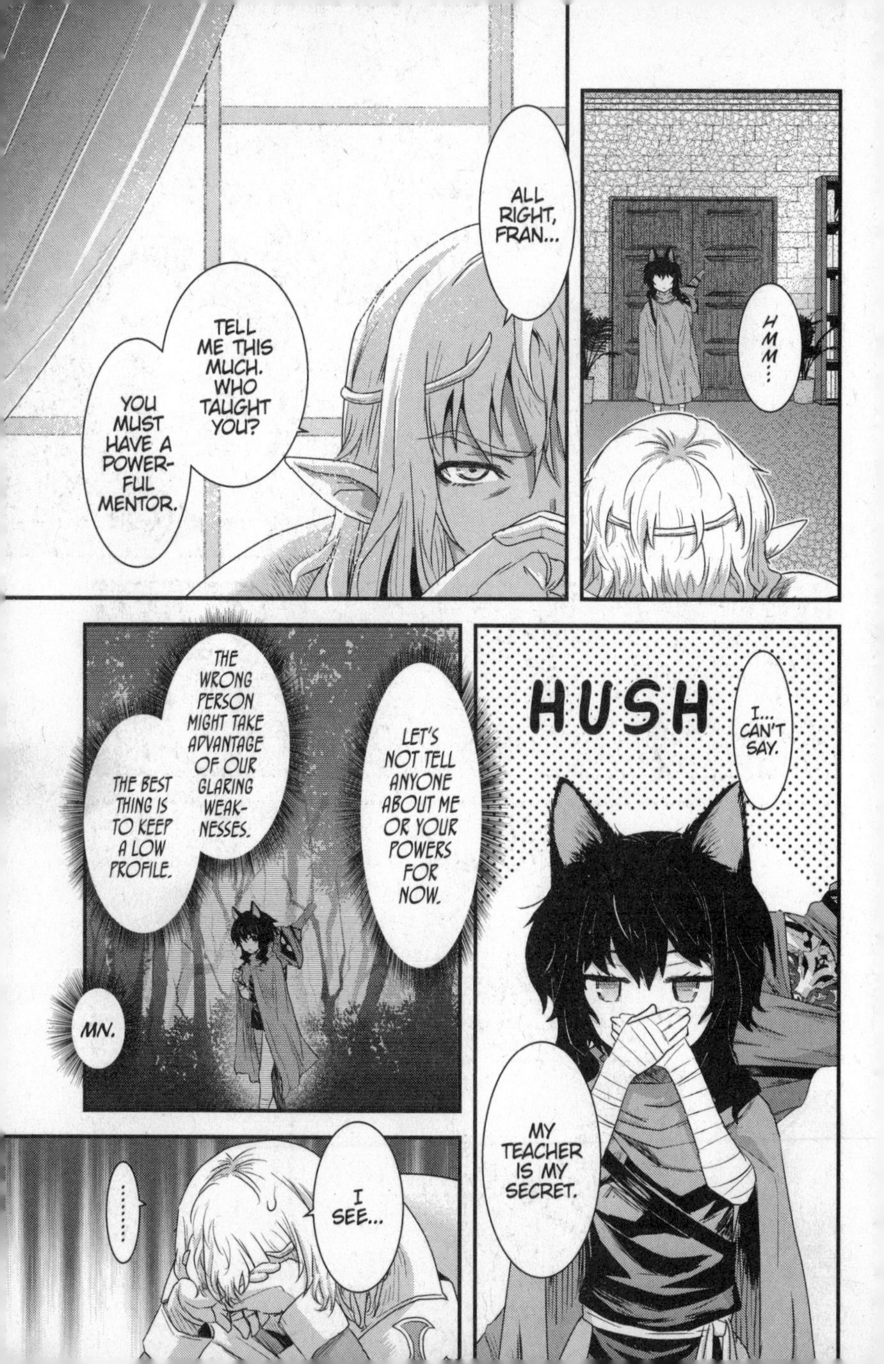
HMM...
ALL RIGHT, FRAN...
TELL ME THIS MUCH. WHO TAUGHT YOU?
YOU MUST HAVE A POWERFUL MENTOR.
HUSH
I... CAN'T SAY.
MY TEACHER IS MY SECRET.
LET'S NOT TELL ANYONE ABOUT ME OR YOUR POWERS FOR NOW.
THE WRONG PERSON MIGHT TAKE ADVANTAGE OF OUR GLARING WEAKNESSES.
THE BEST THING IS TO KEEP A LOW PROFILE.
MN.
I SEE...
......

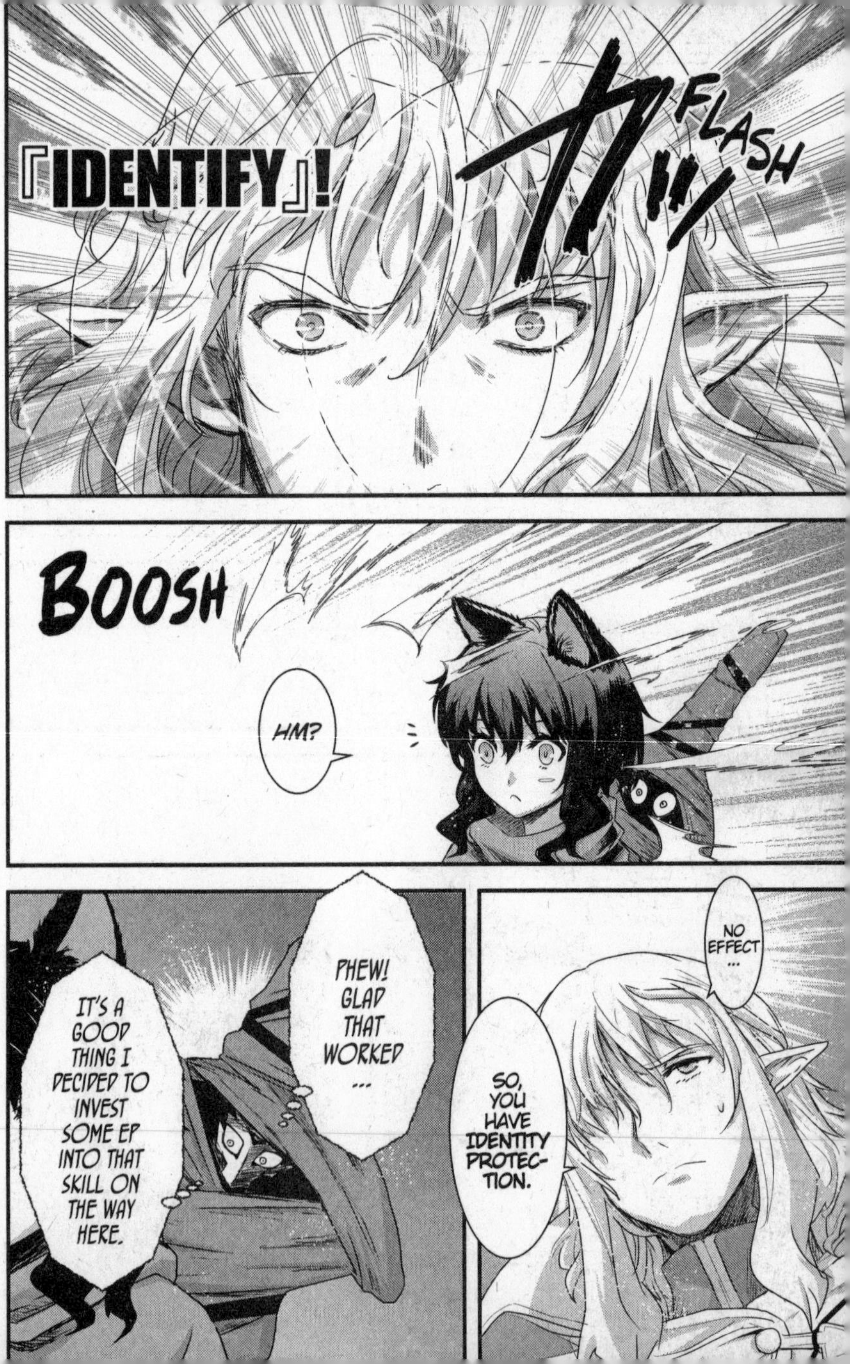
『IDENTIFY』!
FLASH
BOOSH
HM?
NO EFFECT...
SO, YOU HAVE IDENTITY PROTECTION.
PHEW! GLAD THAT WORKED...
IT'S A GOOD THING I DECIDED TO INVEST SOME EP INTO THAT SKILL ON THE WAY HERE.

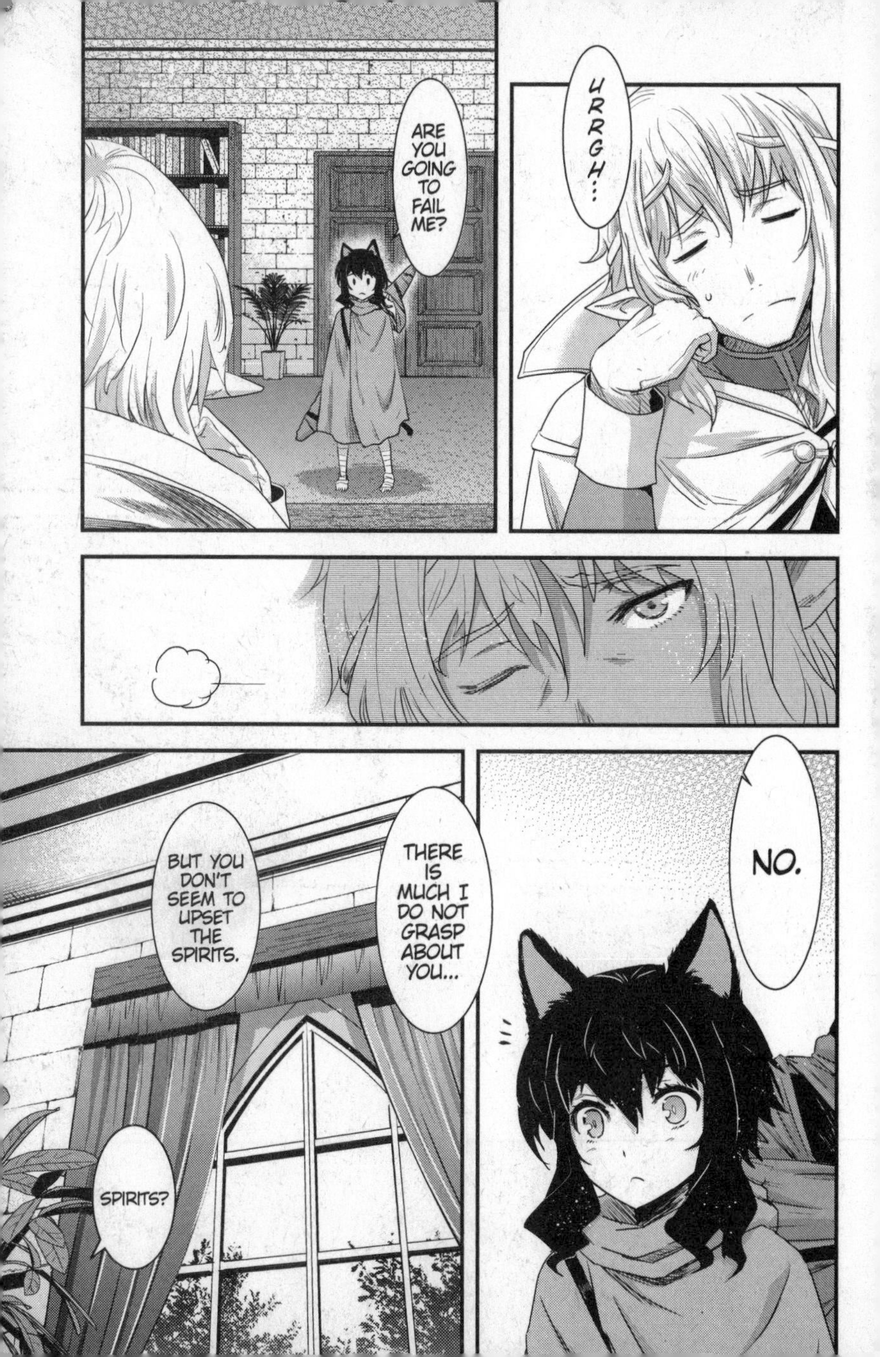
URRGH...
ARE YOU GOING TO FAIL ME?
NO.
THERE IS MUCH I DO NOT GRASP ABOUT YOU...
BUT YOU DON'T SEEM TO UPSET THE SPIRITS.
SPIRITS?

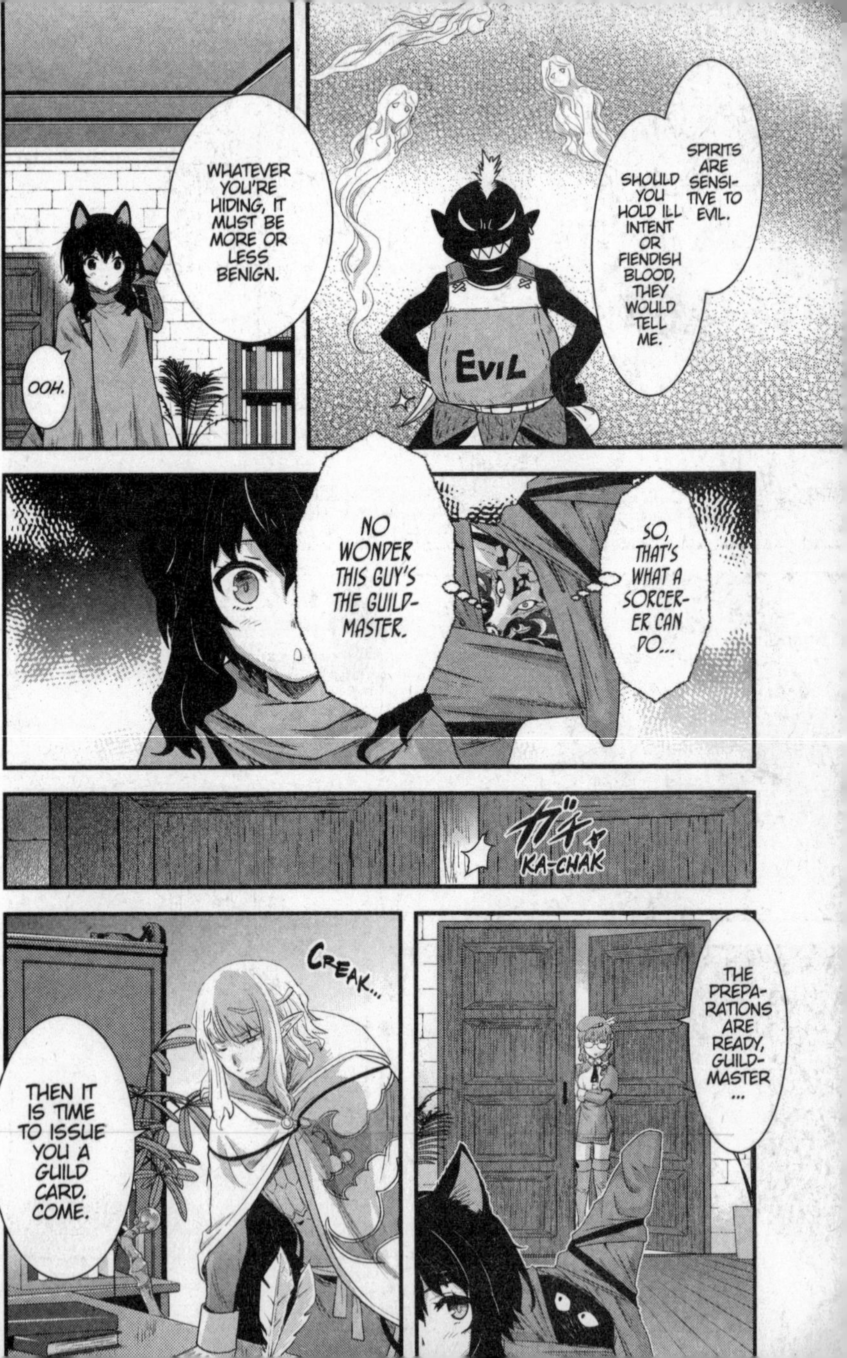
SPIRITS ARE SENSITIVE TO EVIL.
SHOULD YOU HOLD ILL INTENT OR FIENDISH BLOOD, THEY WOULD TELL ME.
EVIL
WHATEVER YOU'RE HIDING, IT MUST BE MORE OR LESS BENIGN.
OOH.
SO, THAT'S WHAT A SORCERER CAN DO...
NO WONDER THIS GUY'S THE GUILDMASTER.
ガチャ
KA-CHAK
THE PREPARATIONS ARE READY, GUILDMASTER...
CREAK...
THEN IT IS TIME TO ISSUE YOU A GUILD CARD. COME.

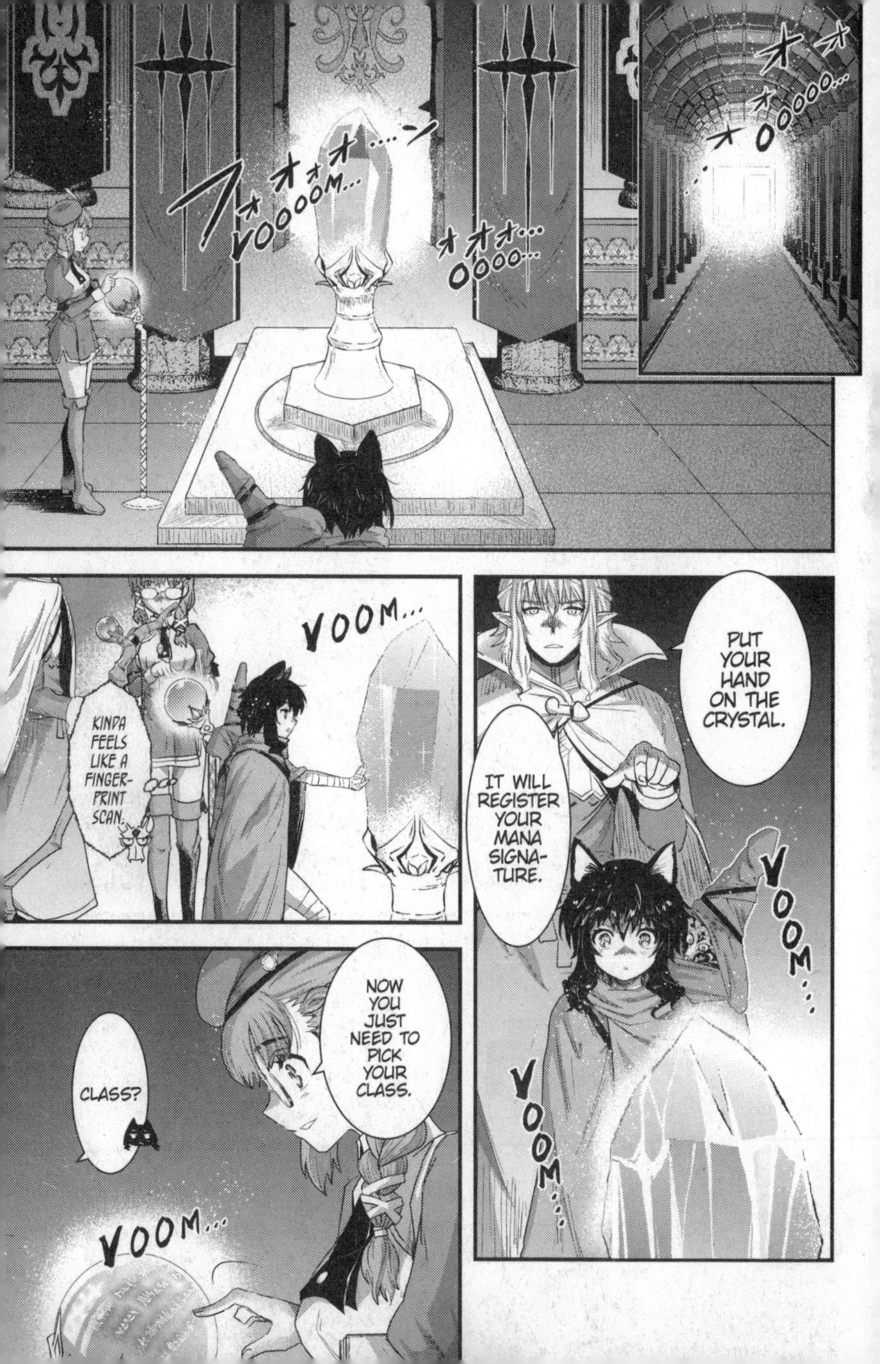
OOOOO...
OOOO...
VOOOOM...
PUT YOUR HAND ON THE CRYSTAL.
IT WILL REGISTER YOUR MANA SIGNATURE.
VOOM...
VOOM...
VOOM...
KINDA FEELS LIKE A FINGER-PRINT SCAN.
NOW YOU JUST NEED TO PICK YOUR CLASS.
CLASS?
VOOM...

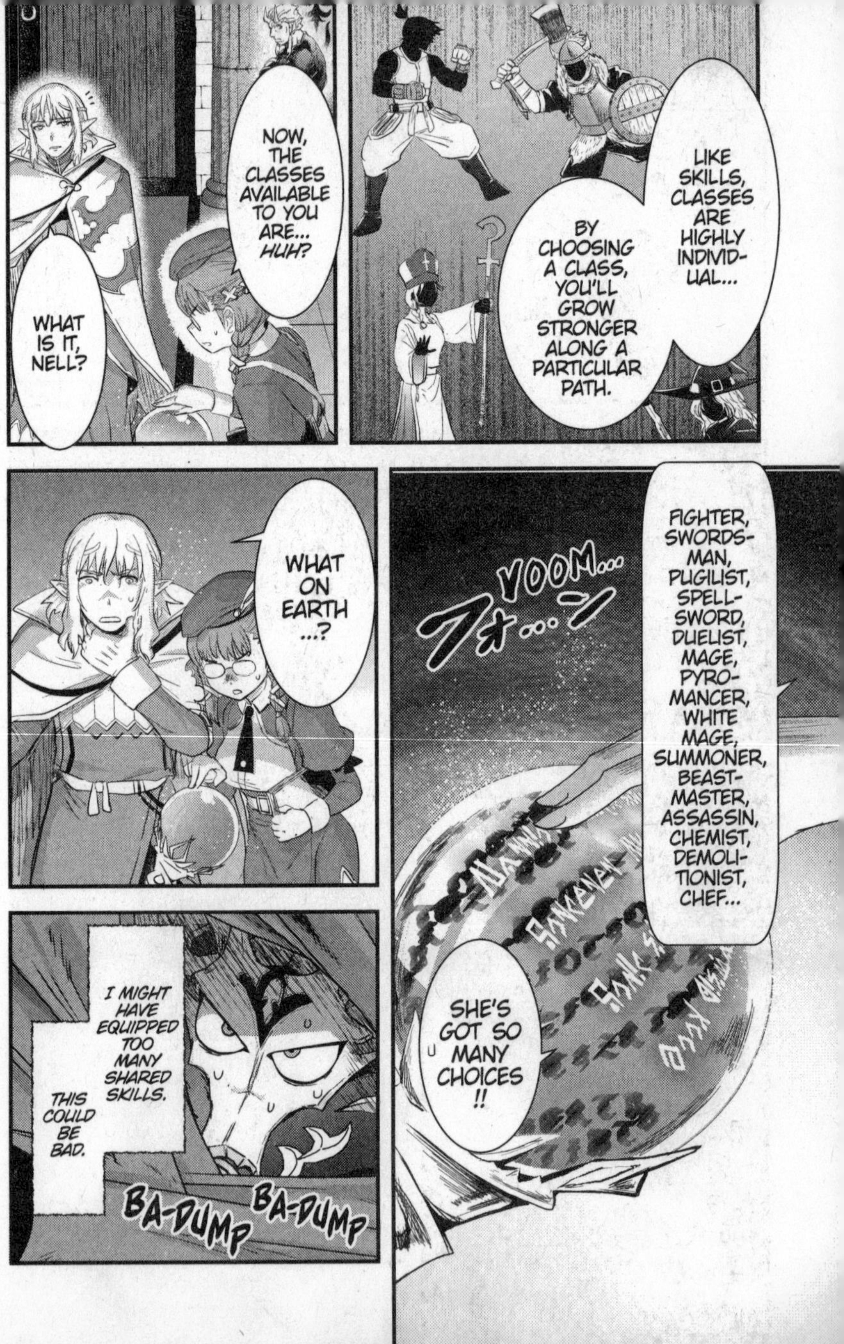
LIKE SKILLS, CLASSES ARE HIGHLY INDIVID-UAL...
BY CHOOSING A CLASS, YOU'LL GROW STRONGER ALONG A PARTICULAR PATH.
NOW, THE CLASSES AVAILABLE TO YOU ARE... HUH?
WHAT IS IT, NELL?
FIGHTER, SWORDS-MAN, PUGILIST, SPELL-SWORD, DUELIST, MAGE, PYRO-MANCER, WHITE MAGE, SUMMONER, BEAST-MASTER, ASSASSIN, CHEMIST, DEMOLI-TIONIST, CHEF...
VOOM...
フォ…ン
SHE'S GOT SO MANY CHOICES !!
WHAT ON EARTH ...?
I MIGHT HAVE EQUIPPED TOO MANY SHARED SKILLS.
THIS COULD BE BAD.
BA-DUMP
BA-DUMP

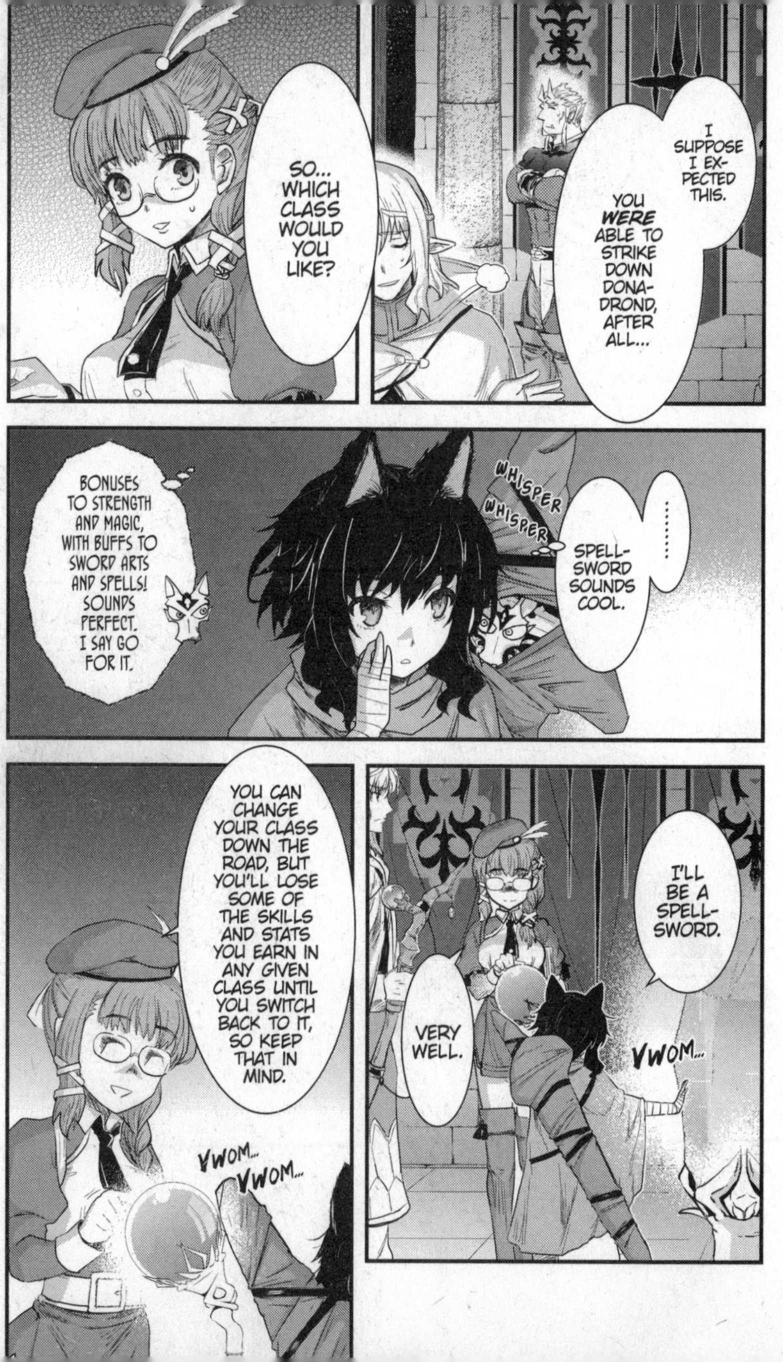
I SUPPOSE I EXPECTED THIS.
YOU WERE ABLE TO STRIKE DOWN DONA-DROND, AFTER ALL...
SO... WHICH CLASS WOULD YOU LIKE?
......
SPELL-SWORD SOUNDS COOL.
WHISPER WHISPER
BONUSES TO STRENGTH AND MAGIC, WITH BUFFS TO SWORD ARTS AND SPELLS! SOUNDS PERFECT. I SAY GO FOR IT.
I'LL BE A SPELL-SWORD.
VWOM...
VERY WELL.
YOU CAN CHANGE YOUR CLASS DOWN THE ROAD, BUT YOU'LL LOSE SOME OF THE SKILLS AND STATS YOU EARN IN ANY GIVEN CLASS UNTIL YOU SWITCH BACK TO IT, SO KEEP THAT IN MIND.
VWOM... VWOM...

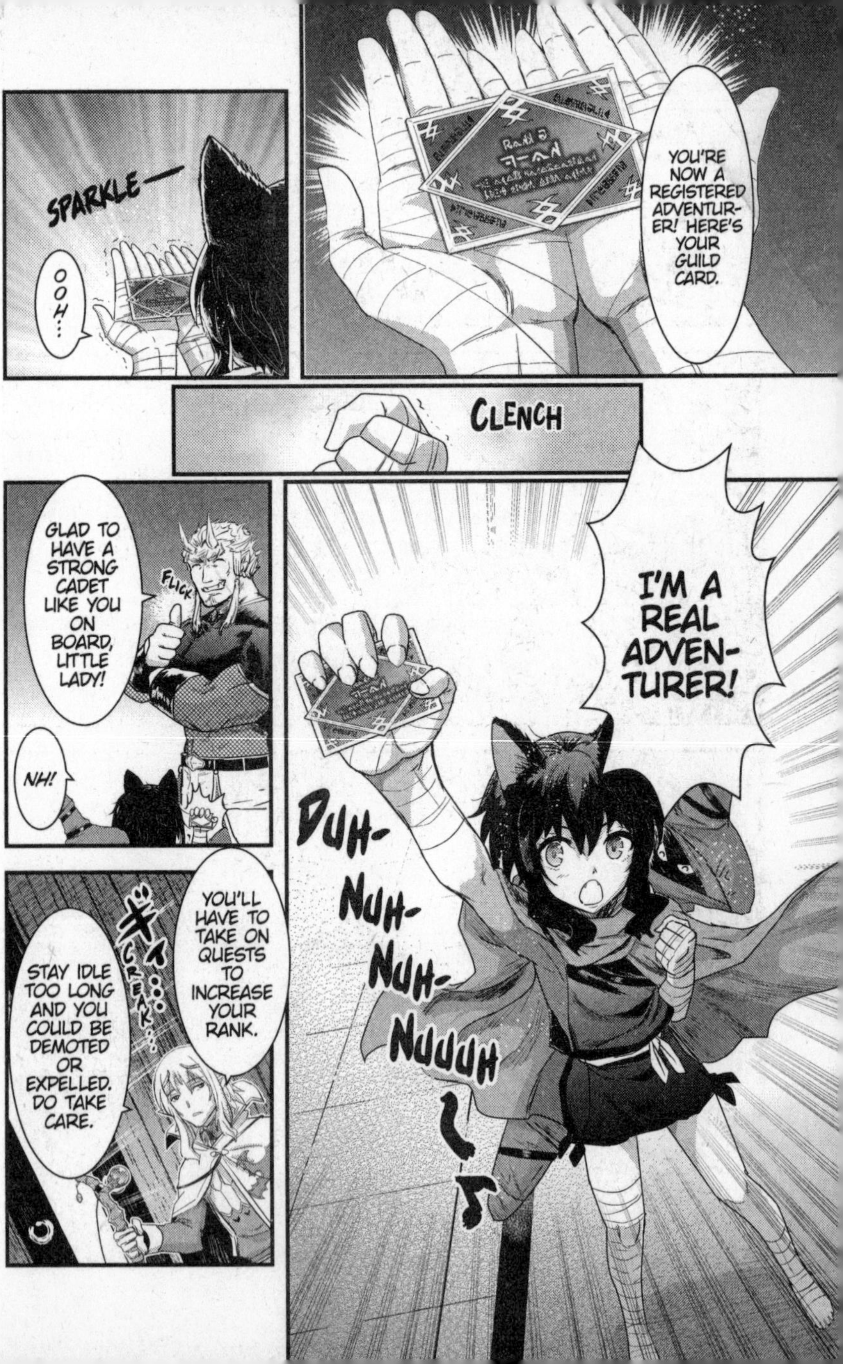
YOU'RE NOW A REGISTERED ADVENTURER! HERE'S YOUR GUILD CARD.
SPARKLE—
OOH...
CLENCH
I'M A REAL ADVENTURER!
DUH-NUH-NUH-NUUUH
GLAD TO HAVE A STRONG CADET LIKE YOU ON BOARD, LITTLE LADY!
FLICK
NH!
YOU'LL HAVE TO TAKE ON QUESTS TO INCREASE YOUR RANK.
STAY IDLE TOO LONG AND YOU COULD BE DEMOTED OR EXPELLED. DO TAKE CARE.
CREAK...

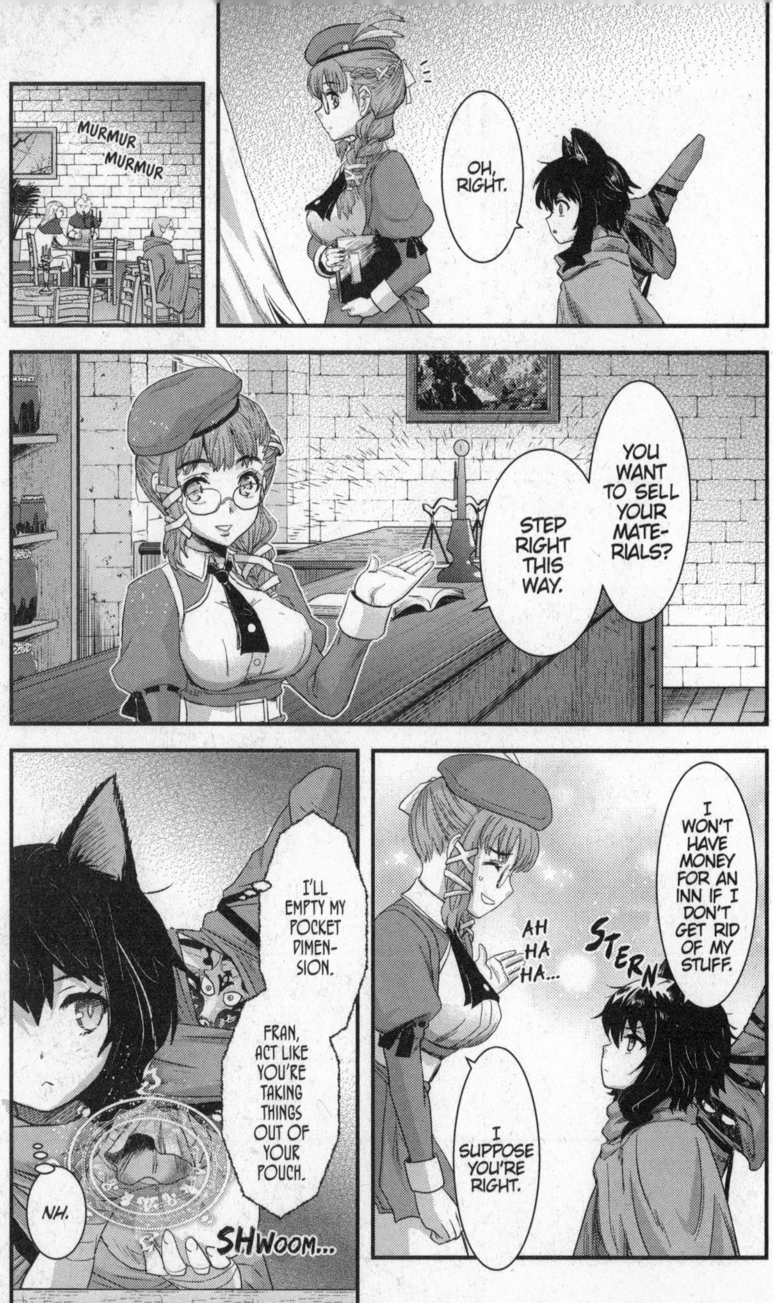
OH, RIGHT.
MURMUR
MURMUR
YOU WANT TO SELL YOUR MATE-RIALS?
STEP RIGHT THIS WAY.
I WON'T HAVE MONEY FOR AN INN IF I DON'T GET RID OF MY STUFF.
STERN
AH HA HA...
I SUPPOSE YOU'RE RIGHT.
I'LL EMPTY MY POCKET DIMEN-SION.
FRAN, ACT LIKE YOU'RE TAKING THINGS OUT OF YOUR POUCH.
NH.
SHWOOM...

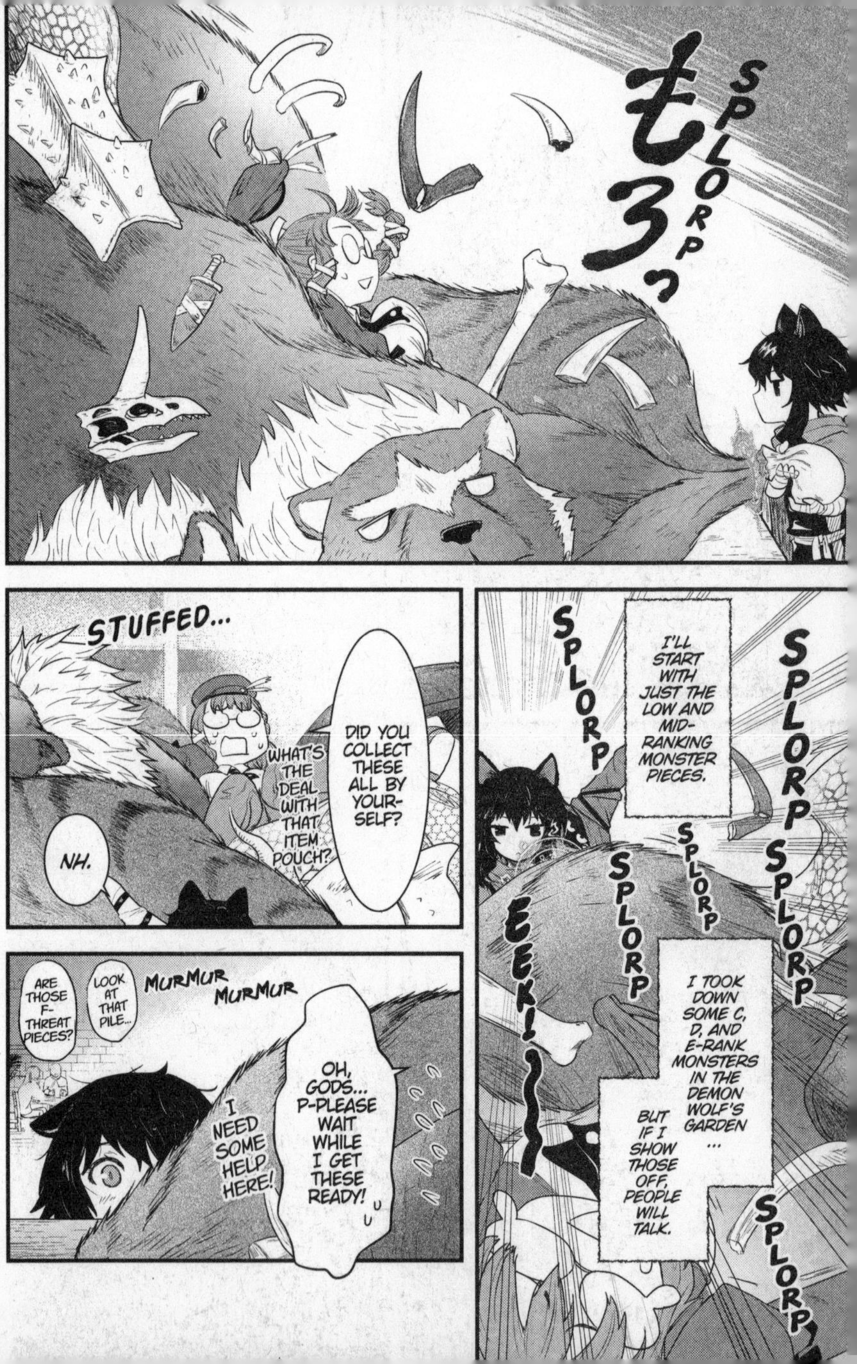

SPLORP
もろっ
SPLORP
I'LL START WITH JUST THE LOW AND MID-RANKING MONSTER PIECES.
SPLORP
SPLORP
SPLORP
SPLORP
EEK!
I TOOK DOWN SOME C, D, AND E-RANK MONSTERS IN THE DEMON WOLF'S GARDEN...
BUT IF I SHOW THOSE OFF, PEOPLE WILL TALK.
SPLORP
DID YOU COLLECT THESE ALL BY YOURSELF?
WHAT'S THE DEAL WITH THAT ITEM POUCH?
STUFFED...
NH.
OH, GODS... P-PLEASE WAIT WHILE I GET THESE READY!
I NEED SOME HELP HERE!
MURMUR MURMUR
LOOK AT THAT PILE...
ARE THOSE F-THREAT PIECES?

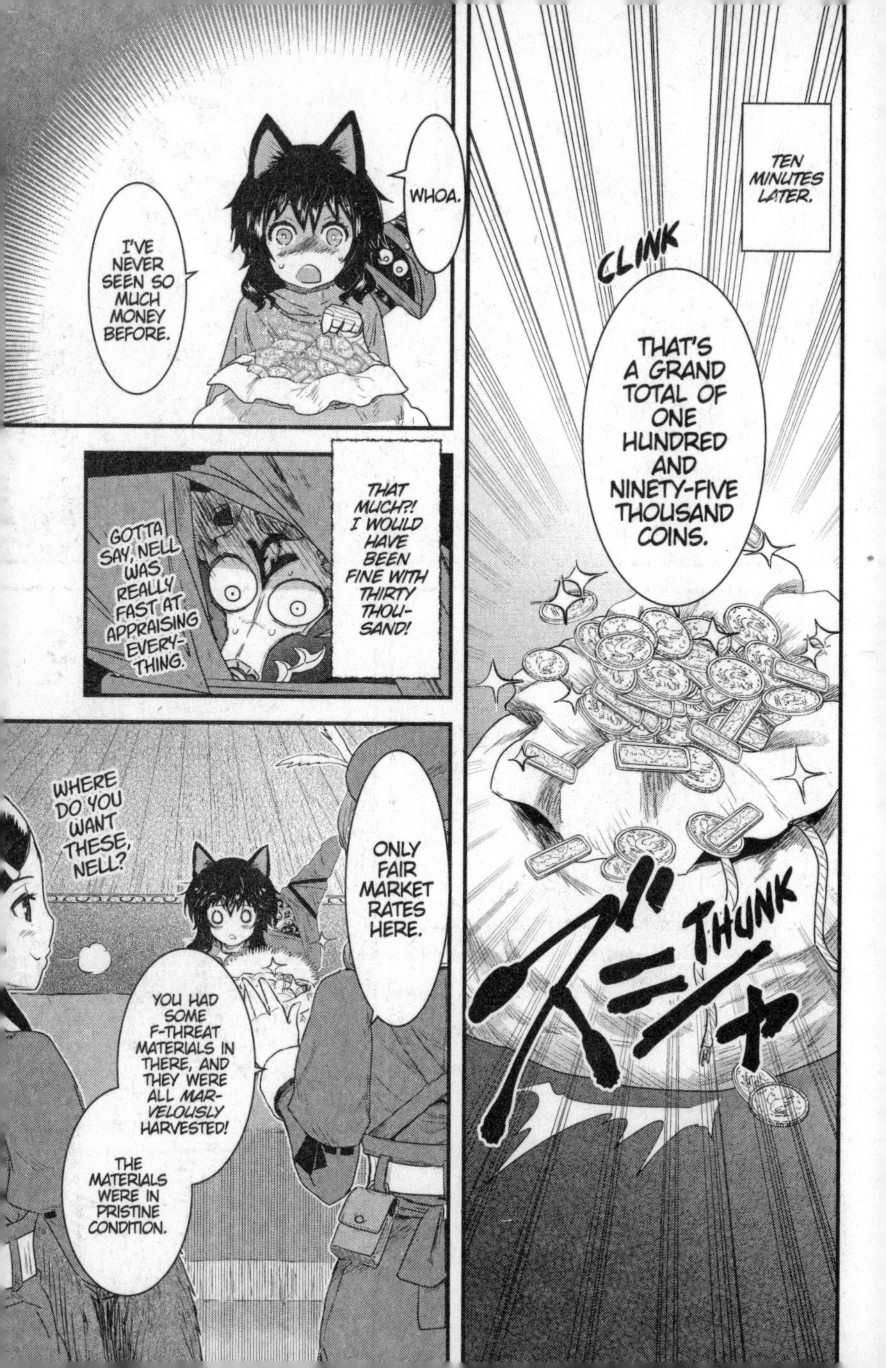
TEN MINUTES LATER.
CLINK
THAT'S A GRAND TOTAL OF ONE HUNDRED AND NINETY-FIVE THOUSAND COINS.
THUNK
WHOA.
I'VE NEVER SEEN SO MUCH MONEY BEFORE.
THAT MUCH?! I WOULD HAVE BEEN FINE WITH THIRTY THOU-SAND!
GOTTA SAY, NELL WAS REALLY FAST AT APPRAISING EVERY-THING.
ONLY FAIR MARKET RATES HERE.
WHERE DO YOU WANT THESE, NELL?
YOU HAD SOME F-THREAT MATERIALS IN THERE, AND THEY WERE ALL *MAR-VELOUSLY* HARVESTED!
THE MATERIALS WERE IN PRISTINE CONDITION.

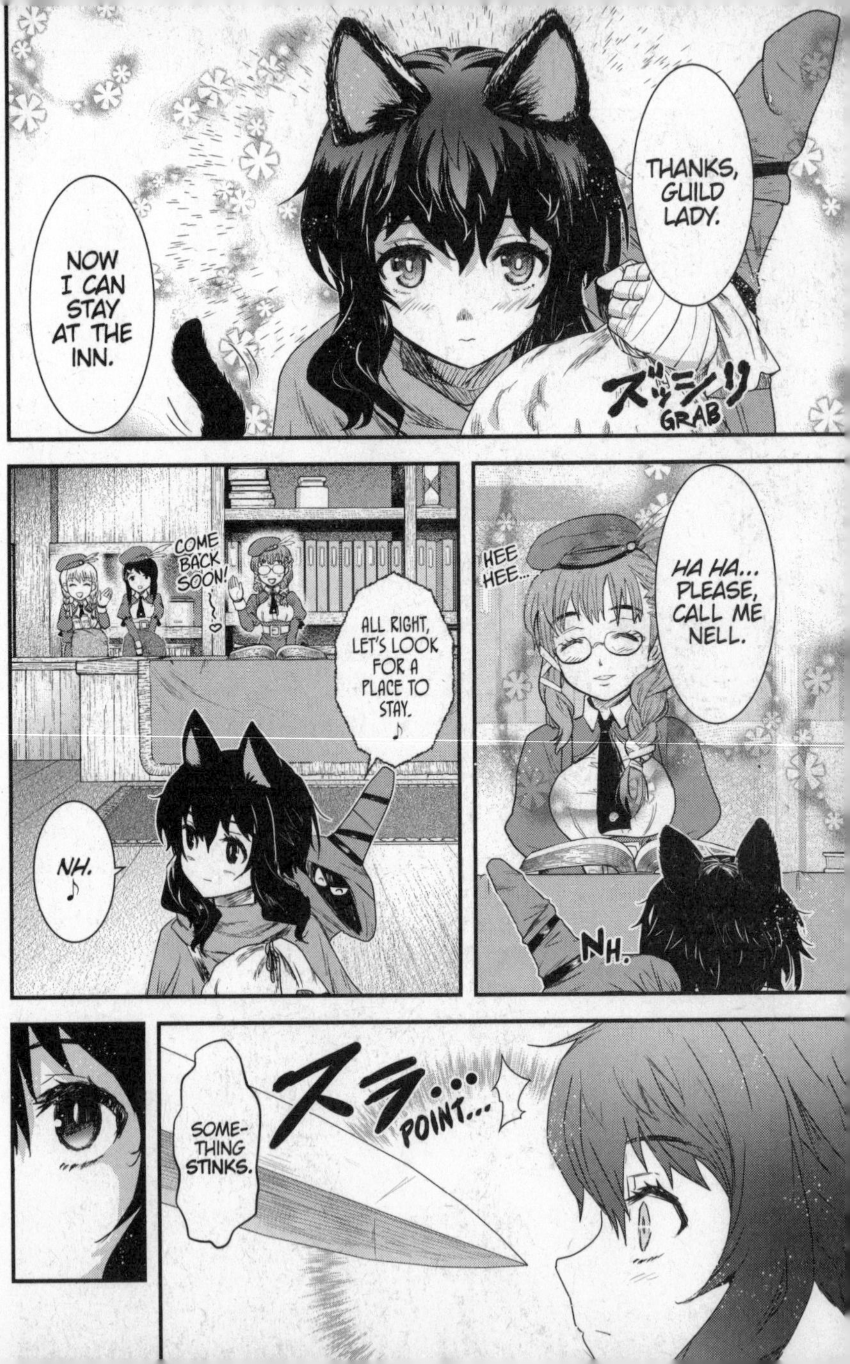
THANKS, GUILD LADY.
NOW I CAN STAY AT THE INN.
ズッシリ
GRAB
HA HA... PLEASE, CALL ME NELL.
HEE HEE...
NH.
COME BACK SOON!
ALL RIGHT, LET'S LOOK FOR A PLACE TO STAY. ♪
NH. ♪
スラ...
POINT...
SOME-THING STINKS.

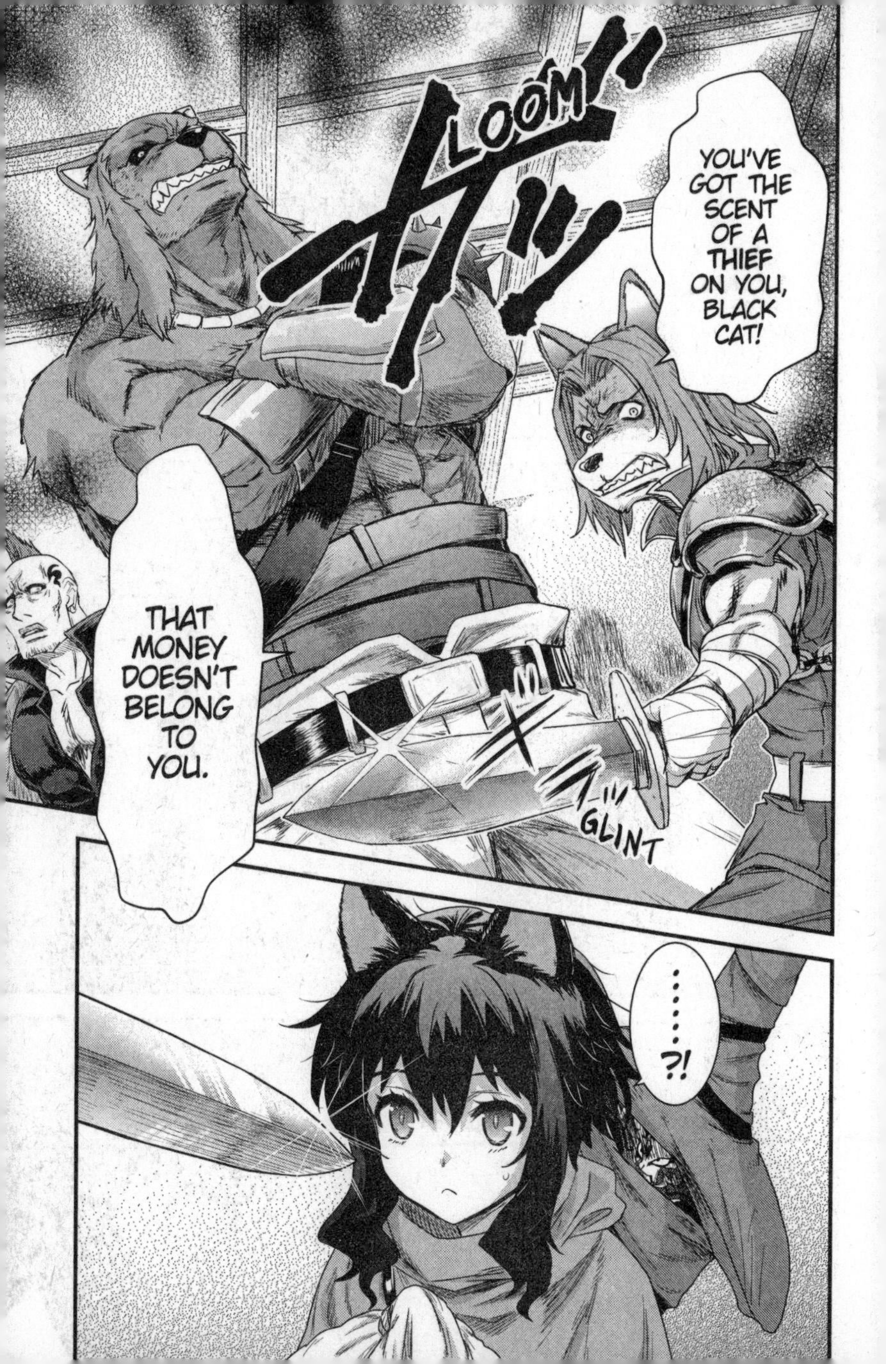
LOOM!!
YOU'VE GOT THE SCENT OF A THIEF ON YOU, BLACK CAT!
THAT MONEY DOESN'T BELONG TO YOU.
GLINT
......?!

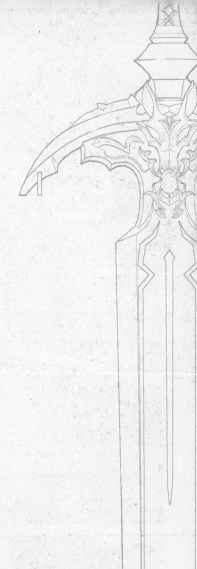

Reincarnated
as a sword

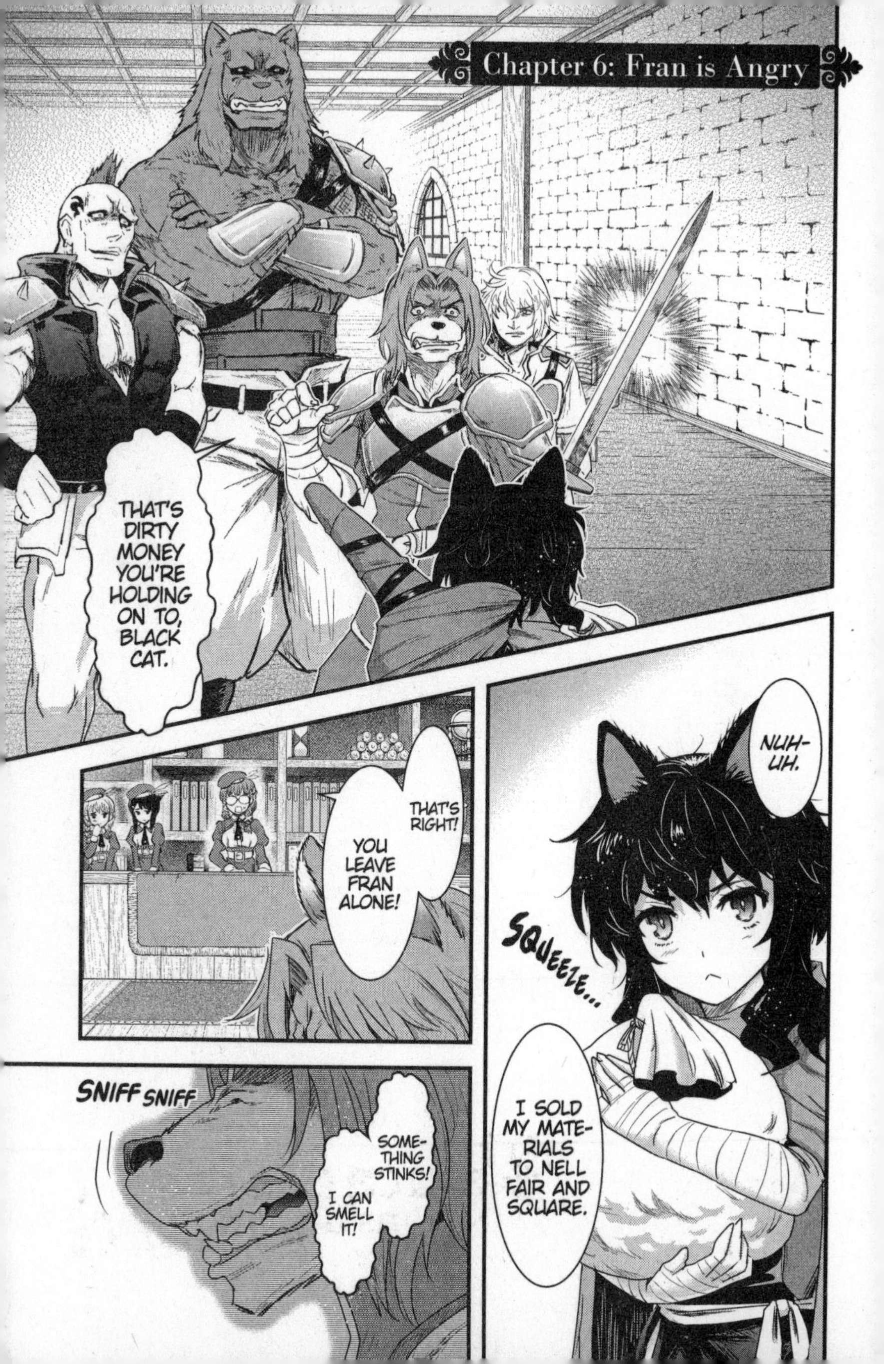
Chapter 6: Fran is Angry
THAT'S DIRTY MONEY YOU'RE HOLDING ON TO, BLACK CAT.
NUH-UH.
SQUEEZE...
I SOLD MY MATERIALS TO NELL FAIR AND SQUARE.
THAT'S RIGHT!
YOU LEAVE FRAN ALONE!
SNIFF SNIFF
SOMETHING STINKS!
I CAN SMELL IT!

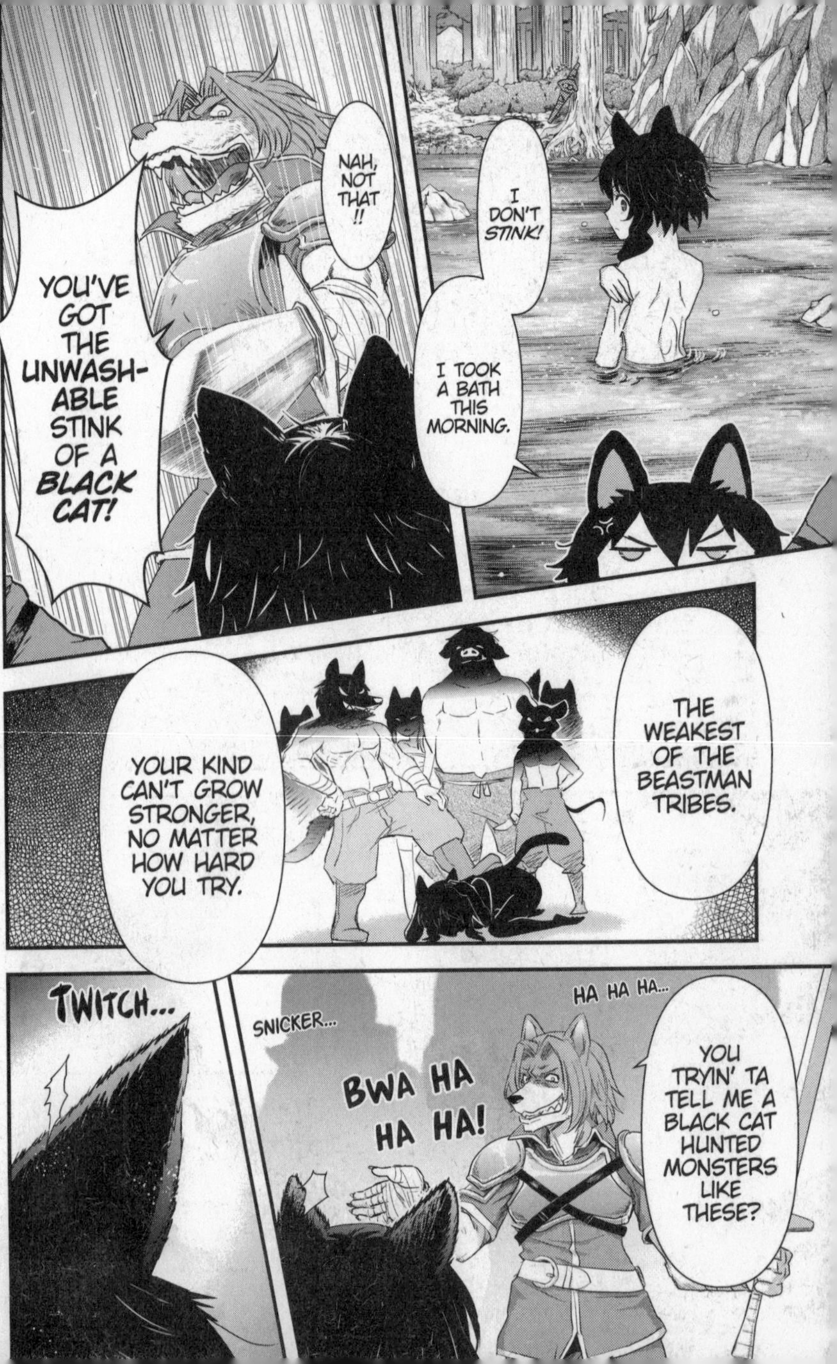
I DON'T STINK!
I TOOK A BATH THIS MORNING.
NAH, NOT THAT!!
YOU'VE GOT THE UNWASH-ABLE STINK OF A BLACK CAT!
THE WEAKEST OF THE BEASTMAN TRIBES.
YOUR KIND CAN'T GROW STRONGER, NO MATTER HOW HARD YOU TRY.
YOU TRYIN' TA TELL ME A BLACK CAT HUNTED MONSTERS LIKE THESE?
HA HA HA...
SNICKER...
BWA HA HA HA!
TWITCH...

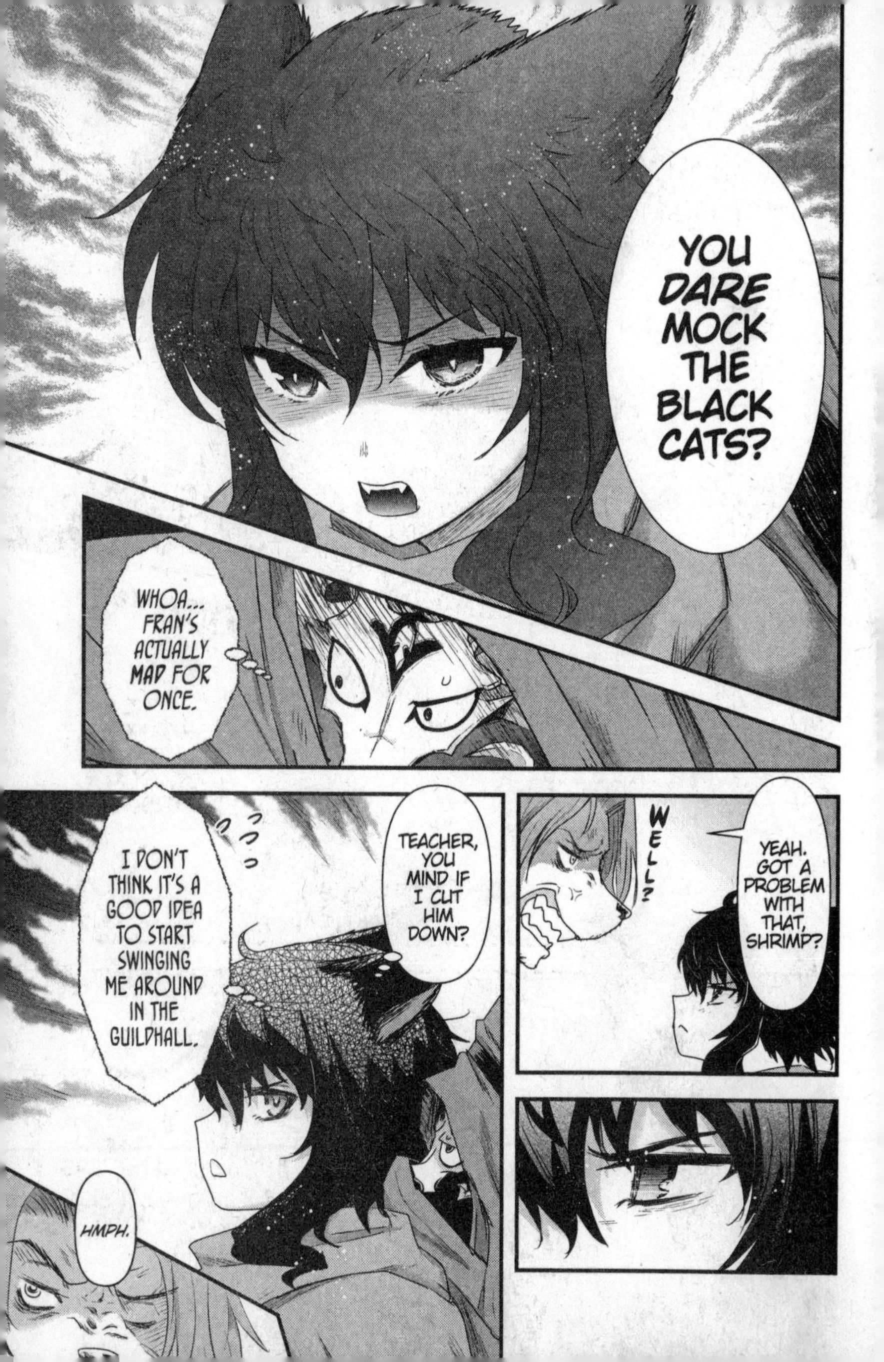
YOU DARE MOCK THE BLACK CATS?
WHOA... FRAN'S ACTUALLY MAD FOR ONCE.
YEAH. GOT A PROBLEM WITH THAT, SHRIMP?
WELL?
TEACHER, YOU MIND IF I CUT HIM DOWN?
I DON'T THINK IT'S A GOOD IDEA TO START SWINGING ME AROUND IN THE GUILDHALL.
HMPH.

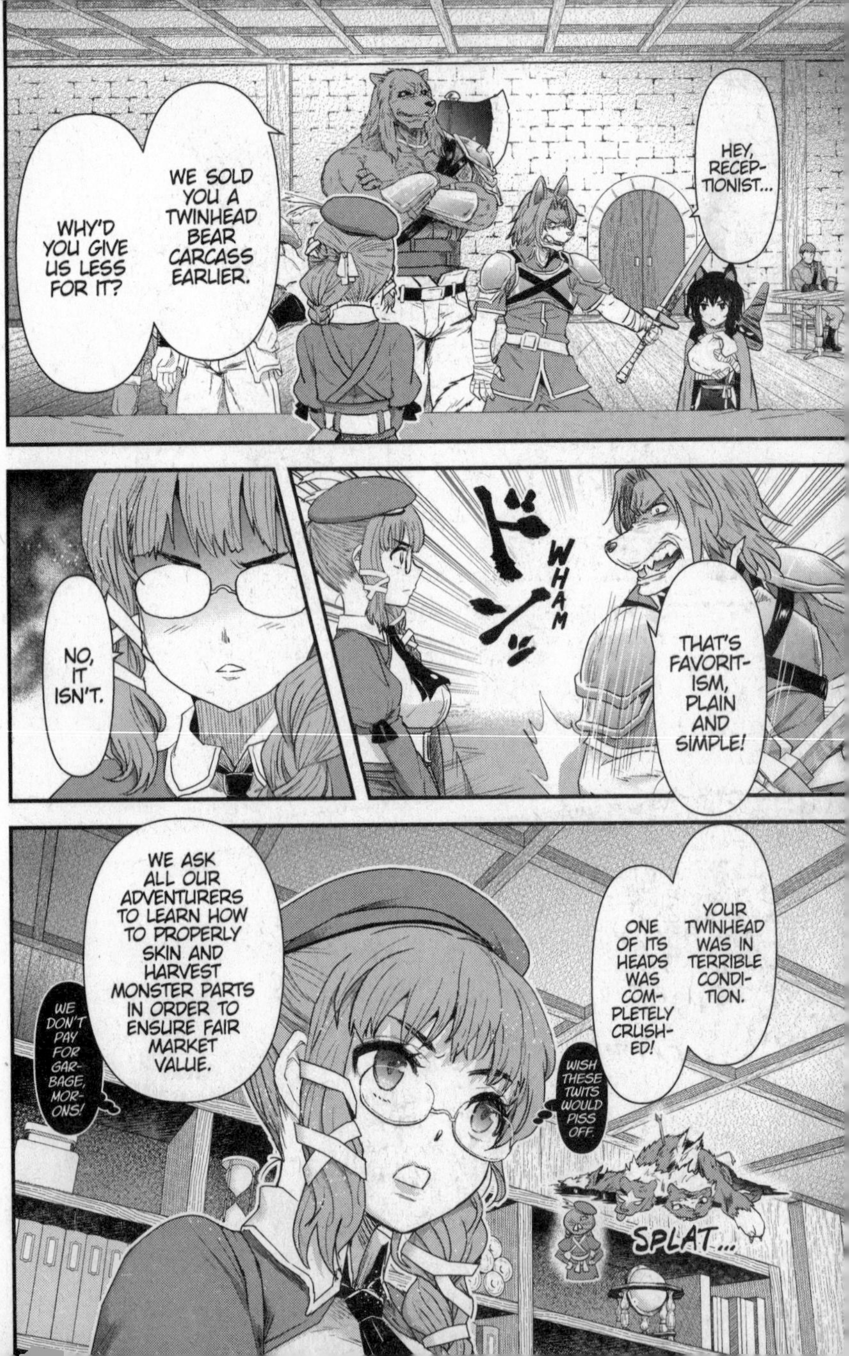
HEY, RECEPTIONIST...
WE SOLD YOU A TWINHEAD BEAR CARCASS EARLIER.
WHY'D YOU GIVE US LESS FOR IT?
ドンッ
WHAM
THAT'S FAVORITISM, PLAIN AND SIMPLE!
NO, IT ISN'T.
YOUR TWINHEAD WAS IN TERRIBLE CONDITION.
ONE OF ITS HEADS WAS COMPLETELY CRUSHED!
SPLAT...
WISH THESE TWITS WOULD PISS OFF.
WE ASK ALL OUR ADVENTURERS TO LEARN HOW TO PROPERLY SKIN AND HARVEST MONSTER PARTS IN ORDER TO ENSURE FAIR MARKET VALUE.
WE DON'T PAY FOR GARBAGE, MORONS!

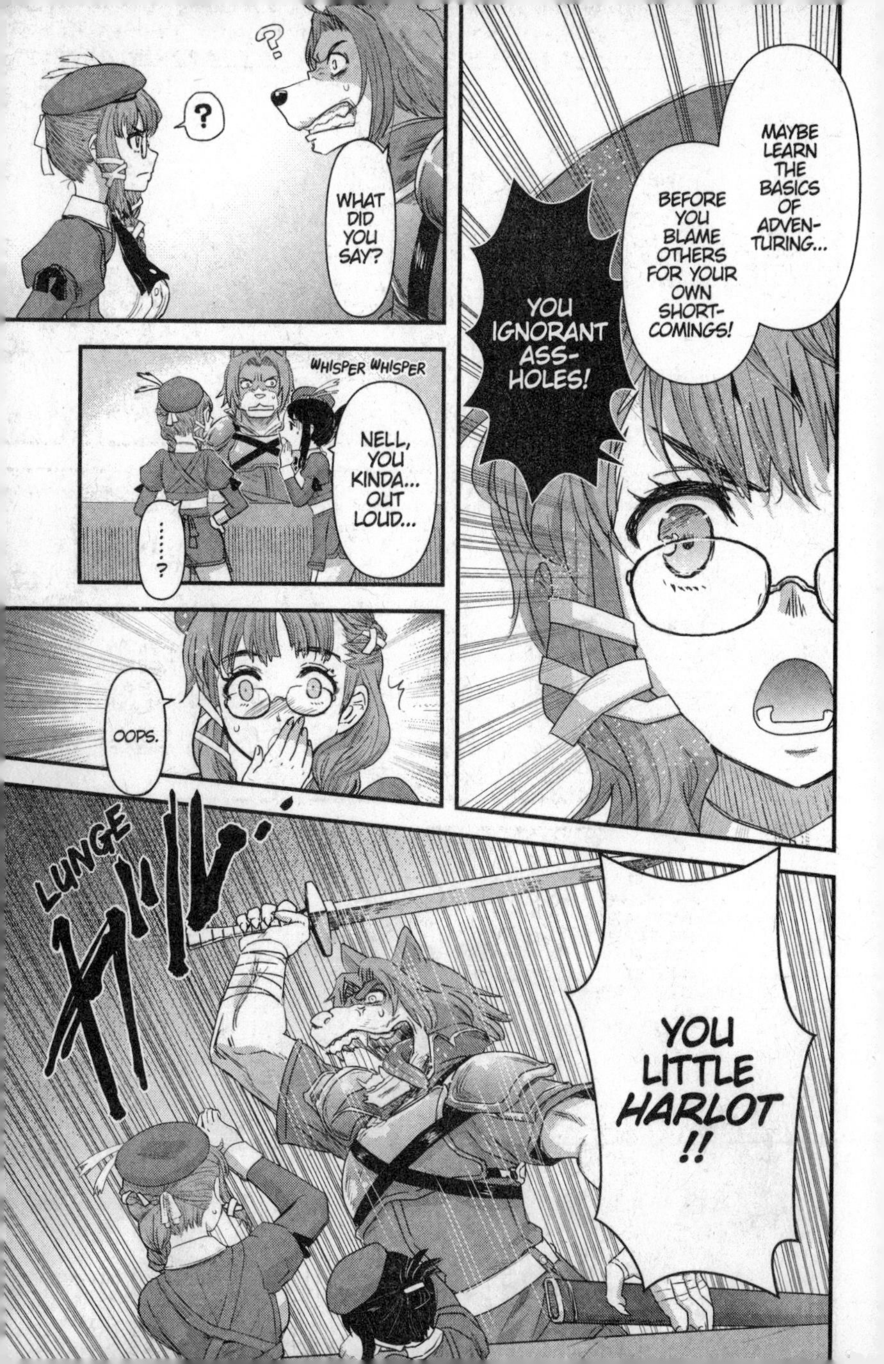
MAYBE LEARN THE BASICS OF ADVENTURING...
BEFORE YOU BLAME OTHERS FOR YOUR OWN SHORTCOMINGS!
YOU IGNORANT ASSHOLES!
?
?
WHAT DID YOU SAY?
WHISPER WHISPER
NELL, YOU KINDA... OUT LOUD...
......?
OOPS.
YOU LITTLE HARLOT!!
LUNGE

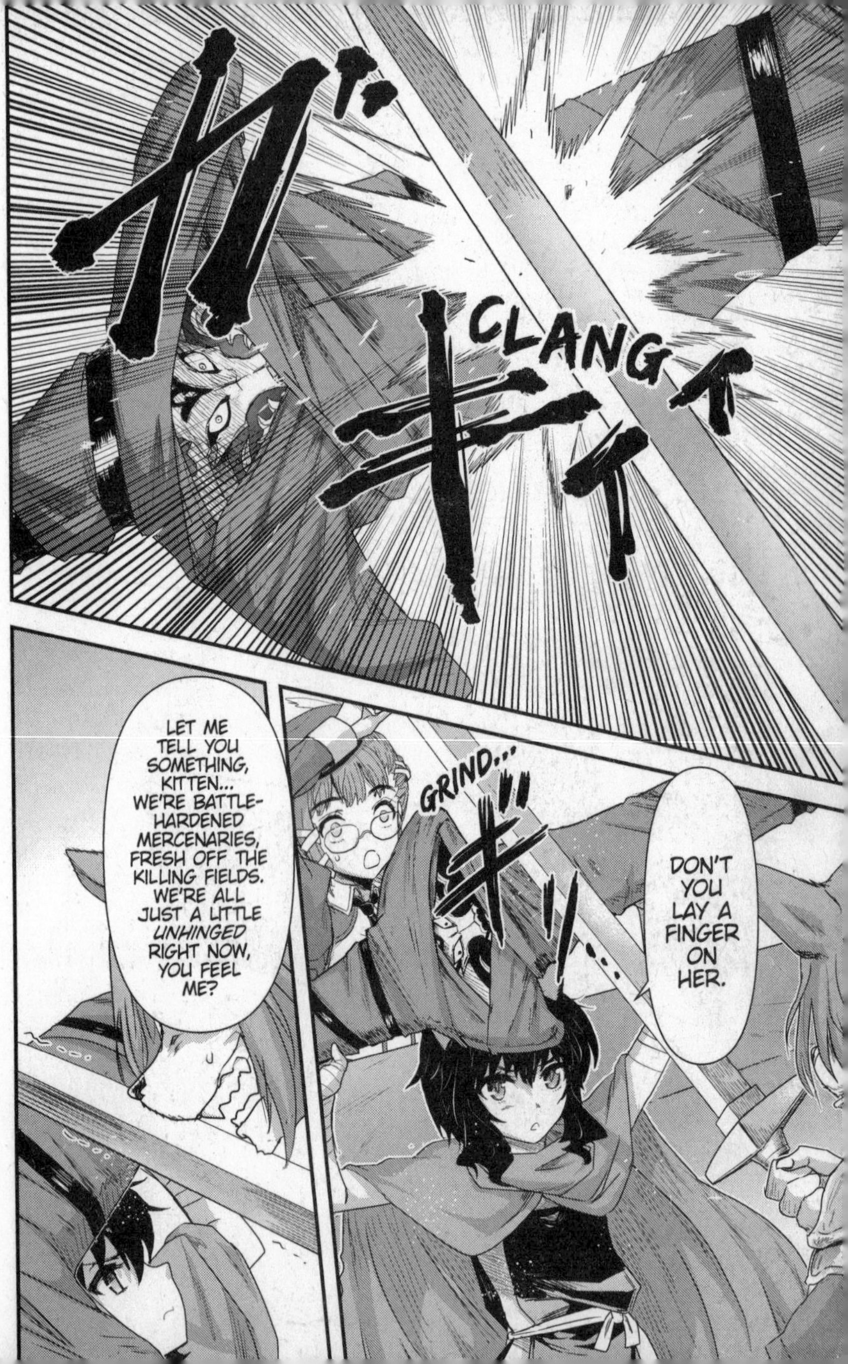
CLANG
GRIND...
DON'T YOU LAY A FINGER ON HER.
LET ME TELL YOU SOMETHING, KITTEN... WE'RE BATTLE-HARDENED MERCENARIES, FRESH OFF THE KILLING FIELDS. WE'RE ALL JUST A LITTLE *UNHINGED* RIGHT NOW, YOU FEEL ME?

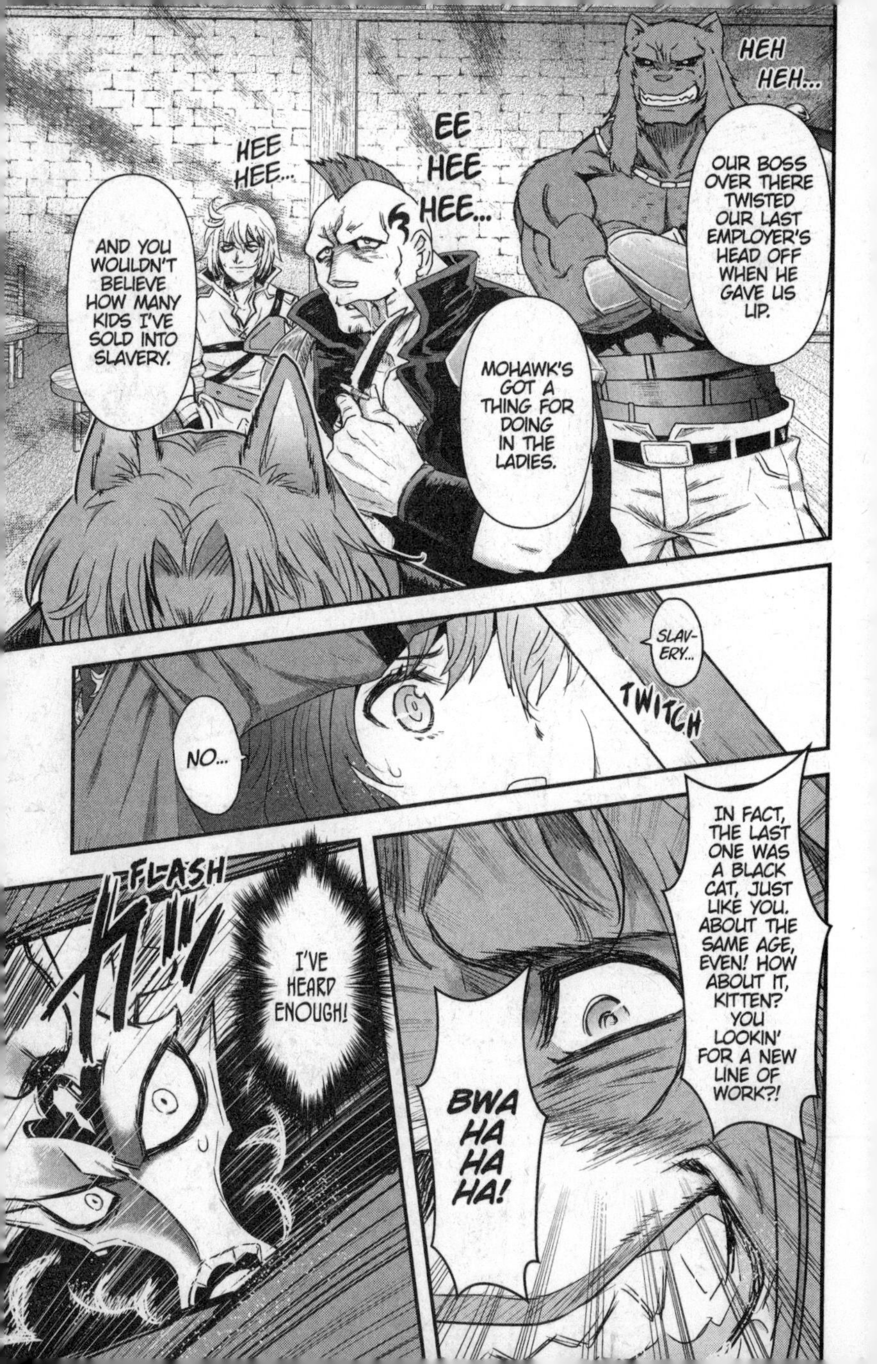

HEH HEH...
OUR BOSS OVER THERE TWISTED OUR LAST EMPLOYER'S HEAD OFF WHEN HE GAVE US LIP.
EE HEE HEE...
MOHAWK'S GOT A THING FOR DOING IN THE LADIES.
HEE HEE...
AND YOU WOULDN'T BELIEVE HOW MANY KIDS I'VE SOLD INTO SLAVERY.
SLAV-ERY...
TWITCH
NO...
IN FACT, THE LAST ONE WAS A BLACK CAT, JUST LIKE YOU. ABOUT THE SAME AGE, EVEN! HOW ABOUT IT, KITTEN? YOU LOOKIN' FOR A NEW LINE OF WORK?!
BWA HA HA HA!
FLASH
I'VE HEARD ENOUGH!

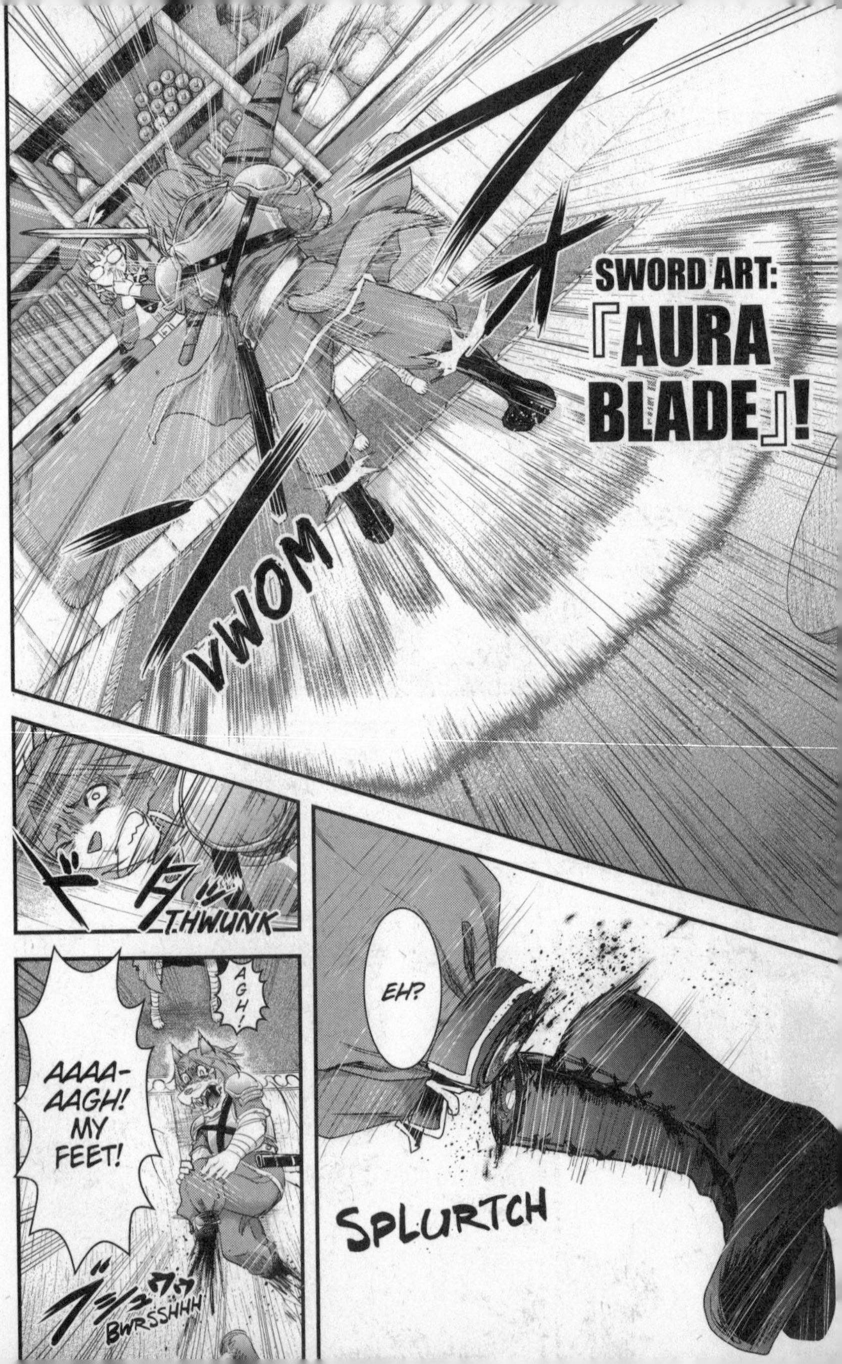
SWORD ART:
『AURA BLADE』!
VWOM
EH?
SPLURTCH
THWUNK
AGH!
AAAA-AAGH! MY FEET!
BWRSSHHH

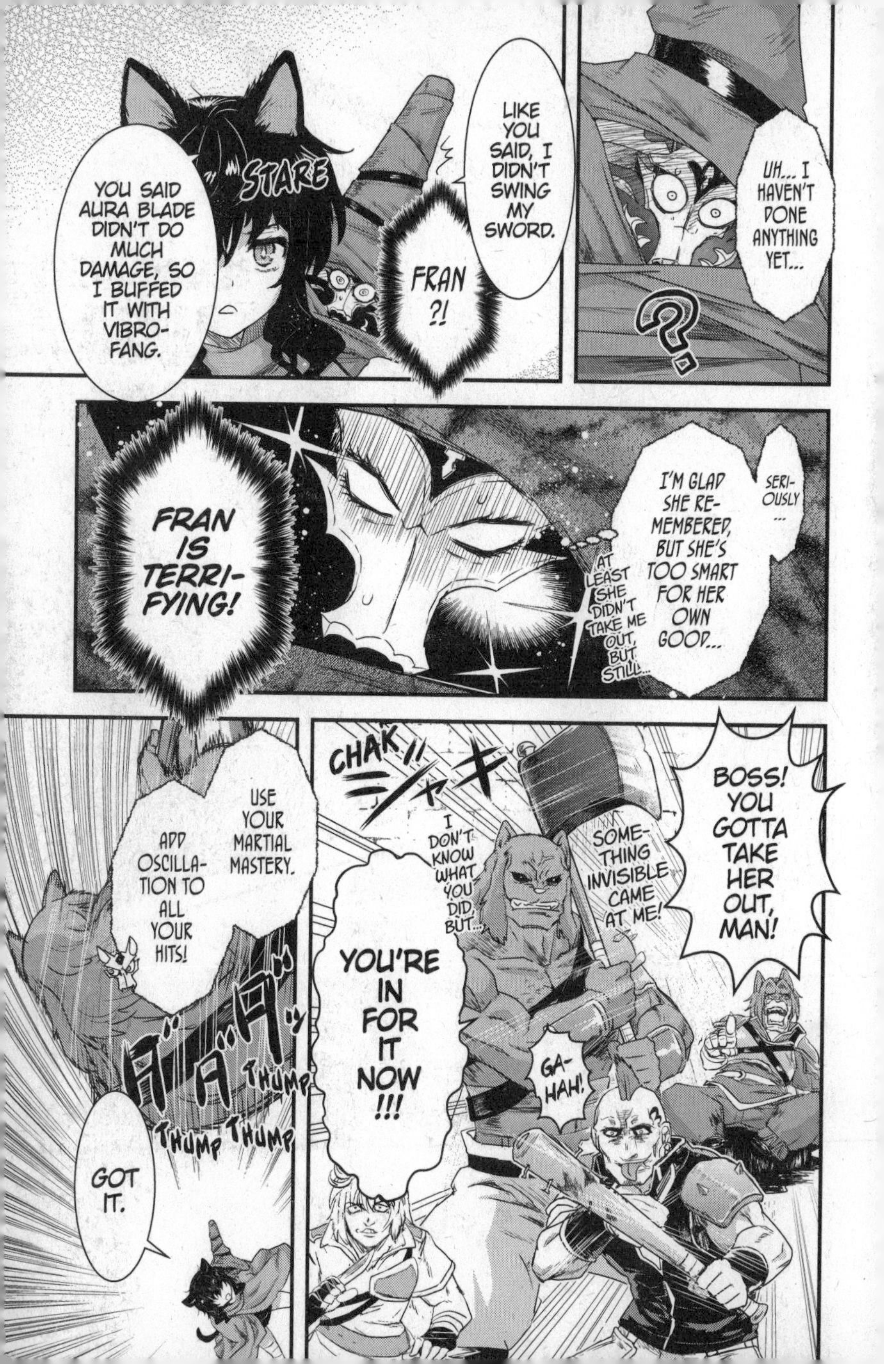
UH... I HAVEN'T DONE ANYTHING YET...
?
LIKE YOU SAID, I DIDN'T SWING MY SWORD.
FRAN ?!
STARE
YOU SAID AURA BLADE DIDN'T DO MUCH DAMAGE, SO I BUFFED IT WITH VIBRO-FANG.
SERI-OUSLY...
I'M GLAD SHE RE-MEMBERED, BUT SHE'S TOO SMART FOR HER OWN GOOD...
AT LEAST SHE DIDN'T TAKE ME OUT, BUT STILL...
FRAN IS TERRI-FYING!
BOSS! YOU GOTTA TAKE HER OUT, MAN!
SOME-THING INVISIBLE CAME AT ME!
CHAK!!
I DON'T KNOW WHAT YOU DID, BUT...
YOU'RE IN FOR IT NOW!!!
GA-HAH!
USE YOUR MARTIAL MASTERY.
ADD OSCILLA-TION TO ALL YOUR HITS!
THUMP
THUMP THUMP
GOT IT.

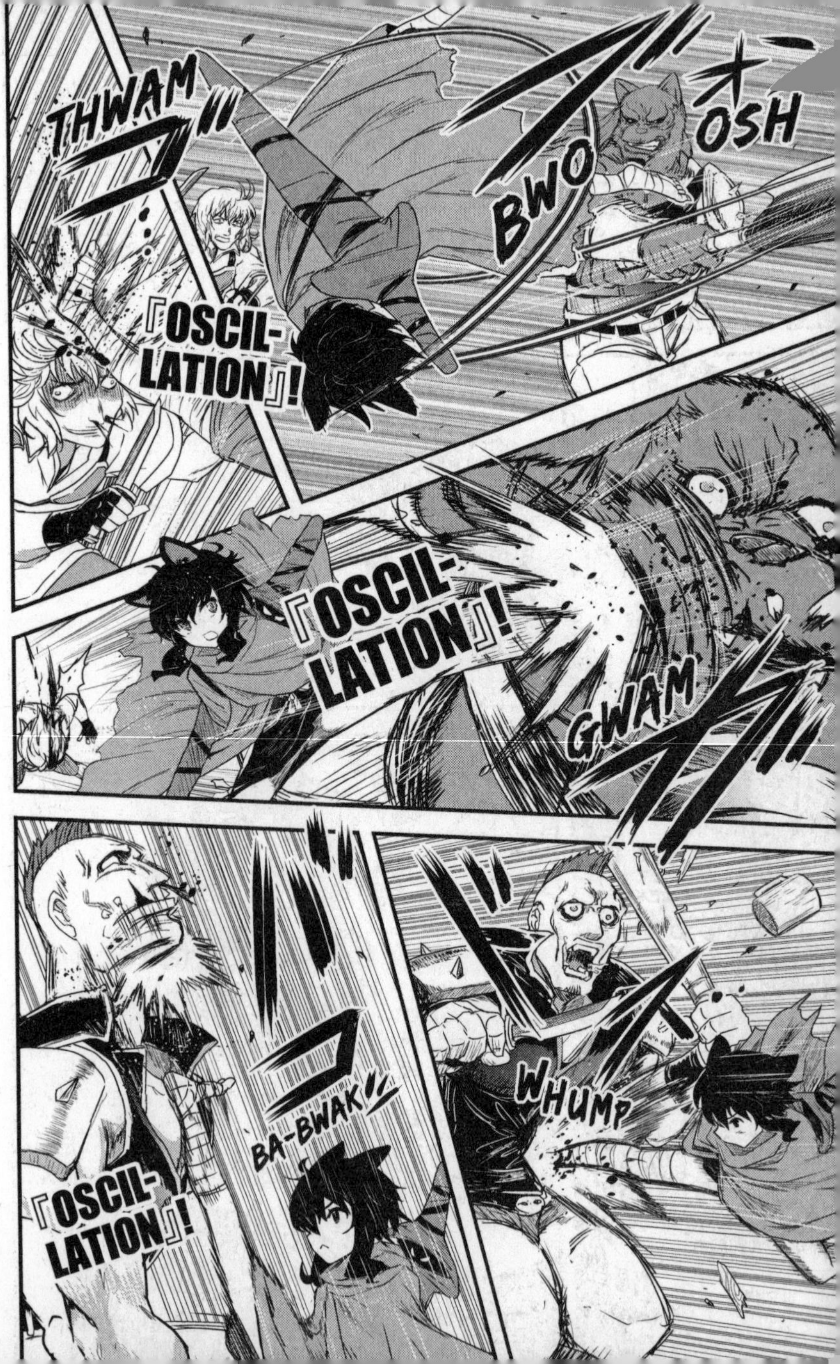

BWOOSH
『OSCIL-LATION』!
THWAM
『OSCIL-LATION』!
GWAM
WHUMP
BA-BWAK!!
『OSCIL-LATION』!

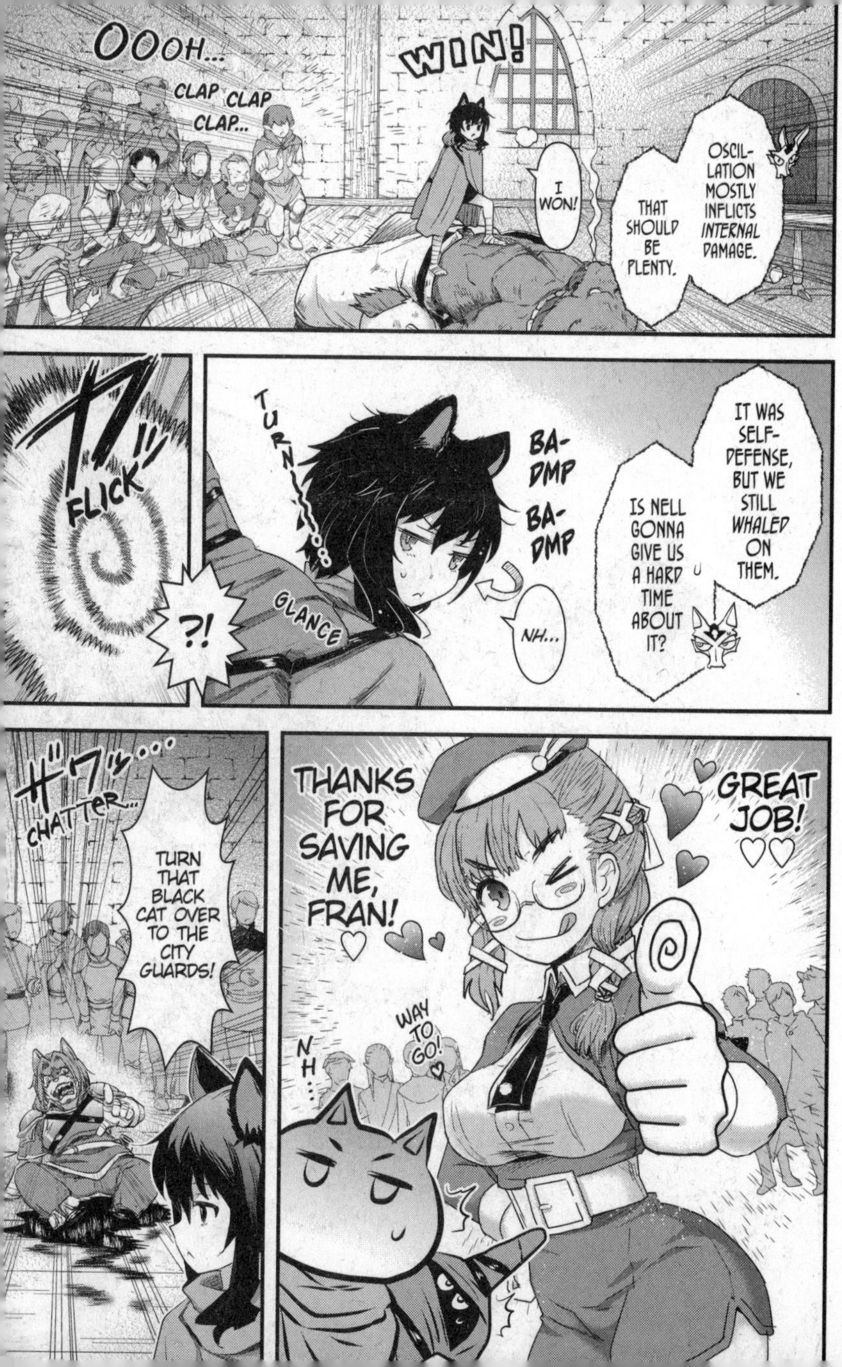
OSCIL-LATION MOSTLY INFLICTS INTERNAL DAMAGE.
THAT SHOULD BE PLENTY.
I WON!
WIN!
CLAP CLAP CLAP...
OOOH...
IT WAS SELF-DEFENSE, BUT WE STILL WHALED ON THEM.
IS NELL GONNA GIVE US A HARD TIME ABOUT IT?
BA-DMP BA-DMP
TURN
NH...
GLANCE
FLICK
?!
GREAT JOB! ♡♡
THANKS FOR SAVING ME, FRAN! ♡
WAY TO GO! ♡
NH...
CHATTER...
TURN THAT BLACK CAT OVER TO THE CITY GUARDS!

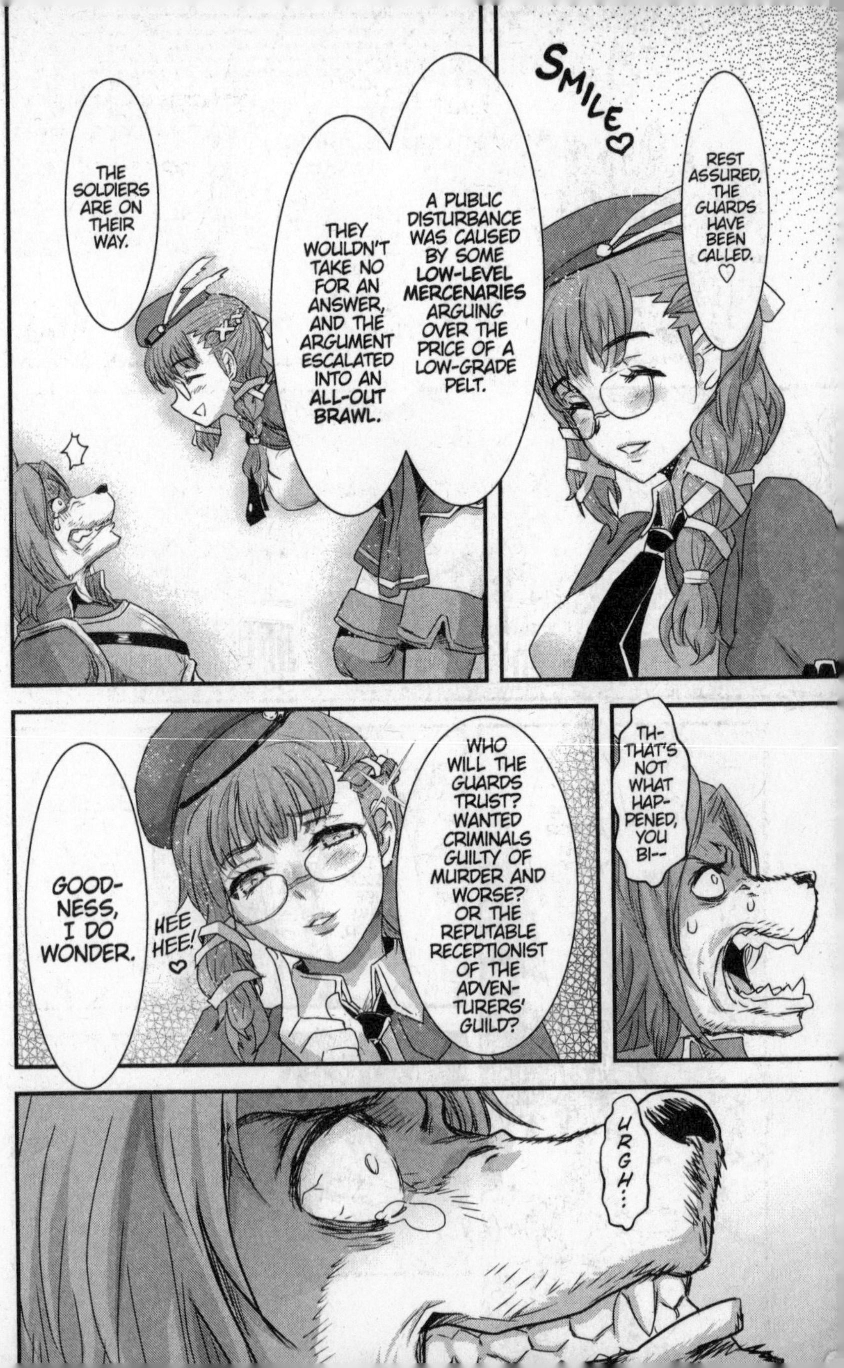
SMILE♡
REST ASSURED, THE GUARDS HAVE BEEN CALLED.♡
A PUBLIC DISTURBANCE WAS CAUSED BY SOME LOW-LEVEL MERCENARIES ARGUING OVER THE PRICE OF A LOW-GRADE PELT.
THEY WOULDN'T TAKE NO FOR AN ANSWER, AND THE ARGUMENT ESCALATED INTO AN ALL-OUT BRAWL.
THE SOLDIERS ARE ON THEIR WAY.
TH-THAT'S NOT WHAT HAP-PENED, YOU BI--
WHO WILL THE GUARDS TRUST? WANTED CRIMINALS GUILTY OF MURDER AND WORSE? OR THE REPUTABLE RECEPTIONIST OF THE ADVEN-TURERS' GUILD?
HEE HEE!♡
GOOD-NESS, I DO WONDER.
URGH...

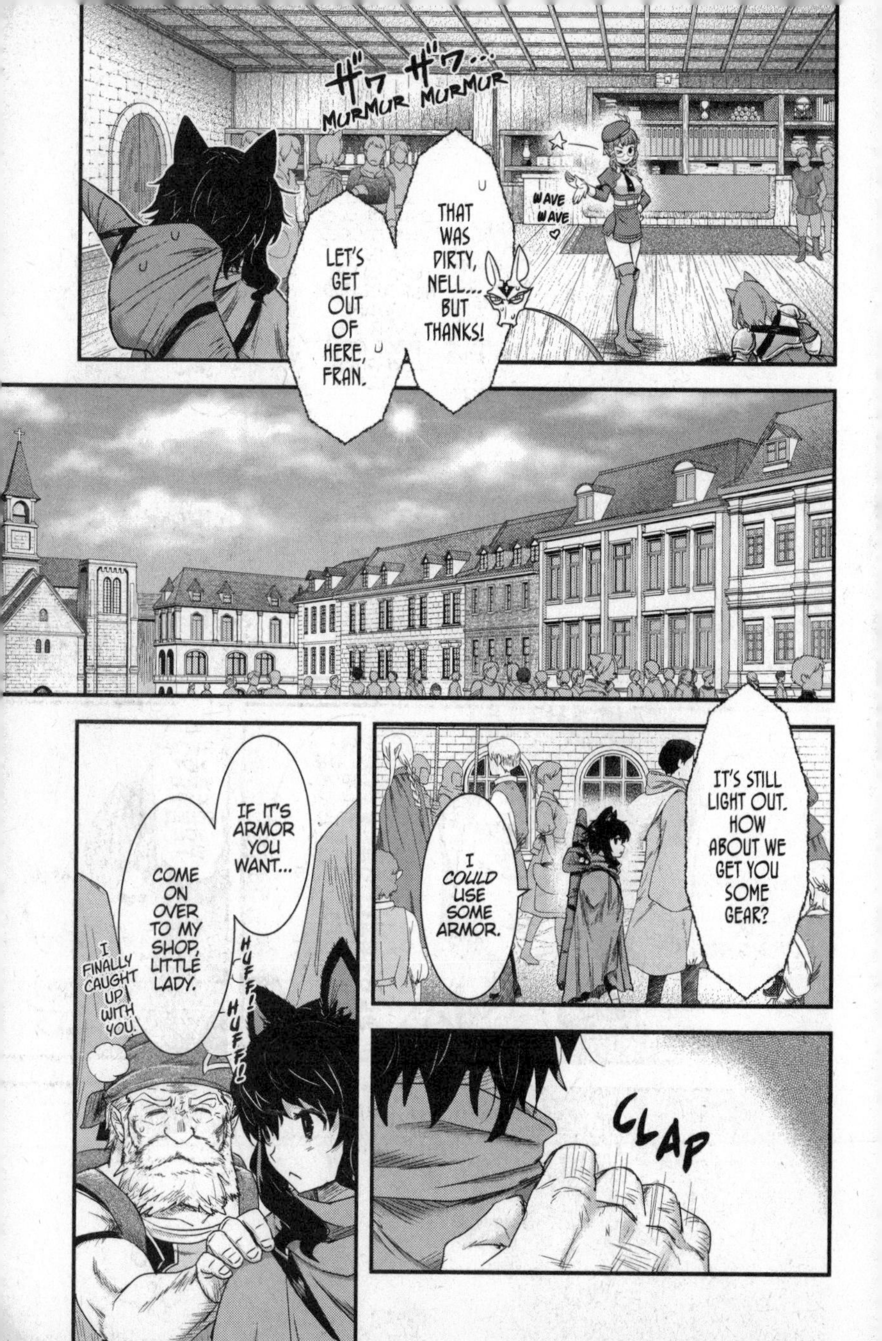
ザワ ザワ…
MURMUR MURMUR
WAVE WAVE
THAT WAS DIRTY, NELL... BUT THANKS!
LET'S GET OUT OF HERE, FRAN.
IT'S STILL LIGHT OUT. HOW ABOUT WE GET YOU SOME GEAR?
I COULD USE SOME ARMOR.
CLAP
IF IT'S ARMOR YOU WANT...
COME ON OVER TO MY SHOP, LITTLE LADY.
HUFF! HUFF!
I FINALLY CAUGHT UP WITH YOU.

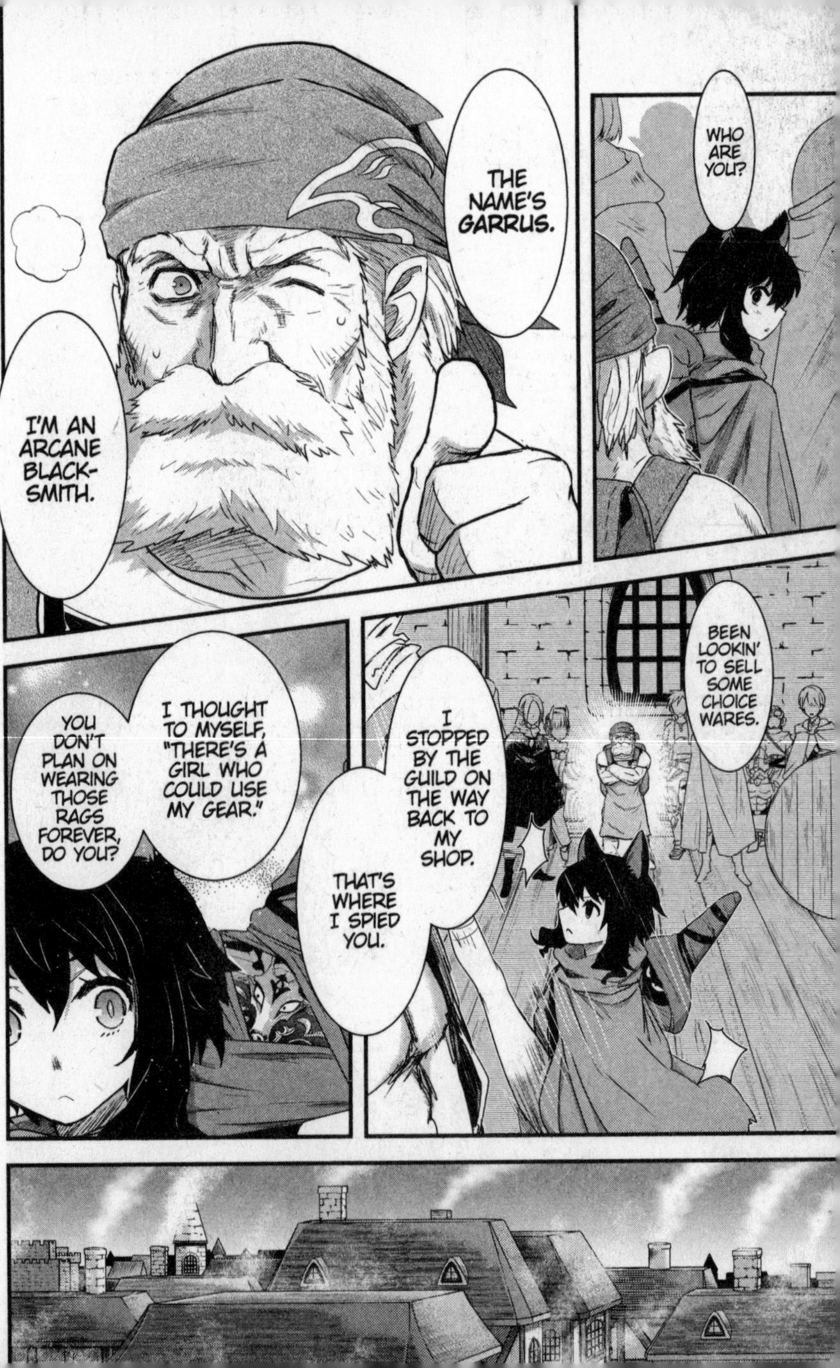
WHO ARE YOU?
THE NAME'S GARRUS.
I'M AN ARCANE BLACK-SMITH.
BEEN LOOKIN' TO SELL SOME CHOICE WARES.
I STOPPED BY THE GUILD ON THE WAY BACK TO MY SHOP.
THAT'S WHERE I SPIED YOU.
I THOUGHT TO MYSELF, "THERE'S A GIRL WHO COULD USE MY GEAR."
YOU DON'T PLAN ON WEARING THOSE RAGS FOREVER, DO YOU?

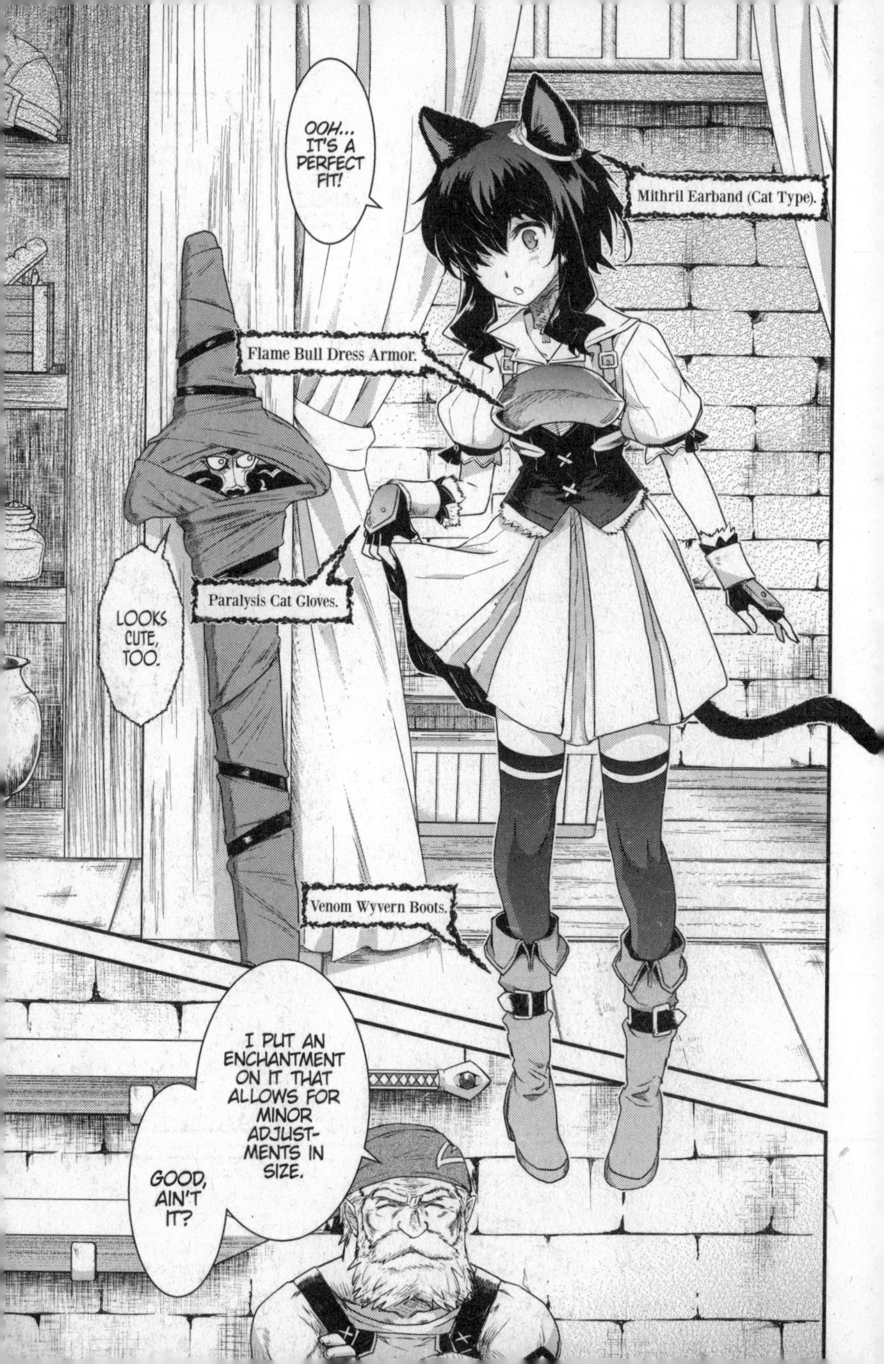
OOH... IT'S A PERFECT FIT!
Mithril Earband (Cat Type).
Flame Bull Dress Armor.
Paralysis Cat Gloves.
LOOKS CUTE, TOO.
Venom Wyvern Boots.
I PUT AN ENCHANTMENT ON IT THAT ALLOWS FOR MINOR ADJUST-MENTS IN SIZE.
GOOD, AIN'T IT?

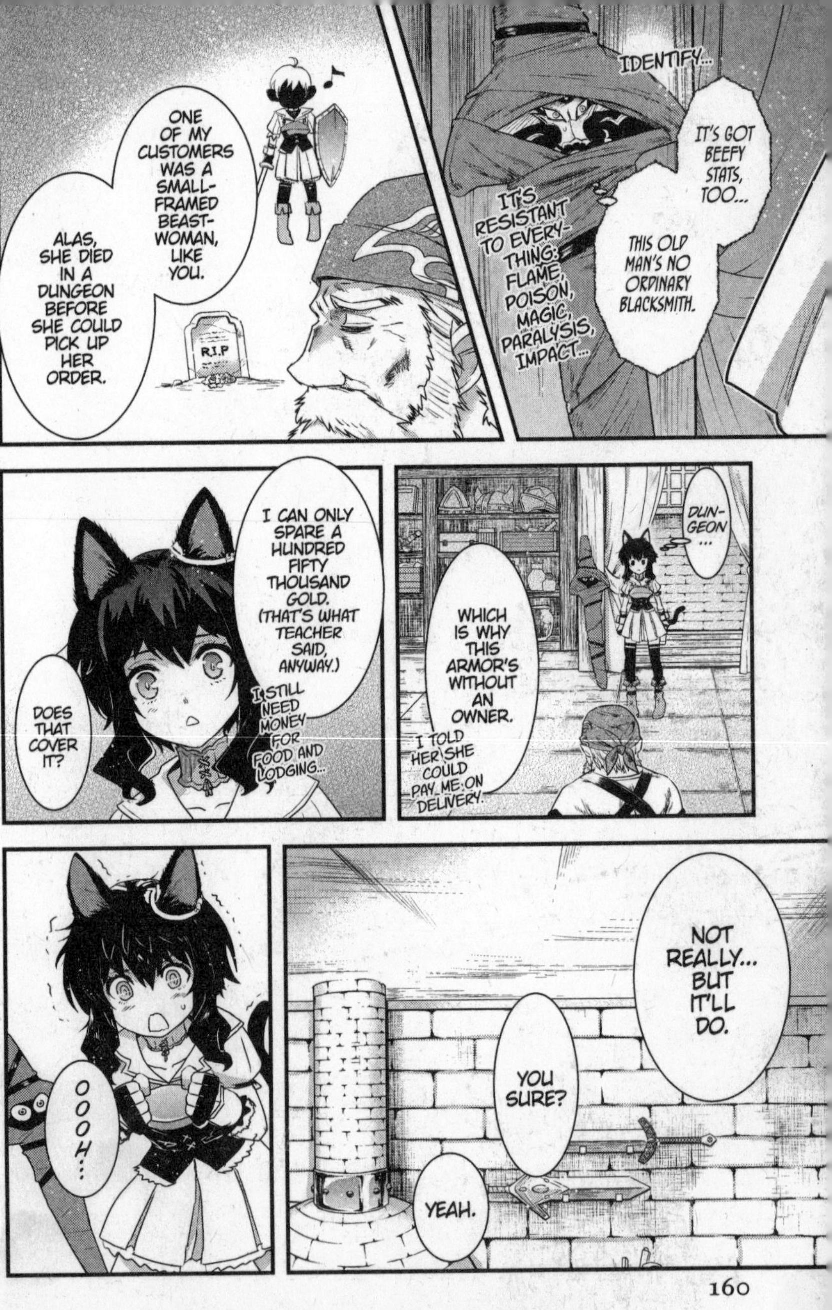
IDENTIFY...
IT'S GOT BEEFY STATS, TOO...
IT'S RESISTANT TO EVERYTHING: FLAME, POISON, MAGIC, PARALYSIS, IMPACT...
THIS OLD MAN'S NO ORDINARY BLACKSMITH.
ONE OF MY CUSTOMERS WAS A SMALL-FRAMED BEAST-WOMAN, LIKE YOU.
ALAS, SHE DIED IN A DUNGEON BEFORE SHE COULD PICK UP HER ORDER.
R.I.P
DUN-GEON...
WHICH IS WHY THIS ARMOR'S WITHOUT AN OWNER.
I TOLD HER SHE COULD PAY ME ON DELIVERY.
I CAN ONLY SPARE A HUNDRED FIFTY THOUSAND GOLD. (THAT'S WHAT TEACHER SAID, ANYWAY.)
I STILL NEED MONEY FOR FOOD AND LODGING...
DOES THAT COVER IT?
NOT REALLY... BUT IT'LL DO.
YOU SURE?
YEAH.
OOOH...

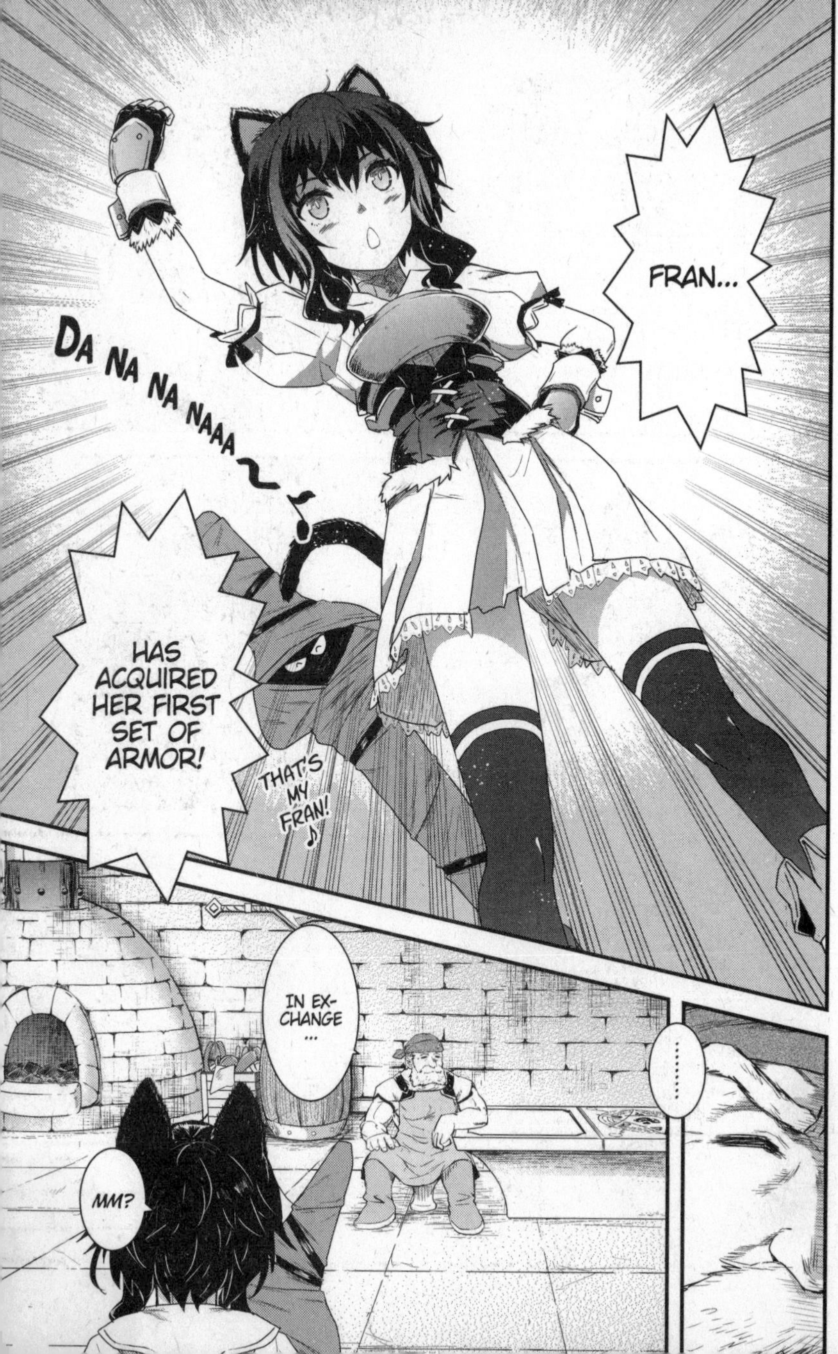
FRAN...
DA NA NA NAAAA ~♪
HAS ACQUIRED HER FIRST SET OF ARMOR!
THAT'S MY FRAN! ♪
......
IN EX-CHANGE ...
MM?

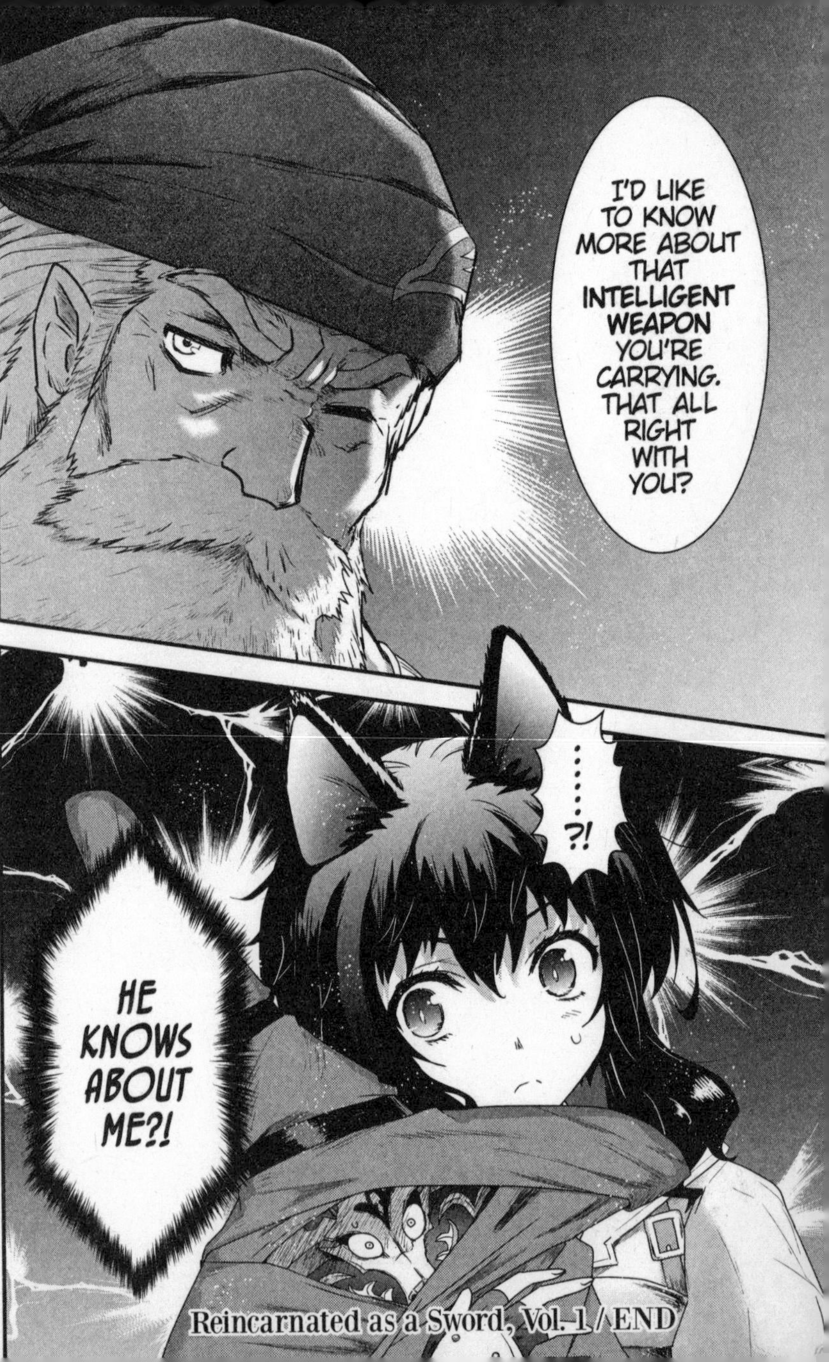
I'D LIKE TO KNOW MORE ABOUT THAT INTELLIGENT WEAPON YOU'RE CARRYING. THAT ALL RIGHT WITH YOU?
......?!
HE KNOWS ABOUT ME?!
Reincarnated as a Sword, Vol. 1 / END

Reincarnated
as a sword

Reincarnated as a sword

Reincarnated as a Sword
Bonus Story
Fran and Pancakes

"These?"

That's right. You wanted the ultimate pancake? Well today, we're adding fruit!

"Oooh, luxurious!"

You said it. Oh, get these, too, while you're at it.

The next thirty minutes were spent shopping. With the ingredients we'd already stowed away in my Pocket Dimension, it was shaping up to be the greatest plate of pancakes I'd make yet.

Upon returning to the inn, I got down to cooking.

Just relax while I get the pancakes ready.

Fran dove into the bed. I pulled a portable stove out of the Pocket Dimension, set it next to the bedside table, and organized my ingredients. Once everything I wanted was within reach of Telekinesis, I started making the pancake batter. I combined flour and sugar into a bowl and mixed it together with monster milk and eggs.

We'll start with a traditional batter.

I lit the stove with a fire spell and poured oil into the frying pan. Once it was up to temperature, I poured the batter into it. Now, flipping pancakes could easily ruin them, but I didn't have to worry about that—not since I'd learned how to move things with my mind. Even if I messed up the flip, I could always save the pancakes by catching and adjusting them mid-air. I'd even used Telekinesis to whisk the batter earlier. It really was the world's greatest skill.

I continued cooking the pancakes while adjusting the temperature. Soon, I had a batch of Fran's favorite regular pancakes. I stacked four of them on top of each other, sliced a square of butter on top, and drizzled them with honey.

I may have outdone myself. This looks absolutely scrumptious.

The stack of pancakes in front of me looked good enough to be the promo shot for an instant batter.

Fran, order u—

"Mm."

Fran was at the table before I could finish my dinner call. I wondered how much her points in Agility contributed to her everyday speed. She was all set and ready, knife in one hand, fork in the other—the picture of a gourmand.

W-well, then. Here's the usual plain pancake.

"Oooh, looks good!"

The stack of pancakes looked perfectly ordinary, but I'd used different ingredients today. I'd used bird monster eggs, monster milk, and even the honey had been harvested from a life-threatening hive of monster bees. Monster ingredients were a luxury, but they were no gimmick. The food made with them actually tasted better. I couldn't confirm this by myself, obviously, but Fran always seemed to enjoy monster meat better than regular beef.

"I'll dig right in."

Eat up.

Munch.

How is it?

Munch, munch, munch!

Fran frantically stuffed her cheeks with pancakes while continuously nodding in approval. All it took was the gleam in her eyes to tell me how much she loved it.

Crap, I have to get started on the next batch.

Another pancake disappeared into Fran's gullet. I got to work, pronto.

The toppings would be the star of this next stack. I whipped up a good amount of cream and poured caramel all over it. Sweet amber oozed down the stiff white peaks, making for a delicious display. Then I remembered the old tradition of topping it all off with a layer of chopped nuts. My pancakes could now stack up against the most popular pancake shops back on Earth!

Next we have the Caramel Whipped Cream with Peanuts Special. My finest work yet!

"Whoooa! It looks amazing!"

Oh, I loved it when Fran's eyes sparkled.

"Can I really have this?"

Of course! I made it for you, after all. I don't see anyone else who could eat it.

"Mm! Thanks."

Fran wasted no time scooping a spoonful of cream. Her eyes lit up even brighter than before, and she began consuming her pancakes at an even faster pace. This stack would soon join the previous one in Fran's stomach. I had to get cooking again, fast!

Next, I made fruit pancakes. I cut up some grapelike fruits, figlike fruits, and applelike fruits and mixed them in bowl. Although similar in appearance, the fruits of this world had different flavors than those on Earth. The grapes tasted like strawberries, the figs like pears, and the apples like grapes. At least, that's what my Cooking skill told me. I don't have a tongue, so I just had to trust it! I cooked up the fruit pancakes and added a layer of custard over them before topping it all off with more fruit. It looked more like a tart than a stack of pancakes.

Here.

"Mm!"

There was no need for words. I set the plate of pancakes in front of Fran and she immediately began eating. Her eyes glowed now, shining with the light of a living star. It was true what they said about the eyes being a window to the soul.

Her earlier munching had been replaced with scarfing.

I continued cooking her pancakes—some flavored with freshly brewed tea, some with more of that monster honey. Fran gobbled it all down as if it were her first meal of the day. We weren't finished yet, though. Oh no. I saved the best for last, Fran!

Feast your eyes on this!

"What…? Whoooaaaaa! That's so awesome. Teacher, you really are the best!"

I couldn't bake a celebratory cake, so I'd dressed a pancake up as one. I thought of Marie Antoinette as I stacked four pancakes high on top of one other and slathered them with a decadent helping of cream and fruit. I called it "Teacher's Special!" It had tea, honey, caramel, and plain pancakes layered with custard and fruit between each level. The tower was fenced in with a hedge of whipped cream.

The monstrous stack was not for the faint of heart, the weak of stomach, or anyone mindful of their waistline.

The confection straddled the line between cake and pancake, but I didn't care, since Fran was so excited to see it. Given that her immediate reaction was to jump out of her seat, I would say she was quite hyped up for it. She'd even started doing a little dance to celebrate. (So adorable!)

"I'm going in!"

She tossed aside her knife and fork, diving face first into the tower. She was living every kid's dream; all she had to do was bite to get a mouthful of dessert. Fran's gluttony sure had a way of making food look delicious!

Fran, come here for a second.

"Mm?"

She was enjoying herself so much that she'd failed to notice the bit of cream on the tip of her nose. I wiped it off, feeling very satisfied.

No need to rush, Fran. It's all for you. But are you

169

sure you won't get bored of this?

"If anything, I'm liking it even more. Eating your pancakes calms me down. I feel warm and fuzzy right here."

Fran sighed, clasping her hands over her chest. She looked absolutely tranquil.

"I'll always remember the taste of your cooking."

To Fran, whose parents had died, and who'd spent four years as a slave, nothing could be more important. I saw the smile of a twelve-year-old return to her lips, and I made up my mind to stay with her—to give her all the memories of pancakes and curries that I possibly could, no matter what adventures might await.

We've got a long road ahead of us, Fran.

"But you'll stay with me the whole way, won't you, Teacher?"

Of course.

Illustration by Llo.

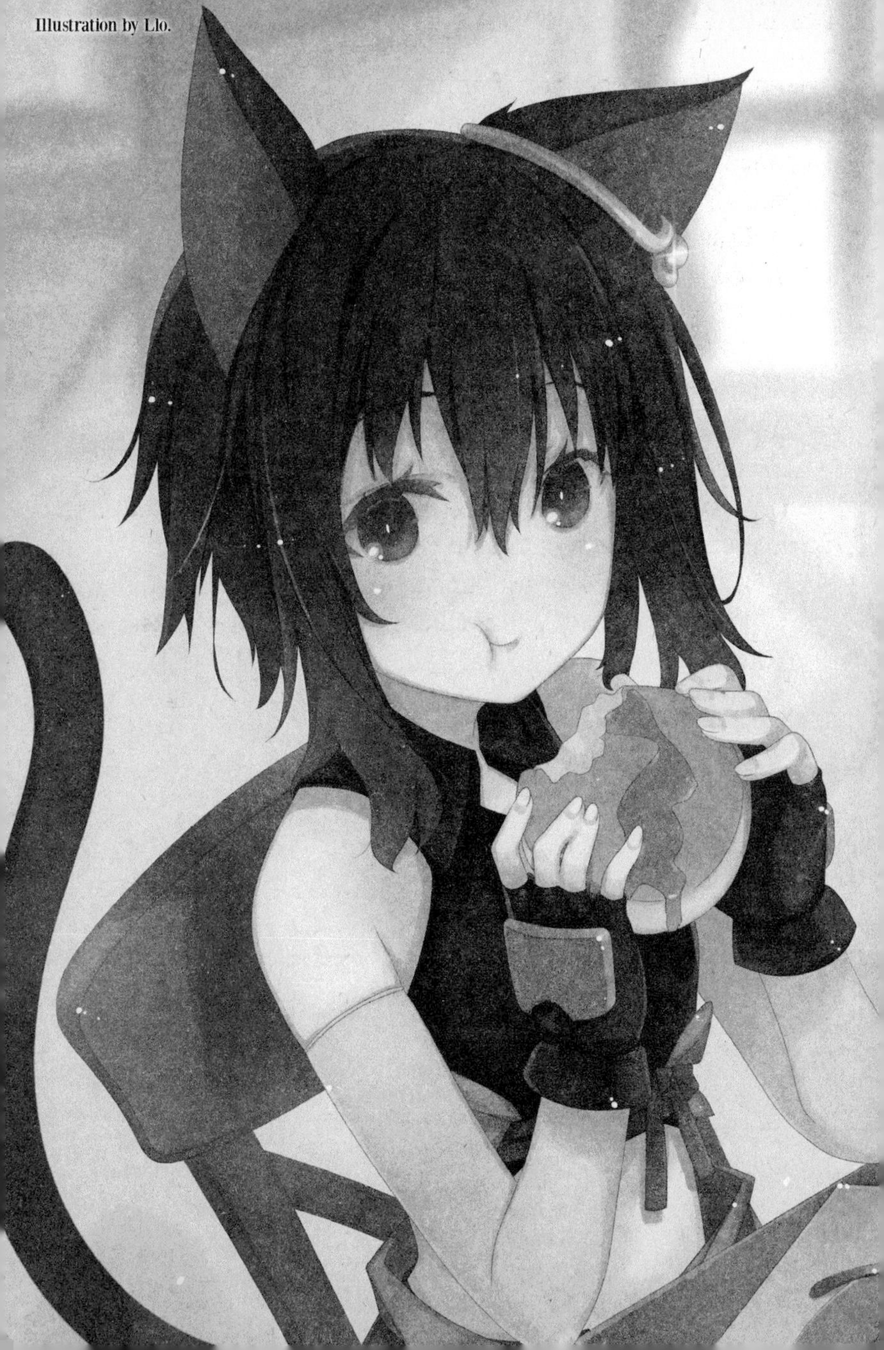

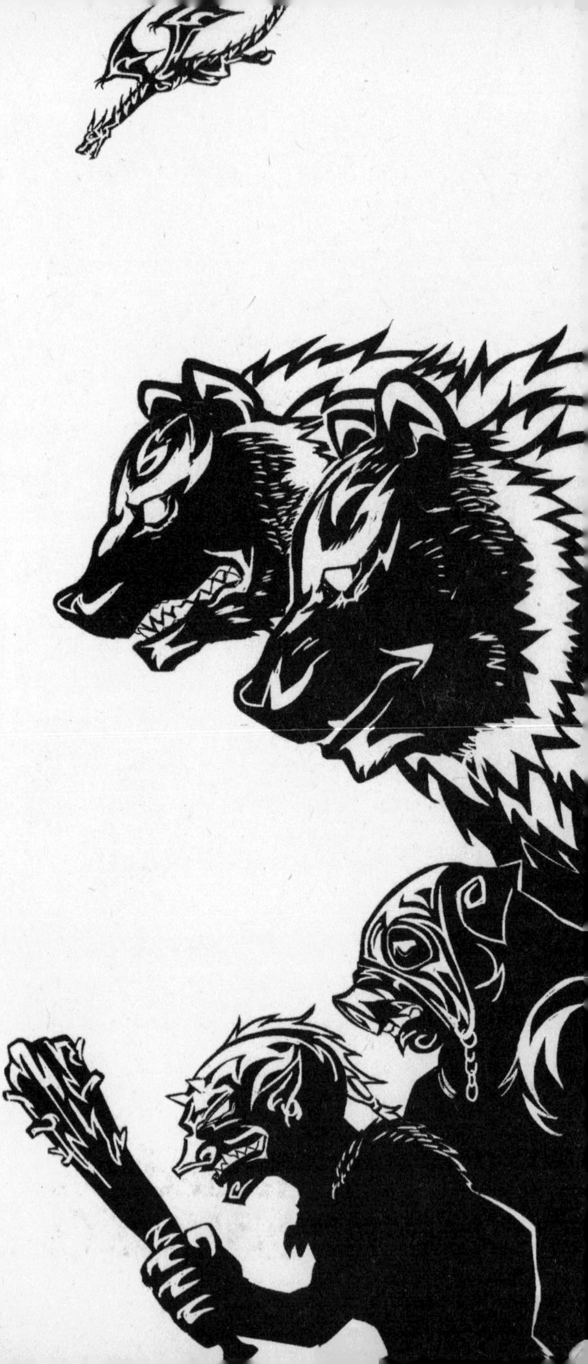

Reincarnated
as a sword

Reincarnated as a Sword

SEVEN SEAS ENTERTAINMENT PRESENTS

Reincarnated as a Sword

story by YUU TANAKA   **art by TOMOWO MARUYAMA**   character designs by **Llo**   **VOL. 1**

TRANSLATION
Mike Rachmat

ADAPTATION
Peter Adrian Behravesh

LETTERING
Rai Enril

COVER DESIGN
KC Fabellon

PROOFREADER
Kurestin Armada
Danielle King

EDITOR
J.P. Sullivan

PRODUCTION MANAGER
Lissa Pattillo

MANAGING EDITOR
Julie Davis

EDITOR-IN-CHIEF
Adam Arnold

PUBLISHER
Jason DeAngelis

TENSEI SHITARA KEN DESHITA Vol. 1
by TANAKA YUU / MARUYAMA TOMOWO / Llo
© 2017 TANAKA YUU, MARUYAMA TOMOWO / MICRO MAGAZINE,
GENTOSHA COMICS INC.
All rights reserved.

Original Japanese edition published in 2017 by GENTOSHA COMICS Inc.
English translation rights arranged worldwide with GENTOSHA COMICS Inc.
through Digital Catapult Inc., Tokyo.

Seven Seas press and purchase enquiries can be sent to Marketing Manager
Lianne Sentar at press@gomanga.com. Information regarding the distribution
and purchase of digital editions is available from Digital Manager CK Russell
at digital@gomanga.com.

Seven Seas and the Seven Seas logo are trademarks of
Seven Seas Entertainment. All rights reserved.

ISBN: 978-1-64275-755-2
Printed in Canada
First Printing: December 2019
10 9 8 7 6 5 4 3 2 1

FOLLOW US ONLINE: *www.sevenseasentertainment.com*

READING DIRECTIONS

This book reads from *right to left*, Japanese style.
If this is your first time reading manga, you start
reading from the top right panel on each page and
take it from there. If you get lost, just follow the
numbered diagram here. It may seem backwards at
first, but you'll get the hang of it! Have fun!!

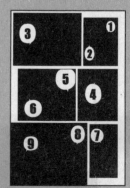